BELIEFS IN GOVERNMENT

Volumes of a Research Programme of the European Science Foundation

Series Editors: Max Kaase, Kenneth Newton, and Elinor Scarbrough

CITIZENS AND THE STATE

This set of five volumes is an exhaustive study of beliefs in government in post-war Europe. Based upon an extensive collection of survey evidence, the results challenge widely argued theories of mass opinion, and much scholarly writing about citizen attitudes towards government and politics.

The **European Science Foundation** is an association of its fifty-six member research councils, academies, and institutions devoted to basic scientific research in twenty countries. The ESF assists its Member Organizations in two main ways: by bringing scientists together in its Scientific Programmes, Networks, and European Research Conferences to work on topics of common concern, and through the joint study of issues of strategic importance in European science policy.

The scientific work sponsored by ESF includes basic research in the natural and technical sciences, the medical and biosciences, the humanities, and the social sciences.

The ESF maintains close relations with other scientific institutions within and outside Europe. By its activities, ESF adds value by co-operation and co-ordination across national frontiers, offers expert scientific advice on strategic issues, and provides the European forum for fundamental science.

This volume arises from the work of the ESF Scientific Programme on Beliefs in Government (BiG).

Further information on ESF activities can be obtained from:

European Science Foundation
1, quai Lezay-Marnésia
F-67080 Strasbourg Cedex
France

Tel. (+33) 88 76 71 00
Fax (+33) 88 37 05 32

BELIEFS IN GOVERNMENT VOLUME ONE

CITIZENS AND THE STATE

Edited by

HANS-DIETER KLINGEMANN

and

DIETER FUCHS

OXFORD UNIVERSITY PRESS

1995

Oxford University Press, Walton Street, Oxford OX2 6DP

Oxford New York
Athens Auckland Bangkok Bombay
Calcutta Cape Town Dar es Salaam Delhi
Florence Hong Kong Istanbul Karachi
Kuala Lumpur Madras Madrid Melbourne
Mexico City Nairobi Paris Singapore
Taipei Tokyo Toronto
and associated companies in
Berlin Ibadan

Oxford is a trade mark of Oxford University Press

Published in the United States
by Oxford University Press Inc., New York

British Library Cataloguing in Publication Data
Data available

Library of Congress Cataloging in Publication Data
Citizens and the state/Hans-Dieter Klingemann and Dieter Fuchs.
—(Beliefs in government; v. 1)
Includes bibliographical references.
ISBN 0–19–827955–8
1. Europe—Politics and government—1945– 2. Political
participation—Europe. 3. Political parties—Europe. 4. Public
opinion—Europe. I. Klingemann, Hans-Dieter. II. Fuchs, Dieter.
III. Series.
JN94.A91C56 1995   320.94'09'045—dc20   95–16227

1 3 5 7 9 10 8 6 4 2

Typeset by J&L Composition Ltd, Filey, North Yorkshire
Printed in Great Britain
on acid-free paper by
Biddles Ltd, Guildford and King's Lynn

FOREWORD

This is one of five volumes in a series produced by the Beliefs in Government research programme of the European Science Foundation. The volumes, all published by Oxford University Press in 1995, are as follows:

i *Citizens and the State*, edited by Hans-Dieter Klingemann and Dieter Fuchs

ii *Public Opinion and Internationalized Governance*, edited by Oskar Niedermayer and Richard Sinnott

iii *The Scope of Government*, edited by Ole Borre and Elinor Scarbrough

iv *The Impact of Values*, edited by Jan van Deth and Elinor Scarbrough

v *Beliefs in Government*, authored by Max Kaase and Kenneth Newton

The first chapter of *Beliefs in Government* presents a brief history of the research project, its general concerns, approach and methods, and an outline of the relationship of each volume to the project as a whole.

All five books share a debt of gratitude which we would like to acknowledge on their behalf. The European Science Foundation (ESF) supported and funded the research programme throughout its five long and arduous years. Eleven of the research councils and academies which are members of the ESF have made a financial contribution to the overall costs of the project—Belgium, Denmark, Finland, France, the Federal Republic of Germany, Ireland, Italy, the Netherlands, Norway, Sweden, and the United Kingdom. We would like to thank the ESF and these member organizations five times over—once for each book.

All five volumes were copy-edited by Heather Bliss, whose eagle eye and endless patience are unrivalled in the Western world. At Oxford University Press we were lucky indeed to have two understanding editors in Tim Barton and Dominic Byatt.

In particular, John Smith, the Secretary of the ESF's Standing Committee for the Social Sciences, and his staff put in huge efforts and gave us encouragement at every stage of the project. Having gone through the process with other ESF research programmes a few times before, they knew when we started what an immense task lay in wait for us all, but were not daunted. We cannot lay claim to any such bravery, and have only our innocence as an excuse.

Max Kaase
Kenneth Newton
Elinor Scarbrough

December 1994

PREFACE

It is generally believed that the relationship between citizens and the state in West European democracies has undergone a fundamental change in the last decades. Many observers regard this change as a challenge to representative democracy. This book addresses the problem from the citizen's perspective. The theoretical validity of the arguments supporting the challenge perspective is examined in the introductory chapter. Ten hypotheses are singled out from the literature. They relate to citizens as participants in the political process; to the intermediary collective actors such as political parties, interested organizations, and social movements, and to generalized attitudes towards politicians, institutions, and the democratic political system as a whole. These hypotheses are tested empirically by a wide variety of data across time and countries in the subsequent chapters.

The evidence is presented in three parts. Part I deals with political involvement, Part II discusses political linkage, while Part III is concerned with the political system. Our results speak against the challenge hypothesis. Citizens of West European societies have not withdrawn support from their democracies. However, rejecting the challenge hypothesis does not mean that there has been no change in the relationship between citizens and the state. The broadening of the action repertory, the increase in political participation, and the decline of party attachment are major characteristics of this change which could be observed in virtually all West European countries. These processes have changed the nature of the interaction between the actors of the polity and the public. Citizens have become more critical towards politicians and political parties, and they are more capable and willing to use non-institutionalized forms of political action to pursue their goals and interests. Thus, parties, interested organizations, and other major political actors have to take this into account, and must constantly and systematically consider voter preferences and opinions. These changes in the nature of the interaction between the citizens and the actors of the polity indicate a process which we call *democratic transformation*. Our arguments are laid out in detail in the concluding chapter.

This book is one of a series based on the work of the Beliefs in

Government (BiG) project, directed by Max Kaase, Science Center Berlin, and Kenneth Newton, University of Essex. They proposed a study of 'Beliefs in Government: Changing Public Attitudes to Government in Western Europe', and our research group took up the topic 'Citizens and the State'. Their intellectual and steering contributions are gratefully acknowledged. However, both the general project and this volume are of a genuinely collaborative nature. *Citizens and the State* has fifteen authors who come from nine different countries. They worked together from 1989 to 1993. They met nine times in various places to present and discuss their analyses. The meetings took place in Berlin (October 1989; December 1990), Rome (April 1990), Oxford (November 1992), Budapest (March 1993), and Strasbourg (June 1993). Special thanks go to our hosts, the Science Center Berlin, the Italian Science Foundation, the Academia Internacional Liberdade e Desenvolvimento, the Monastry of Idhra, University of Essex, Nuffield College, the Central European University, and the European Science Foundation and its staff. The University of Gothenburg hosted a meeting of the editors and the convenors of the three parts of the book in the spring of 1993 and we want gratefully to acknowledge this too.

For marvellous help in the editorial work, we admire and appreciate the contribution of Elinor Scarbrough, University of Essex. Elinor Scarbrough also served as the Research Co-ordinator of the BiG project. Without her organizational talent, her firm commitment, and her kind understanding this book would not have seen the light of day. We owe her a lot. And we gratefully acknowledge the services provided by John Simister, Research Officer, and by Christine Wilkinson, Helen Sibley, and Sharon Duthie, who, at different times, provided excellent secretarial assistance.

The European Science Foundation proved to be an ideal support structure for the project. Its Standing Committee for the Social Sciences helped to launch the BiG programme and to bring together the groups of scientists to work on it. We are also well aware of the ESF's generous financial support. Special thanks go to John Smith, Secretary to the ESF who, in that capacity, was responsible for the BiG project. His administrative skills and flexibility were truly remarkable. It is within this type of infrastructure that large-scale comparative research can flourish and become reality.

Konstanza Prinzessin zu Löwenstein of the Science Center Berlin has been the good spirit of Group 1. She eased our lives as editors and acted behind the scenes when group dynamics made that necessary. We also want to thank Ekkehard Mochmann and the staff of the Zentralarchiv für empirische Sozialforschung Köln for the help they gave us. They served the project well.

Other colleagues have been generous with their advice and counsel, in particular William Miller, University of Glasgow, and Bengt Gunnar Sjöblom, University of Copenhagen, who reviewed our draft manuscript.

Much has been said about the social functions of comparative research. In this project we have experienced what it really means. It means suffering through meetings, wining and dining, going abroad and making friends, and being proud of a joint product. This period of our lives we shall not forget.

Hans-Dieter Klingemann
Dieter Fuchs

December 1994

CONTENTS

LIST OF FIGURES

LIST OF TABLES

ABBREVIATIONS

CDA	Christian Democratic Appeal [Netherlands]
CDU	Christian Democratic Union [Germany]
CSU	Christian Social Union [Germany]
CEU	Central European University
CPS–NES	Center for Political Studies—National Election Study
CSSD	Czechoslovak Social Democratic Party [Czechoslovakia]
DP	Proletarian Democracy [Italy]
DS	Democratic Party [Serbia]
EC	European Community
ECPR	European Consortium for Political Research
ESF	European Science Foundation
EVSSG	European Value Systems Study Group
FDF	Francophone Democratic Front [Belgium]
FDP	Free Democratic Party [Germany]
FKGP	Independent Small Holders Party [Hungary]
FIDESZ	Federation of Young Democrats [Hungary]
HSD–SMS	Movement for Self-Governing Democracy—Rally for Moravia and Silesia [Czech Republic]
HZDS	Movement for Democratic Slovakia [Slovakia]
KDH	Christian Democratic Movement [Slovakia]
KDNP	Christian Democratic People's Party [Hungary]
KDU–CSL	Christian Democratic Union—Czech People's Party [Czech Republic]
KLD	Liberal-Democratic Congress [Poland]
KPN	Confederation for an Independent Poland [Poland]
KSCM	Communist Party of the Czech and Moravian Lands [Czech Republic]
LO	Landesorganisasjon [Norwegian trade-union confederation]
LO	Landesorganisationen [Swedish trade-union confederation]
LSU	Liberal Social Union [Czech Republic]
MDF	Hungarian Democratic Forum [Hungary]

MKM–EWS–MLS	Hungarian Christian Democratic Movement—Coexistence—Hungarian People's Party [Slovakia]
MRG	Left Radicals [France]
MSI	Social Movement [Italy]
MSZP	Hungarian Socialist Party [Hungary]
NATO	North Atlantic Treaty Organization
ODA	Civic Democratic Alliance [Czech Republic]
OECD	Organization for Economic Co-operation and Development
ODS	Civic Democratic Party [Czech Republic]
ODU	Civic Democratic Union [Czech Republic]
PC	Centre Alliance [Poland]
PLI	Liberals [Italy]
PR	Radicals [Italy]
PRI	Republicans [Italy]
PRL	Francophone Liberals [Belgium]
PSC/Fr.	Christian Socialists [Belgium]
PSDI	Social Democrats [Italy]
PSL	Polish People's Party
RPR	Gaullists [France]
SDL	Party of the Democratic Left [Slovakia]
SdRP	Social Democratic Party of Poland [Poland]
SGP	Political Reformed Party [Netherlands]
SNS	Slovak Nationalist Party [Slovakia]
SPD	Social Democratic Party [Germany]
SPR–RSC	Republican Party [Czech Republic]
SZDSZ	Alliance for Free Democrats [Hungary]
UD	Democratic Union [Poland]
UDF	Union for French Democracy [France]
VU	People's Union [Belgium]
VVD	People's Party for Freedom and Democracy [Netherlands]
ZChN	Christian National Unity [Poland]

Standard country abbreviations used in the tables and figures

AU	Austria
BE	Belgium
DK	Denmark
FI	Finland
FR	France
GB	Britain
GE	Germany
GR	Greece
IC	Iceland
IR	Ireland
IT	Italy
LU	Luxembourg
NL	Netherlands
NO	Norway
PO	Portugal
SP	Spain
SV	Sweden
SW	Switzerland

LIST OF CONTRIBUTORS

KEES AARTS, Lecturer in Political Science, Faculty of Public Administration and Public Policy, University of Twente.

ROBERTO BIORCIO, Reseacher, Department of Sociology, University of Milan.

DIETER FUCHS, Associate Professor of Political Science, Free University of Berlin, and Senior Research Fellow, Science Center Berlin.

GIOVANNA GUIDOROSSI, Researcher, POLEIS Centre, Bocconi University, Milan.

SÖREN HOLMBERG, Professor of Political Science—Electoral Research, and Director, Swedish Election Study, Department of Political Science, University of Göteborg.

HANS-DIETER KLINGEMANN, Professor of Political Science, Free University of Berlin, and Director of the Research Unit on Institutions and Social Change, Science Center Berlin.

OLA LISTHAUG, Professor of Political Science, Department of Sociology and Political Science, University of Trondheim.

RENATO MANNHEIMER, Professor of Political Sociology, Department of Political Science, University of Genova.

HERMANN SCHMITT, Research Fellow, Zentrum für Europäische Sozialforschung, and Director, Mannheimer Zentrum für Europäische Umfrageanalysen und Studien, University of Mannheim.

PALLE SVENSSON, Senior Lecturer, Department of Political Science, University of Aarhus.

JACQUES THOMASSEN, Professsor of Political Science, Faculty of Public Administration and Public Policy, University of Twente.

GÁBOR TÓKA, Lecturer, Department of Political Science, Central European University, Budapest.

RICHARD TOPF, Reader in Politics, and Director, Centre for Comparative European Survey Data, London Guildhall University.

MATTI WIBERG, Associate Professor of Political Science, Department of Political Science, University of Tampere.

ANDERS WIDFELDT, Doktorandtjähnst, Department of Political Science, University of Göteborg.

1

Citizens and the State: A Changing Relationship?

DIETER FUCHS AND HANS-DIETER KLINGEMANN

We try to answer two different types of question in this book. The first is descriptive: has the relationship between citizens and the state in West European democracies undergone a fundamental change in the last two or three decades? Several influential studies claim that it has; if that is true, it would have serious consequences for the condition of these democracies. The second question is related to these consequences: are there grounds for believing that the nature and scope of changes in the relationship between citizens and the state constitute a challenge to representative democracy in Western Europe?

These two questions are discussed at some length in this introductory chapter. The empirical analyses presented in the chapters which follow look at different aspects of the relationship between citizens and the state, examining the political involvement of citizens, the linkages between citizens and the state established by political parties and interest groups, and the level of generalized support among citizens which these democracies can count on. These chapters shed light on the first question. The extent to which these changes constitute a challenge to representative democracy, our second question, is discussed in the concluding chapter.

This chapter has been discussed extensively with members of Group 1 of the Beliefs in Government project and with colleagues at the Science Center Berlin. We especially wish to thank Jürgen Gerhards, Sören Holmberg, Max Kaase, Bill Miller, Elinor Scarbrough, Jacques Thomassen, and Richard Topf for their extremely helpful comments.

Citizens and the State

The General Issue

In democracies, the relationship between citizens and the state is necessarily a precarious one, in which the nature of democracy is kept permanently open. This holds true at least since the transformation from democratic city-states to democratic nation-states, which Dahl (1989) refers to as the 'second transformation'. This transformation was actuated, and presumably even imposed, by the increase in scale of these democracies and the increase in complexity of these societies. It was characterized by the conjunction of the idea of democracy and the idea of representation. At the institutional level, it led to the differentiation of a specific system to assume the business of governing a community of citizens on their behalf. Within the framework of the formal rules in this system of government, collectively binding decisions are made by elected actors. By election, the community of citizens delegates its sovereignty to representatives who are empowered to make decisions. This second democratic transformation was completed only at the beginning of this century with the introduction of universal suffrage and the emergence of modern party systems. Dahl describes the democracies which represent the provisional outcome of this long historical process as 'polyarchies', and all contemporary Western European democracies are such polyarchies. In so far as their general and defining feature is representation, they can also be designated by the somewhat less artificial term *representative democracy*.

The precariousness of the relationship between citizens and the state lies in this essential feature of representation.[1] Representative government inevitably establishes distance between the rulers and the ruled, implying the possibility that this distance may attain such proportions that it would be difficult to continue to speak of democracy. Political processes in democracies therefore can, and must, always confront the question of whether they satisfy democratic criteria. How responsive are these political processes to the demands of citizens, and to what extent can citizens control this responsiveness?

If only because of this fundamental structural problem, the relationship between citizens and the state is the object of permanent public and academic scrutiny. The intensity of this scrutiny varies, depending on how the relationship appears to be faring. In modern societies, both the public and the scientific community are, among other things, critical agents who are able to discharge a democratic control function by observing the operation of political processes. The type of observation which each of these agents performs is necessarily different in nature.

The concept of *congruence* can serve as a point of reference for observing the relationship between citizens and the state. Congruence usually arises on at least two, hierarchically related, levels. The lower level of congruence is that of everyday political *processes* in a country. These processes, in turn, are controlled by the *structures* of the system of government, which constitute the higher level. Congruence at the level of political processes exists where the specialized actors (parties, governments, politicians), who are the vehicles and organizers of these processes, can give citizens what they want. If they can do so, they satisfy the democratic criterion of responsiveness. In return, these actors receive a corresponding degree of support from the citizens. This, in its turn, is one of the conditions for democratic processes to function. However, there are two reasons why democratic processes must systematically generate a greater or lesser degree of dissatisfaction among citizens. First, because the resources available to any government to implement its policies are limited and, secondly, because implementing a particular policy necessarily rules out others.

The institutional mechanism which is supposed to regulate system-atically generated dissatisfaction in representative democracies is that of government and opposition. The effectiveness of this mechanism depends on how many citizens regard at least one party as suitable and competent to represent their interests, and how many citizens believe that 'their' party has a real chance of assuming government in the foreseeable future. The more effectively the government/opposition mechanism operates, the easier it is to limit and canalize dissatisfaction to avoid its generalization to the higher levels of the system—that is, to dissatisfaction with the formal, constitutionally determined, structures of government.

Congruence between citizens and the state at the level of the formal structures exists when citizens perceive these structures as commensurate with generally accepted values and norms. The more pronounced the commensurability, the greater will be the support which citizens give to the formal structures. This is the core consideration in almost all concepts of legitimacy.

It is evident, then, that congruence between citizens and the state and the support accorded to the state by its citizens refer to quite different levels and have quite different sources. Nevertheless, the two levels are systematically related in a manner which is crucial to the functioning of democracy in any country. Acceptance of the formal structures is the precondition for the outcomes of political processes being acknowledged as binding, even when they are not condoned. Such acknowledgement is rooted in the understanding that outcomes come about on the basis of legitimate rules of procedure. The acceptance of formal structures is also a precondition for transforming the inevitable dissatisfaction of a section of the citizenry with the outcomes of political processes into behaviour which is consistent with the system; that is, into appropriate electoral behaviour. This has already been characterized as the government/opposition mechanism.

Moreover, if there is lasting serious dissatisfaction at the process level which cannot be channelled within the government/opposition mechanism, it is unlikely that formal structures can—enduringly—be legitimated on the basis of values and norms. The probable consequence would be the more or less pronounced generalization of dissatisfaction with the formal structures. In discussing the relationship between citizens and the state, both the fundamental distinction between the structural level and the process level, and the interdependence of the two levels, must thus be taken into account. Easton (1965) has already pointed this out, and it must be kept in mind in the treatment of crisis theories which follows.

At the process level, congruence between citizens and the state is disturbed when the state can no longer satisfy the demands of its citizens. However, this type of disturbance is inherent in the system. Such disturbances lead to a *crisis* of the state, and in our case this means to a crisis of representative democracy, when they can no longer be absorbed by existing institutional mechanisms (e.g. the government vs. opposition mechanism) but require quite new institutional solutions. Since the end of the allegedly quiet 1950s, much influential comment from among the public and the academic community has been heard to the effect that the representative democracies of modern societies are indeed in this situation. However, before one joins in this crisis rhetoric on the basis of this or that evidence, it is advisable to remember that the rhetorical figure of crisis is promoted by the specific rationality of actors in the various arenas of society.

Under the conditions of a competitive party system, for example, it is perfectly rational for opposition parties to postulate a societal or political crisis to convince voters of the urgency of removing the governing parties from power. In the mass media, talk of crisis is one of the surest ways to attract the attention of the public. Generating attention is, in its turn, one of the guiding lights for actors in the mass media. In the scholarly debate, too, the diagnosis of a crisis presumably has a greater chance of gaining attention than merely ascertaining conflict. The latter point is relatively trivial, since democracy means, and needs, conflict by its very nature. Thus, because of the tendency to stylize conflict as crisis, it is important to distinguish between the rhetoric and the substance of crisis.

Yet the fact that there are mechanisms to generate or stabilize the rhetoric of crisis does not preclude the possibility that an actual crisis exists. In the scholarly debate, such separation can be effected in two ways. In the first place, we can examine the theoretical validity of the arguments supporting a crisis hypothesis. We do this in the following section. Secondly, and above all, we can do it by empirically testing the hypothesis. This is the task of the subsequent chapters in this volume.

The Theoretical Argument

The scholarly debate on the crisis in Western representative democracies reached a climax around the mid-1970s, at least as far as its theoretical elaboration was concerned. Almost in parallel, a number of crisis hypotheses were advanced, such as the legitimation crisis (Habermas 1973, *inter alia*), the governability crisis (Brittan 1975; King 1975, *inter alia*), and the crisis of democracy (Crozier, Huntington, and Watanuki 1975, *inter alia*). Although the ideological and theoretical bases for these crisis hypotheses varied greatly, their diagnoses concurred in one essential point: the demands made by citizens on democratic governments were increasing, and doing so irreversibly, while, at the same time, the capacity of governments to realize their policy objectives was declining due, among other things, to lower economic growth. However, the crisis hypotheses postulated by critics differed widely in locating the societal causes for these alleged problems.

Arguing in a neo-Marxist vein, Habermas (1973) believed that the cause of the legitimation crisis lay in a fundamental contradiction in late capitalist societies between social production and private appropriation. At the level of the political system, this contradiction took the form of collective taxation along with the highly particular expenditure of scarce tax revenues. This contradiction, which cannot be legitimated by prevailing values and norms, could, according to Habermas, be kept latent only by compensating citizens with continuous growth in income, leisure, and security. Habermas argued that, for various reasons, the governmental system is increasingly less successful in fulfilling the growing demands of citizens. One of the causes was lower economic growth; another, that the state has assumed an increasing number of functions. In consequence, the scope for making demands on the state has grown.

Whereas Habermas's hypothesis of a legitimation crisis located the causes, primarily, outside the political system, Crozier *et al.* (1975) saw endogenous causes for the crisis of democracy which they postulated. The crisis was due to governments being overloaded by the growing demands of citizens. One of the decisive factors in this development, they argued, was the limited capacity of the state to select between demands which are equally legitimate. Another factor is grounded in one of the vital institutional elements of representative democracy: the system of party competition forces parties constantly to outbid one another in terms of their policy programmes, thus inflating the demands of citizens. Consequently, according to Crozier *et al.*, the institutional arrangements for limiting and canalizing demands in a representative democracy operate in reverse.

Although different reasons were advanced, all the crisis theories in this debate assumed an overloading of the state by the escalating demands of citizens, with a consequent shortfall in the performance of the state. But to speak of a crisis of representative democracy makes sense only when dissatisfaction with the democratic process is generalized to apply to the structures of democracy, thus threatening their survival in the long term. However, the gloomy forecasts—that an impending crisis threatened representative democracies in Western societies—were not corroborated by developments in the years that followed. Moreover, apart from the obvious fact that all these democracies continued to operate, the development of a crisis could be refuted on less dramatic evidence.

First of all, and contrary to theoretical assumptions, a number of countries succeeded in fending off and reducing the demands made on the state. This did not lead to breaches of legitimation, as the predominant findings from systematic survey data show. Western democracies obviously still had a reserve of legitimation at the structural level which provided a sufficient buffer against the shortfall in performance at the process level. A further reason for the inaccurate predictions of the crisis theories is the absence of a credible alternative to these democracies. If not before, this became dramatically apparent upon the collapse of the socialist regimes in Eastern Europe, generally regarded as the major alternative political order to the representative democracies of the West. The question of the continued existence of these democracies in their basic institutional structures can be shelved for the time being.

Over the past decade, critical assessments of the condition of Western democracies have formulated the issue of the proper relationship between citizens and the state quite differently, coming to quite different conclusions about their future development. The essence of these analyses is that the institutions of representative democracy, and the professional political actors within that structural framework, have not reacted adequately to the processes of societal change, or have yet to do so.[2] We deal with these processes of change in greater detail later. At this stage, it only needs to be noted that these analyses concluded that the supposed adaptation problems imply a *challenge* to representative democracy. What, in detail, constitutes this challenge and how it is to be met is stated with varying degrees of clarity and definition. Reference to a challenge, however, is precise only if it relates not simply to more or less serious problems, but also embraces the assumption that, owing to the nature of their institutional structures, these democracies are unable to react adequately to the problems they face. In contradiction to the crisis theories, this 'structural deficit' can be seen to relate not to representative democracies as a whole, but only to particular structural components or to the structure of subsystems— as, for example, the party systems.

On the premiss that there are structure-related problems about adapt ing to societal processes of change, in the sense outlined above, two quite different consequences may be anticipated, depending on whether or not there are structural alternatives acceptable to the citizens. If no credible alternatives are available, the problems of structural adaptation must induce growing dissatisfaction among citizens with the institutions of democracy and the major actors of democracy. This might well lead to paralysis in the political decision-making processes without any structural change taking place, let alone the system collapsing. Under these conditions, the challenge to representative democracy would go no further than the permanent articulation of criticism or political apathy among a more or less extensive section of the citizenry. Hirschman (1982) assumes that both phenomena occur in cycles of commitment and withdrawal. This kind of challenge, an *ignis fatuus* with no point of reference, can be described as a 'soft' challenge.

The situation is different if the critique of representative democracy is made from the perspective of an alternative with some prospect of winning favour among a majority of the population. This can be regarded as a real challenge, since it means that structural change is both conceivable and possible. In defining democratic alternatives, a distinction is often drawn between direct and indirect democracy. Cohen (1971) understands this as the fundamental analytic distinction in describing democracies. This distinction underwent a far-reaching shift in emphasis in the critical debate about democratic theory during the 1980s. Indirect democracy, and in our case this means Western representative democracies, is confronted less by various forms of direct democracy than by a mixed form containing both indirect and direct institutional elements. Among critics making this point, this is particularly true of Beck (1986), and Rödel, Frankenberg, and Dubiel (1989), but other analyses also point in this direction. The practical necessity of representative democracy is to a large extent accepted in this critique.[3] Thus the representative system is understood as the indispensable institutional framework within which the institutions of direct democracy can, or even must, be introduced in order to restore congruence between citizens and the state. However, a precise description of the shape taken by this alternative form of democratic order is to a large extent waived. It is seen more as the relatively open terminus in an evolutionary process. This is also the view espoused by Dahl, to whom we shall return in our final chapter.

If representative democracy is essentially accepted, even though, because of practical constraints, it may be the second-best solution, a further type of challenge becomes apparent. What is then challenged is not representative democracy as such, but merely a certain form of institutionalization in a particular country or group of countries. The alternative is provided by other forms of institutionalization in other countries. Comparisons between existing democracies in particular countries have inestimable advantages: not only do alleged merits represent a future possibility, but they can be scrutinized within the democratic reality of the countries concerned. This sort of challenge is perfectly capable of bringing about a considerable and far-reaching systemic change within the general category of representative democracies, as shown by the transformation of the Fourth French Republic into the Fifth Republic. This was a shift from a parliamentary system with a proportional voting system to a presidential system with a majority system, substantially modifying the character of politics in France.

Our point of departure is the frequently advanced hypothesis that societal change generates problems for Western representative democracies which disturb the congruence between citizens and the state, and which the institutional mechanisms of representative democracy alone can no longer resolve. Notwithstanding these three different types of challenge, the concept of challenge contains a meaning which distinguishes it decisively from the concept of crisis. The issue of the survival of representative democracy as a form of political order in Western European countries is not on the agenda. Rather, what is at issue are the relative merits of variants of representative democracy in comparable countries, or of a mixed form in which the institutions of a representative system are complemented by the institutions of direct democracy. But these changes, too, would considerably influence the operation of democratic processes in individual countries. It is, therefore, pertinent to question whether, and to what extent, a challenge to Western representative democracies actually exists.

In particular, the challenge hypothesis can be confronted by a *normality* hypothesis. This supposes that Western representative democracies are perfectly capable of absorbing and assimilating growing pressure from societal problems. If this is indeed the case, the forms of political expression taken by such pressure could be understood as the normal manifestations of democracy in complex societies. Differences in dealing with problems are then best attributed to differing structural arrangements in existing democracies. We have described this possibility as a 'soft' challenge because possible structural reforms relate only to alternative variants of the same type of democracy. The differences could, however, also be attributable merely to political factors. These would include the fundamental ideological orientation of particular governments, or the specific policies implemented in different countries.

In the scholarly and the public debate, this normality hypothesis is still masked by the challenge hypothesis. The reason for this is to be found not only in the systemic mechanisms mentioned, which reward the diagnosis of crisis-like situations, but also in the considerably more serious consequences for the further development of Western democracies if the challenge hypothesis adequately reflects reality. The general issue of this volume, then, is the challenge to representative democracy. It provides the overriding and integrating terms of reference for the specific questions addressed in the empirical analyses presented in the subsequent chapters. We return to this general issue and the normality hypothesis in the final chapter, where we attempt to provide some answers.

The Specific Issues

The general issue of the challenge to representative democracy cannot be investigated directly in this volume. A definitive account could only be achieved with hindsight—once Western representative democracies have been modified to such an extent that they represent a significantly different type of democracy which can no longer be regarded as representative. Should this occur, the issue would be settled. In the empirical analyses in this volume, specific issues have been formulated which can be subjected to empirical scrutiny here and now.

These specific issues are concerned with the fundamental and specific political attitudes and modes of behaviour among citizens which must be assumed to exist if the challenge hypothesis is correct. In defining these issues, we shall to a large extent rely on what the diagnoses underlying the challenge hypothesis have to say on the matter. The findings of the empirical analyses on specific issues can then be considered together, and interpreted, in relation to the general issue. This we shall do in the final chapter.

The relationship between citizens and the state is bilateral, so it can be disturbed from either direction. But we shall assume to begin with that the relationship has been fundamentally modified and has given rise to disturbances in congruence *because citizens have changed*. The state is thus, at least temporarily, a constant factor in the relationship. There are two reasons for this approach. First, most of the critiques we cite have assumed that the challenge to representative democracy is caused primarily by changes in attitudes and modes of behaviour among citizens. Secondly, a challenge to the institutional structure of a given democracy is conceivable only if its citizens are dissatisfied and behave accordingly. This is also true if the final cause of such change lies with the state and its actors.

The critical analyses which are our reference points differ considerably in type and emphasis. We have identified the most important components of these analyses, which are depicted schematically in Figure 1.1. Our explication of this schema provides the basis for formulating the specific issues addressed in the empirical chapters. Thus we summarize the main arguments of the major critiques and

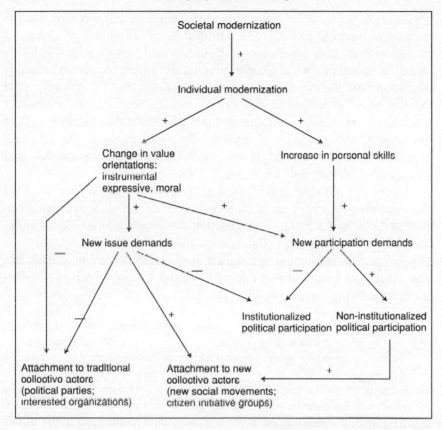

FIGURE 1.1. *Modernization processes and political orientations*

transform those arguments, if need be, in a way which allows us to test them with the data at hand. But we should emphasize that the arguments expressed here are not necessarily what we ourselves would advocate. Rather, they are arguments with wide currency, and in the final chapter we shall discuss how they have survived the empirical tests.

In constructing Figure 1.1 we have adapted and modified the general frame of reference developed by Inglehart (1990*a*: 6) for analysing the processes of social and political change. This general frame of reference can be regarded as a transposition and concentration of the various arguments relating to the micro-level of the individual citizen—even if one does not agree with the details of Inglehart's theory. Almost all the critical analyses assume that the changes which citizens undergo are caused by the processes of societal modernization, even if the term 'modernization' is not explicitly mentioned. However, of the several terms available for describing societal change, 'modernization' is the most appropriate to characterize a multitude of individual processes of change in both their interconnected effects and significance. Inglehart identifies economic growth, technological development, rising levels of education, and the expansion of mass communication as the changes at the system level which have a systematic influence at the individual level. Other processes of modernization which we consider relevant in this context are the development of the welfare state, the growing importance of the service sector, and increasing geographical and social mobility (see Bell 1973; Beck 1986, *inter alia*).

In formulating the specific issues, we concentrate on the outcomes of these systematic processes of change occurring at the individual level, as postulated in the critical analyses. By analogy to societal modernization, we refer to these processes collectively as *individual modernization*,[4] a concept elaborated by Inkeles. He describes a personality with a high degree of 'individual modernity' in the following terms (Inkeles and Smith 1974: 190ff.; see also Inkeles 1983: 12ff.):

[An] informed participant citizen; he has a marked sense of personal efficacy, he is highly independent and autonomous in his relations to traditional sources of influence, especially when he is making basic decisions about how to conduct his personal affairs, and he is ready for new experiences and ideas, that is, he is relatively open-minded and cognitively flexible . . . the modern man is also different in his approach to time, to personal and social planning, to the rights of persons dependent on or subordinate to him, and to the use of formal rules as a basis for running things.

This comprehensive description of individual modernity—or individual modernization, if one conceives all this as a developmental process implying a more or less marked modernity in individual personalities—can be analytically simplified and specified. Individual modernization has both a formal and a substantive dimension. The formal dimension consists in an increase in personal skills; the substantive dimension in a change in value orientations. These are precisely the two individual-level changes which Inglehart (1990*a*: 6) posits as the consequences of system-level changes.

For the moment we shall follow Inglehart's argument. By changes in value orientation, he means a 'shift from Materialist to Postmaterialist value priorities . . . from giving top priority to physical sustenance and safety toward heavier emphasis on belonging, self-expression, and the quality of life' (Inglehart 1990*a*: 66). In Figure 1.1, postmaterialism is allocated to expressive and moral value orientations; we deal with this allocation later. The 'increase in personal skills' refers especially to higher cognitive competence, such as the increased ability to process complex information and an increase in knowledge about one's own scope for action in the various arenas of society.

The two aspects of individual modernization identified in Figure 1.1 are general in nature, taking different forms in the subsystems of society. In the political system, they result in citizens making new demands on the democratic process and its specialized actors. New issue demands are to be understood as the political specification of general value orientations, which anticipate being taken into account and implemented in the decision-making process. What this involves, in detail, depends on the current political agenda. The most important new issue demands to have arisen in the past two decades on the basis of postmaterialist value preferences have been concerned with the abolition of nuclear energy, disarmament, and various ecological problems.

The problem for the relationship between citizens and the state, however, lies not in the emergence of such new issue demands but in the extent of responsiveness among the most important collective actors. In a representative democracy, these actors articulate the demands of citizens in relation to the political decision making process, and introduce these demands into the system. In this context we are referring to political parties, and also to interest groups. The lower the degree of responsiveness of these actors to the demands of citizens, the weaker is the attachment of citizens to them likely to be. At least two reasons are given for the presumed inadequate responsiveness of these intermediary actors in the political system.

It is claimed, first, that there is a certain inertia on the part of historically rooted political parties and interest groups in the face of new problems and interests produced by social change. This thesis was advanced some time ago and has many advocates, especially in the context of 'frozen cleavages' in Western European party systems. However, it precludes postulating a challenge to representative democracy, for inertia is necessarily a transitory phenomenon. The very logic of competition among intermediary actors to gain citizen support requires such actors, in the long run, to adapt their platforms to changes in citizen interests. Should they fail to do so, new political parties and new interest groups are likely to emerge. But both the programmatic adaptation of established intermediary actors and the formation of new actors of the same type are forms of adaptation to societal change which are inherent in the system. Thus, both forms of adaptation tend to be more in accord with the normality hypothesis. But this is not the primary reference point for our analyses.

There must, then, be a second cause for the inadequate responsiveness of the actors in the system of interest intermediation. The system of representative democracy, in its current form, can be called into question only when these intermediary actors are insufficiently responsive to new issue demands for structural reasons. However, the critical analyses hardly address the question of where the structurally determined limits to responsiveness lie. But such limits must be assumed if the challenge hypothesis is to be upheld. Thus, as we show in Figure 1.1, with regard to the relationship between citizens and intermediary actors, we expect a weakening of the attachment of citizens to political parties and interest groups—the two major types of traditional collective actors. Such weakening would have to be expected as long as the premiss of inadequate responsiveness can be upheld, regardless of whether it proves a transitory phenomenon or a structural one.

While the critical analyses we address substantially agree that there has been a change in value orientations among citizens, they differ widely on the direction of this change. To bring a modicum of system to these differences, we resort to Parsons' (1951) analytical typology, which distinguishes three universal modes of evaluative orientation towards objects: instrumental, moral, and expressive. This general typology can reasonably be specified and applied in relation to political objects (Fuchs 1993*a*). In a moral orientation, universal criteria are applied, directed towards the generation of collective goods which no one may be excluded from using. With instrumental and expressive orientations, utilitarian criteria are applied, and the goods to which people aspire are generally individual goods. An expressive orientation involves the expectation of immediate gratification through the object, whereas an instrumental orientation is dominated by longer-term cost–benefit calculations. Inglehart's postmaterialist values are best described as moral orientations. The new issue demands arising from postmaterialist values, as noted above, relate to fundamental risks in modern societies. It is not a matter of particular group interests, but of concerns which affect everyone, and which sometimes even involve the issue of human survival. This quality determines the unconditionality and prescriptiveness that are the essential attributes of moral evaluations.

However, there is a problem with the self-actualization component in Inglehart's concept of postmaterialism, which he regards as a central constituent of postmaterialism. Although it is conceivable that the self-actualization of individuals is also grounded in moral orientations, the manifestations of self-actualization over the past decades are more appropriately understood as evidence of expressive or hedonistic orientations. Bell (1976) has described the growing importance of hedonistic value orientations as an essential characteristic of the 'cultural contradictions' in modern societies. Huntington (1974) had previously advanced a similar argument. And the hypothesis of an increase in hedonistic self-actualization has been addressed again in more recent discussions of postmodernism. In Inglehart's concept of postmaterialism, the moral and hedonistic dimensions of value change are not separated, which has the advantage that 'postmaterialism' is compatible with the most heterogeneous phenomena. But it also, therefore, suffers the disadvantage of conceptual fuzziness in relation to this heterogeneity. In Figure 1.1, we have followed Inglehart in combining the two dimensions of value change because several of the critical analyses present arguments similar to those of Inglehart, at least at the micro-level. At a later stage, however, we will formulate a hypothesis based only on the assumption of the growing dominance of expressive or hedonistic value orientations.

In Figure 1.1 we show a negative effect implying that an instrumental value orientation increasingly determines the nature of ties between citizens and the traditional collective actors. This is based primarily on the analysis by Streeck (1987), which addresses and synthesizes a multitude of individual lines of argument. Observing the dissolution of traditional social milieux, Streeck concludes that the loyalties of citizens to established political actors is declining precisely because such loyalties are generated and stabilized by traditional social milieux. Streeck describes this development figuratively as 'the draining of pre-organizational sources of formal organizations' (1987: 475; our translation). According to Streeck (see also Crook, Pakulski, and Waters 1992: 8), moral and affective loyalties are being displaced by an increasingly instrumental orientation towards these actors; and an instrumental orientation means that citizens calculate the costs and benefits of investment in such actors. This investment can take the form of contributions to campaign funds, payment of party dues, of votes in elections, or merely rhetorical support in everyday talk. The growth of instrumental orientations also makes citizens more exacting and more critical towards the activities of collective political actors. The collective actors in question—parties or interest organizations—cannot count on the unconditional loyalty of specific groups in society. Rather, they have to win this loyalty by their performance and efficiency. Streeck suggests solving this problem by transforming political parties and interest groups into service organizations which cultivate their members and clientele systematically and professionally. Regardless of whether such a transformation could succeed, the assumption of Streeck's analysis must be that, until the transformation occurs, traditional political actors are insufficiently responsive to citizen demands of whatever type.

The issues addressed in the empirical analyses in this volume, with only one exception, relate to the end points of the causal tree shown in Figure 1.1. The exception is the hypothesis of a strengthening of the individualist aspects of democratic values and a weakening of the collectivist aspects (see Figure 1.2). According to Jacques Thomassen, in Chapter 13, individualist and collectivist democratic values differ in several respects. In the first case, the dominant value is liberty, in the second case it is equality; in the first case the desirable political goods are individual, but in the second they are collective goods; political participation is a means to an end in the first case, but self-fulfilment is an end in itself in the second case. In terms of the three universal modes of object evaluation, individualistic democratic values are to be counted among instrumental orientations. The dissolution of traditional social milieux posited by Streeck can be regarded as one of the reasons why instrumental orientations are generally spreading, and why there is a related increase in individualistic democratic values. Further factors favouring this development are the individualization of life situations (Beck 1986) due to societal modernization, and the consequent particularization of interests, and also auto-dynamic evolutionary cultural processes, which Crook *et al.* (1992) describe as rationalization processes. The specific issue of democratic orientations addressed in Chapter 13 thus has its place within the framework we have developed.

Whereas new issue demands relate to the substantive dimension of political decision-making processes, new participation demands are assigned to the formal dimension of political decision-making processes. Demands for more participation, and for new forms of participation, arise as a consequence of both dimensions of individual modernization. In Inglehart's concept of postmaterialism, the need for more political participation is a defining element. But even setting aside the claims made for postmaterialism, it seems obvious to regard greater participation in political decision-making processes as the political

Object of analysis	Hypotheses	Parts of the book
Ego as a participant	1. Decline in institutional political participation 2. Increase in non-institutionalized political participation 3. Increase in political apathy	Part I: Political involvement
Intermediary collective actors	4. Decline in the attachment to interest organizations 5. Decline in the attachment to political parties 6. Increase in the attachment to new collective actors	Part II: Political linkage
Institutions, system, and values	7. Decline in support (trust) for politicians 8. Decline in support (trust) for governmental institutions 9. Decline in support for the democratic system 10. Increase in support for individualistic democratic values	Part III: Political system

FIGURE 1.2. *Synopsis of the main hypotheses*

expression of the general value of self-actualization. The emergence of new participation demands can, therefore, be seen as one consequence of the increasing importance of individual self-actualization, regardless of whether this arises from hedonistic, moral, or post-materialist orientations.

In Figure 1.1, we show that the second reason for the emergence of new participation demands is the increase in personal skills. This, too, is in keeping with Inglehart's theory, but it is also backed up by political participation research, especially by analyses based on value-expectation theories. The more highly people evaluate their competence in a given field, the more likely they are to attain their goals in this field through their own efforts (see Krampen 1988 *inter alia*). New participation demands can thus be understood as a political consequence of the value of self-actualization and the subjective ability actively to organize one's own life.

Two possible consequences of the demand for more participation can be distinguished. First, the significance of voting as the most important institutionalized form of participation would have to diminish. Voting is a highly routine political act, which takes place relatively seldom, and relates only indirectly to envisaged goals. The feeling that political decisions are not much influenced by their votes is reinforced if citizens, in addition, believe that the contending parties do not take into account the new issue demands. The second consequence of demands for more participation can be seen in the emergence of non-institutionalized forms of political action. But there are two essential differences between non-institutionalized forms of participation and the institutionalized act of voting.

In the first place, non-institutionalized forms of participation can be deployed in all phases of the political decision-making process to influence potential and actual decision makers. Moreover, it is up to citizens themselves whether or not to get involved. Secondly, non-institutionalized participation is related directly to the realization of goals. Thus non-institutionalized forms of participation are more appropriate for the expression for self-actualization values in the political arena, and more effective for attaining specific political goals, than institutionalized involvement. Thus, with the emergence of new issue demands, one expects participation in elections to decline and involvement in non-institutionalized forms of political involvement to increase.[5]

Non-institutionalized action is not as a rule undertaken by single individuals but as collective action. The most important collective actors to have emerged outside the party systems in most Western societies since the early 1970s are generally referred to as 'new social movements'. The arrival and consolidation of new social movements has been interpreted by many social scientists as the expression of a fundamental change in the relationship between citizens and the state (Cohen 1985; Offe 1985; Keane 1988; Melucci 1989; Neidhardt and Rucht 1993, *inter alia*). The term 'new social movement' characterizes a multifaceted phenomenon (Klandermans, Kriesi, and Tarrow 1988; Rucht 1991; Schmitt-Beck 1992) which encompasses not only the successful course of mobilization, but also the structural conditions facilitating mobilization, including the organizational infrastructure, networks of interaction, mobilization potentials, and opportunity structures.

For the purposes of our analysis, however, we need only emphasize that new social movements formulate new issue demands as the goals of their action, and embrace non-institutional forms of action. What especially distinguishes new social movements from the traditional collective actors—political parties and interest organizations—is that they espouse more flexibly the new issue and participation demands of citizens which the traditional collective actors have not, hitherto, adequately taken into consideration, and which, in some respects, they could not systematically take into account. Thus, if we proceed on the assumption that new issue demands and new participation demands have emerged, as we have done in Figure 1.1, citizens can be expected to show increasing attachment to these new collective actors.

In addition to new social movements, Figure 1.1 includes citizen initiative groups. Although citizen initiative or action groups may be elements of a new social movement, they need not be. A new social movement can only be said to exist where popular mobilization has some degree of permanence and is networked beyond the regional level on the basis of common organizational structure and common political goals. However, there are numerous citizen action groups or other types of collective actors that cannot be regarded as social movements of this type but are autonomous collective actors. They can come into being on the basis of quite different goals from those of the new social movements which appeared in the 1970s and 1980s. The long-term significance of this new type of collective actor consists less in its articulation of specific goals but, rather, in the flexibility of its organization and its non-institutionalized forms of action which can be used to pursue very different goals (Fuchs 1993*b*).

Thus citizen initiative groups cannot be equated with new social movements. The latter are characterized by their ideological direction, or tendency, one of the reasons why they are called new social movements. Citizen action groups, on the other hand, because of their organizational flexibility and openness to all manner of issues, are a specifically modern form of collective actor. From the citizen's perspective, they allow efficient interest representation under time constraints; from the perspective of the political system, they are a collective political actor which is capable of adapting more quickly than formal organizations to the changing constellation of problems.

So far, in explicating Figure 1.1, we have formulated five hypotheses relating to the individual citizen as an active participant in political events and in the relationship between citizens and collective political actors. The individual hypotheses are set out in Figure 1.2. But we have yet to address the hypothesis, shown in Figure 1.2, of an increase in political apathy. This hypothesis derives from the assumption that Western societies have reached a turning point in the modernization process which leads to quite different societal and political forms of expression. By contrast, the other five hypotheses are formulated on the premiss that Western societies are in a process of continuing modernization.

The central argument underlying the political apathy hypothesis is that the developed societies of the West are already in a stage of so-called postmodernization (Crook *et al*. 1992). Theorists of postmodernization claim that a fundamental cultural change is occurring which results in the dissolution of the integrated value patterns that provide the basis for the legitimacy of societal subsystems, and for the common and binding terms of reference for all actors within, for example, the economic and political systems. What postmodernization theorists see as remaining after the dissolution of these integrated value patterns is the development of life-styles centred on personal self-actualization.[6]

Bell (1976) has analysed theoretically such (post)modernization effects, and has described hedonism as the axial principle of (post)modern cultures (Turner 1989). Postmodern culture thus consists in structurally amorphous and transitory packages of life-styles directed towards hedonistic self-actualization. Elements of this new cultural orientation are the desire for the immediate gratification for one's own actions, and the priority given to individual goods over collective goods (Reimer 1989). Thus, within the framework of postmodernization theory, an increase in *expressive* evaluation standards is assumed. These standards, in effect, constitute a contrast hostile to moral standards of evaluation. If for no other reason, the two should be kept analytically separate and not confused as occurs in Inglehart's concept of postmaterialism.

Postmodernization theorists have relatively little to say on the possible political consequences of these developments. Gibbins (1989: 15ff.) and Crook *et al*. (1992: 222) observe that, in principle, the formalization, organization, and rationalization of modern politics is hardly compatible with expressive self-actualization. We attempt to specify this very general assertion. Neither participation in elections, nor the mechanism by which citizens select parties and politicians for decision-making positions, nor the results of government action, offer individuals convincing incentives to seek hedonistic self-actualization. The utility of voting can only be realized in the upcoming legislature, which makes the realization of utility uncertain because it relies on future government action; and governments act under highly complex, and not entirely predictable, conditions. Moreover, individual utility is rather low because most government action delivers collective goods; individual goals may be only vaguely connected to collective goods.

Against this background, two conclusions can be drawn about hedonistically oriented citizens, depending on the degree of dissociation of such citizens from the state and politics. First, they are marked by a lack of political interest and low political participation; or, alternatively, by low political interest along with primarily non-institutionalized participation which happens only occasionally and lacks clear and stable goals. Kaase and Barnes (1979: 526) labelled these two variants 'political apathy' and 'expressive political action'. According to their analysis, 'political apathy' and 'expressive political action' are considerable in all five of the Western democracies they examined. If it is the case, as they claim, that system-conformity involvement—or instrumental political action—is still predominant, the potential for 'expressive political action' would nevertheless be alarming for future developments (Kaase and Barnes 1979: 533).

However, this outcome can readily be interpreted within the framework of postmodernization theory, above all if 'political apathy' and 'expressive political action' have increased since the 1974 surveys were conducted. Postmodernization theory assumes that this increase has occurred, and hypothesis 3 has been formulated accordingly (see Figure 1.2).

Seven hypotheses have been specified in relation to the micro-level of citizens. Confirmation of these hypotheses would be a necessary condition for us to conclude that a challenge to representative democracies really does exist. But note that hypotheses 2 and 3 are to be regarded as mutually exclusive since they derive from quite different theoretical approaches. We should also note a modification of the necessary condition: all hypotheses could be confirmed despite there being no challenge to representative democracy. A slight decline in the importance of traditional collective actors and institutionalized forms of involvement, and an increase in the importance of new collective actors and non-institutionalized forms of participation, can also be the expression of a differentiation of the democratic process within the institutions of the representative system and its formal structure of rules. This would be in the manner of adapting to processes of social change and the societal and individual modernization which is inherent in, and in

conformity with, the existing system. It would also be in accord with
the normality hypothesis. A challenge to representative democracies
can, therefore, be postulated only in connection with supplementary
assumptions.

A decisive supplementary assumption relates to the generalization of
citizen dissatisfaction. We assume that this occurs with the successive
spreading of dissatisfaction to more and more system levels. It would
first be evident if citizens believe that the politicians and political
parties as a whole are neither able to solve vital societal problems
nor prepared to add new issues and participation demands to their
agendas. If such beliefs are widespread, the normal interplay between
government and opposition—as the institutional means by which representative democracies absorb dissatisfaction—will no longer function.
If such a situation persists for a long period of time, a further generalization to the institutions of government seems possible. In line with the
challenge argument, hypotheses 7 and 8 in Figure 1.2 postulate that this
generalization of dissatisfaction has taken place in West European
democracies during the past two decades. These two hypotheses have
been tested using indicators of levels of trust in relevant political
objects. Trust is defined as the subjective probability of a citizen
believing that the political system, or parts of it, will produce preferred
outcomes even if this citizen takes no part in its production (Gamson
1968: 8). Based on this definition, Easton (1975: 447) has postulated
trust as a subdimension of diffuse political support. A sufficient
reservoir of diffuse support for political actors and institutions is, in
turn, a precondition for not calling them into question.

A higher level of the generalization of dissatisfaction would be
reached if it went beyond dissatisfaction with particular institutions
and specific actors to include democracy as a political system. Whether
or not such a process of generalization has indeed happened in West
European democracies will be shown when testing hypothesis 9 in
Figure 1.2. Only if a substantive decline in support for the democratic
system can be demonstrated empirically would it be possible to talk
about a challenge or, even more serious, a crisis of democracy.

The ten hypotheses which we have discussed are summarized in
Figure 1.2, which also shows how they are related to the three parts
of the book. In this chapter, we have set out as hypotheses the specific
questions which are dealt with in this volume. The subsequent chapters
take up these hypotheses in turn and try to test them empirically. In the
final chapter, we come back to the question of whether or not changes in

the relationship between citizens and the state constitute a challenge to representative democracy.

NOTES

1. We use the term 'state' as a colloquial expression for the differentiated govern-mental system.
2. See, *inter alia,* Kaase (1984, 1990); Offe (1985); Beck (1986); Held (1987); Streeck (1987); Dalton (1988); Gibbins (1989); Rödel, Frankenberg, and Dubiel (1989); Dalton and Küchler (1990); Inglehart (1990*a*); Crook *et al.* (1992).
3. This also applies in varying degrees to prominent representatives of a model of participatory democracy among normative democratic theorists. The proposals put forward by writers such as Pateman (1970), Macpherson (1977), Poulantzas (1978), and Barber (1984) aim to extend participation rather than to replace representative institutions.
4. Since the West European societies we are dealing with have all, for a long time now, been classified as modern, a more precise term would be 'continued societal or individual modernization'. For linguistic reasons we prefer the simpler term.
5. The two Political Action studies have demonstrated that the willingness of citizens in Western democracies to engage in non-institutionalized forms of action has increased. See Barnes, Kaase, *et al.* (1979); Jennings, Van Deth, *et al.* (1989).
6. See Featherstone (1988); Gibbins (1989); Harvey (1989); Crook *et al.* (1992); Lash and Friedman (1992).

PART I

Political Involvement

2

Electoral Participation

RICHARD TOPF

In this chapter we examine trends in electoral turnout across Western Europe during the post-war period. The first hypothesis set out in Chapter 1 (see Figure 1.2) predicts a general trend towards lower levels of turnout. We test this hypothesis in some detail, beginning with a discussion of the importance of elections in representative democracies, followed by a description of the demographic changes which have occurred in West European countries over the last forty years or so. We then go on to examine the relationship between changes in turnout levels and demographic change. Our main findings raise serious doubts about the declining turnout hypothesis, which is far from confirmed by the general trends we have found. Rather, we conclude that such changes as there have been in turnout levels may be accounted for, above all, in terms of the changing demographic composition of West European electorates.

Democratic Participation

National elections are powerful symbols of the democratic legitimacy of a nation-state. It has become commonplace for international organizations to send observers to report on the conduct of such elections by regimes claiming to have adopted the democratic creed, and for these reports to form the basis for the regime's recognition, or otherwise, by the international community. It is equally commonplace for such reports to reveal that a putatively democratic, national electoral process has involved violent deaths, imprisonments, and many varieties of corruption.

From the perspective of citizens of the West European states which are the concern of this chapter, such strife may often seem so remote as to be incomprehensible. We now live in a calm sea of political tranquillity where few would question that all eighteen countries in Western Europe qualify as legitimate members of the international democratic community, and that all eighteen are stable regimes when judged by the criteria which observers apply to the wider world.[1] This is not to say, of course, that malpractices in the conduct of national elections never occur in Western Europe but, rather, when they do, they are of a different order from events reported of the less developed world.

We should not forget, however, that the universality of democratic regimes in Western Europe is a recent development. Just over thirty years ago, when Lipset first outlined his thesis on the possible relationships between the processes of societal modernization and the conditions for a democratic order, only half the states of Western Europe met his definition of a stable democracy. Lipset (1959: 48) defined stable democracies as states with a democratic political system since the First World War, and the absence over the past twenty-five years of a major political movement opposed to the democratic rules of the game. By these criteria, Austria, Finland, France, Greece, West Germany, Iceland, Italy, Portugal, and Spain were all categorized as being still unstable democracies or dictatorships.

Of course, Lipset's empirical analyses were grounded in the conventional notion of liberal democracy of the time. From this theoretical perspective, the most important challenge facing post-war political sociology was to determine the most suitable economic, societal, and institutional conditions for sustaining and enlarging the family of stable, pluralist, liberal democracies (Topf: 1989*b*). Lipset's prognosis was that stable liberal democracy could best be achieved through the processes of societal modernization. Through modernization, he proposed, the political efficacy of the mass citizenry is increased, especially by the expansion of education. Citing Dewey, Lipset (1959: 56) argued that education not only increased people's tolerance and restrained them from adhering to extremist doctrines, but also increased their capacity to make rational electoral choices and promoted their adherence to democratic values. Thus societal modernization was seen, in effect, as a complete solution to the core problem.

While there was considerable consensus among analysts who adhered to system-functionalist models of society about the systemic benefits of informed political involvement by citizens, there was less agreement about what would constitute the ideal level of political participation. At the core of the notion of pluralist democracy was the idea that through political participation, especially in elections, the individuals and groups who comprise a modern society must be able to express their choices for differing public policies, and thereby their differing visions of the good society. Indeed, political participation was often defined in terms of instrumental acts (cf. Topf 1989*b*), and voting in national elections was regarded as the prototypical form of such instrumental activity.

Yet the normative question of what, from a systemic perspective, would constitute an ideal level of electoral turnout in a liberal democracy remained unspecified. Many analysts, Lipset included, took the view that once a stable liberal democracy is established, it is unnecessary, even dangerous, for instrumental participation to be maximized. Rather, low electoral turnout might be taken as an indication of satisfaction with the existing political system, while high turnout might indicate destabilizing levels of societal conflict (Tingsten 1937: 225; Lipset 1959: 32; Dittrich and Johansen 1983). On this basis, Almond and Verba (1963) defended what they termed 'the myth of civic competence', whereby what counts in a stable liberal democracy are not politically active citizens, but politically competent citizens who believe that they can, if they so choose, influence the political process.

Clearly, however, there is an inherent analytical tension between the notion of political participation, especially voting, defined in instrumental terms and participation in elections as symbolic, even ritualized events, which reproduce and concretize the collective identity of the national community (Parsons 1959; Edelman 1964). From this latter perspective, electoral participation is conceptualized as a form of symbolic action which lends generalized support to the political system. Thus, for example, Dalton writes: 'Voting is the one activity that binds the individual to the political system and legitimizes the rest of the democratic process' (1988: 41). It follows that symbolic participation should, ideally, involve the entire electorate.

We find a parallel to this tension in contemporary approaches to the analysis of political participation. On the one hand, researchers investigating voting behaviour, primarily seeking to explain partisanship, remain divided over the relative merits of sociological and rational

choice models of electoral behaviour (Tullock 1967; Riker and
Ordeshook 1968; Crepaz 1990). On the other hand, research into the
wider field of political action in the tradition of Almond and Verba, or
Barnes, Kaase, *et al.* (1979), in which the central questions are the
challenges to representative democracy, often eschews consideration
of voting *per se*. The reasons which Marsh and Kaase (1979: 86), for
example, gave for excluding voting from their analysis of 'conventional political participation' are enlightening:

Voting is a unique form of political behaviour in the sense that it occurs only
rarely, is highly biased by strong mechanisms of social control and social
desirability enhanced by the rain-dance ritual of campaigning, and does not
involve the voter in informational or other costs . . . As a consequence we did
not include 'voting' in our conventional participation scale.

Although such a decision may be valid for the development of a
social-psychological portrait of political activism, it precludes the
analysis of exactly those indicators which might show changes in the
'strong mechanisms of social control and desirability' attached to
voting. Yet the thesis that there may be a radicalization of the democratic process associated with modernizing processes, raises the prospect of a weakening of such societal mechanisms, and hence of the
legitimating functions of the electoral process.

In this chapter, we focus on levels of participation in national
elections as an indicator of the relationship between national political
cultures and political institutions. We are concerned with aggregate
levels of participation; that is turnout rather than partisanship. In
particular, we are concerned with changes over time in levels of
participation. We take it as axiomatic that, for the reasons we shall
review below, no West European political system is at present facing
systemic crisis, despite the well-known differences between countries
in their typical levels of electoral turnout. Thus our concern is to
explain and interpret any *changes* in the levels of national electoral
participation, rather than to explore the reasons for cross-national
differences in absolute levels.

Of course, participation in national elections is by no means the
only form of institutionalized linkage between citizens and the state.
All West European countries hold local elections, several also hold
regional elections, and many of them now participate in elections for
the European Parliament. In addition, there is the range of quasi-
institutionalized interactions with politicians and public bodies which

Marsh and Kaase categorized as conventional political action. But we know from a number of studies, including Political Action, that voting in national elections remains the most all-embracing activity: 'contacting' is far less common in Western Europe (Dalton 1988; Parry, Moyser, and Day 1992). Our decision to exclude these other forms of political participation from this chapter, and the next, is not intended to diminish their significance in the processes of intermediation between citizen and state. It is due simply to the paucity of comparative time-series data.

The term 'democratic national election' embraces a variety of different institutional provisions and practices. National elections in Western Europe are held in unitary and federal states. The elections may be for presidents or for members of legislatures. Voters may face a choice between individual party candidates or between party lists. The elections may take place at constitutionally determined intervals, or on dates determined by the government of the day within certain fixed time limits. Although there is now universal adult suffrage, the voting age still varies, as do the criteria for the disenfranchisement of certain groups, especially immigrants. Similarly, although most national elections in Western Europe are conducted under systems of proportional representation, electoral arrangements vary quite widely.

Some of these differences in electoral arrangements may contribute to the differences between countries in levels of overall electoral turnout. Compulsory voting may produce higher levels of turnout, and changes in the franchise or in electoral arrangements may have similar effects. The enfranchisement of women, only some twenty years ago in Switzerland, Spain, and Portugal, and the widespread reduction of the voting age to 18 during the 1960s and 1970s, are also possible causes of changes in turnout.

Differences between countries in their constitutional and institutional arrangements for elections, as well as changes within individual countries over time, may have important consequences for electoral turnout. According to Lane and Ersson (1990), Tingsten (1937) was the first to suggest that obligatory participation affects voting behaviour (cf. Powell 1980). Campbell *et al.* (1960) reviewed the hypothesis that in the United States, procedural barriers to registration may account for non-voting. Such ideas persist in many interpretations of the lower turnouts in the United States compared with other Western countries (Kelley, Ayres, and Bowen 1967; Powell 1986). More recently, multivariate analyses have been used to assess the significance of institutional factors when comparing voting behaviour cross-nationally, and for comparing the relative importance of institutional and individual-level factors (Bartolini and Mair 1990; Dittrich and Johansen 1983; Flickinger and Studlar 1992; Jackman 1987; Lane and Ersson 1990; Pedersen 1983; Powell 1980, 1986). There are multiple threads running through this literature. Some analysts address the themes raised by Tingsten and by Campbell (Powell 1980), others focus on the relationships between party systems and voter volatility. For example, Bartolini and Mair (1990: 146ff.) examine changes in electoral turnout in order to assess the stability of party affiliations.

It is beyond the scope of this chapter to examine this debate. Moreover, rather than explaining cross-sectional differences in levels of turnout between countries, our concern is with longitudinal trends in electoral turnout (cf. Crewe 1981; Flickinger and Studlar 1992). Crewe concluded that electoral turnout had been remarkably stable in liberal democracies throughout the period from the 1940s to the 1970s. More recent studies, however, have often concluded that turnout is declining and, for some (Martikainen and Yrjönen 1991), worryingly so. We turn now to examine the data.

Dynamics of Demographic Change

It is commonplace in the literature to find a distinction between macro, aggregate-level, and micro, individual-level, hypotheses about electoral participation (Weber 1949; Lane and Ersson 1990). Yet often consideration of the macro level takes place solely in terms of institutional and socio-economic variables. Equally important for the analysis of mass participation in elections are differences between, and changes in, the demographic structure of countries. This is certainly the case for postwar Western Europe.

The analyses of electoral participation in this chapter focus on comparative changes in voting percentages and ratios among eligible populations. The overall numerical demography of those populations, however, has often changed, and continues to change, in significant ways which may be masked by our presentation of the electoral data in terms of percentages and ratios. For example, the statistic that there was a drop of some 4 percentage points in mean electoral turnout in Western Europe between 1950 and 1990 completely masks the statistic that the overall population of Western Europe increased over the same period by some 22 per cent, and the enfranchised population by even more, from 143 million to 263 million. In order to put the data on electoral participation in context, our first task is to consider the dynamics of demographic change in Western Europe. We examine overall population change, and changes in the age, gender, and education profiles of these populations.

Population Change

The total population of all West European countries has grown over the last fifty years. In some cases this growth has been quite dramatic. The French population, for example, increased by some 15 million between 1940 and 1990, an increase of 36 per cent on the 1940 base. As important, however, are the rates of population change. These are illustrated in Figures 2.1a–2.1c,[2] which show the peak of the so-called 'baby boom' around 1970 in the more developed countries, such as Britain,[3] Italy, and the Scandinavian countries, followed by a declining rate of growth through the 1990s. Less economically developed countries, such as Greece and Ireland, show a comparable pattern a decade later, peaking around 1980. By the year 2000, all Scandinavian countries will approximate to zero population growth, while in the remainder of Western Europe, overall growth will continue for longer at some 2–3 per cent per decade. The exception is Ireland, with a continuing growth rate of around 10 per cent per decade and still slowly climbing (Simons 1992: 50ff.; United Nations 1989).

However, for present purposes, our particular interest is the changing composition of the adult, enfranchised population. The most obvious development is the entry into the voting population in the early 1990s of the age cohorts of the 1970s baby boom. But the age structure of West European populations is changing more radically. Throughout the post-war period, and especially since the 1970s, life expectancy has been increasing from a mean of 68 years in 1950 to 78 years in the 1990s. At the same time, the total fertility rate, even controlling for changes in infant mortality rates, has declined from a West European mean of 2.8 children in the mid-1960s to a mean of 1.7 children by the 1990s. This is well below the mean of 2.1 children required for population replacement. Indeed, only in Ireland is there now a positive population birth rate, and it is predicted that the negative birth rate throughout the rest of Western Europe will continue for at least a further generation.

Political Involvement

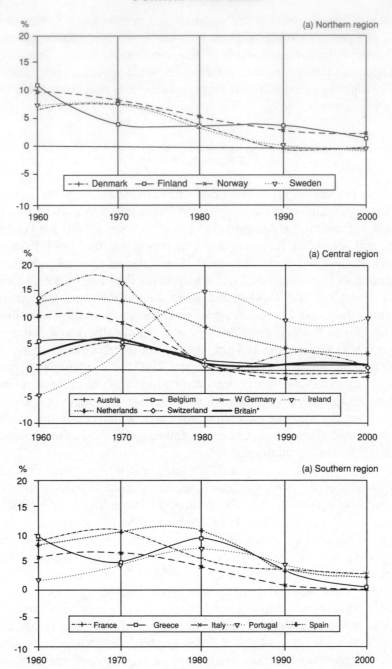

See facing page for caption.

This means that the figures for the overall rate of population change mask a compound effect. In the first place, an increasingly large proportion of the populations of Western Europe are older people who live longer; secondly, and at the same time, there is a sharper rate of decline in the birth rate than the charts might imply. In crude terms, compared with 1950, by the millennium the proportion of the population below voting age will have halved, while the proportion above retirement age will have doubled (United Nations 1989). Thus the overall size of West European electorates doubled during the post-war period. Moreover, in so far as electoral turnout may prove to be age related, then statistics which show that, over time, the same proportions of the young and the old vote, may actually be masking the rapid increase in the total numbers of older people going to the polls.

The immediate post-war populations in Western Europe showed a gender skew in favour of women. This ranged from some 14 per cent more women than men in Austria, to just 1.5 per cent more women in Denmark. Ireland alone showed a very modest male skew of just under 2 per cent. The most significant general factors accounting for this skew are the greater life expectancy of women and the effects of the Second World War on the male populations of many countries. Over the last forty years, however, in all countries without exception, the constant general trend has been the convergence of the sexes. Projections of this trend indicate that sometime next century, Western Europe as a whole is likely to stabilize with a gender skew towards women of only some 2–3 per cent. Among older populations, however, due to their greater life expectancy, women continue to outnumber men.

Quantifying changes in the demography of education is more diffi-cult. Systems of compulsory and higher education differ considerably between Western European countries, and have often been changed during the lifetime of the current population. In general, the trend has been towards longer periods of compulsory education. However, even today the age at which school attendance must begin varies from 5 years of age in the Netherlands and Britain to 7 years in Denmark and Germany. Similarly, the school-leaving age varies from 14 years in Ireland, Portugal, and Spain, to 18 years in Belgium and Germany.

FIGURE 2.1. *Percentage population growth over decade base, 1960–2000*
Sources: Tabah (1990); United Nations (1991); World Bank (1992).

Again, the age at which university first degrees are generally obtained varies between 21 and 24 years of age (OECD 1992; Chisholm 1992). It follows, therefore, that for any given period, cross-national comparisons using either years of full-time education or school-leaving age will be seriously deficient. The problem is even greater for comparisons over several decades.

One tempting alternative is to compare the type of education received, either by comparing the educational institutions people have attended or the qualifications they have obtained. Unfortunately, these indicators prove to be no better for constructing comparative categories: educational institutions and the qualifications they award have often changed, and they differ markedly between national educational systems. These difficulties are compounded by the way most education data are compiled which makes it difficult to proceed, reliably, from single-point, national cohort data to a demographic profile of education among West European populations as a whole.[4] At present, we must turn to survey data for estimates of educational levels.

In this chapter and the next, we have cut through the Gordian knot of these difficulties by adopting a pragmatic, tripartite categorization of national education levels, using whichever appeared to be the most appropriate data for the time point and country concerned. We have three categories, or levels, of education: 'minimal', 'intermediate', and 'higher'. Entries in these categories may draw on data for the number of years of full-time education, the age of completion of full-time education, or the highest educational qualification achieved. Moreover, these data are tested against macro-demographic sources when these are available, but rely solely on survey data where they are not.

Of course, data of this sort would not be suitable for any detailed analysis of the importance of education—over time or cross-nationally—for political culture and participation. Our three categories would be too crude to justify, say, cross-national comparisons of the values and actions of the most highly educated. But we do not attempt that here. Rather, the categories are used to construct a ratio of the proportion of the highly educated over that of the minimally educated in a sample of national populations at a given time. This ratio increases as the proportion of the highly to the minimally educated increases. This is our indicator of education effects. Thus if this calculation were applied to the British data, for example, the ratio of graduates to those with no qualifications would be 0.01 in 1959, 0.14 in 1971, rising to 0.29 by the late 1980s.

In Figures 2.2*a* and 2.2*b* we plot this ratio for samples of the adult populations of West European countries over the last twenty years.[5] This is the period during which the rapid expansion of post-war education begins to become evident in the educational profiles of adult populations, although, of course, the rates of change in the educational ratios for the total adult population are much slower than for generational cohorts. None the less, the figures clearly show the differences in educational expansion between countries like Denmark, the Netherlands, and Belgium, with over half of today's cohorts now entering some form of higher education, and other countries, such as Greece, Ireland, and Britain where still a quarter or less do so (OECD 1992).

Implications of Demographic Change

Clearly, then, Western Europe is going through a process of considerable change in its demographic profile. The rate of overall growth in national populations is declining towards zero by the beginning of the next century. At the same time, the cross-sectional profile of these populations is changing as a result of negative birth rates, increasing life expectancy, and a small gender skew due to the longer life expectancy of women. The net results of these changes are populations with an increasing proportion of older to younger people, with a ratio of the order of 2 : 1 or higher being reached during the 1990s in the more developed countries. The educational profile is also changing, but more variably than the age and gender profiles, owing to different national education policies. Moreover, there is no consistent relationship between levels of economic development and national policies on higher education. Countries such as Britain, say, may rank highly on measures of economic development, but are still grouped with Ireland and Spain in a ranking of the proportions entering higher education. None the less, throughout Europe, the proportion of each generational cohort entering higher education is increasing rapidly, albeit against different baselines, while the proportion with just minimal education is declining even faster.

These demographic changes have important consequences for the analysis of political participation. As we shall see below, it has long been recognized that there is a direct, almost linear, relationship between voting and age (Crewe, Fox, and Alt 1977; Dalton 1988; Parry, Moyser, and Day 1992; Verba and Nie 1972). At least up to

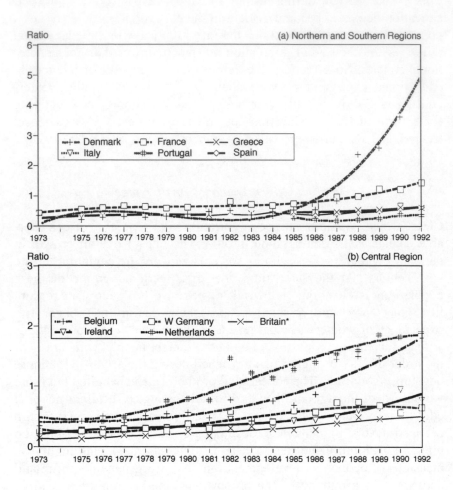

FIGURE 2.2. *Education in EC countries: ratio of higher to minimal levels,*
1973–92

Sources: Eurobarometer cumulative file (1973–91, ZA Study 1684B); OECD (1993).

the age of infirmity, the likelihood of voting increases with each successively older age cohort. Thus, changes in demography suggest that the absolute numbers of citizens likely to vote should be increasing. Broadly similar considerations apply as a result of the changing educational profile. Again, it is conventionally held that the likelihood of voting is closely related to education levels. Thus we expect age and education to have a composite effect. We shall examine the evidence shortly.

In Chapter 3, when we turn to other types of political participation, the effects of demographic change may well turn out to be more complicated. Many analysts (Beer 1982; Crozier, Huntington, and Watanuki 1975; Dalton 1988; Dalton and Küchler 1990) have reported that direct political action, such as taking part in protest marches or occupations, is largely an activity among younger, better educated citizens. The demographic trend, however, is towards increasingly better educated populations, but with steadily smaller ratios of younger to older age cohorts. These trends could well have opposite effects on political participation. We examine the survey evidence for net effects in the next chapter.

Post-war Electoral Trends

It was noted earlier that at any one period in time, there are always marked differences between countries in levels of electoral turnout. In the late 1980s, for example, the range was between 47 per cent of the eligible population in Switzerland to 94 per cent in Belgium, with a mean level of 80 per cent for all eighteen West European countries.[6] But it was also suggested that a country-by-country comparison of overall levels of turnout is not a particularly useful way of studying the dynamics of electoral participation. While cross-national comparisons of turnout are important for some purposes, what matters in our analysis is a comparison of the trends in turnout within countries over time. If the data can be presented in this way, we shall be able to interpret rates of change, if any, in electoral participation using a universal comparative measure.

As a basis for measuring the trends in electoral turnout over the post-war period, we calculated the mean level of overall turnout for each country in all national elections since 1945.[7] Since national elections across Western Europe have taken place at different times, we have adopted five-year time periods as a presentational device. Then, for each country, we calculated the difference between the turnout for the national election(s) which took place within each five-year period, averaging the figures in cases where there was more than one election, and the overall mean level of turnout for the post-war period in that country (cf. Bartolini and Mair 1990; Flickinger and Studlar 1992). This technique also allows us to determine the mean level of turnout for Western Europe as a whole.

Taking all eighteen countries together, including the three southern countries which have not routinely held elections since 1945, turnout in the post-war period is 83 per cent. Against this overall mean, during the last five-year period when all countries held national elections, 1985–9, the West European mean was 80 per cent, the lowest for any five-year period. The highest mean for any five-year period was 85 per cent for 1960–5. Thus, as Figure 2.3 shows, there has been a recent decline in overall turnout when measured against the post-1945 mean level. But a decline of some 3 percentage points is a very small change indeed. Bearing in mind the many demographic changes in these populations during the last forty years, the most telling conclusion must be that a decline of less than 3 percentage points around the overall mean of 83 per cent indicates remarkable stability in turnout throughout the post-war period.

Inevitably, the overall measure conceals greater variation in electoral turnout for individual countries. In Figures 2.4*a*–2.4*c* we show the variations from the post-1945 national mean turnout level for northern, Central, and southern European countries respectively. Our expectation of greater variation than in the overall level is confirmed. However, when Switzerland and the more recently democratized southern countries are excluded, the variation only increases from less than 3 percentage points to less than 8 percentage points.

Turning to the trends over time, the plots show that within none of the three regions is there any consistent pattern of variation over time from the overall mean turnout. Some countries within each group do show a drop below the overall mean during the last decade. In the north, this applies especially to Finland, where the major decline took place in the early 1970s (cf. Martikainen and Yrjönen 1991). In the Central region it applies to Switzerland and—to a much lesser extent—to West Germany. And it also applies, in so far as such data are meaningful, to the newly democratized countries of Portugal and Spain. As important, however, if Portugal, Spain, and Switzerland are excluded as

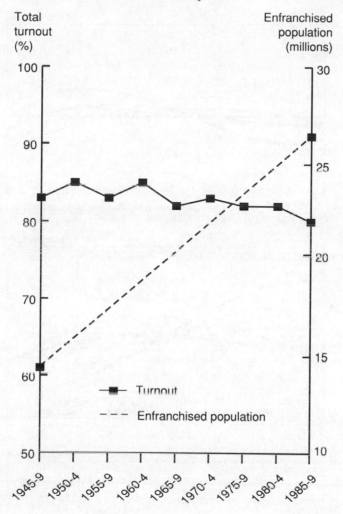

Figure 2.3. *West European electoral turnout, 1945–90*
Sources: Mackie and Rose (1991); World Bank (1992); national election returns.

exceptional cases, is that in the remaining fifteen countries the trends
in turnout for the last decade divide equally between those that are
falling and those that are stable or rising.

The evidence suggests, then, that it is not the case that over recent
years there is a *general* trend towards declining electoral participation
in Western Europe as a whole. This is equally true if we consider
Europe in regional categories, or in terms of measures of modernity.

Political Involvement

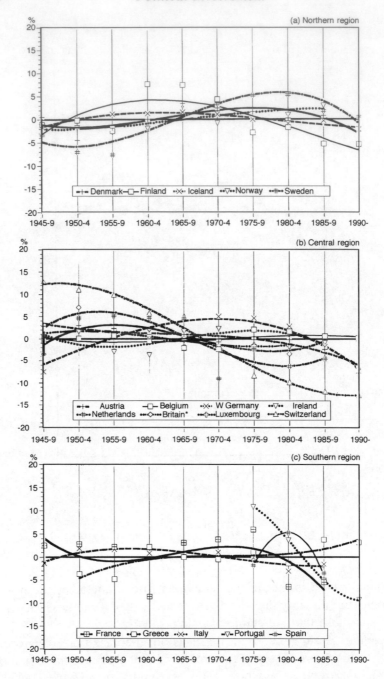

See facing page for caption.

For example, among the more developed countries, the trend is slightly downwards in Germany and Sweden but slightly upwards in Britain.

Voting and Age

It may well be, of course, that the overall stability in electoral turnout during the post-war period masks trends which have not yet become evident. Such trends could arise simply as a result of the macro-demographic changes in the composition of populations which we outlined earlier; for example, there is likely to be a strong correlation between electoral participation and the age of the voter. For whatever reason, the young are less likely to vote than the old. Typically, the relationship is linear, with each successively older cohort being more likely to vote.

It follows, then, that as the ratio of older to younger cohorts increases, so overall turnout levels may be expected to increase. However, we noted earlier that the theory of societal modernization foresees the possibility of rather different changes in political behaviour. This thesis suggests that in advanced industrial societies, new modes of political participation may not just supplement, but also replace, participation through institutionalized channels such as political parties. Thus, if the factors which produce and sustain such a political subculture were to spread through society as the result of inter-generational change, then over time electoral participation would decline.

In order to provide the basis for examining this thesis in greater detail in later chapters, it is important to establish whether, although trendless overall, the socio-demographic composition of West European voters is changing. For this, we draw on survey data, rather than published electoral returns. Once again, our interest is focused on changes over time rather than cross-national differences which may remain constant over time. Our unit of measurement is again a ratio, this time the ratio of the percentage who vote among the youngest enfranchised cohort at any one point in time as against the percentage who vote among an older cohort. Specifically, we have taken a ratio of the 20–30 year old

FIGURE 2.4. *National elections turnout since 1945: percentage variation around mean turnout*

Sources: Mackie and Rose (1991); World Bank Tables (1992); national election returns.

Political Involvement

TABLE 2.1. *Electoral turnout in national elections:*
ratios of younger to older age cohorts, 1960–92

	1960–5	1970–4	1979–81	1985–9	1990–2	1992
Northern Europe						
Denmark	—	—	0.72	0.86	—	0.99
Finland	—	0.88	0.90	0.81	0.75	—
Norway	0.96	0.93	0.89	0.88	—	0.87
Sweden	0.90	0.97	0.92	0.91	0.94	0.94
Central Europe						
Belgium	—	—	—	0.87	—	1.00
Britain	0.91	0.84	0.84	0.88	0.93	—
West Germany	0.90	0.91	0.90	0.84	—	0.90
Netherlands	—	0.64	0.91	0.80	—	0.89
Ireland	—	—	—	0.56	—	0.86
Austria	—	0.64	0.73	—	—	—
Switzerland	—	0.71	—	—	—	—
Southern Europe						
France	—	—	0.83	0.77	—	0.80
Greece	—	—	—	0.47	—	0.90
Italy	0.72	0.41	0.81	0.71	—	0.66
Portugal	—	—	—	0.67	—	0.91
Spain	—	—	—	0.63	—	0.83
Mean	0.88	0.77	0.84	0.74	0.87	0.89

Notes: A ratio of 1.00 would indicate that the same percentage of both cohorts voted. The reliability of the 1970–4 data for Italy, based on the Political Action survey, is uncertain. The 1990–2 ratios are based on national election studies. The 1992 ratios are based on turnout in the most recent national elections as reported in Eurobarometer, No. 37.

Sources: national election surveys in Denmark, Finland, Britain, Netherlands, Norway, Sweden, and West Germany; Civic Culture (1959); Political Action (1973–6); ISSP (1985); Eurobarometer, No. 31.

cohort as against the cohort of 50 years and older.[8] Whenever possible, the data used here have been drawn from national post-election surveys, but when these were not available we have used data from more general comparative surveys during the relevant period. The latter surveys have not always been conducted immediately after a national election.

As we can see from Table 2.1, using survey data means that we are unable to calculate age ratios for all West European countries and time periods. Moreover, survey responses on reported voting are less reliable than official voting returns (but see Swaddle and Heath 1989). None the less, the data in Table 2.1 provide clear confirmation of the general thesis that younger people are less likely to vote than older people. No entry in the table shows a ratio of above 1.00, which would occur if a higher percentage of the younger rather than the older age cohorts said they had voted in their last national election. Indeed, the only entries in the table approaching a ratio of 1.00 are from a Eurobarometer survey in 1992. The overall mean ratio for all time points is 0.82.

In view of the nature of our data, a more detailed interpretation of Table 2.1, in terms of cross-national comparisons and trends over time, must be cautious. At first sight, one striking difference is between the ratios for the countries of northern and southern Europe, placed respectively in the top and bottom halves of the table. These suggest that, in general, the differences in voting behaviour between younger and older age cohorts are much greater in the southern countries than in the northern countries of Western Europe. However, these differences may well be an artefact arising from the fact that the data for the northern countries are taken largely from national election surveys, while such specialized data are not available for southern Europe.

For those countries where election survey data are available—Finland, Norway, Sweden, Britain, Germany, the Netherlands—the trends over time show no consistent pattern, and certainly no general trend towards declining electoral participation among the youngest cohort. The continuing decline in Finland is exceptional, falling from 0.90 in 1979–81, to 0.81 in 1985–9, and to 0.75 in 1991 (cf. Martikainen and Yrjönen 1991). In Britain, on the other hand, after declining in the late 1960s, the ratio has been increasing since the late 1970s, reaching 0.93 for the 1992 election (cf. Crewe, Fox, and Alt 1977; Heath and Topf 1986). Our data clearly confirm, therefore, that throughout Western Europe for at least the last thirty years, the youngest electors are less likely to vote than older electors. But we have found no evidence of any general trend towards an increasing difference between these groups over time. Rather, we find minor fluctuations, with both increasing and decreasing ratios over the last decade or so.

It is beyond the scope of this chapter to consider what factors may explain the country-by-country differences we have found. However, in the case of Britain, we have survey data for the late 1980s on the electorate's beliefs about voting in a national election. In the 1987 British Election Study, respondents were asked to say which of the following statements came closest to their views about voting:

In general elections:

(1) It's not really worth voting.
(2) People should only vote if they care who wins.
(3) It is everyone's duty to vote.

Only 3 per cent of respondents chose the first option, and over 75 per cent chose the third. Moreover, of the people who said they had not voted, only 16 per cent chose the first option. But there were differences between the age cohorts. Just 2 per cent of older respondents believed it was not worth voting in general elections, but 6 per cent of the youngest respondents took this view. Moreover, whereas some 84 per cent of those 50 years or older believed there is a duty to vote, this dropped to 60 per cent among the 20–30 year olds.

Britain may not, of course, be typical of other West European political cultures. In so far as it is, however, clearly there is little evidence of a subculture among the young which is so apathetic towards the electoral process that they see no point in voting. Where younger and older electors do differ is in their reasons for voting, with the young less likely to express the notion of a duty to vote. This should be no cause for alarm about the democratic process among defenders of pluralist theory.

Voting and Gender

There is an intriguing disagreement among scholars about the significance of gender in voting. The conventional wisdom of electoral studies is that gender is not significant. In their analysis of British elections, Butler and Stokes (1974) simply did not consider gender. A decade later, Heath, Jowell, and Curtice (1985: 23) concluded that, so far as voting is concerned, 'It is the absence of gender differences which is striking'. By contrast, in their study of wider forms of political action, from which voting was excluded, Marsh and Kaase stated that 'Conventional participation is most heavily influenced by sex' (1979: 106). A decade later, Dalton asserted, 'Gender is also an important determinant of political activism. Men are more politically active than women in virtually all Western democracies' (1988: 49). Both views may, of course, be correct within the terms of their different perspectives on political participation.

Our findings on electoral participation are unequivocal. For the entire period from the 1960s onwards, we have found no country for which there is a statistically significant gender effect on electoral turnout. Moreover, where and when there are small gender differences in the data on self-reported voting, it is as common to find that more women than men say they have voted as vice versa. Ironically, in four of the eight countries surveyed for Political Action, the data show that more women than men stated they had voted. Similarly, in the most recent data, there is no discernible pattern of gender effects. Where small differences do appear, they may be counter-intuitive. In the late 1980s, for example, there was a slightly greater likelihood of men voting in Germany, but a modestly higher proportion of women stated they had voted in Britain, Spain, and Portugal.

This is an important finding. First, bearing in mind the modest demographic gender ratio in favour of women, the absence of a gender skew in electoral participation means that, in absolute numerical terms, somewhat more women than men may be expected to vote in national elections. This may well be significant not only for politicians who set the policy agenda of national elections, but also for the processes of system legitimation. Secondly, it has been argued by feminist critics of pluralist democratic theory that women and men participate in politics in different ways (Norris 1990; Phillips 1991). Women, it is claimed, engage in different norms of citizenship, preferring consensual, group activities to the conflictual and competitive aspects of politics, typified by elections (Chapman 1990). This debate is well beyond the scope of this chapter, but the evidence we have adduced on electoral turnout lends no support to the general notion that women are less involved in voting than men. Indeed, the clear trend towards equal electoral participation, and sometimes even higher participation among women than among men, suggests there are no inherent gender differences in notions of citizenship.[9]

Voting and Education

Education has long been seen as the key to resolving the inherent tensions between consensus and conflict in the modern democratic process. Lipset, for example, drew on Dewey to argue that education would enable citizens to understand the need for tolerance, restrain them from adhering to extremist doctrines, and increase their capacity to make rational choices. Similarly, Almond and Verba considered that 'the educated classes possess the keys to political participation and involvement' (Almond and Verba 1963: 381; cf. Lipset 1959: 56; Heath and Topf 1986: 546). Moreover, numerous studies of the 1960s and 1970s confirmed that, at least for American elections, there was a highly significant correlation between levels of education and electoral participation. Kirkpatrick (1979: 278), for example, demonstrated a consistent 30-point separation in turnout between people with less than nine years education and those with over twelve years. Several studies of West European countries have identified similar correlations between education levels and voting, but they also identified anomalies and methodological problems. Kavanagh (1980) re-analysed the Almond and Verba data to demonstrate that, in Britain, the least educated had the highest levels of political competence. Indeed, re-analysis of these data shows that in none of the three European states surveyed—West Germany, Italy, Britain—is there a clear, positive relationship between educational levels and reported voting in the last national election.

The data on education and electoral participation presented in Table 2.2 have been constructed on the same basis, and from the same sources, as those in Table 2.1. Again, the measure is a ratio, this time showing turnout among the least well educated cohort as a ratio of turnout among the most highly educated cohort.

Our findings are clear. Throughout the last thirty years, across Western Europe, the mean ratio of voting, for the lowest educational cohort compared with the highest, varies less than 0.05 from unity.[10] That is, we find no generalized educational effect for voting, and no generalized trend over time. Table 2.2 shows country-specific differences and country-specific time trends. It appears from the three data-points we have available that in Austria and Switzerland the least well educated are far less likely to vote than the most highly educated, but these data are derived from general cross-national surveys, so they cannot be checked against national election surveys. Perhaps more significantly, we find no general pattern which distinguishes between, say, northern and southern Europe, nor between the more and less developed countries. The data for Ireland, Portugal, and Sweden look much the same. The very modest trends over time in West Germany and Sweden are in opposite directions.

In Western Europe, then, there is no significant correlation between educational attainment and electoral turnout. To put the same point in

TABLE 2.2. *Electoral turnout in national elections: ratios of minimal to higher educational levels, 1960–92*

	1960–5	1970–5	1979–81	1985–9	1990	1992
Northern Europe						
Denmark	—	—	1.01	0.98	—	0.81
Finland	—	0.93	—	—	1.02	—
Norway	0.95	0.96	0.97	0.98	—	0.85
Sweden	0.94	0.96	0.97	1.00	0.96	—
Central Europe						
Belgium	—	—	0.80	1.00	—	0.97
Great Britain	0.97	0.95	0.90	0.98	1.09	—
West Germany	1.03	0.96	0.96	0.96	—	0.84
Netherlands	—	0.82	0.93	0.95	—	0.80
Ireland	—	—	—	1.05	—	0.90
Austria	—	0.92	0.76	—	—	—
Switzerland	—	0.68	—	—	—	—
Southern Europe						
France	—	—	0.96	1.05	—	0.82
Greece	—	—	—	1.02	—	0.87
Italy	1.12	1.40	0.94	0.91	—	0.60
Portugal	—	—	—	0.98	—	0.90
Spain	—	—	—	1.05	—	0.93
Mean	1.00	0.95	0.92	0.99	1.02	0.84

Note: See Table 2.1.

Sources: See Table 2.1.

different terms, the evidence for Western Europe suggests that, since the 1960s, people of all educational levels possess the skills to participate in national elections. When the parallel data are reviewed in the next chapter, we may well find confirmation of the hypothesis that educational attainment is highly significant for other forms of political activity. This would then lend weight to the argument that voting is fundamentally different from other forms of political participation. By the same token, however, the clear evidence is that, in general, West European citizens of low and high levels of education are equally as likely to vote in national elections.

Conclusion

This chapter has reviewed the evidence for change in the overall level of electoral turnout in Western Europe against a background of several, shorter-term, country-specific studies, which have demonstrated declining levels of turnout in recent years. While the evidence from such studies is not questioned, the conclusion we draw is that there is no evidence of a general trend towards lower levels of electoral turnout. Rather, the trend lines are remarkably stable, particularly when set in the context of significant changes in the institutional arrangements and demographies of West European countries during the post-war period.

As to the dynamics of societal change, we have shown that gender and education have no significant effect on the probability of voting, but age very clearly does. Consistently and universally, older people are more likely to vote than younger people. However, this is a long-standing phenomenon and, again, we have found no evidence of a generalized trend over time towards a changing ratio in the propensity to vote between the age cohorts.

On the basis of these data, therefore, the evidence suggests that West European national elections are in little danger of losing the capacity to bind citizens to the political system. Rather, provided the strong relationship between voting propensity and age continues to hold, then as the mean age of West European populations continues to rise for at least a further generation, so levels of electoral turnout may well follow.

NOTES

1. Northern Ireland is, perhaps, a significant exception to this generalization. Even in this case, however, the political violence is not directly related to national elections in Britain.
2. The percentage population growth over decade base refers to the percentage increase in the size of the population from one decade to the next, that is, from 1950 to 1960, from 1960 to 1970, and so on. Thus the figures for 1960 represent the growth from the 1950 baseline. Polynomial plots show the best fit of a line through the data-points where it cannot be assumed that the relationship is linear.
3. In this chapter, the term 'Britain' is used rather than 'the United Kingdom'. All the analyses drawing on macro-level data and electoral returns refer to the United Kingdom, which includes Northern Ireland. But the analyses based on survey data

do not include Northern Ireland since it was not included in most of the original surveys.

4. The education statistics published by international bodies such as the OECD and UN, based on returns by national governments, typically show the distribution of levels of education within specified age cohorts in national educational systems. It is comparatively easy to extract from such publications data on the patterns of educational participation for, say, 15–19 year olds, or the number of university first degrees awarded in a given year. Thus, for example, we know that in the late 1980s, even in the most developed countries, there remained wide differences in national educational provision for 15–19 year olds, with almost two thirds of all 19 year olds in Germany in full- or part-time education compared with a quarter in Britain (OECD 1992; Chisholm 1992). But relating the annual data on educational provision to overall levels of education in the entire adult population, however long ago they completed their education, requires highly complex calculations. There is research in progress, such as the OECD International Education Indicators Project (OECD 1992), which will eventually make the task easier, but even this project is designed to facilitate contemporary rather than historical research.

5. The data for Figures 2.2a and 2.2b are based on the Cumulative Eurobarometer 1973–91 survey data (ZA Study 1684) and *Education at a Glance* (OECD 1992). There are no comparable time series data for non-EC European countries. The plots are based on curvilinear regression analysis where the relationships are assumed to be non-linear.

6. Turnout statistics may be calculated on several bases. The most commonly used, and the basis adopted for this chapter, is the gross number of voters as a percentage of the registered electorate. The latter figure may be somewhat higher than the total population eligible to vote, based on macro-demographic data, but has the advantage of clarity and consistency with the primary data sources (for a computation of the differences between the two measures for the 1970s, see Powell 1986). It produces a lower figure than the percentage of 'valid' votes cast, a statistic also commonly found in the literature. For present purposes, a vote is a vote—whether or not it is a 'spoilt' one.

7. The data were recalculated from Mackie (1992) and Mackie and Rose (1991), and published national election returns.

8. The youngest age selected was set at 20 years rather than 18 years in order to exclude from the percentage of non-voters those respondents who were not eligible to vote at the time of the last election before the survey was conducted. It also included cases where, at the time and in the country concerned, 18 year olds were not enfranchised.

9. Alternatively, these findings might be incorporated within the thesis by interpreting women's participation as expressive; that is, women vote expressively while men vote instrumentally.

10. The data on which this figure is based do not include the data from Eurobarometer, No. 37 (1992), which show considerable discrepancies from equivalent national election surveys.

3

Beyond Electoral Participation

RICHARD TOPF

In this chapter we turn from the analysis of post-war trends in electoral participation to look at wider forms of participation in the democratic process. Again, our focus is on trends throughout Western Europe as a whole, rather than country-by-country comparisons. Our conclusion will be that, whereas electoral turnout in Western European countries has remained remarkably stable, political participation beyond voting has been rising dramatically.

It has become common practice to refer to political activities beyond electoral participation as being, in some sense, unconventional participation. It is important not to forget, however, that such notions are historically relative. The peaceful modes of activity identified in survey analyses as having become increasingly prevalent since the 1960s often have culturally embedded roots which pre-date mass democracy. Petitioning is an obvious example. Even less peaceful forms of action, such as the occupation of buildings and road barricades, may have cultural links in many countries with the revolutionary history of democracy itself. Thus, what is significant about such activities is not that they are novel—although some forms of action clearly are new—but rather their relationship to the development of representative democracy.

Participation and the Model of Representative Democracy

The model of representative democracy, as outlined in Chapter 1, incorporates an inherent tension in its notion of political participation. On the one hand, it holds that citizens should be sufficiently informed about, and involved in, the political process such that they perceive the principles of pluralist democracy to be realizable. Thereby, citizens reproduce support for the democratic system, and hence ensure its stability. On the other hand, this 'myth of democratic competence' requires, above all, that mass participation should be moderate in its frequency and its forms; too little or too much participation could equally threaten the delicate balance of the system.

As we noted in the previous chapter, the historical evidence of the post-1945 period reveals that Western representative democracies have proved far more robust than many political analysts feared. The purportedly fragile, re-emergent democracies of the post-war period have survived the initially low levels of mass political involvement which were thought to undermine their viability. Similarly, all survived the rise of the protest movements of the late 1960s onwards, which again it was feared might have overloaded their political systems.

However, this is not to say that in Western democracies the relationships between citizens and state have remained unchanged over the last fifty years. As Fuchs and Klingemann (Chapter 1) demonstrate, it is certainly arguable that while the problems of stability may no longer be a central issue, the very success of the processes of societal modernization—diagnosed as the key to successful representative democracies—may themselves have created new problems. In particular, it has been argued that the emergence of a postmodern political culture is likely to be accompanied by a radicalization of the democratic process to which the institutional structures of democratic systems may be unable to adapt.

At the core of all such theoretical analyses, of course, are questions about the nature of political participation. In the last resort, it is not what people believe *per se* which will shape the future of our democracies, but what they do, and do not do, as the result of their beliefs and perceptions. Indeed, as we shall consider later, it was the propensity of analysts to over-interpret attitudinal survey data into behavioural predictions that led to many of the crisis prognoses of the 1970s (Beer 1982; Crozier, Huntington, and Watanuki 1975; cf. Barnes, Kaase, *et al.* 1979).

The contemporary pattern of political participation is now well known and very similar throughout Western democracies (Parry, Moyser, and Day 1992; Dalton 1988; Fuchs 1990). It is illustrated for one country, Britain, in Table 3.1. Voting in elections remains by far the most frequent form of activity, but other forms of engagement with

TABLE 3.1. *Types and levels of political participation in Britain*

Percentage saying they had done the action at least once			
Voting		Group activity	
Vote general	82.5	Informal group	13.8
Vote local	68.8	Organized group	11.2
Vote European	47.3	Issue in group	4.7
Party campaigning		Protesting	
Attended rally	8.6	Signed petition	63.3
Fund raising	5.2	Attended protest meeting	14.6
Canvassed	3.5	Organized petition	8.0
Clerical work	3.5	Political strike	6.5
		Protest march	5.2
Contacting		Political boycott	4.3
Councillor	20.7	Contact media	3.8
Town Hall	17.4	Blocked traffic	1.1
MP	9.7	Physical force	0.2
Civil servant	7.3		
			$(N = c.1,570)$

Source: Parry *et al.* (1992).

political parties are rare. In so far as British citizens make direct contact with other political institutions, some one in five say they have approached their local councillor or town hall, although such approaches are more likely to be about municipal services than policy inputs.

It is, of course, the final two categories of political participation presented by Parry *et al.*—'group activity' and 'protesting'—which are regarded as radical. These types of participation are the principal focus of this chapter.

Modernist and Postmodernist Theses

The postmodernist thesis posits a set of hypotheses about the future of political participation (see Figure 1.2). The first of these hypotheses is that the emergence of a postmodernist political culture will be accompanied by a decline in institutionalized political action and hence a decline in support for the traditional institutions linking citizen and state. The empirical evidence for this thesis was examined in the previous chapter, using electoral turnout as the typical form of such participation. Our clear conclusion was that, although there are country differences, there is no support for the view that electoral participation is declining generally. Trends in attachment to political parties are examined in later chapters in this volume.

The second key postmodernist hypothesis divides into two, integrally related, parts. The first part holds that in postmodern political cultures, there is likely to be an increase in 'further political participation'; that is, participation in the political process through channels other than formal institutions such as political parties and public bureaucracies. Such 'direct' participation may take forms which were considered unconventional a generation or so ago. The second part concerns the rationality which motivates such participation. It is premised on the notion that while 'modern' political participation is instrumentally oriented towards specific political goals, 'postmodern' participation may be informed by expressive or hedonistic rationalities. This orientation towards action matters, it is argued, because of the potential dangers inherent in a mismatch of rationalities between those of politically active citizens, and those of the target political institutions.

We addressed the first thesis in the previous chapter, the second will be considered here. It will be argued that while there are analytical and methodological problems in using survey data to examine this thesis, the direction of the evidence is none the less very clear.

Measuring Political Participation

Estimating the full range and level of political participation is not straightforward. It means using survey data based on questions about what people have done, or would do, which counts as *political*. Questions about 'conventional' action, such as voting or attending party meetings, present few problems. But responses to questions about activity which is less clearly political depends on the format of the question. Inviting respondents to tick items from a list of actions risks, for example, including petitions to the committee of a social club as political action. By contrast, responses to a question specifying that it is about political action (e.g. 'I'm going to read out some different forms of political action that people can take, and I'd like you to tell me . . .') might depend too much on the respondent's conception of what is political. For example, mothers blocking a road to secure a school crossing may not see that as a political act. Focusing questions on policy issues, such as taxation or nuclear weapons, clarifies the purpose of action, but the data are then limited to just those policy areas. In brief, different understandings of what constitutes political action, and the array of concerns that might stimulate people to do more than just vote, make it difficult for surveys to capture the whole spectrum of political action.[1]

The data used in this chapter are taken from comparative survey research spanning over thirty years. The earliest data are from Almond and Verba's 1959 survey for *The Civic Culture* (1963), which was concerned primarily with democratic stability. Hence the questions about political participation beyond voting set the topic in the specific context of actions directed at influencing some perceived, legislative injustice. Respondents were asked what they might do if a 'very unjust or harmful' law was being considered by parliament. Almond and Verba also wanted to encompass their respondents' perceptions of their own political efficacy and the corresponding responsiveness of political institutions. Thus questions were asked, first, about what respondents believed they could do about such an injustice, then what they would do and what they perceived to be effective, and finally what they had ever actually done.

This kind of question format continues to be used, not least because subsequent researchers wished to develop comparable data over time (see Appendix 3.1 for details). Inevitably, however, questions about some non-specific, perceived injustice will not capture many other types of political activity, for the reasons outlined. Unfortunately, there are few survey data which would enable us to compare responses to the 'legislative injustice' form of question with similar types of activity directed at other issues on the political agenda. Some indication of how these compare may be gleaned from the 1986 British Social Attitudes Survey, in which respondents were asked an identical battery of questions about political activities in two different contexts in separate sections of the questionnaire: in one section, in the context of legislative injustice; in another section, in the context of environmental pollution. The responses showed that almost half the respondents purported to have taken some form of action against a perceived legislative injustice, and a quarter to have acted over environmental protection. However, while two-thirds of respondents had engaged in at least one political act over one issue or the other, less than a fifth had done so over both issues

(Topf 1992). The evidence here, then, is that there is little overlap on the two types of issues.

Protest Potential and Political Obligation

In the survey for *The Civic Culture*, Almond and Verba asked their respondents what political actions they had performed, what they believed they could do, what they would do, and what they believed would be effective. However, this battery of questions underwent a crucial transformation when the core concern of social scientists moved away from questions about which form of political culture best supports democratic stability to examine the significance of the political protests of the late 1960s.

For his seminal Protest and Political Consciousness study, Marsh developed a much-extended battery of questions about types of political action, ranging from signing a petition, through demonstrating and occupying buildings, to damaging property and personal violence. In the survey questionnaire, Marsh placed such actions in the context of 'pressing for changes'. Moreover, and crucially, he adapted the questions about what respondents 'would do', to 'would do . . . if [the issue] were important', and used these data to construct a measure of 'protest potential'. Marsh's (1977) study was confined to Britain but the research framework played an important role in the crises theories of the 1970s. Data showing high levels of potential for unconventional forms of political protest, including illegal and violent activities, were widely cited. Beer (1982), for example, reproduced Marsh's key data in full to sustain his argument that British democratic culture had 'collapsed'.

Clearly the notion of protest potential is capable of sustaining two, interrelated but analytically distinct, interpretations. On the one hand, it may be used to predict the likely frequency of different types of political protest at some future date. Thus, for example, Beer interpreted Marsh's figures that some 40 per cent would never join a demonstration and only some 75 per cent would never occupy buildings or block traffic, as indicating that 60 per cent and 25 per cent respectively of the British population might engage in such activity in the future. Only 6 per cent and 1 per cent, respectively, had said that they had actually done these things. Almost twenty years later, with the benefit of hindsight, we know that no Western political system suffered a collapse of its democratic institutions as a result of the upsurge of protest activity in the late 1960s. Moreover, as we shall see, replications of the original survey work show that reported levels of extreme protest activity have not increased from the 1970s to the 1990s (Barnes, Kaase, *et al*. 1979; cf. Jennings, Van Deth, *et al*. 1989; Fuchs 1990; Kaase 1992).

The second interpretation of protest potential data concerns psychological predispositions. That is to say, responses to survey questions asking what people believe they would do, in some specified but hypothetical situation, may be interpreted as indicating their orientation towards both that situation and certain types of action. This raises intriguing conceptual and methodological issues about the meaning of questions about action potential, which we can only touch on in this chapter. One possibility is to interpret their meaning at face value. Thus action potential data do, indeed, indicate the perceptions of respondents about their future behaviour. The significant differences found in all surveys between levels of potential and levels of reported action are then explained by the absence of the political trigger which would convert potential into action. In the case of the typical form of the question outlined above, this would mean that respondents had not perceived an issue of legislative injustice which would warrant taking action.

However, such a position is difficult to sustain in the face of the accumulated survey data we now have. In the first place, numerous analyses of comparative data over the last twenty years have failed to identify any narrowing of the gap between potential and action. Rather, times-series data show that positive responses to questions about hypothetical future actions are poor indicators of what actions people do subsequently perform (Jennings, Van Deth, *et al*. 1989; Fuchs 1990; Kaase 1992). As importantly, we now have a sufficient variety of survey materials about action potential to show that there are design and context effects which point to at least one alternative interpretation of the materials.

One aspect of this problem is the effect of juxtaposing questions in surveys about what respondents say they 'would do' and 'have done' in a given situation. There is now considerable evidence that the context of the former influences responses to the latter (Topf 1992). A second aspect emerges when alternative wordings are substituted for the term 'would do' in the question battery. The conventional questions about legislative injustice were posed in the 1987 British Election Study but—

in contrast to the 1986 and 1989 British Social Attitudes Surveys—instead of asking respondents what 'would you do', people were asked 'which, if any, of the following things do you think people ought to do'. The effect of this change of wording was to increase very significantly the proportion of positive responses. Not only was there near unanimity that people ought to sign petitions and contact their Members of Parliament over harmful or unjust legislation, but the proportions claiming to have performed these actions were more than twice as high as in the 1986 and 1989 surveys when the conventional 'would do' phrase was used.

Taking these two aspects together, such data suggest that action measures may be better interpreted as cultural indicators of dimensions of political obligation rather than as predictors of future levels of actual behaviour. In other words, responses to the 'legislative injustice' battery of questions are informed by the respondents' sense of their democratic obligations. The 'action potential' of individuals reflects not what they will do but what they think they ought to do (Topf 1989*b*, 1992). This aspect of the relationship between citizens and the state is considered in later chapters in this volume.

The Data

The data used in this chapter are of two types. We look first at political discussion as one discrete type of non-institutionalized political action. For this variable, we used data from the Eurobarometer surveys, which have regularly asked respondents how frequently they discuss politics when together with friends. We have also analysed data which—as far as possible—are functionally equivalent to the battery of items on 'unconventional' political action, as developed by Marsh. For this, we used the Civic Culture data as an indicative baseline, and used data from the Political Action Study (1973–6), European Values Survey (1981), Eurobarometer, No. 31 (1989), and the World Values Survey (1990) in order to examine trends over time.[2] In each of these surveys, the battery of items on unconventional action was created with the same core structure, although for the reasons discussed earlier, we did not include the items on action potential. However, the surveys differed, both in the way questions on political action were contextualized, and in whether a time period was specified for reported actions (see

Appendix 3.1 for details). Thus detailed comparisons of trends should be treated with caution.

Political Discussion

In the previous chapter we noted the continuing debate about whether or not its ritualistic elements precludes voting as a useful measure of political involvement. We find similar disagreements about political discussion with family, friends, and colleagues. Almond and Verba (1963), for example, followed the tradition set by Mill in regarding the skills needed to engage in political discussion as valuable elements of democratic citizenship. Moreover, they saw the freedom to engage in discussion as an important indicator of the absence of totalitarian restraints in the political system. Thus, in *The Civic Culture*, political discussion was treated as one form of activity among many in a composite notion of democratic participation. The same principle informed the interpretation applied by Barnes, Kaase, *et al.* (1979), who grouped political discussion together with activities such as reading about politics in newspapers, working with people in the community to solve local problems, and party activities (but not voting) as conventional political participation.

In contrast, Verba, Nie, and Kim (1978) posited a sharper analytical distinction between the notion of political involvement, under which they grouped both an interest in politics and discussions about politics, and political participation itself, which they defined as activities directed at influencing the governmental process. On this basis, they saw voting and political discussion as lying at opposite poles of their classification of political activity (Verba, Nie, and Kim 1978: 75). In terms of the analytical framework for political participation outlined by Fuchs and Klingemann, and discussed above, the difference which Verba *et al.* highlight may be seen as one between voting as the archetypal form of instrumental action, and discussion about politics with friends, colleagues, and family, as non-instrumental, expressive action. However, while such a categorization is clearly one possibility, it is by no means necessarily the only one.

On the one hand, as we have noted, not all analysts would agree that voting must also be informed by an instrumental motivation; on the other hand, as Parry *et al.* (1992: 40) point out, political discussion may be either instrumental or expressive. Thus political discussion could be aimed at persuading friends and family to vote in a particular way, which would, presumably, be equally as instrumental as the act of voting itself. But equally, many survey respondents would probably also regard gossip about the latest ministerial scandal as political discussion. Parry and his colleagues decided that the inherent uncertainty about how to interpret political discussion meant that this is 'a dangerous and potentially flawed measure' (1992: 40). Hence, they excluded it from their analyses of political participation (see Table 3.1 above).

We treat political discussion in two different ways. First, whether or not political discussion should be categorized as instrumental or expressive action, trends over time in the distribution and levels of political discussion are indicators of the vitality of *homo politicus* in Western Europe. Thus, we begin by analysing political discussion as a discrete mode of political participation in the democratic process. In the next section, however, we have excluded political discussion from our composite measure of direct political action, thus ensuring the comparability of our measures with those of other analysts. Finally, in the last section, we return to include political discussion in our composite measure, which is designed specifically to address the postmodernist thesis.

Dynamics of Political Discussion

According to Almond and Verba's data (1959) some 15 per cent of Britons, 11 per cent of Germans, and 4 per cent of Italians said they frequently discussed politics; 29 per cent, 39 per cent, and 68 per cent, respectively, said they never did so. The Eurobarometer data yield comparable figures for all EC member states from 1973 onwards. These figures (not shown here; see Volume iv, Figure 14.1) reveal that for the European Community as a whole, averaged over the entire period 1973–92 (with each new member state included as it joined the Community), 17 per cent said they discussed politics frequently, and 34 per cent said that they never do so. Viewed on a year-by-year basis, the figures remain remarkably stable, varying by under 3 per cent from the overall mean throughout the twenty years surveyed. The picture remains much the same when we compare individual countries. There are, naturally, some variations. Using the mean level of political discussion as our measure (based on a three-point scale of frequently, occasionally, never), a ranking of the EC countries shows that political discussion is most frequent in Greece and least common in Portugal and Spain. The remaining EC countries do not differ greatly, and there is no evidence to support notions of cultural tendencies, such as some contrast between silent northerners and loquacious southerners.

As in the previous chapter, we restrict our analyses of the social demography of political participation to age, gender, and education. These variables represent significant changes in West European societies, and it would be important if they were found to be correlated with political participation beyond voting. They are also the key variables which many analysts have associated with the so-called 'participatory revolution'.

We are interested first in examining whether the lesser propensity to vote among young people applies equally to discussion about politics. If that is the case, it would add weight to the claim that the young are disillusioned with politics. However, such a finding would not tell us whether the politics of the young is informed by instrumental or expressive motives. What we find, however, is that age is not a significant indicator of the frequency with which people engage in political discussion. Indeed, on our scale—ranging from 1.0 to 3.0— the differences in the mean levels are typically below 0.1 between the youngest and the oldest age cohorts. Moreover, in most EC member countries, including Spain and Portugal, the young are more likely to discuss politics frequently than older people. Only Britain, Ireland, and the Netherlands show a negative ratio of the youngest to the oldest age cohorts.

The trends over time are equally stable. In so far as there is any variation in the differences between the age cohorts, the explanation is not that younger people are tending to discuss politics less frequently in the 1990s compared with the early 1970s; rather, it is that older people are doing so more frequently. This is most noticeable in southern Europe, especially in Greece—and in Portugal and Spain, although our data for these two countries cover only the last decade.

As political discussion with friends principally takes place in informal social settings, rather than within the structured framework of more instrumentally organized political activities, then we may expect its frequency to be affected by traditional gender roles. Van Deth (1989: 302) draws on Rosenberg's evocative phrase, 'the threatening consequences of politics', in seeking to explain why women may express a lower interest in conventional politics than men. Thus gender differences in political participation may serve as one indicator of the penetration of modernization into national political cultures.

We have again used an index of mean difference to clarify our findings. This male-female mean difference measure is constructed by subtracting the mean level of frequency of political discussion among women from that among men. Thus a negative number shows that women are likely to discuss politics less frequently than men. The position is unambiguous. Figure 3.1 shows that there has been a significant negative mean difference in all EC member countries over the last twenty years. In other words, fewer women than men say they discuss politics. The difference is largest in the countries of southern Europe, and smallest in the Netherlands.

However, as against our earlier finding of highly stable overall levels of political discussion, in the case of gender the difference is narrowing in all EC countries. Moreover, during the 1980s, the male-female gap was closing at an increasing rate, especially in those countries with previously large differences. The one exception is, again, the Netherlands, where there has been a modest increase in the gender difference index since 1987. The overall trend, therefore, is of increasing convergence, possibly even towards the elimination of gender differences altogether by the mid-1990s.

Finally, we look at differences according to education levels. Almond and Verba found, in the 1959 data, a close relationship between the frequency with which people discussed politics and their level of educational attainment. They noted, especially, very large differences in all five countries studied between the proportion who never discussed politics among those with only minimal education, compared with people with higher levels of education. In Western Europe, among respondents reporting that they never discussed politics, the ratios for the higher educated over the minimally educated cohorts were 0.48 in Britain, 0.09 in West Germany, and 0.30 in Italy.

Many subsequent studies have confirmed the direction of this finding, and we would expect to find that the Eurobarometer data reveal similar patterns. To clarify the picture, we have again categorized education according to three levels (see Chapter 2 for details) which allows us to compare people with minimal and with higher levels of education. We then used as our measure the difference between the mean level of political discussion among the more highly educated and the minimally educated.

Yet again, the outstanding feature of these data, shown in Figure 3.2,

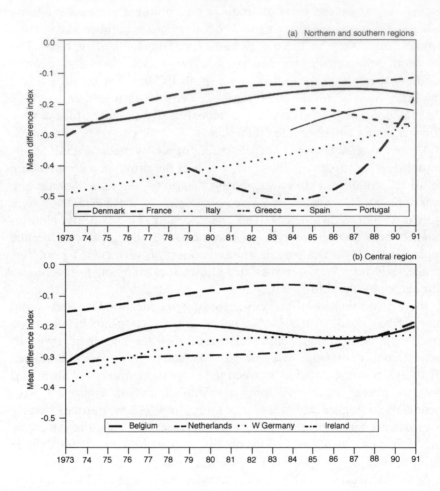

FIGURE 3.1. *Gender differences in levels of political discussion, 1973–91*
Sources: Eurobarometer cumulative file (1973–91, ZA Study 1684B); OECD (1993).

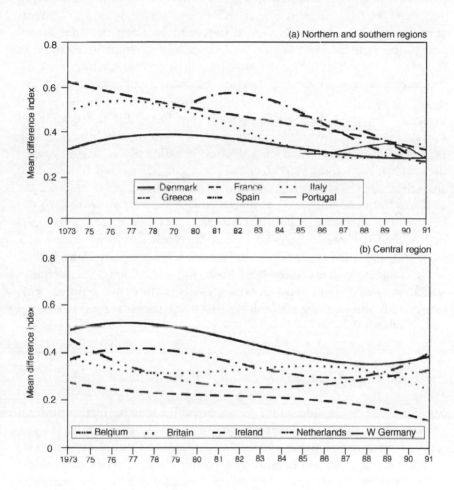

FIGURE 3.2. *Education differences in levels of political discussion, 1973–91*
Sources: See Fig. 3.2.

is their stability. In all countries and at all time points, the better educated are more likely to discuss politics frequently than those with minimal education, with the difference index remaining within a narrow band of between 0.1 and 0.5 for all countries and all time points. Even so, the regression lines in Figure 3.2 indicate a very modest convergence over time, with declining differences between the educational categories, principally in the newer democracies of southern Europe. In so far as these trends are significant, they arise for two distinct reasons. In Greece, where political discussion has consistently been most frequent among EC countries, those with minimal education have been closing the gap on those with higher levels during the last decade. In Portugal and Spain, where the frequency of discussion is lowest among member states, there has been a decline in political discussion among the better educated, at least over the short period covered by our data, from 1985 to 1991.

If the frequency of political discussion is, indeed, a measure of the health of a democratic political system—whether directly or indirectly—then the evidence so far is that the West European patient has been in a remarkably stable state, at least over the last twenty years. Such changes as there have been over the period are in a direction which suggests an increasing homogeneity within the political cultures, with diminishing differences between the sexes and between educational levels.

Typologies of Political Participation

So far, we have considered all forms of political participation beyond voting indiscriminately, except to note that survey data rarely, if ever, report violent action rising above 1 or 2 per cent. Intuitively, however, it seems reasonable to operationalize some scale of types of political action in terms of, say, their degrees of difficulty and the skills required to perform them, or their levels of formal legality, or their perceived legitimacy. One such typology, based on Parry *et al.* (see Table 3.1), distinguishes four categories of political participation apart from voting: party campaigning, contacting politicians or officials, group activities, and protesting. This last category also forms the basis for the political action battery first developed by Marsh, and is often subdivided into further categories, such as 'legal', 'civil disobedient', and 'violent' (Fuchs 1990; Kaase 1992).

Unfortunately, once we set aside the rare acts involving violence, the empirical world hardly complies with such typologies. The problem with hierarchies of action premised upon skill or difficulty is that these are subculturally relative. What is 'second nature' to the educated middle classes may be beyond the abilities of people with minimal education. Similarly, what is second nature in the working-class trade union movement may be unachievable by the individualistic middle classes. Again, the problem with action categories based on legality is that what is formally legal is country-specific. Moreover, in applying such a schema, it has to be assumed that the political actors themselves are aware of what is legal within their national laws. The Political Action study, for example, classed 'wildcat strikes' and 'occupying buildings' as illegal actions, but prior to the spate of industrial relations legislation which began in 1979, Britain had a long and entirely legal tradition of spontaneous industrial action by local union members. Similarly, the British law on trespass has long been complicated, with entering other people's property often being a civil rather than a criminal offence.[3] As legal advisers to many British universities have found to their chagrin, students may well not have been breaking the criminal law when they occupied university property. As importantly for our purpose, students cannot have been assumed to know their legal status when they took such action.

This leaves two possibilities for constructing a hierarchy of unconventional political actions. We could distinguish between violent and non-violent actions. However, given the extremely low levels of self-reported violent action, the classification would not be very useful. Alternatively, a hierarchy could be premised upon the notion of perceived legitimacy. But perceptions of legitimacy, again, are culturally and subculturally relative.[4]

We are interested in cross-national comparisons of trends in political participation over the last thirty years or so. Our comparisons are based on the battery of questions first used for cross-national comparisons of unconventional political participation in Barnes, Kaase, *et al.* (1979). This comprises a list of possible types of political action, ranging from signing a petition to political violence, which respondents were asked if they had ever performed. As we noted earlier, in different surveys this battery of questions varies in terms of the specificity of the context within which the action is set, the past period of time, if any, to be recalled, and the inclusion of 'action potential' questions within the same battery (see Appendix 3.1 for details). We also noted that the battery of items may be considered to form an ascending scale of the difficulty of the action (Fuchs 1990), or the action types may be grouped in various ways (see Table 3.1; cf. Barnes, Kaase, *et al.* 1979; Kaase 1989). However categorized, it is important to bear in mind that, in all variants, the question battery is a measure of the single performance by a respondent of a type of action; it does not indicate the frequency with which the respondent has engaged in that type of action. It does not distinguish between people who have, say, once signed a petition or are habitual petition signers, or those who go to political meetings every week and those who have been only occasionally. All these types of action show as a 'single act' response. Thus, the battery measures an action repertoire; it does not yield a measure of the level of activism.

The available secondary materials allow us to compare data for three principal time periods, 1974, 1980, and 1989/90. We can also set these against Almond and Verba's 1959 data. In order to enhance comparability, in each case we have constructed a single cumulative index from all the action items in the relevant batteries. We then reduced this index to three categories: (i) people who have engaged in none of these forms of political participation; (ii) people who have engaged in some (i.e. one or two) of these forms; (iii) people who have engaged in several (i.e. three or more) of these actions. Our findings are set out in Table 3.2.

The 1959 data are for Britain, Italy, and West Germany only. They show that in these three West European countries 85 per cent of respondents had engaged in no activities aimed at influencing the policies of national or local government; by 1990, and for a much larger number of countries, that percentage had almost halved to 44

TABLE 3.2. *Political participation in Western Europe, 1959–90*

	1959	1974	1981	1990
None	85	69	55	44
Some	11	27	38	46
Active	4	4	7	10
N	2,734	6,148	13,315	15,107

Notes: Entries are aggregate percentages. All the original data have been re-analysed.

Sources: Civic Culture (1959); Political Action (1973–6); European Values Survey (1981); World Values Survey (1990).

per cent. By the same token, activists were just 4 per cent in 1959 through to 1974, but rose to 10 per cent by 1990.[5]

Table 3.3 presents the same data disaggregated to the level of countries. This shows that compared with Britain, West Germany, and Italy the three countries for which we have data for all four time points—the trend set out in Table 3.2 was underspecified. In each of these three countries, the likelihood of citizens engaging in some form of political participation apart from voting increased about fourfold between 1959 and 1990. Thus the data in Table 3.2 retain their force.

Analysis of the disaggregated country data for each action type add little to the aggregate picture. The distributions are set out in Appendix 3.2, Table 3.A1. Such differences as there are between countries are best explained in terms of cultural differences. For example, the propensity to occupy and blockade only rises above 5 per cent in France and Italy, but these levels have not changed over the last decade. Political violence throughout Europe is at least as low as shown in Table 3.1 for Britain. Finally, the trend towards an extension of the participatory repertoire is consistent across all countries for which we have data, and for all time points. Only in Finland and Spain, between 1981 and 1990, has there been no increase.

TABLE 3.3. *Political participation in Western Europe, by country, 1959–90*

	1959	1974	1981	1990
Denmark	—	—	48	59
Finland	—	26	40	38
Iceland	—	—	40	55
Norway	—	—	58	68
Sweden	—	—	58	74
Belgium	—	—	27	51
Britain	18	31	66	77
Ireland	—	—	32	46
Netherlands	—	28	37	54
West Germany	16	34	48	57
France	—	—	52	57
Italy	10	34	50	56
Spain	—	—	32	32

Note: Entries are percentage of adult population who engage in some form of political participation beyond voting.

Sources: See Table 3.2.

Political Involvement

Dynamics of Increasing Participation

The various theories we considered earlier suggest that the participatory revolution we have now measured was to be expected, and that the motor of this revolution is the newly emerging generation of young and better educated citizens. To examine this thesis, we have again applied the difference ratio measure for age cohort, gender, and educational attainment. The results are summarized in Table 3.4.

The findings reveal a more intriguing story than the broad brush of theory led us to expect. The ratio of the youngest to oldest age cohorts has increased for the non-active but declined consistently for both categories of active participants, albeit at markedly different rates. For the politically inactive, the ratio of 1.1 in the 1959 data was reversed to 0.8 by 1974, reaching 0.7 by 1990. In contrast, among the most active (setting aside the statistically unreliable data for activists in 1959), the age difference ratio stood at nearly 4.0 in 1974 but fell to 1.9 by 1990. In other words, differences in the levels of political activism between the youngest and oldest cohorts have halved over the last two

TABLE 3.4. *Political participation in Western Europe by age, gender, and education, 1959–90*

	1959	1974	1981	1990
Age				
None	1.13	0.79	0.75	0.73
Some	(0.31)	1.49	1.26	1.23
Active	(0.29)	3.95	3.62	1.93
Gender				
None	0.89	0.92	0.81	0.83
Some	1.82	1.35	1.18	1.07
Active	2.77	2.65	2.09	1.68
Education				
None	1.52	1.66	1.58	1.81
Some	(0.45)	0.55	0.67	0.72
Active	(0.15)	0.16	0.33	0.30

Notes: Entries are ratios. Where there are fewer than 100 cases, the entries are shown in parentheses. The ratios for age are based on aged 18–30 : aged 50 and older; for gender, on men : women; for education, on minimally educated : higher educated. In each case, a ratio of 1.00 indicates equal levels of participation; below 1.00 indicates that more of the first group (young, or men, or minimally educated) than the contrasted group participate; above 1.00 indicates the converse.

Sources: See Table 3.2.

decades. This is not because the young are becoming less active but because the older age cohorts are becoming more active.

A very similar picture emerges for gender differences. Again, for the inactives the ratio stood at 0.9 in 1974, reaching 0.8 in 1990, while the ratio difference for the active fell from 2.7 in 1974 to 1.7 in 1990. This means that whereas the proportion of women in the large but shrinking pool of political inactivism is growing, simultaneously the predominance of males in the expanding pools of activism is declining. The outcome is that almost as many women as men in Western Europe as a whole are now moderately active.

The data for the education groups follow the same pattern, although in this case the pattern is counter-intuitive. Whereas the theoretical arguments predicted that political activism would become the domain of the better educated, the difference ratios show a consistent decline in the predominance of the better educated in both categories of activism. For the actives, the ratio which stood at 0.2 in 1974 was reduced to 0.3 in 1980 and remained unchanged in 1990. This means that proportionately twice as many of those with minimal education were politically active in 1990 compared to 1974. Recall that the proportion of 'actives' increased overall from 4 per cent to 10 per cent over the same period (see Table 3.2).

It is important to be clear about what these data mean. They show that at the aggregate level, just as for each country separately, and at each time point separately, there are still significant differences in levels of political participation between age, gender, and educational cohorts. However, just as recent country-specific times series analyses have shown that multi-dimensional techniques do not confirm that age, gender, or education explain much variance in actual political participation (Fuchs 1990; Kaase 1989), so these data confirm that these socio-demographic variables are becoming less significant over time.

These trends amount to the steady de-skilling of political activism. This process is especially telling for the postmodernist thesis. This was premised on the notion that activism will become the preserve of skilled élites embodying postmaterialist, expressive, and hedonistic values. Of course, our findings do not refute that thesis, but, rather, reflect the differential time scales for the rate of increase in political activism as against the overall penetration of the educated élite into the general population. Table 3.3 shows that Britain, for example, has by far the lowest level of inactivism in Western Europe yet also one of the lowest proportions of university graduates in the population (OECD 1993).

Rationalities of Political Action

We noted at the beginning of this chapter that a key tenet of the postmodernist thesis is an analytic distinction between instrumental and expressive action. Such distinctions have been made by social scientists ever since Weber's (1968) seminal work on the sociology of action. However, when we turn to recent attempts to test this distinction empirically, one crucial aspect of such theories has to be kept in mind.

From a rationalist—and hence modernist—perspective, it is axiomatic that all individual action may be interpreted in instrumental, goal-oriented terms. This is not to say that rationalists deny that individual action may be simultaneously expressive, in that the choice of both means and ends may be informed by an individual's values and sense of the moral order. It is a different matter, however, to argue that, at the systemic level, the development of a postmodernist political culture would be accompanied by such relativism that rationalism no longer holds sway. Barnes and Kaase (1979: 526) interpreted Huntington's (1974) predictions about 'postindustrial politics' as implying this kind of development. Were such a radical position to be maintained it would mean that we had entered an era of incommensurability in which survey techniques were no longer valid.

A less radical claim is that while individuals may still give a rational account of their actions, none the less expressive rather than instrumental rationality will come to predominate at the level of the political and social systems. It is from such an analytic perspective that the 'heroic assumptions' of Barnes, Kaase, *et al.* (1979)—that expressive styles may be displacing instrumental purposes in political action—may best be viewed. Barnes and Kaase tested this thesis, using a single survey item on expressed political interest to distinguish between instrumentally and expressively informed political participation. What makes this attempt heroic is the notion that people who say they are uninterested in politics yet say they are politically active must be acting expressively rather than instrumentally.

However, the simplicity of this approach gives it force. We have attempted to replicate the Barnes and Kaase analysis, within the limitations of our data, in order to test whether the developments predicted by postmodernist theory can be verified. There are two notes of caution, however. First, the 'double negative' position—no interest and no action means apathy—is relatively easy to defend, but the 'double positive' position—interest and action means instrumental-ism—is less convincing. Its weakness lies in the absence of any further indicator to refute the alternative conclusion that a positive expression of interest in politics constitutes expressive action.

The second note is methodological. In some of our data, the item on interest in politics with the closest equivalence to the Barnes and Kaase item uses the phrase 'interested and active in politics' as the first option for respondents. Analysis of the data reveals a sizeable category of respondents who are 'very interested and active', yet say they have performed none of the actions in the political action battery. It is entirely possible for these replies to be accurate: respondents may engage in other, unlisted types of political participation, or they may have a different understanding of what it is to be active in politics. Either way, in examining the data, we have to be aware that we are looking at a snapshot of what might be only part of the political domain.

Hedonistic Activists?

We have referred to the attempt by Kaase and Barnes (1979) to operationalize an empirical test of Huntington's notion of the hedonistic activist. This was well before the emergence of current debates about the political consequences of societal postmodernization. They used a single survey item—expressed level of interest in politics—as a general indicator of political involvement, together with an aggregate measure of political participation, to generate four modes of political involvement. These they identified as:

(1) political apathy = no interest + no action
(2) political detachment = interest + no action
(3) expressive activist = no interest + action
(4) instrumental activist = interest + action

They then used the ratio of instrumental over expressive political action to compare levels of hedonistic activism between countries.[6]

Now, we have already noted that one significant postmodernization thesis holds that contemporary changes in West European political cultures may be less than benign for Western representative democracies. On the one hand, there is the danger inherent in an increase in political apathy; on the other hand, the danger of an increase in expressive—as opposed to instrumental—political action. So, finally in this chapter, we report an analysis of the 1981 and 1990 data which is functionally equivalent to the analysis of the 1974 data by Kaase and Barnes. While our test is by no means definitive, according to the postmodernization thesis we should find that both political apathy and hedonistic action has increased proportionally since 1974; that is, we expect the ratio of instrumental to expressive political participation to have declined.[7]

The results of our test are shown in Table 3.5. The upper half of the table shows our recomputation of the 1974 Political Action data for the four countries for which we have data at all three time points. In the lower half, we include all the countries for which we have data for at least two time points.

In the four Political Action countries, political apathy stood at 27 per cent in 1974, peaked at 32 per cent in 1981, and then dropped to 23 per cent by 1990. Across Western Europe as a whole, political apathy increased only slightly from 27 per cent to 29 per cent between 1974 and 1990. The proportions of the detached remain much the same throughout the period among both sets of countries. Levels of expressive participation increased generally from around 20 per cent to around 25 per cent. As for instrumental activists, the proportions dropped rather

TABLE 3.5. *Modes of political involvement, 1974–90*

Mode of involvement	1974	1981	1990
Four Political Action countries			
Apathetic	27	32	23
Detached	13	12	12
Expressive	19	28	25
Instrumental	42	29	41
N	5,118	5,105	6,620
Western Europe			
Apathetic	27	36	29
Detached	11	14	11
Expressive	21	23	24
Instrumental	41	27	35
N	7,713	16,282	20,054

Notes: Entries are average percentages. The entries in the upper part of the table are for West Germany, Netherlands, Italy, and Britain. The entries in the lower part are for up to fourteen countries.
Sources: See Table 3.2.

steeply during 1974–81 but had largely recovered to earlier levels by 1990.

Our findings, then, are quite clear: instrumental action remains the dominant mode of political involvement. Although this has not been consistently so, as the 1981 data reveal, instrumental action has been predominant for most of the period. At the same time, however, for Western Europe as a whole, the gap between instrumental and expressive action narrowed from 20 percentage points in 1974 to 11 points in 1990—due to a drop in the level of instrumental action and some increase in the level of expressive action. This trend is not altogether surprising when we bear in mind the considerable overall increase in levels of political participation, together with the much larger number of countries in the 1990 data set.

Even so, there are also differences between the upper and lower parts of the table. In particular, the level of instrumental action is lower and apathy greater in both 1981 and 1991 across Western Europe as a whole compared to the four Political Action countries. These differences are best interpreted by looking at more detailed, country-by-country breakdowns. These are set out in Appendix 3.2, but we note two broad brush conclusions here. First, comparing 1981 with 1990, we find, in almost every case, an increase in instrumental participation and a decline in political apathy. The exception is Spain, where the position barely altered. Yet there was no comparably clear pattern for the other two participatory modes—detachment and expressive action—over the decade; these modes increased in some countries and declined in others.

Secondly, at first sight the broad geographical groupings in the table would appear to draw out significant differences between recent patterns of participatory modes, with instrumental action most prevalent in northern and Central regions of Western Europe, while apathy ranked highest in southern Europe. For example, by 1990 in Norway 57 per cent of the population were instrumental activists and 11 per cent apathetic, while in Spain, 54 per cent were apathetic and 19 per cent were instrumental activists. Moreover, except for Britain in 1981, for all three time periods and every country in the table, the highest ranking mode is always either instrumental participation or apathy, never detachment or expressive action. In 1990, for example, instrumentalism was the most prevalent mode of participation in all countries of the northern and Central regions apart from Belgium and Ireland where, as in France, Italy, and Spain, apathy appears foremost.

However, when we turn to consider the relationship between instrumental and expressive modes of participation, which is at the core of the postmodernization thesis, the data reveals a more complicated situation with significant variations between countries and time points (see Appendix 3.2, Table 3.A2). Therefore, like Kaase and Barnes (1979: 529ff.), we recomputed the data in terms of ratios. In Table 3.6 we present the rank order, for 1990, of instrumental to expressive participation for all the countries for which we have time series data. As we can see, West Germany ranks highest, with a ratio of 4.0, reflecting the 52 per cent of instrumental activists over 13 per cent of expressive activists. Ranked lowest with a ratio of 0.7 is Belgium, where, in 1990, the expressive mode was more prevalent than the instrumentalist mode.

When we view the overall ranking of countries for 1990, one point bearing directly on the postmodernization thesis stands out above all others. For some six of our fourteen countries—Germany, Norway, the Netherlands, Austria, Finland, and Denmark—the instrumental over expressive ratio lies between 4.0 and 2.0, which means that instrumental participation is at least twice as prevalent as expressive participation. For a further five countries—Iceland, Sweden, Britain, France, and

TABLE 3.6. *Ratio of instrumental to expressive political participation,*
1974–90

	1974	1981	1990
West Germany	3.8	1.7	4.0
Norway	—	1.2	3.6
Netherlands	3.2	1.5	3.1
Austria	3.0	—	2.6
Finland	1.4	1.5	(2.0)
Denmark	—	1.1	2.0
Iceland	—	1.3	1.4
Sweden	—	1.2	1.2
Britain	1.5	0.7	1.1
France	—	3.2	1.1
Spain	—	1.2	1.1
Ireland	—	0.7	0.9
Italy	1.0	0.8	0.7
Belgium	—	1.1	0.7

Notes: Entries are ratios based on percentage of electorate who participate instrumentally and expressively. Entries in parentheses are based on a sample size which is too small to be statistically significant.

Sources: See Table 3.2.

Spain—the ratio is above 1.0. Only for Ireland, Italy, and Belgium is the ratio in a band between 0.9 and 0.7, showing that the expressive mode is more prevalent than the instrumental mode.

Turning to trends over time, perhaps the first point to be noted is the markedly lower ratios for 1981 compared with both 1974 and 1990, especially for those countries in the upper part of the table. In some measure, this may be an artefact arising from differences in the questionnaire design which we noted earlier. But it may also parallel the general dip in the late 1970s and early 1980s in measures of other dimensions of political culture, such as satisfaction with democracy and postmaterialism (see Commission of the European Communities 1994; Inglehart 1994).

However, taking these data at face value, we see that, even in 1981, the instrumentalist over expressive ratio was higher than 1.0 for ten of the thirteen countries surveyed. Moreover, between 1981 and 1990 the ratios fell in only four countries—France, Spain, Italy, and Belgium— all of which, significantly, lie in the lower part of our table. Finally, when we review the four countries for which we have reliable data for all three time points—Germany, the Netherlands, Britain, and Italy—a bifurcation emerges. For Germany and the Netherlands at the top of the table, the ratios for 1974 and 1990 are at roughly the same levels, with instrumentalism more than three times more prevalent than expressivism; for Britain and Italy, the ratios are lower in 1990 than in 1974, albeit only by the order of 0.3. In the case of Italy, this means that the ratio of 1.0 in 1974 fell to 0.8 in 1981, and remained at 0.7 for 1990— equal bottom with Belgium.

On the basis of this analysis, therefore, we find no evidence of a general trend across Western Europe over the last two decades towards increasing levels of political apathy or hedonistic modes of participation. Rather, what does emerge is a clear ranking among West European countries in the ratios of different participatory modes according to the schema developed by Kaase and Barnes. In 1974, Germany and the Netherlands were at one pole of this ranking, Belgium was at the other pole, with Britain at the mid-point. In 1990, despite the much expanded list of countries surveyed, this ordering remained unchanged.

On their own, of course, our data on political participation are not a sufficient basis to reach firm conclusions about the validity of the postmodernization thesis. That would require us to draw upon additional materials about changes in political values in the countries we have examined. That task is well beyond the scope of this chapter. None the less, what may be said with some confidence is, first and foremost, that if processes of postmodernization have indeed been taking place in Western Europe over the last two decades, then those processes have not been accompanied by increasing political apathy or hedonistic political participation. Secondly, there is a sharp, and seemingly stable ranking of West European countries in terms of instrumental as against expressive political participation. Again, however, without further independent data, we may only speculate upon whether this country ranking parallels other classifications of Western political cultures, in terms, say, of postmaterialism or postmodernism. In their analysis of the Political Action data, Kaase and Barnes (1979: 526) highlighted 'the potential hedonism and irrationality of postindustrialism'. However, if the most recent empirical work of analysts such as Inglehart and Abramson (1994) on classifying countries according to correlations between their economies and their political cultures is any guide, then the rankings we have identified would seem to undermine rather than support the postmodernization thesis.

Conclusion

In the previous chapter, we challenged the widely held thesis that levels of electoral participation are declining in Western Europe. In contrast, in this chapter we have confirmed unequivocally the parallel thesis of a participatory revolution. Levels of non-participation in modes of political action beyond voting have declined to such an extent across Western Europe over the last thirty years that non-participants now comprise a minority of national electorates. In several countries, such as Britain, Norway, and Sweden, well over two-thirds of their electorates are now participants in some mode or other of what, but recently, was labelled unconventional activity.

Of equal importance, as levels of political participation have increased to involve the majority of the population in many European countries, so there has been a concomitant de-skilling of political activism. In contrast to the view that beyond voting, the social demography of political activism is primarily skewed in favour of younger, better-educated men, our evidence points to the conclusion that such gender, age, and educational differences are diminishing. Quite possibly, by the mid-1990s, in many West European countries political participation will prove to be evenly spread, equally involving men and women, young and old, early school leavers and graduates.

We also addressed the so-called postmodernization thesis, according to which the participatory revolution we have identified may threaten the stability of European democratic institutions. We have found scant evidence to support postmodernist concerns that the rise of political activism has been primarily a rise in expressive and hedonistic modes of action at the expense of instrumental participation. On the contrary, our analyses, constructed in the postmodernists' own terms, produced country rankings which may well show instrumentalism rather than expressivism to be the major correlate of so called postmodernization. At the very least, what is already clear is that political apathy and putatively expressive modes of political participation are most prevalent in the less developed countries of Western Europe. Instrumentalism, not hedonism or irrationality, accompanies postindustrialism.

APPENDIX 3.1
Political Participation Questions

The wording of the political participation questions in the surveys used in this chapter is as follows:

Civic Culture Study 1959

Q26 Open question: Suppose a law were being considered by the Parliament which you considered to be very unjust or harmful, what do you think you could do? . . . (if needed) Anything else?

The categories imposed were:
   Nothing
   Work through informal, unorganized groups: neighbours, friends. Get neighbours or friends to write letters, attend meetings, sign a petition, talk to people
   Work through a political party
   Work through other formal, organized group: trade union, professional group, church, etc.
   As individual talk to, write letters, or contact representatives, councilmen, and/or other political leaders or the press, etc. (activities for which respondent does not mention getting others to join him)

As individual talk to, or write letters to authorities, administrative depart-
ments
Consult a lawyer, use legal (juristic) means, go to court
Vote
Take some violent action: protest march, rebellion, active resistance,
assassination, riots
Other
Don't know/n.a.

Q27 If you made an effort to change this law, how likely is it you would
    succeed?

Very likely
Moderately likely
Somewhat likely
Not at all, impossible
Likely only if others joined in
Other
Don't know

Q28 If such a case arose, how likely is it you would actually try to do
    something about it?

Very likely
Moderately likely
Somewhat likely
Not at all likely, impossible
Depends on the issue
Other
Don't know
n.a./refused to answer

Q29 Have you ever done anything to try to influence an Act of Parliament?

Often
Once or twice, a few times
Never
Don't know/n.a.

Q30 Suppose several men were trying to influence a government decision.
    Here is a list of things they might do [see below]. The first man works
    through personal and family connections with government officials. The
    second one writes to government officials explaining his point of view.
    The third tries to get people interested in the problem and to form a
    group. The fourth man works through his party. A fifth man organizes a

protest demonstration. Which one of these methods do you think would be the most effective?

None
Writing to government officials
Getting people interested; forming a group
Working through a political party
Organizing protest demonstrations
Other
Don't know

Political Action Study 1973–6

Q18 Now please place the playing cards on this card to show me the extent to which these actions may be effective when people use them in pressing for changes. Are they usually very effective, somewhat effective, not very effective or not at all effective?

Signing a petition
Joining in boycotts
Attending lawful demonstrations
Refusing to pay rent or taxes, etc.
Joining in wildcat strikes
Painting slogans on walls
Occupying buildings or factories: 'sit-ins'
Blocking traffic with a street demonstration
Damaging things like breaking windows, removing road signs, etc.
Using personal violence like fighting with other demonstrators or the police

Q19 Finally, please place the cards on this scale to show me, first, whether (1) you have actually done any of the things on the cards during the past ten years; (2) you would do any of these things if it were important to you; (3) you might do it in a particular situation or (4) you would never do it under any circumstances.

European Values Survey 1981

Q267 Now I'd like you to look at this card. I'm going to read out some different forms of political action that people can take, and I'd like you to tell me, for each one, whether you have actually done any of these things, whether you would do it,* might do it, or would never, under any circumstances, do any of them.

Signing a petition
Joining in boycotts
Attending lawful demonstrations
Joining unofficial strikes
Occupying buildings or factories
Damaging things like breaking windows, removing road signs, etc.
Using personal violence like fighting with other demonstrators or the police

World Values Survey 1990

Replication of question from European Values Survey 1986.

British Social Attitudes Survey 1983

Q10a Has there ever been an occasion when a law was being considered by Parliament which you thought was really unjust and harmful? Yes/No

If Yes:

 b Did you do any of the things on this card? Any others?
 c Suppose a law was now being considered by Parliament which you thought was really unjust and harmful, which, if any, of the things on this card do you think you would do? Any others?
 d Which one of the things on this card do you think would be the most effective in influencing a government to change its mind?

Contact my MP
Speak to an influential person
Contact a government department
Contact radio, TV or newspaper
Sign a petition
Raise in an organization I already belong to
Go on a protest or demonstration
Form a group of like minded people
None of these

*The published questionnaire includes the 'whether you would do it' part of the question but responses to this question were not included in the response codes. Only 'have done' (1), 'might do' (2), 'would never do' (3), and 'don't know' (4) were coded.

British Social Attitudes Survey 1984

Q6*a* Suppose a law was now being considered by Parliament which you thought was really unjust and harmful. Which, if any, of the things on this card do you think you would do? Any others?

   d Which one of the things on this card do you think would be the most effective in influencing a government to change its mind?

List as for British Social Attitudes 1983.

British Social Attitudes Survey 1986

Q86*a* Suppose a law was now being considered by Parliament which you thought was really unjust and harmful. Which, if any, of the things on this card do you think you would do? Any others?

   b And have you ever done any of the things on this card about a government action which you thought was unjust or harmful? Which ones? Any others?

List as for British Social Attitudes 1983 and 1984.

Q87 Please use a phrase from this card to say how effective you think each of the following would be in influencing a government to change its mind? How effective would it be to . . .

List as above.
Response categories: very effective; quite effective; not very effective; not at all effective.

British Election Study 1987

Q6*a* Suppose a law was being considered by Parliament which you thought was really unjust and harmful. Which, if any, of the following things do you think people ought to do? People ought to . . .

Contact their MP?
Sign a petition?
Go on a demonstration?
Join a protest group?

   b And which of these things have you ever done?

British Social Attitudes Survey 1989

Full replication of British Social Attitudes Survey 1986.

APPENDIX 3.2

TABLE 3.A1. *Modes of political involvement in thirteen West European countries, 1974–90*

	Apathetic	Detached	Expressive	Instrumental	N
Finland					
1974	32	8	34	36	1,001
1981	37	21	17	25	901
1990	32	19	17	33	343
Denmark					
1974	—	—	—	—	—
1981	29	14	28	30	867
1990	23	11	22	43	928
Norway					
1974	—	—	—	—	—
1981	25	14	28	33	1,101
1990	11	16	16	57	1,065
Sweden					
1974	—	—	—	—	—
1981	26	14	28	33	815
1990	17	5	36	43	839
Iceland					
1974	—	—	—	—	—
1981	35	21	19	25	869
1990	29	13	25	34	655
Austria					
1974	24	11	16	48	918
1981	—	—	—	—	—
1990	30	14	16	40	1,244
Britain					
1974	30	9	24	37	1,267
1981	20	11	41	29	1,109
1990	14	7	37	42	1,369
Germany					
1974	22	20	12	46	2,034
1981	30	14	21	35	975
1990	17	18	13	52	1,535
Netherlands					
1974	25	12	15	48	1,019
1981	39	16	18	27	998
1990	24	18	14	44	959

TABLE 3.A1. *Cont.*

	Apathetic	Detached	Expressive	Instrumental	N
Belgium					
1974	—		—	—	—
1981	58	13	14	15	841
1990	39	8	31	22	2,243
Ireland					
1974	—	—	—	—	—
1981	52	14	20	14	984
1990	35	14	27	24	929
Italy					
1974	52	14	15	18	778
1981	41	6	30	23	993
1990	34	6	34	25	1,529
France					
1974	—		—	—	—
1981	23	22	13	42	1,017
1990	32	8	29	31	822
Spain					
1974	—	—	—	—	—
1981	52	10	17	20	1,612
1990	54	9	18	19	1,750

Notes: Entries are percentages. The 1990 Finnish survey was administered only to respondents with personal computers. The sample is too small for the analysis to be considered statistically reliable. Thus, the 1990 Finnish figures are included for information only.

Sources: Political Action (1973–6); European Values Survey (1981); World Values Survey (1990).

TABLE 3.A2. *Modes of further political participation in sixteen West European countries, 1959–90*

	1959	1974	1981	1989	1990
Denmark					
Join the citizen's action group			—	14	—
Sign petition			44	30	51
Join boycott			19	11	11
Attend lawful demonstration			19	17	27
Join rent/tax strike			—	1	—
Join unofficial strike			9	10	17
Occupy building			3	1	2
Block traffic				2	—
Damage things			2	1	—
Use personal violence			1	0	—
N			1,116	955	1,012
Finland					
Sign petition		20	30		(41)
Join boycott		1	9		(14)
Attend lawful demonstration		6	14		(14)
Join rent/tax strike		0	—		—
Join unofficial strike		5	6		(8)
Occupy building		0	1		(2)
Block traffic		0	—		—
Damage things		1	5		—
Use personal violence		0	1		—
N		1,088	977		(200)
Norway					
Sign petition			56		61
Join boycott			7		12
Attend lawful demonstration			20		20
Join unofficial strike			3		24
Occupy building			1		1
Damage things			2		—
Use personal violence			1		—
N			1,216		1,205
Sweden					
Sign petition			54		72
Join boycott			9		17
Attend lawful demonstration			15		23
Join unofficial strike			2		3
Occupy building			0		0
Damage things			1		—
Use personal violence			1		—
N			934		960

TABLE 3.A2. *Cont.*

	1959	1974	1981	1989	1990
Iceland					
Sign petition			37		47
Join boycott			7		21
Attend lawful demonstration			14		24
Join rent/tax strike			—		—
Join unofficial strike			3		5
Occupy building			0		1
Block traffic			—		—
Damage things			1		—
Use personal violence			0		—
N			912		692
Austria					
Sign petition		39			48
Join boycott		3			5
Attend lawful demonstration		7			10
Join rent/tax strike		1			—
Join unofficial strike		1			1
Occupy building		0			1
Block traffic		1			—
Damage things		0			—
Use personal violence		0			—
N		1,400			664
Belgium					
Join the citizen's action group			—	26	—
Sign petition			24	47	47
Join boycott			3	10	9
Attend lawful demonstration			14	16	23
Join rent/tax strike			—	4	—
Join unofficial strike			4	4	6
Occupy building			3	2	4
Block traffic			—	5	—
Damage things			1	1	—
Use personal violence			1	1	—
N			1,012	866	2,632

Political Involvement

TABLE 3.A2. *Cont.*

	1959	1974	1981	1989	1990
Germany					
Join the citizen's action group		—	7	14	—
Sign petition		31	47	30	57
Join lawful demonstration		9	15	9	21
Join boycott		4	8	5	11
Join rent/tax strike		1	—	1	—
Join unofficial strike		1	2	0	2
Occupy building		0	2	0	1
Block traffic		2	—	2	—
Damage things		0	1	0	—
Use personal violence		0	1	0	—
One such act—local	15				
One such act—national	3				
N	959	2,196	1,253	971	2,030
Britain					
Join the citizen's action group		—	—	11	—
Sign petition		23	63	69	75
Join lawful demonstration		6	10	10	14
Join boycott		6	7	13	14
Join rent/tax strike		2	—	3	—
Join unofficial strike		5	7	6	10
Occupy building		1	3	2	2
Block traffic		1	—	3	—
Damage things		1	2	2	—
Use personal violence		0	1	1	—
One such act—local	15				
One such act—national	6				
N	915	1,378	1,217	934	1,457
Ireland					
Join the citizen's action group			—	10	—
Sign petition			29	35	42
Join boycott			7	6	7
Attend lawful demonstration			13	7	17
Join rent/tax strike			—	4	—
Join unofficial strike			5	2	4
Occupy building			2	2	2
Block traffic			—	3	—
Damage things			1	0	—
Use personal violence			0	0	—
N			1,152	921	985

TABLE 3.A2. *Cont.*

	1959	1974	1981	1989	1990
Netherlands					
Join the citizen's action group	—	—		17	—
Sign petition	22	35		52	51
Attend lawful demonstration	7	13		14	25
Join boycott	6	7		8	9
Join rent/tax strike	4	—		5	—
Join unofficial strike	2	2		2	3
Occupy building	1	2		1	3
Block traffic	1	—		2	—
Damage things	1	1		1	—
Use personal violence	0	1		0	—
N		1,121	1,152	942	1,002
France					
Join the citizen's action group			—	26	—
Sign petition			45	56	54
Join boycott			12	13	13
Attend lawful demonstration			27	20	33
Join rent/tax strike			—	6	—
Join unofficial strike			10	9	10
Occupy building			7	8	8
Block traffic			—	10	—
Damage things			1	2	—
Use personal violence			1	2	—
N			1,162	901	959
Greece					
Join the citizen's action group				28	
Sign petition				52	
Join lawful demonstration				28	
Join boycott				3	
Join rent/tax strike				2	
Join unofficial strike				8	
Occupy building				4	
Block traffic				4	
Damage things				1	
Use personal violence				1	
N				883	

TABLE 3.A2. *Cont.*

	1959	1974	1981	1989	1990
Italy					
Join the citizen's action group		—	—	29	—
Sign petition		17	42	42	48
Join boycott		2	6	3	11
Attend lawful demonstration		19	27	19	36
Join rent/tax strike		2	—	1	—
Join unofficial strike		1	3	4	6
Occupy building		5	6	5	8
Block traffic		2	—	5	—
Damage things		1	1	1	—
Use personal violence		0	2	1	—
One such act—local	9				
One such act—national	2				
N	911	1,017	1,202	974	1,851
Portugal					
Join the citizen's action group				24	
Sign petition				19	
Join boycott				2	
Attend lawful demonstration				18	
Join rent/tax strike				0	
Join unofficial strike				1	
Occupy building				1	
Block traffic				1	
Damage things				1	
Use personal violence				1	
N				848	
Spain					
Join the citizen's action group			—	20	—
Sign petition			24	32	23
Join boycott			9	9	5
Attend lawful demonstration			25	22	23
Join rent/tax strike			—	3	—
Join unofficial strike			7	2	6
Occupy building			3	2	3
Block traffic			—	9	—
Damage things			1	1	—
Use personal violence			1	1	—
N			1,992	859	2,141

Notes: Entries are percentages. For exact question wording, see Appendix 3.1. The size of the 1990 Finnish sample is too small to be statistically significant. The data for Britain exclude Northern Ireland.

Sources: Civic Culture (1959); Political Action (1974); European Values Survey (1981); Eurobarometer, No. 31; World Values Survey (1990).

NOTES

1. In their study of political participation in Britain, Parry, *et al.* (1992) used open-ended questions to elicit respondents' perceptions of the political domain. But such research is expensive and difficult to design for comparisons over time or between countries. Moreover, the findings suggest that there is no universally shared perception of what counts as 'political', and hence no ideal form of survey design which would encompass the entirety of 'political participation'.

2. The Political Action collected, in most countries, in 1974. The data from Eurobarometer, No. 31 (1989), were used to verify the data from the 1990 World Values Survey where this was possible. Participation data from both surveys are reported in Appendix 3.2, Table 3.A2. All the data presented in the tables are based on re-analysis of the original data. Details of question wordings are given in Appendix 3.1. In some instances, our findings may differ from those published by the original investigators.

3. The 1994 Criminal Justice Act in Britain—itself the subject of considerable and sometimes violent protest—includes provisions intended to remove such uncertainties. However, at the time of writing, these provisions have yet to be tested in the courts. The National Union of Students in Britain has continued to use 'occupations' as a form of political protest.

4. It is, of course, possible to use statistical techniques, such as factor analysis, to generate groupings which may be interpreted as the basis for a schema of action types (Fuchs 1990; Kaase 1992; Parry *et al.* 1992; Topf 1992; Westle 1992). But such schema are nation-specific, and do not hold good when 'external' types of action are introduced which were not included in the original closed list put to respondents.

5. One technical point about these data should be noted (see also the notes to Table 3.2). Table 3.2 includes only countries for which we have data for at least two time points. None the less this means that our data for 1959 are for just three countries, and those for 1974 for just five. This weakens the statistical significance of the time trends.

6. There are, of course, significant differences in the definition of concepts such as 'expressive' and 'instrumental'. Our usage follows the definitions explicated by Fuchs and Klingemann (Ch. 1) who, in turn, premised their distinction on Kaase and Barnes (1979). This usage differs in important respects from that developed elsewhere (Topf 1989*b*, 1993; cf. Street 1994) in which 'expressive action' is defined in terms of its moral component.

7. While we have endeavoured to achieve functional equivalence with Kaase and Barnes's analyses, there are some differences. First, Kaase and Barnes's composite measure of political action included both genuine behavioural measures of participation, and conative items, namely, measures of action potential. For reasons we have already rehearsed, we also used a composite measure of action but excluded the conative items. Secondly, Kaase and Barnes were able to include in their measure an extended list of forms of conventional participation akin to the types set out in Table 3.1. We lack comparable data for 1981 and 1990. However, like Kaase and Barnes, we have included an indicator of political discussion in our composite measure.

PART II

Political Linkage

4

Political Parties in Decline?

HERMANN SCHMITT AND SÖREN HOLMBERG

Some twenty years ago Giovanni Sartori (1976) characterized political parties as the major linkage mechanism between citizens and the state. Since then, new forms of interest mediation are challenging the functions of political parties (Dalton and Küchler 1990), and the links between parties and people are said to have weakened (Dalton, Flanagan, and Beck 1984; Crewe and Denver 1985). This is evident, it is claimed, in the waning of partisanship and the decline of party membership. In this chapter, we examine developments in partisanship; trends in party membership are investigated in the next chapter.

The aspect of political linkage we are concerned with is the attachment of electors to political parties. Using indicators of the strength of party identification—or party attachment—as our principle analytic tool, we trace the development of partisanship in some fifteen party systems in post-war Western Europe. The focus in the first section is on theory and concepts; in the second section, on changes across time and differences between countries. Party differences are highlighted in the final section.

The name of the game is primarily charting and tracking. The more

The analyses of national election surveys conducted in Western Europe and the United States reported in this chapter were provided by colleagues from the respective countries. They are John Curtice, University of Strathclyde; Donald Granberg, University of Missouri; Ola Listhaug, University of Trondheim; Palle Svensson, University of Aarhus; and Jacques Thomassen, University of Twente. Their support is most gratefully acknowledged; we would not have been able to re-analyse the massive body of these surveys without it. We analysed the Eurobarometer data ourselves. Angelika Scheuer and Inge Weller provided skilful research assistance.

difficult task of explaining changes and differences in the strength of party identification is not overlooked, but is less emphasized. However, we deliberately avoid 'structural' avenues of explanation and speculation. In those terms, a possible downturn in the strength of party identification has been said to be caused by such diverse factors as the expansion of mass education, the growing reach of the mass media, a value change towards postmaterialism, the proliferation of political skills, and new forms of societal participation (Dalton 1988)—characteristics generally regarded as the correlates of modernization (see Figure 1.1). The baseline of such arguments is that the emerging class of young, educated, politically skilful, and self-confident 'new citizens' (Barnes 1984) needs less political organization and therefore less often establishes durable ties with political parties.

The explanatory paths we pursue in this chapter are less crowded, and follow signposts which are political rather than socio-structural. But before addressing such questions, we investigate the actual state of partisanship in West European countries. Has there really been a general erosion of partisan ties?

The availability of appropriate data, by necessity, limits the number of countries in our study. First, there are countries with well established election studies: Britain, West Germany, the Netherlands, Norway, Denmark, and Sweden. Secondly, all member states of the European Community are covered by the Eurobarometer surveys, which, since 1975, regularly include a question on party attachment. The United States, which has the world's longest time series on party identification, is also included to give a backdrop to the results for Western Europe.

Partisanship and What It Is For

Partisanship is anything but an under-researched area. None the less, there is hardly anything about partisanship which is not undisputed. Scholars even disagree over what partisanship is. The 'basic' (Miller 1991) and now classic notion of partisanship goes back to at least *The American Voter* (Campbell, Converse, Miller, and Stokes 1960). There, partisanship was conceived as an individual's psychological identification with, or affective orientation towards, an important group object in his or her environment (pp. 121 ff.). This psychological 'membership' is assumed to be acquired through primary political socialization, via parental transmission, and to crystallize into stable alignments as a consequence of growing electoral experience, such as repeated voting for the same party (Converse 1969). Originally, party identification was conceived as an exogenous variable in models of party choice, colouring attitudes about issues and evaluations of candidates, and thus affecting the vote both directly and indirectly (Campbell *et al.* 1960: 136 ff.).

A different understanding was formulated about two decades later (Page and Jones 1979; Fiorina 1981; Franklin and Jackson 1983; Franklin 1984). Partisanship was then portrayed as an endogenous variable, affecting current political evaluations and the vote and being affected by them at the same time. Most of the work establishing this revisionist view is well in line with the rational choice paradigm of political behaviour, attributing changes in partisanship largely to cognitive processes of issue evaluation. Recent time-series evidence indicates, however, that issue evaluations cannot account for everything and certainly not for short-term changes in partisanship, which, rather, should be seen to originate in changing affective or emotional views (Whiteley 1988; Pomper 1992).

The most plausible conclusion from this debate is that the driving forces in the dynamics of partisanship may vary, depending on the time-frame applied and the political setting. Even changes in the very short term, in response to campaign events for example (cf. Allsop and Weisberg 1988; Brody and Rothenberg 1988; Stewart 1992), do not necessarily damage a revised model of voting behaviour which removes partisanship from the exogenous, antecedent position once assigned to it.[1] Rather, partisanship is allowed, conceptually, to covary with the course of politics. This new orthodoxy, however, is not yet observed everywhere, as the recent controversy over macro-partisanship demonstrates. The core of this dissension is about whether macro-partisanship (the two-party division among all party identifiers) varies systematically over time—even if one relies on the 'right' (CPS/NES) rather than on the 'wrong' (Gallup) time series and question wording (cf. MacKuen, Erikson, and Stimson 1989, 1992; Abramson and Ostrom 1991).

Neither the phenomenon of partisanship nor the study of it is restricted to the United States. Partisanship in Western Europe, however, is often understood to be different from the US example. When cleavage politics was alive and well, it was portrayed as a derivative of the subcultural identities of citizens; as a reflection of the location of voters in the cleavage structure rather than as a personality trait *per se* (Campbell and Valen 1966; Berger 1977; Thomassen 1992). Many West European scholars felt that the study of a derivative pays little dividend and went on to the real thing. Others continued within the Michigan framework, often along with American co-authors (Butler and Stokes 1969; Klingemann and Taylor 1977; Heath and Pierce 1992).

Early applications of the Michigan survey instrument in Western Europe assembled mixed evidence (Budge, Crewe, and Farlie 1976). Moreover, serious problems about the measurement of partisanship became apparent. In particular, it was found that the US standard survey instrument[2] is unsuitable for use in countries with more than two parties—which means that it is unsuitable everywhere except in the United States. Various European operationalizations of partisanship were designed subsequently which proved less stable than the American prototype, and in the Dutch case even less stable than the vote (Thomassen 1976; Butler and Stokes 1969; LeDuc 1985; Holmberg 1992).[3] The fact that these measures coincided almost perfectly with measures of vote preference questioned the conceptual independence of partisanship from the vote in Western Europe (Borre and Katz 1973; Thomassen 1976). Furthermore, it became evident that the presumed exogenous position of partisanship in models of vote choice was not borne out by data for West European electorates (Schleth and Weede 1971; Thomassen 1976).

Judged by the new orthodoxy, these findings cause considerably less concern about the concept of partisanship. Later work demonstrated the suitability of measures of subjective partisanship for the explanation of voting behaviour in Western Europe, although for some countries— Britain, France, Germany, and Sweden[4] among them—more than others.[5] Recent comparative work supports this notion. Based on panel data from the Political Action studies for the United States, the Netherlands, and Germany, Barnes (1989) emphasizes the similarity of individual-level dynamics in the development of partisanship. Analysing British, Dutch, and German panel data, Richardson (1991) agrees with Barnes in describing partisanship as responsive to the characteristics of national party systems—just as US partisanship can be seen to reflect the characteristics of American institutional arrangements.

According to both Barnes and Richardson, two features in particular contribute to the specificity of partisanship in Western Europe: the existence of minor parties and the cleavage roots of the two major party alternatives. Concentrating on these traditional cleavage parties, Richardson portrays European partisanship in the following manner (1991: 753–4):

Where systemic alternatives reflect traditionally deep societal divides, mutually opposing value systems and ideologies, and relatively durable and consistent position taking by parties, the cognitive, affective, and evaluative portion of individuals' partisanship should be well developed and internally consistent. Moreover, high levels of interparty affective hostility between supporters of traditional cleavage parties should be found . . . Party loyalties comfortably fit the characteristics of an affect-laden schema . . . Stored in the structure are (1) positive affective feelings toward favored parties (termed affective tags by some researchers); (2) negative feelings toward nonfavored parties; (3) evaluative images favoring the supported party and not favoring other parties; and (4) political values and issue positions congenial to pre-ference for a particular party.

One might object that this picture describes West European partisan-ship of the 1950s better than that of the 1990s. Interrelated processes of socio-political change over the past two decades (cf. Inglehart 1977, 1990a; Barnes, Kaase, *et al.* 1979; Jennings, Van Deth, *et al.* 1989) have contributed to a gradual erosion of the traditional social founda-tions of party support (Dalton *et al.* 1984; Franklin, Mackie, and Valen, *et al.* 1992). A new generation of partisans has emerged in most West European party systems which does not fit into the schema outlined by Richardson. Change happens gradually though, and a cleavage-based understanding of partisanship might still adequately describe the way in which most—or at least many—partisans in Western Europe relate to their parties.

What do we know once we have investigated the dynamics of European party attachments? Or, stated differently: what would the consequences of a significant decline in partisanship look like? There are several aspects to this question. At the individual level, partisanship has been known as a vehicle for political participation: party identifiers are generally more likely to vote, to attend campaign events, and care about the election result (Campbell *et al.* 1960; Verba, Nie, and Kim 1978; Dalton 1988). On this view, a decline in partisanship would either signal rising political apathy, or the proliferation of protest behaviour as a potential challenge to the prevailing political order, or both (Kaase and Barnes 1979; Kaase 1989).

A related view argues that one of the many important functions of

political parties is to socialize and integrate citizens into the political
system (Neumann 1956). To the degree that this is achieved, partisanship will breed positive attitudes towards the political system and,
indirectly, trust in the political regime (Miller and Listhaug 1990).
Declining partisanship, on the other hand, can be expected to promote
political cynicism.

Most obviously, partisanship contributes to stability in individual
voting behaviour—according to whichever orthodoxy. Declining partisanship, therefore, is equivalent to the dwindling of the stabilizing
elements in electoral behaviour. When partisanship is declining, electoral volatility is likely to increase—to the degree permitted by the
structure of party competition in a given country.[6] And, a downturn in
partisanship improves the electoral prospects for new parties, contributes to the further fractionalization of party systems, and thereby tends
to complicate coalition building and government formation processes.

Partisanship thus contributes to the mobilization of citizens in conventional political participation,[7] and gives individual party choice
some firm ground. Depending on the performance of party government, partisanship seems to promote beliefs about legitimacy and
political trust, and thus helps to integrate citizens into the political
order. Partisanship contributes directly to the stability of party systems, and indirectly to the stability of the political order itself. This
is what is at stake if partisanship fades away.

National Election Studies and Eurobarometers

Reliable information about the evolution of partisanship is available
from two major data sources, national election studies and the Eurobarometer series. Based on these data series, we distinguish three
classes of countries. One class consists of those countries for which
we use only Eurobarometer data: Ireland, Belgium, Luxembourg,
France, Portugal, Spain, Italy, and Greece. For a second class of
countries, national election study data are available but Eurobarometers are not: these are Norway, Sweden, and the United States. Both
types of survey data are available for the third class of countries, to
which belong Denmark, Britain, the Netherlands, and West Germany.

For each of our two data sources, we distinguish between all
identifiers and strong party identifiers. The latter are drawn from the
strongest response category in national election studies, and the two

strongest categories in the Eurobarometer data.[8] Strong identifiers are a subset of the larger group of party identifiers.[9]

The Trend is Down in Many Countries, but . . .

Visual inspection of Figure 4.1, graphs *a–q*, reveals that the strength of party identification is declining in many countries of Western Europe. A quick look can give a false impression, however. To give our conclusions a firmer footing, linear regression analyses were performed, treating strength of party identification as the dependent variable and time (the year of the survey) as the independent variable. Separate analyses were run for the Eurobarometer data and the national election studies, and for strong identifiers and all identifiers, respectively.

One could object that linear modelling might not be the most appropriate strategy to describe the actual distributions. The loosening of partisan ties might happen in phases rather than as a continuous process. However, our interest in this first step is merely in the direction and the magnitude of change; declining party attachments should show up in significant negative trends fitted to the empirical distributions.

The results of our trend analysis are fairly varied. Although they generally point to a decline in partisanship across Western Europe, it is obvious that the depth and spread of this development are quite different in different countries and for different periods of time. The trend lines, no doubt, do tend to decline. As we show in Table 4.1, fifteen of the seventeen regression coefficients calculated from the time series based on national election studies are negative. Moreover, one of the two exceptions the increase in all identifiers in Germany from 1961 onwards—is questionable because the wording of the item was changed. We come back to this problem later.

This, however, is not the whole story in the national election studies data. If we consider not only the strength of these weights, but also their robustness as indicated by tests of significance, things suddenly appear much less uniform. Of the six countries with a long-standing tradition of national election studies, just two—Sweden and Britain—exhibit significant, steep declines. Irrespective of short-term movements, linear trend estimates suggest that party attachments are rather stable in Norway, Denmark, and the Netherlands. And they are either modestly rising (according to the longest time series from 1961 onwards) or modestly declining (according to the strictly comparable time series

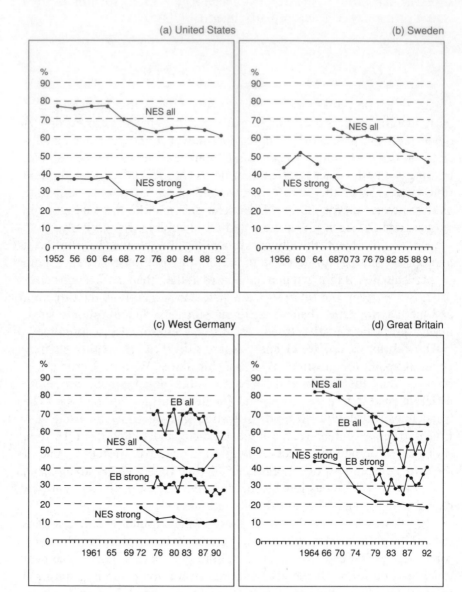

(a) United States   (b) Sweden

(c) West Germany   (d) Great Britain

See over page for caption.

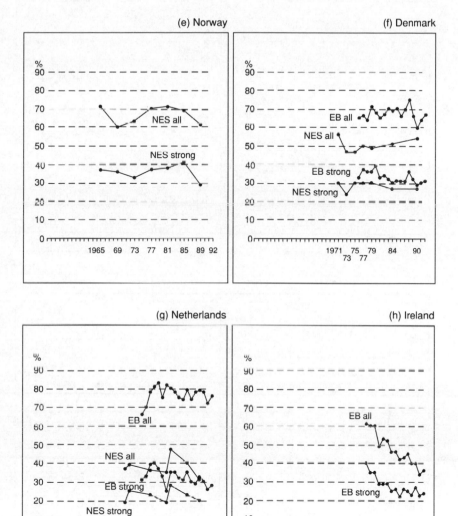

See over page for caption.

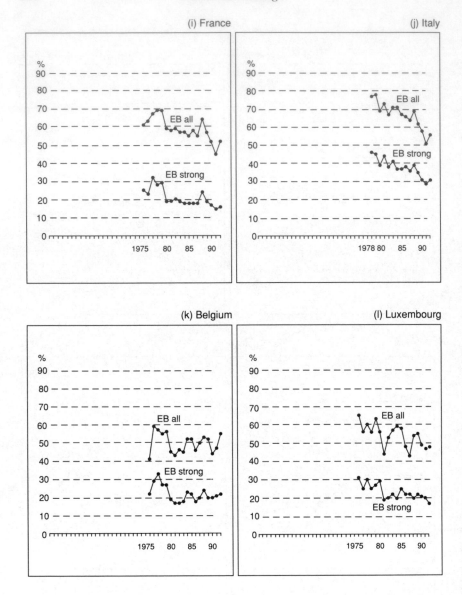

See facing page for caption.

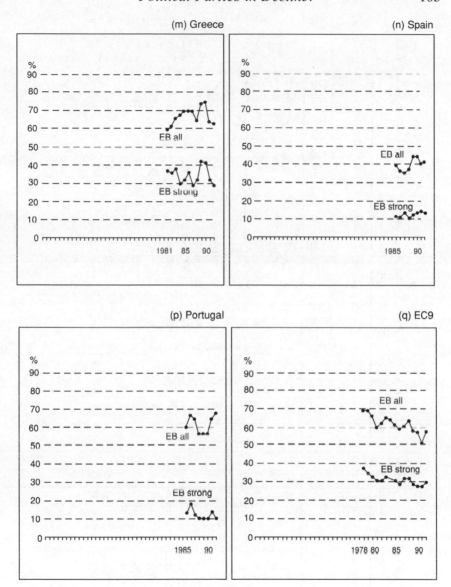

FIGURE 4.1. *Country-specific evolution of party attachment*

Notes: Strong and weak identifiers compared on the basis of national election studies and Eurobarometer data as available. NES 1975 data for Britain are for October 1974.

Sources: data from Tables 4.A1 and 4.A2.

TABLE 4.1. *Evolution of partisanship across time in fourteen West European countries and the United States: linear regression analysis using national election studies and Eurobarometer data*

Country	Data source	Time span cover	No. of observations	Strong identifiers		All identifiers	
				Intercept	b-values	Intercept	b-values
USA	NES	1952–92	11	36.7	−0.25*	78.4	−0.44**
Ireland	EB	1978–92	15	35.6	−0.96***	61.8	−1.83***
Italy	EB	1978–92	15	45.8	−1.00***	78.6	−1.50***
France	EB	1975–92	18	26.9	−0.60*	66.9	−0.86***
Britain	NES	1964–92	9	46.0	−1.21**	92.0	−0.78***
	EB	1978–92	15	33.4	0.02	60.5	−0.81*
Sweden	NES	1956–91	12	48.6	−0.65***	n.a.	n.a.
	NES	1968–91	9	38.0	−0.49*	66.1	−0.70**
Luxembourg	EB	1975–92	18	28.5	−0.56***	61.9	−0.74*
Germany	NES	1961–90	9	n.a.	n.a.	38.6	0.26
	NES	1972–90	6	16.1	−0.38	52.8	−0.66
	EB	1975–92	18	33.2	−0.26	69.8	−0.52
Netherlands	NES	1971–89	6	22.4	−0.01	38.9	−0.11
	EB	1975–92	18	36.3	−0.42*	75.7	0.09

Norway	NES	1965–89	7	36.9	−0.08	66.9	−0.04
Denmark	NES	1971–89	7	28.9	−0.07	50.3	0.07
	EB	1976–92	17	36.7	−0.37*	67.4	0.01
Belgium	EB	1975–92	18	25.7	−0.37	50.8	−0.10
Portugal	EB	1985–92	8	14.8	−0.62	60.3	0.18
Greece	EB	1981–92	12	35.6	−0.17	63.0	0.52
Spain	EB	1985–92	8	10.5	0.37*	35.9	0.81
EC-9	EB	1978–92	15	35.6	−0.47*	71.2	−0.89**

*p < 0.05   **p < 0.005. Two-tailed *t*-tests applied.

Notes: Country-specific OLS regressions were performed with proportion of party identifiers as the dependent variable and year as the independent variable. 'Number of observations' means number of elections in the case of NES, and number of years covered in Eurobarometers. For NES, the number of elections is not equivalent to the number of surveys; in some cases, more than one survey contained the party identification measure, and the findings are averaged; in other instances (e.g. in Denmark), some election studies did not include the party identification measure. Some data for Sweden 1956–91 and for Germany 1961–90 cannot be estimated because of changes in question wording. EC-9 is the 'old' European Community of nine member-countries (Belgium, Denmark, France, Germany, Ireland, Italy, Luxembourg, Netherlands, and Britain). For these countries, equivalent Eurobarometer data are available from 1978 onwards; pooled analyses are run on the basis of weighted data with national sample sizes adjusted to the relative population weight within the Community. We used the Irish 'closely attached' to exemplify how to read these figures. Strong party identifiers comprised, in 1978, an estimated 35.6 per cent of the adult population. This level has been declining by approximately 1 per cent per year since (precisely −0.96 per cent) and approaches the 20 per cent mark in 1992 (35.6 +(15*−0.96)).

from 1972 onwards) in West Germany. But the German trends are insignificant, whichever way we look at the data.

The evidence from the Eurobarometer data is not very different, at least on first sight. Seventeen of the twenty-four regressions shown in Table 4.1 produce a negative slope, indicating that party attachments in the EC member countries have been generally declining over the last fifteen years. Again, not all these negative trends are statistically robust. Indications of a reliable downwards trend are manifest in just five of the twelve EC countries. Ireland certainly belongs in this dealigning group, both with respect to strong party identifiers and less strongly involved citizens. A substantial decline of both strong and weak identifiers is also found in Italy; a similar but somewhat less pronounced decline is evident in France and Luxembourg as well. The Eurobarometer evidence also suggests that British partisanship is best characterized as a process of peripheral dealignment: strong identifiers do not follow any systematic trend while the proportion of weak identifiers shows marked decline.

The second and larger group of countries generally shows doubtful and insignificant trends. Most, but not all, of these trends point in a negative direction. Germany belongs to this group as well as the Netherlands, Denmark, and Belgium. The latter three countries, in particular, exhibit similar trends in the Eurobarometer data, characterized by a continuing fall in strong identifiers and a modest increase of more loosely involved partisans.[10] It is well known, however, that these party systems underwent dramatic changes during the 1960s and 1970s, so it is tempting to interpret these particular developments in partisanship as a consequence of realignment processes (cf. Schmitt 1989).

Greece, Spain, and Portugal might also be counted in this 'doubtful' group. On the other hand, relying on somewhat less rigid criteria, one could as well entertain the argument that partisanship in these new democracies is on the increase. Spain is a prime case in support of Converse's (1969) hypothesis about the association between ageing and the growth and stabilization of partisanship: between 1985 and 1992, the estimated increase in the proportion of strong identifiers in Spain amounts to 40 per cent.

The distributions from the national election studies for the United States, Britain, Germany, and Sweden suggest that the loosening of partisan ties seems to happen in phases rather than as a steady secular process. The British 'decade of dealignment' (Särlvik and Crewe 1983) occupied the 1970s; partisan ties in the United States deteriorated somewhat earlier, from the mid-1960s until the mid-1970s; and German partisanship declined somewhat later, from the mid-1970s until the early 1980s. A periodic decline of partisanship is also apparent in Sweden. Attachments to Swedish parties deteriorated during the 1960s and again during the 1980s, but with a period of stability in the 1970s. Such period-specific downturns in party attachments are not evident for the Netherlands, Denmark, and Norway, all countries which experienced significant changes in their party systems.

If there is an overall tendency, then, it is of loosening partisan bonds. This is testified by the negative trend estimated for the European Community of the Nine (Figure 4.1*q*). The evidence also indicates, however, that political parties are ailing more in some countries than in others. The decline of partisanship is not a uniform process. This conclusion is in line with findings from previous research (cf. Denver 1985; Reiter 1989; Schmitt 1989). Comforting as this may be, however, we must bear in mind that those earlier studies relied on much the same data bases, and were just as restricted by the limitations of the data, as this study. For many countries we simply lack the data necessary for a diachronic perspective appropriate to identifying long-term change.

None the less, some estimates are possible. Sweden stands out in showing an almost continuous decline of partisanship since the 1960s. Irish, Italian, and French evidence is less revealing, but data for the past fifteen years suggest that party attachments in those countries also have declined more or less continuously. Strong, period-specific, and less long-lasting falls in party attachments are evident in the United States, Britain, and Germany. In each of these cases, periods of party decline lasted about a decade, with some recovery thereafter. The Netherlands, Denmark, and Belgium exhibit no signs of such a dramatic decline, although short-term shocks to partisan ties—such as the 1973 electoral upheaval in Denmark—cannot be overlooked.

Finally, we note the modest growth of partisanship in the new democracies of southern Europe. Spain is the clearest case. As Barnes *et al.* (1985) observed earlier, 'Spaniards have been slow to identify with parties', which they attribute, among other things, to the smoothness of the transition to democracy. They concluded that 'continuity and tranquillity are not the stuff of heroic myths, of massive mobilization, of the flowering of political passions' (p. 715). The empirical evidence available by the early 1990s suggests, in addition, that the slow growth of partisanship might be best suited to building a more partisan electorate in the long run.

Political and Other Explanations

Partisanship is tending to decline. What we find, however, is anything but a smooth and uniform decline across Western Europe. Sweeping macro-level explanations which, for example, talk of the importance of rising educational levels, increased penetration of the mass media, and the coming of the new postindustrial age, cannot do justice to all these differing trends. We are not arguing that macro-sociological explanations of this kind are irrelevant; in all likelihood, they play some role as driving forces behind the long-term trend in partisanship. What we doubt, however, is that they play major roles. In our opinion, the leading role belongs not to sociology but to politics and political explanations.

Political factors like the extent of party competition and the content of ideological conflicts, the evolution of new parties, changes in political leadership, and the scope of politics are the key considerations to understanding shifts in mass partisan ties, both in the short term and in the longer perspective. However, these processes are extremely difficult to analyse, largely because the relevant independent variables are inadequately measured. Our endeavours to analyse the development of party identification across countries and over time, reported in Table 4.2, demonstrate these difficulties.

We tested four hypotheses. The first states that the degree of polarization in a political system is related to the level of mass support for parties. A decline in polarization should lead to a loosening of partisan ties among the electorate. The second and third hypotheses are similar to the first, but they deal more directly with the heart of the matter: the level of political conflict. Declining levels of ideological and issue conflict undercut the relevance of both parties and partisan ties, hence they should have a negative effect on the strength of party identification. The fourth hypothesis deals with changes in the number of parties, which is an important aspect of the structure of the party system. An increase in the number of parties is expected to lead to declining aggregate levels in the strength of party identification, since the adherents of new parties, compared to supporters of old established parties, have had less time to develop strong psychological attachments to their party.[11]

The data for classifying countries according to changes in the levels of polarization and the degree of issue conflict were obtained from Lane and Ersson's (1991) analyses. The polarization index, originally

TABLE 4.2. *Change in political system factors in relation to change in the aggregate level of party identification*

Political system factors	Party identification		
	Stable or increasing	Declining	
Political polarization			
Increasing	**GE BE GR NO SP**	GB SW	8 out of 13 cases accord with hypothesis
Declining	DK NL PO	**IR IT FR**	
Ideological conflicts			
Stable or increasing	**GE BE DK PO SP**	GB FR	9 out of 13 cases accord with hypothesis
Declining	NL GR	**IR IT LU SW**	
Issue conflicts			
High	**BE PO SP**	GB	7 out of 13 cases accord with hypothesis
Low	GE NL DK GR NO	**IR IT FR SW**	
Number of parties in parliament			
Increasing	SP DK	**IR IT LU**	9 out of 14 cases accord with hypothesis
Broadly stable	**BE GE GR NL[a] NO PO**	FR SW GB	

[a] declining.

Notes: Data on strength of party identification are based on Eurobarometer results (all attached), except for Sweden and Norway where NES results (all identifiers) were used. The classification of countries regarding change in political polarization and the level of issue conflicts is based on data presented by Lane and Ersson (1991: tables 5.5, 8.1, and 5.3). The classification of countries regarding change in the number of parliamentary parties is based on data provided by Volkens and Schnapp (1991). Change is established over the following time periods: Belgium (1971–87); Denmark (1971–88); Germany (1972–90); France (1973–88); Greece (1985–9): Ireland (1973–89); Italy (1972–87); Luxembourg (1974–89); Netherlands (1971–89); Norway (1965–89); Portugal (1983–7); Spain (1982–9); Sweden 1968–88); and Britain (1974–87). The classification according to change in ideological conflicts builds on left–right self-placement data from the Eurobarometers. Distances between party means for major parties have been used to construct the ideological left–right distance variable. Trend coefficients (betas; predictor variable is the sequence of Eurobarometer surveys) are as follows: Denmark +0.56; France +0.47; Portugal +0.27; Britain +0.10; Denmark +0.10; Spain +0.01; Belgium −0.00; Ireland −0.08; Luxembourg −0.11; Greece −0.33; Italy −0.44; Netherlands −0.65. Countries printed in bold type behave as hypothesized.

devised by Taylor and Herman (1971), is sensitive to ideological left–right distances between parties as well as to the vote shares of parties. The issue conflict variable derives from Lane and Ersson's tentative coding of the occurrence of major issues across sixteen West European countries. Taking account of properties such as frequency, intensity, and duration, they classified levels of issue conflicts along an ordinal scale from 1 to 5 (pp. 290–1). We disregard the time-series dimension of Lane and Ersson's analysis and use only their level estimates for the most recent period in their study (1965: 89).

We constructed two variables, the number of parties and the level of ideological conflict. The first is straightforward, simply counting the number of parties represented by at least one seat in parliament, and establishes whether this number increased or declined during the period for which equivalent survey evidence is available. The ideological conflict variable is based on left–right self-placement data from the Eurobarometer series (national election study data for Sweden). The distances between the major parties have been used to construct an ideological left–right distance variable over time and across EC countries. The distances between the means of the electorates[12] of the major parties[13] on the 10-point left–right self-placement scale are used as proxy measures of the intensity of ideological conflict in different party systems and at different points in time.[14] This allowed us to relate developments in the strength of party identification to changes in political system factors in thirteen West European countries.

Our results are not very impressive. While all relationships point in the predicted direction, they are generally rather weak. Three of our hypotheses dealt with the impact of ideological and issue conflicts on the development of party identification. The analysis suggests that increasing ideological polarization—no matter how it is measured—leads to growing partisanship in a majority of cases. Our fourth hypothesis dealt with the relationship between changes in the party system and aggregate changes in partisanship. The analysis reveals that stable party systems tend to coincide with stable partisanship, while an increase in the number of parliamentary parties tends to coincide with declining partisanship.

The ideological conflict variable provides us with true time-series data. For most EC countries we have biannual measurements of both ideological conflict and party attachments going back to the mid- or late 1970s. Thus, in nine countries, we can apply a stronger test than the simple four-fold analysis. Regression analyses appropriate to correcting for autocorrelated errors were applied to examine the relationship between the proportion of party identifiers on the one hand and the intensity of ideological conflict and the passage of time on the other.[15] The results are presented in Table 4.3.

Again our findings suggest that an increase in the level of ideological conflict between the two major party alternatives leads to stronger partisan attachments in most countries. The regression analysis yields positive coefficients in seven of the nine countries under investigation. These coefficients, however, reach statistical significance in only two of the nine countries: Denmark and the Netherlands. In these countries, an increase in the mean ideological distance of one scale point between the two major party alternatives coincides with a growth of party attachments of about 5 percentage points. In Italy, Ireland, Britain, France, and Germany, an increase in the mean ideological distance between the two major party alternatives leads to an increase in partisanship of between 2 and 3 percentage points. These effects are comparatively weak and statistically not significant. In Belgium and Luxembourg,

TABLE 4.3. *Impact of the degree of ideological conflict on the evolution of party attachments*

Country	Constant	Autoregression/ attenuation	Ideological conflict	Time trend
Denmark	55.1	+0.2	+5.7*	−0.1
Netherlands	59.9	+0.2	+5.2*	+0.1
Italy	75.4	+0.2	+2.8	−0.8**
Ireland	67.9	−0.0	+2.7	−0.9**
Britain	58.1	+0.6**	+2.0	−0.4
Germany	63.2	+0.4*	+1.9	−0.5**
France	66.2	+0.3	+1.7	−0.3
Belgium	56.6	+0.0	−0.5	−0.2
Luxembourg	62.6	+0.0	−0.6	−0.3*

*$p < 0.05$ **$p < 0.005$

Notes: Entries are unstandardized regression coefficients. Data base is the Eurobarometers up to No. 37. The dependent variable is the proportion of all attached as monitored by these surveys. The ideological conflict variable is the difference in mean left–right self-placement of voters for the two major party alternatives in each party system (see Table 4.2 for details). The time-trend variable is the sequence of Eurobarometer surveys. The ideological conflict variable is used here in its synchronous (non-lagged) values to predict the proportions of all attached to a party. As the Eurobarometer time series for Greece, Spain, and Portugal are still too brief for this type of analysis, these countries are not included. Time-series regressions were performed with the AREG algorithm provided by SPSS-PC+; maximum likelihood estimation was used.

party identification seems hardly affected by the temperature of ideological conflicts.

The downturn of party identification in Sweden is also strongly related to the lessening of ideological conflict between the political parties (data not shown here). Based on national election study data about people's perceptions of left–right distances between parties, there is little doubt that ideological conflict has become less acute in Sweden. For example, the average distance between the Conservatives and the Social Democrats on the left–right scale (ranging from 0 to 10) has gone down from 6.1 in 1982 to 5.7 in 1988, and down again to 5.1 in 1991. The Social Democrats are placed more to the right today than ten years ago, while at the same time, the Conservatives are placed somewhat more to the left. Indeed, the correlation between ideological conflict and strength of party identification seems to be stronger in Sweden than for the EC countries, as monitored by the Eurobarometer series. According to data from the Swedish election studies for the period 1979–91, when five elections were held, the correlation is 0.75. Moreover, if we use data about how people place parties on the left–right scale—rather than left–right self-placement—the correlation increases to 0.82.

An essential, but sometimes overlooked, individual-level prerequisite of political explanations for the decline of party identification is that partisanship has to have political content. The strength of party identification should be related, preferably strongly related, to such political factors as the ideological closeness of voters to the parties and their evaluation of the policies of parties on specific issues. Among Swedish voters, the strength of party identification has a distinctly political flavour. People who place themselves close to their preferred party on the left–right scale, and who evaluate their party's issue positions favourably, tend to have stronger party identification than other people. However, the strength of the relationship varies across the parties. The highest correlations are registered for the two largest Swedish parties, the Social Democrats and the Conservatives—about 0.40 for both parties on both the ideological and the policy evaluation tests. The correlations are modest, but given the attenuating effect of measurement error, they are quite impressive.

The strong relationship between political factors and the strength of party identification in Sweden means that we would expect declining levels of party identification to go hand in hand with perceptions of increased distances on the left–right scale between voters and their parties. That is exactly what we find. Comparing the distance between where people place themselves and where they place their preferred party on the left–right scale shows that most parties were perceived by their own voters to be further away in 1991 than in 1979. Among Social Democratic voters, for example, 51 per cent located themselves and the party in the same place on the left–right scale in 1979. In 1991, the comparable result was only 42 per cent. The conclusion from the Swedish case is quite obvious: increased political distance between voters and parties, in ideological and policy terms, is one of the factors behind the rapid decline in partisan ties during the 1980s.

This can also be seen in America. According to national election study data, the proportion of Americans perceiving party differences was at its lowest in the 1970s.[16] During the Reagan years, more people perceived party differences than previously (63 per cent in 1984 compared with 50 per cent in 1952), and partisanship rose again. A minor set-back was observed with the 1992 election, which was attributed to the third candidate, Ross Perot, taking a strong anti-party stance (Wattenberg 1994).

Issues and policies are not the whole story, however. Political leaders and dramatic events can be equally important for the evolution of party attachments. The steep increase in the strength of party identification in Germany in 1972 is an excellent case in point. That year, for the first time in the history of the Federal Republic, a vote of no-confidence (*konstruktives Mißtrauensvotum*) was demanded in parliament, intended to replace Willy Brandt's SPD–FDP government with a CDU–CSU government led by Rainer Barzel.[17] The vote was defeated but early elections were called, which resulted—after a very lively and stimulating campaign ('*Willy wählen*')—in the re-election of Willy Brandt. The consequence was an extraordinarily high politicization of society at large.

Unfortunately, the impact of these events on German party identification is somewhat difficult to assess due to a change in the wording of the partisanship question between the 1969 and the 1972 election surveys.[18] None the less, it seems plausible to assume that the change in the instrument would affect the relative proportions of party identifiers equally. As to the effect of the 1972 events, euphoria about the defeat of the *Mißtrauensvotum* and confirmation of the Brandt government are likely to have boosted Social Democrat identification, but it should either have modestly depressed identification with the Christian Democrats or left it unaffected.

The evolution of party identification in West Germany is depicted in

Figure 4.2. The proportion of Christian Democratic identifiers in the electorate remains basically stable at about 18 or 19 per cent, irrespective of the change in question wording in 1972. It is attachment to the Social Democratic Party which fluctuates remarkably. From 19 per cent in 1969, identifiers rose to 31 per cent in 1972, but fell back to 22 per cent in 1976 when Helmut Schmidt took over as leader; it fell even further to 16 per cent in 1983 when the Social Democrats were in opposition with Hans-Jochen Vogel as leader.[19] It was not until 1990 that Social Democratic levels of affective support improved again, from 16 to 20 per cent, when Oskar Lafontaine stood and lost against Helmut Kohl in the highly politicized reunification election.

Thus the steep decline in West German partisanship during the 1970s and early 1980s is mainly a phenomenon associated with the Social Democrats. The levels of affective support assembled by Willy Brandt in 1972 were eroded, gradually but steadily, thereafter. (For another account of these developments, see Norpoth 1984; also Baker, Dalton, and Hildebrandt 1981.)

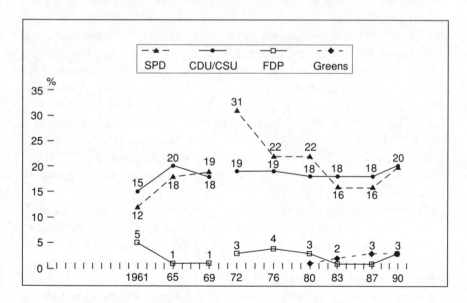

FIGURE 4.2. *Party specifics in the evolution of West German party identification, 1961–90*

Note: Entries are percentages of identifiers (*Anhänger*) before 1972 and percentages of 'strong' and 'fairly strong' identifiers after 1972.

Sources: national election studies.

Changes in the social structure of Western societies are known to affect the way people relate to politics and to political parties. Social change is assumed to cause what may be called the structural decline of partisanship. Structural decline cannot but proceed slowly. We do not investigate these processes, but take them for granted. But, if partisanship in Western Europe were affected only by structural change, a more or less uniform picture of minor decline should emerge everywhere. This is not so. Our measures of partisanship fluctuate considerably over time, and trends in partisanship vary quite remarkably between countries. This cannot be explained by broadly uniform processes of structural change. The specific properties and processes of different political systems need to be considered.

Our analyses find that the degree of political polarization and both ideological and issue conflict positively affect levels of partisanship in a majority of countries. Stable party systems and stable partisanship run in parallel, while declining partisanship is associated with party system change—as measured by a significant increase in the number of parliamentary parties. The importance of political factors is underlined by the Swedish and West German cases. The extraordinary decline in Sweden results largely from the ideological alienation of voters and the increasing ideological similarity of the parties; and there is hardly anything of greater generality behind the German trend other than the erosion of the Social Democratic support assembled by Willy Brandt in the early 1970s.

Partisanship among Party Electorates

Party identification need not necessarily develop at the same pace, nor in the same direction, across different parties. Neither can it be expected to reach the same levels for different kinds of parties. This, at least, is what the German case suggests. It is to this aspect of partisanship that we turn in this final section.

In considering partisanship among the electorates of specific parties, we can think of two different aspects: level and trend. The level of partisanship refers to the proportion of party identifiers among voters for a party; the trend in partisanship is the direction of developments in this proportion over time. Earlier research suggests that the size of parties influences partisanship among their voters. Barnes (1989) found that attachments to large parties become more stable and stronger as people grow older whereas bonds with smaller parties are weaker, more volatile, and tend to wane as people grow older. These differences arise largely because 'it is much easier to switch identification or vote, or both, to and from a minor party than from one major party to another' (p. 243).[20] Studies of voting behaviour in the 1989 European elections found that large parties are conspicuous for their ability to mobilize both their identifiers (Schmitt 1990) and their broader electoral potential (van der Eijk and Oppenhuis 1991). This again suggests that there is something different about attachments to large parties. Even if it is not clear what accounts for the difference between major and minor parties, obviously we need to consider the size of parties as one criterion differentiating the levels of partisanship enjoyed by parties. We distinguish between large, middle-sized, and small parties.[21]

Another factor affecting partisanship is the age of parties. We know that it takes time for individuals to acquire stable ties with political parties (Converse 1969). Transposing this individual-level insight to the level of the political party[22] suggests that young parties cannot yet rely on a stable core of identifiers, while older ones can—although, for several reasons, they need not. We differentiate between old parties (operative at least since the end of the Second World War), middle-aged parties (in between old and young), and young parties (operative since the late 1970s or the 1980s).

A further factor which plausibly differentiates between the level of partisanship enjoyed by parties is their ideological position. The more extreme the ideological position taken by a party, the more likely it is to attract true believers rather than volatile pragmatists. Empirically, we classify parties as far left, left, centre, right, and far right according to the mean left–right self-placement of their electorate.

A final criterion is the political family to which a party belongs. Functional considerations suggest that partisanship has socio-structural correlates other than age (cf. Miller 1976). Confronted with the complexities of politics, electors who are less well educated, less skilful, and less interested in politics are generally thought to be in greater need of the simplifying device of partisanship. To the extent that this holds true, we expect identificative support for parties with a traditional working-class or lower middle-class electorate, such as socialist or Christian democratic parties, to exceed that of parties with a middle-class appeal, as in the case of liberal or ecological parties. Moreover, bearing in mind the processes of socio-structural change and cognitive mobilization (Dalton 1984), we may also expect the former party families—which happen to coincide with large parties and to some degree with old parties—to suffer a disproportionately strong decline in party attachment.

We can be brief in reporting the results of this final step of our analysis, shown in Table 4.4.[23] First, there is no statistically significant association between level and trend in party specific partisanship. It is not the case that highly partisan parties have experienced decline while the partisanship of other parties has remained stable or increased. The two aspects vary independently of one another.

Secondly, the predictors of size, age, ideological position, and party family account for a significant proportion of the variance in the level of partisanship (59 per cent) but they are less illuminating about trend differences (31 per cent). Thirdly, as we expected, large parties have a somewhat more partisan following than small and medium-sized parties. However, the size of a party has no major impact *per se* on the partisanship of its supporters. This is evident in the multivariate analysis. Moreover, large parties do not progressively lose affective support, as might have been expected. Rather, other things being equal, they have been able to attract partisan attachments over the last two or three decades. So have the small parties. Above all, it is the middle-sized parties which have lost adherents over time.

Our results show, fourthly, that there is not much to the argument that young parties have not had the time or the opportunity to build partisan electorates. The ageing hypothesis, borrowed from analyses of the individual voter, is only weakly supported by our data. The age effect, while being quite impressive in the bivariate analysis, almost disappears in the multivariate analysis. Nor is age related to trends in partisanship. Counter-intuitive as it may be, we find that the overall decline in party attachments is not concentrated around the old dinosaurs among the parties.

Fifthly, the evolution of affective support for a party is best explained by its ideological position. Parties occupying a position near the poles of the left–right spectrum—the 'ideological parties'—show growing numbers of identifiers, while more centrist or moderate parties have lost a proportion of their identifiers over time. The largest increase in identifiers is observed for parties on the far right, but parties near the left pole also did better than average. This cross-national comparative finding obviously provides strong support for our earlier interpretation of the Swedish *malaise*: partisanship grows best on ground well

TABLE 4.4. *Partisanship in different categories of parties: correlates of levels and trends (multiple classification analyses)*

Independent variables and categories	Number of parties	Dependent variables			
		Level of parties' partisanship		Trend in parties' partisanship	
		Unadjusted deviation from grand mean[a]	Deviation adjusted for other independent variables[a]	Unadjusted deviation from grand mean[b]	Deviation adjusted for other independent variables[b]
Party size					
Small	46	−0.40	−0.28	0.37	0.34
Medium	23	0.27	0.25	−0.59	−0.84
Large	16	0.78	0.44	−0.21	0.23
		eta=0.40	beta=0.26	**eta=0.33**	**beta=0.41**
Party age					
Young	24	−0.58	−0.18	0.06	−0.19
Middle	15	−0.10	−0.06	0.04	0.23
Old	46	0.33	0.12	−0.05	0.02
		eta=0.33	beta=0.11	eta=0.04	beta=0.11
Ideological position					
Far left	13	0.96	1.03	0.34	0.37
Left	20	0.01	−0.05	−0.39	−0.34
Centre	23	−0.73	−0.08	−0.02	−0.39
Right	20	0.21	−0.40	−0.29	−0.18
Far right	9	−0.04	−0.30	1.11	1.61
		eta=0.46	**beta=0.39**	**eta=0.36**	**beta=0.49**
Party families					
Communist	12	1.13	0.39	0.19	−0.11
Extreme right	2	0.96	1.67	0.11	−1.86
Christian democrat	11	0.69	0.88	−0.08	−0.24
Socialist	16	0.46	0.22	−0.64	−0.16
Conservative	5	0.36	0.42	0.11	0.17
Regionalist	3	−0.04	0.26	0.11	0.32
Left-socialist	6	−0.37	−0.52	0.27	−0.20
Liberal	17	−0.74	−0.54	−0.07	0.26
Agrarian	1	−1.04	−1.32	0.11	1.31
Green	10	−1.24	−0.79	0.41	0.35
Progress	2	−2.04	−0.128	1.61	0.53
		eta=0.71	**beta=0.54**	eta=0.33	beta=0.32
Variance explained			**59%**		**31%**

[a] grand mean (level) = 3.01
[b] grand mean (level) = 2.93

Notes: Descriptive information on the dependent variables is given in Tables 4.A3 and 4.A4, in the appendix to this chapter. Eighty-nine parties were coded altogether. A few missing data result in the multivariate MCA being based on eighty-five cases. Pearson correlation between level and trend of individual parties' partisanship is −0.0713 and not significant. Coefficients in bold type are significant above 0.05. An example might help to explain the figures: sixteen big parties rank considerably above average as regards their level of partisanship, with a mean deviation of +0.78 from the grand mean of 3.01. The scale ranges from 1 = strong partisan parties to 5 = unpartisan parties (cf. Table 4.A1). This positive deviation is reduced to +0.44 in the multivariate analysis when the effects of all other independent variables are removed in advance. In a bivariate analysis, the size of parties is significantly related to their level of partisanship (eta = 0.40); in a multivariate analysis of variance, however, this effect diminishes (eta = 0.26) and becomes insignificant.

fertilized with ideological conflict, and is bound to deteriorate where such nourishment is lacking.

The ideological position of a party is also related to its level of partisanship. The partisanship of electorates situated on the far left of the ideological spectrum figures well above average, while attachments to right-wing parties (both far right and right) are below average. This coincides with the form of political organization originally adopted by the different social and ideological movements in Western Europe. The thoroughly organized mass-membership party (*von der Wiege bis zur Bahre*) originates in the political traditions of the socialist and labour parties associated with the working-class left, while the more loosely assembled cadre party, such as the early conservative and liberal parties, is associated with the traditions of right-wing politics.

This leads us, finally, to the relationship between party family and partisanship. Party family is the strongest predictor of the level of attachment to individual parties, but it is not significantly related to trends. Indeed, the pattern that emerges seems to be based on functional requirements rather than political traditions. The electorates 'closest' to their party are, on average, less well educated, less wealthy, and less involved in politics. Being mostly composed of working-class and lower middle-class voters, the electorates of Christian democratic, communist, conservative, and socialist parties are above average in their partisanship. Middle-class voters, on the other hand, who are known to be more skilful politically, are over-represented among green, liberal, and left-socialist parties; the electorates of these parties are considerably less partisan than the average voter.

Temporary Phenomenon or Permanent Change?

If there is an overall tendency in Western European partisanship, it is of loosening partisan bonds. But specific developments, by country and by party, are so varied that any general 'overall' view disguises more than it discloses. The evidence presented in this chapter suggests that party attachments are in steady and steep decline in Sweden, Ireland, Italy, and France. Sharp, period-specific downturns in partisanship, as well as signs of subsequent recoveries, are evident in Britain and Germany (and the United States). Stable partisanship is characteristic of the Netherlands, Denmark, Norway, and Belgium. And there are some modest signs of growing partisanship in the new democracies of southern Europe, notably in Spain.

This variety of country-specific findings, we argue, cannot be explained by broadly uniform processes of social-structural change. Instead, we considered political factors, and found that the degree of political polarization and ideological conflict affect levels of partisanship positively in a majority of countries—most clearly so in the Netherlands, where partisanship is, in any case, comparatively buoyant. We found also that partisanship varies considerably between parties. Supporters of the mass-membership Christian democratic, conservative, communist, and socialist parties are more partisan than supporters of other parties. Finally, we found that ideologically distinct parties, both small and large, have been able to increase the number of partisans in their electorate.

Reviewing these findings, one cannot help wondering whether it is the Swedish or the Dutch, the Irish, or the Danish examples which provide the model for future developments. Are we witnessing the first signs of a general phenomenon of partisan decline or is declining partisanship confined to particular countries under particular circumstances?

Modern democracy has been built upon competing political parties. In the wake of theorizing about 'post-industrial' society, however, the need for parties has been questioned. The newly independent and resourceful postmaterialist citizen is expected to be ready to challenge the authority of political institutions and not to be in need of representation through political parties. To the extent that collective efforts will be required, it is argued, alternative organizations and *ad hoc* issue groups will emerge. Even if they do not disappear entirely, political parties will be reduced, at least, to bare electoral vehicles or mere political ritual.

As we are sceptical about sweeping theories of this grandeur and remain faithful to an old and wise rule in political science, we refrain from trying to foretell the future. We suspect, however, that political parties will prove to be far more tenacious than many expect. The reasoning underlying our view is that the decline in partisanship has not been uniform and linear across Western Europe. General macrosociological explanations cannot do justice to all the different patterns in our findings. Political factors of short or middle range have to be taken into consideration as well. For example, there is a noticeable relationship between degrees of partisanship among voters and degrees of polarization and ideological conflict among the political parties. When ideological conflicts between parties diminish, peoples' need of parties abates and partisanship becomes less intense. Thus, one would expect partisanship and the relevance of political parties to increase again, if and when ideological differences and issue conflicts flare once more and become more acute. Political conflicts are the *raison d'être*, the breath of life, for political parties. Without conflicts parties languish.

These observations are well in line with our evidence that the ideological distinctiveness of parties is the single most powerful predictor of flourishing partisanship. This suggests that the parties themselves, more than any anonymous process of socio-structural change, are in a position to determine the future of partisanship in Western Europe.

METHODOLOGICAL APPENDIX

In view of our experience in the research for this chapter, we add a note on the problems of comparability which arise when analysing survey measures of partisanship.

Apart from the well-known difficulties of cross-national comparisons, several specific problems of comparability arise when analysing measures of partisanship. Probably the most obvious is in comparing levels. It is hardly possible to compare levels of party attachment which have been measured with different survey instruments. This applies to comparisons using data from the Eurobarometer series and national election studies. In each survey series, party attachment is measured differently—according to different national traditions of electoral research, on the one hand, and according to the Eurobarometer standard, on the other. This is also a problem in each of the two data sources taken separately. Changes of question wording took place in the national series of elections studies (for example, in 1972 in Germany, in 1968 in Sweden) as well as in the Eurobarometer series (see Katz 1985 and Schmitt 1989 for details). This makes it impossible to compare the level estimates of party attachment obtained by these two series of surveys. The best we can do is compare the trend lines.

Cross-national comparisons are no easier. The strength of party identification, in most instances, has been monitored differently across countries. In this respect, the Eurobarometer surveys are the least problematic. Care has been taken to use functionally equivalent questions across the countries participating in the Eurobarometer surveys. Language differences and translation difficulties cannot be overlooked, however. Translation to ensure the identical meaning of expressions like 'feeling close to a particular party' is difficult to achieve in all West European languages. Consequently, estimates of the level of partisanship in cross-national comparisons have to be used with extra caution.

A further problem is that it is not obvious how to arrive at the data-points constituting the actual trend lines to be compared. National election studies, for example, are usually conducted in a series of waves, either as true panel surveys or a series of consecutive cross-sectional surveys. A measure of party identification is often included more than once. Judging from the German data (and also, but less clearly so, from the Swedish data), it appears that post-electoral levels of partisanship tend to exceed pre-electoral levels. For both the German and the Swedish cases, our strategy was to average the proportions across the different waves—which tends to balance out both the effects of political mobilization and (more technically) of panel mortality, and to give a more summary picture of the election at hand. This average figure then constitutes the finding for that election year. The annual figures derived from the Eurobarometer data are the averages of the findings in the spring and fall survey.

A comparison of the data from the national election studies and the Eurobarometers show differences which merit looking at more closely. The first emerges with regard to strong identifiers in Britain: according to the British Election Study, this group has declined; according to the Eurobarometer data, this group is remarkably stable. However, this apparent contradiction stems from the different time frames of the two series: the BES started in 1964 but comparable Eurobarometer data for Britain are available only from 1978 onwards. Inspection of the actual distributions rather than the linear trend estimates suggests that the British 'decade of dealignment' (Särlvik and Crewe 1983), which corresponded roughly to the 1970s, was almost completed when the Eurobarometer series started. At the beginning of the 1980s a new and considerably lower plateau of partisanship was reached which is evident in both data sources. Thus, while the longer BES series is heavily shaped by massive withdrawals from partisanship in the 1970s, the Eurobarometer series portrays a period of relative stability in party affiliations during the 1980s.

Clearly, then, the apparently contradictory evidence is actually consistent. Even more nicely, the fluctuations of Eurobarometer identifiers between election years make some sense. They seem to indicate partisan demobilization when general elections are distant, and the well-functioning mobilization of partisanship when they come close. While this is not exactly what the old orthodoxy of party identification was intended to measure (although what it did measure was, in many instances, exactly the same phemomenon; see Butler and Stokes 1972: 470), it is compatible with the new orthodoxy which allows partisanship to vary in response to political stimuli.

A second difference is found, again with regard to strong identifiers, for the Netherlands and Denmark. While national election studies there do not reveal any stable long-term trend, the Eurobarometer data show strong identifiers to be in moderate decline. Both the time span covered by the two survey series and the level estimates derived from them are sufficiently close to one another that they can hardly cause this discrepancy. What probably makes the difference is that national election studies are conducted in times of high mobilization and politicization, while Eurobarometer surveys are conducted irrespective of elections being close or distant. Parties in these post-realignment environments (see Schmitt 1989) might still be able to mobilize their strong identifiers at election time, but progressively lose this ability in more quiet phases of the political cycle. However, overall partisanship in these countries is in good shape according to both data sources.

The German case, finally, is a particularly good example to demonstrate that the absence of a consistent long-term trend should not be taken to signify stability. The contrary may well be the case, and party attachments over a given period may grow and decay in compensating ways which prevent an overall trend emerging. German party alignments strengthened during the 1960s in general, and, in particular, after the alternation in power of 1969 (cf. Norpoth 1984). Many of these additional partisan attachments faded away in the second half of the period of SPD–FDP governments; more precisely, under the chancellorship of Helmut Schmidt between the mid-1970s and the early 1980s. From then on, German party attachments seem to have regained more stable ground again.

Another problem is comparing the partisanship of party electorates across system borders. One way to escape from measurement specifics is to compare party deviations from the overall national pattern. To arrive at an estimate of the level of partisanship among the electorate of a specific party, the party-specific proportions of attached voters have to be averaged over the available surveys and compared to the system-specific average level of partisanship. Unbiased trend estimates can be arrived at by comparing party-specific regression slopes (*b*-values) to overall regression slopes. These procedures can be applied to both the Eurobarometer and national election study data.

Two additional rules were applied in the analysis of the partisanship of individual parties. First, in order to get some balanced picture, the partisanship scores of party electorates were compared with the partisanship scores for all prospective voters rather than with the scores for all entitled to vote. Prospective non-voters—found in varying proportions in different systems—are known to be less partisan, and party-specific deviations from an overall level of partisanship would, in some countries, hardly produce any party with below-average partisanship. The second rule has to do with the linguistic and cultural segmentation of Belgian society. When we treated Belgium as one system and considered deviations from an overall average, we found that Flemish and Walloon parties are well ordered in two distinct partisan groups. Belgium was therefore treated as two systems, one consisting of Walloon voters and parties, the other of Flemish voters and parties.

TABLE 4.A1. *The development of strength of party attachment in the twelve EC countries: proportion of Eurobarometer respondents closely attached to party and all attached, 1975–92*

Year	Eurobarometer number	IT	FR	GE	DK	NL	GB	LU	IR	BE	GR	SP	PO	EC-9 average
Closely attached (very and fairly close)														
1975	4	—	25	29	—	31	—	31	—	22	—	—	—	—
1976	5–6	—	23	35	33	33	—	25	—	29	—	—	—	—
1977	7–8	—	32	31	37	39	—	30	—	33	—	—	—	37
1978	9–10	46	28	29	36	40	40	25	40	27	—	—	—	37
1979	11–12	45	29	31	36	37	34	27	35	27	—	—	—	34
1980	13	39	19	32	39	33	37	29	35	19	—	—	—	32
1981	15	44	19	27	33	25	32	21	29	17	37	—	—	30
1982	17–18	38	20	35	34	35	26	21	29	17	36	—	—	30
1983	19–20	41	19	36	32	35	34	22	29	18	38	—	—	32
1984	21–22	37	18	36	30	32	29	20	25	23	30	—	—	30
1985	23–24	37	18	34	31	31	30	25	26	22	32	11	13	30
1986	25–26	38	18	32	31	35	26	22	22	18	36	11	18	28
1987	27–28	36	18	32	31	30	36	22	26	20	29	13	12	31
1988	29–30	39	24	27	36	29	35	21	25	24	32	10	10	31
1989	31–32	35	19	25	32	33	31	23	23	20	42	12	10	28
1990	33–34	31	17	28	29	30	32	22	27	20	41	13	10	27
1991	35–36	29	18	26	30	26	37	20	23	21	32	14	13	27
1992	37–38	31	16	28	31	28	41	17	24	22	29	13	10	29

All attached *(very and fairly close, and sympathizers)*

Year	EB													
1975	4	—	61	69	65	66	—	65	—	41	—	—	—	—
1976	5–6	—	63	71	66	70	—	56	—	59	—	—	—	—
1977	7–8	—	67	63	66	73	—	60	—	57	—	—	—	—
1978	9–10	77	69	58	64	81	68	56	61	55	—	—	—	68
1979	11–12	78	69	68	71	83	62	63	60	56	—	—	—	69
1980	13	69	59	72	68	75	63	56	60	45	—	—	—	66
1981	15	73	58	59	65	82	48	44	49	43	59	—	—	60
1982	17–18	67	59	69	67	80	50	53	53	46	61	—	—	62
1983	19–20	71	57	70	70	78	60	57	52	45	65	—	—	65
1984	21–22	71	57	72	69	75	56	59	46	52	67	—	—	64
1985	23–24	67	55	69	70	74	48	58	46	52	69	39	60	61
1986	25–26	66	58	67	66	75	41	48	42	46	69	36	66	59
1987	27–28	64	55	68	70	74	52	43	43	50	69	35	64	60
1988	29–30	69	64	61	75	78	56	54	45	53	64	37	56	63
1989	31–32	62	57	60	66	78	48	55	40	52	73	44	56	58
1990	33–34	58	52	59	60	78	54	49	40	44	74	44	56	57
1991	35–36	51	45	54	64	72	48	47	34	47	64	40	64	51
1992	37–38	56	52	59	67	76	55	48	36	55	63	41	67	57

Notes: Entries are yearly averages in percentages. Data base is the Eurobarometer surveys. Respondents are aged 18 and over; national representative weighting routines are applied if available. Displayed are the proportions of those close to party among all respondents; don't knows and no replies are treated as not close. For most years, results from two Eurobarometer surveys have been collapsed and a mean result is given. When computing the EC-9 average, an additional weight was applied to adjust national sample sizes to the relative population weight of each country within the Community.

Political Linkage

TABLE 4.A2. *The development of party attachment in eight Western countries: proportion of national election study respondents classified as identifiers and strong identifiers, 1952–92*

Election year	SV	GE	GB	NL	DK	NL	USA
1952							77 (37)
1953							
1954							
1955							
1956	– (44)						76 (37)
1957							
1958							
1959							
1960	– (52)						77 (37)
1961		29 (–)					
1962							
1963							
1964	– (46)		82 (44)				77 (38)
1965		40 (–)		71 (37)			
1966			82 (44)				
1967							
1968	65 (39)						70 (30)
1969		40 (–)		60 (36)			
1970	63 (33)		79 (42)				
1971					56 (30)	37 (19)	
1972		56 (18)				39 (25)	65 (26)
1973	60 (31)			63 (33)	47 (24)		
1974			74 (30)				
1975			73 (27)		47 (30)		
1976	61 (34)	49 (12)					63 (24)
1977				70 (37)	50 (30)	36 (23)	
1978							
1979	59 (35)		68 (22)		49 (30)		
1980		45 (13)					65 (27)
1981				71 (38)		35 (19)	
1982	60 (34)					47 (28)	
1983		40 (10)	63 (22)				
1984					51 (27)		65 (30)
1985	53 (30)			69 (41)			
1986						40 (23)	
1987		39 (10)	64 (20)				
1988	51 (27)						64 (32)
1989				61 (29)		33 (20)	
1990		47 (11)			54 (27)		
1991	48 (24)						
1992			64 (19)				

Notes: Data bases are national election studies. The percentage of strong identifiers is shown in parentheses. Tabular information on party attachment was provided by John Curtice for Britain; Ola Listhaug for Norway; Palle Svensson for Denmark; Jacques Thomassen for the Netherlands; Donald Granberg for the United States; and for Germany and Sweden by the authors. The Swedish question wording is documented in Holmberg (1992). The measurement problems with the German data are described by Kaase (1976) and Falter (1977). The British instrument is documented in Crewe, Day, and Fox (1991: 471–2). The Norwegian instrument is described in Listhaug (1989: Ch. 7). The US question is given in n. 2. Significant changes in question wording affecting this table occurred in Sweden from 1968 on, and in Germany from 1972 on. The '1975' election in Britain is that of October 1974.

TABLE 4 A3. *Deviations from average levels of partisanship in party electorates, 1975–90*

	NO	SV	DK	NL	GE	GB	IR	LU	BE	FR	IT	SP	PO	GR
Strong partisan (10% + >average)	ChrD	SD	DKP SD[c] V	RelR[d]					PCB	PC	PCI MSI		CDU	KKE EPEN
Partisan (5% to 9%)	SD			PvdA[c] CDA[c]	SPD[c]	Lab	FF FG	PC	PSB PSC	RPR	DC	IU Reg[e]		
Average (4% to –4%)	Cent Con	Con ChrD Com	VS[b] KF SF[c] KrF[c]	VVD LftG[c] Green	CDU[c] Green	Con Green Natl	Lab Green PrD Natl	PD POSL PSC	BSP PLP VU RW	PS UDF FN	DP PR PSI PSDI	PSOE (A)PP	PS CDS PSD PRD	
Rather unpartisan (−5% to −9%)	ScLft	Cent	RF[b] RV[c]			Lib	Workers		PVV CVP	PSU	PRI PLI	CDS		PASOK ND
Nonpartisan (−10% and less)	Lib Progr	Lib Green[a] CD	FrP[a] Green	D'66	FDP[c]			Ecolo	Ecolo	Ecolo	Green			DIANA

[a] Three data points only.

[b] Only Eurobarometer data available; otherwise both sources are considered.

[c] Eurobarometer and national election study classification suggest different placements. The latter is accepted because it covers a longer time period.

[d] RelR = SGP + GPV + RPF.

[e] Reg = mainly CIU and HB

Notes: Sources are Eurobarometer surveys covering, for most countries, the period 1975–90, and national election studies series (as available). Average partisanship is a nation-specific measure, computed as the average (across surveys) of the proportions of identifiers (very and fairly close for Eurobarometers; strong and ordinary identifiers for national election studies) among voters. Party specific averages (of proportions of identifiers among party voters) are compared with the overall measure.

TABLE 4.A4. *Party-specific deviations from national trend in partisanship*

	NO	SV	DK	NL	GE	GB	IR	LU	BE	FR	IT	SP	PO	GR
Strongly increasing (+0.31 and more)	SocL Progr		FrP[c] VS[b] DKP SF[c]	RelR[d] VVD[c]	Green[c]		PrD	PC	PCB Ecolo	FN			PRD	ND
Increasing (+0.11 to +0.30)	Con	ChrD Green[a]	RF[b]	CD[c]	CDU[c]		FF	Ecolo	RW	Ecolo	PSI PSDI PRI DC	PSOE CDS	CDS	PASOK EPEN
Average (−0.10 to +0.10)	Cent	Com SocD Cent Con	RV KF[c] KrF[c]	D'66		Con[c] Lab[c] Lib[c]	FG Lab		PSB PLP VU PSC	PC RPR	PR PLI Green	Reg		
Declining (−0.11 to −0.30)	SocD	Lib	V GRE	PvdA[c] LftGr[c]	FDP[c]	Natlst		PD	PVV PSC	PS PSU	PCI MSI	IU	CDU	
Strongly declining (−0.31 and less)	Lib ChrD		SD	CDA[c]	SPD[c]	Green	Workers	LAB	BSP CVP	UDF	DP	PP	PS PSD	KKE DIANA

[a] three data points only.

[b] Only Eurobarometer data are available; otherwise both sources are considered.

[c] Eurobarometer and national election study classification suggest different placements. The latter is accepted because it covers a longer time period.

Notes: The criterion variable for regression analyses was proportion of identifiers (strong and ordinary) within party electorates. For other details, see notes to Table 4.A3.

NOTES

1. But it does question the viability of the concept of a 'normal vote' (Converse 1966) which necessitates—logically but not empirically—a truly independent (i.e. causally antecedent) measure of partisanship in order to estimate election-specific, short-term deviations.

2. In the University of Michigan's CPS/NES electoral surveys, the respondent is asked: 'Generally, do you think of yourself as a Republican, a Democrat, an independent or what?' Those naming a party are asked: 'Would you call yourself a 'strong' [Republican/ Democrat] or a 'not very strong' [Republican/Democrat]?' Independents or 'other' are asked: 'Do you think of yourself as closer to the Republican or Democratic party?' Typically, a seven-category variable is constructed from these responses, ranging from strong Republican through moderate Republican, independent Republican, Independent, and so on to strong Democrat. This 'treasure of American electoral research' (Barnes *et al.* 1988: 227) has been heavily criticized. More recent work in this field includes Miller (1991) who proposes concentrating on what he calls the 'root question' ('Generally speaking . . .'), rather than on the seven-point index involving the follow-up questions, which results in a much more stable variable; the revisionists' case, he argues, rests largely on this noisy measurement. Barnes *et al.* (1988) demonstrate that the US findings from the party closeness question in the Political Action study, and included in a number of other comparative studies, are well in line with the CPS/NES instrument but lack the dimensionality or independence problem which plagued US research for some time. Johnston (1992) demonstrates that prompting for independence produces measurement artefacts which are avoided when alternative measures of partisanship are used.

3. A recent methodological experiment suggests that those findings are, in part, artefacts—at least for Britain—of a false question order in the questionnaires (Heath and Pierce 1992).

4. For Britain, see Särlvik and Crewe (1983); Alt (1984); Clarke and Stewart (1984); Heath and McDonald (1988); for France, see Inglehart and Hochstein (1972); Lewis-Beck (1984); Converse and Pierce (1986); for Germany, see Klingemann and Taylor (1977); Norpoth (1978, 1984); Falter and Rattinger (1983); for Sweden, see Holmberg (1981); Holmberg and Gilljam (1987).

5. For example, the Netherlands. Thomassen (1976) forcefully formulated his initial critique on the basis of a panel survey of Dutch voters. Using additional empirical evidence, Van der Eijk and Niemöller (1983, 1985) found that a considerable proportion of Dutch voters 'identify' with multiple parties which, typically, were very close ideologically. They concluded that Dutch voters tend to identify with ideological positions rather than with particular parties. However, Barnes (1989) found Dutch partisanship well behaved and attributed earlier anomalies to 'identity problems' which Dutch parties, especially the religious ones, experienced during the 1960s and 1970s.

6. In their study of the 1987 election, Heath *et al.* found that growing dealignment in Britain did not translate directly into rising volatility (1991: ch. 2). We are inclined

to attribute this finding to the fewer options for British voters compared to voters in multiparty systems operating under proportional representation.

7. But see Finkel and Opp (1991) who demonstrate, using the German Greens as an example, that parties not only integrate individuals into institutionalized electoral behaviour, but also mobilize their followers to engage in unconventional protest behaviour.

8. The standard Eurobarometer party attachment question in English reads: 'Do you consider yourself to be close to any particular party?' [If so:] 'Do you feel yourself to be very close to this party, fairly close, or merely a sympathizer?' See Table 4.A1 for how the Eurobarometer data sets were prepared for analysis. Also see Table 4.A2 on documentary sources for the wording of the party identification question in national election studies.

9. Although we used the term partisanship in the conceptual discussion, we use the terms party attachment and party identification interchangeably to denote empirical measurements.

10. This is signified in Table 4.1 by the fact that the trend towards declining partisanship is less strong among all identifiers than among strong identifiers.

11. Another, equally plausible, process which yields the same result involves turning the argument around: declining mass support for established parties increases the chances of new parties succeeding.

12. The Eurobarometer surveys regularly ask respondents to place themselves on a left–right scale ranging from (1) on the left to (10) on the right. Party electorates are identified by another standard Eurobarometer question on respondents' vote intention 'if a general election were held tomorrow'.

13. These parties are: Fianna Fáil and Fine Gael, Ireland; Christian Democratic Union/ Christian Social Union and Social Democratic Party, Germany; Christian Social People's Party and Socialist Workers' Party, Luxembourg; Christian Democrats and Communists, Italy; Christian Democratic Appeal and Labour in the Netherlands (Catholic People's Party instead of CDA before 1977); Conservative and Labour, Britain; Conservative People's Party and Social Democrats, Denmark; Gaullists (RPR) and Socialists, France; Christian People's Party (Flemish) and Socialist Party (Walloon) in Belgium; Popular Alliance/People's Party and Socialists, Spain; Social Democratic Party (centre-right) and Socialist Party, Portugal. A few decisions may be debatable, particularly treating Belgium as one political system with the major party alternatives represented by the more 'radical' of each pair of (linguistic) parties.

14. A linear trend coefficient was estimated for each of these distance variables indicating the over-time evolution in the intensity of ideological conflict in a particular socio-political setting. These coefficients were dichotomized and cross-tabulated with the dichotomized distribution of national trends in the strength of party attachments.

15. A number of experiments with different lags for ideological conflict were performed on the Eurobarometer data. In the end a uniform procedure across the countries was preferred as country-specific lags are hard to justify theoretically. Moreover, opinion formation processes which extend over one year (lag 2) or a year and a half (lag 3) are equally problematic. Thus, the final alternative was reduced to a synchronous (i.e. non-lagged) and a diachronous approach with a lag

of one survey; i.e. predicting current party attachments from the intensity of ideological conflict six months earlier. The synchronous approach was preferred for presentation as it produced the more clear-cut result. Time (measured as the sequence of Eurobarometer surveys) was considered as an additional predictor in order not to blur the autocorrelation term with time trends known to exist from earlier stages of the analysis.

16. The exact figures are: 50 per cent in 1952; 50 per cent in 1960; 51 per cent in 1964; 49 per cent in 1968; 46 per cent in 1972; 47 per cent in 1976; 58 per cent in 1980; 63 per cent in 1984; and 60 per cent in 1988 (Wattenberg 1990: 145).

17. Two SPD members could not follow Willy Brandt in his *Ostpolitik*. They left the SPD parliamentary group and joined the CDU/CSU camp. Erich Mende, a former president of the FDP, had joined the CDU/CSU for the same reason two years earlier. As a result, the governing coalition no longer commanded a parliamentary majority.

18. The earlier instrument asked, as a follow up to the party choice question, whether the respondent was a convinced supporter (*Anhänger*) of the party they voted for. In 1972, the instrument was changed to: 'Many people are close to a particular party over an extended period of time, though they might occasionally vote for a different party. How about you? Generally speaking, are you close to a particular party? If so, which one?' The precodes are: party *a*, party *b*, other party; no, don't know, refused. All those naming a party are then asked: 'All in all, how strongly or weakly do you feel towards this party?' The precodes are: very strongly, fairly strongly, moderate, fairly weakly, very weakly; don't know, no answer.

19. This suggests that instrument change alone only marginally affected the measurement. Such a view is broadly supported by the findings of a different but related instrument, the party sympathy rating scales. These scales, which are known to produce even more volatile results than measures of party identification usually do, were administered in identical format in both the 1969 and the 1972 surveys, and show the SPD gaining (from 23 to 31 per cent) and the CDU moderately loosing (from 22 to 17 per cent) popular support.

20. Richardson—mistakenly, we feel—attributes the same differences to the cleavage roots of large parties while disregarding such origins for smaller parties (1991: 759 and Table 4.4). Small liberal parties, for instance, are no less cleavage-based than most of their larger competitors.

21. Parties are defined as large when they gained over 30 per cent of the vote in a majority of elections after the Second World War, middle-sized when they gained between 10 and 30 per cent, and small when they achieved less than 10 per cent.

22. For this transposition to be justified, it has to be assumed that new parties attract only 'new' voters or, in cases where this does not hold, that 'old' voters switching their identification behave as 'new' ones. The former assumption is obviously unrealistic, the latter untested.

23. Descriptive results are displayed in Tables 4.A3 and 4.A4. The strategy applied to arrive at meaningful party scores is documented in some detail in the Methodological Appendix.

5

Party Membership and Party Representativeness

ANDERS WIDFELDT

Political parties and interest organizations have a central role as intermediaries in the relationship between governing élites and ordinary citizens. Developments in the relationship between voters and parties were examined in the previous chapter, but the vitality of intermediary organizations is provided by their members. In this chapter, we look at parties from that rather different perspective, examining developments in party membership. In a subsequent chapter, Kees Aarts examines developments in interest organizations. The common theme of both chapters is the concept of political linkage.

Although the concept of political linkage is frequently used, it lacks a universally accepted definition. In an anthology dealing with various aspects of political linkage, Kay Lawson concludes that, at least, we can speak of linkage as 'a connection, usually with a connotation with interaction' (Lawson 1988: 33). In representative democracies direct linkages are usually extraparliamentary actions, while intermediary organizations constitute indirect linkages. However, the linkage function of parties is a diverse matter. Lawson identifies four basic kinds of party linkages: participatory, electoral, clientilistic, and directive

I thank Sami Borg (University of Tampere), Martin Bennulf and Per Hedberg (University of Göteborg), and Ola Listhaug and Beate Huseby (University of Trondheim) for supplying data from national election studies. I also thank Torbjörn Berglund and Iris Alfredsson of the Social Science Data Bank at Göteborg University for their assistance with the Eurobarometer data.

(Lawson 1988: 16ff.). While the directive linkage is primarily relevant to authoritarian or dictatorial regimes, the other three are all associated with democracy. The key distinction here, for our purposes, is between the participatory linkage on the one hand, and electoral and clientistic linkages on the other, which can be summarized as representative linkages.

The distinction we have drawn is analogous to the dichotomization of parties commonly used in the literature on party organization. One type of party is described as emphasizing its members and their contribution to the party's activities. Such parties are organized, at least formally, in a 'bottom-up' way, with decisions and appointments emanating from the grass roots, and party activities are not confined to election campaigns. In this type of party much effort is invested in recruiting a large number of members, who are well aware of the party's ideology and policies, and who are able and willing to convey these ideas to the public. Such parties are usually referred to as 'mass' or 'party democracy' parties (Duverger 1954: 63ff.; Epstein 1967: passim; Wright 1971: 17ff.). They form linkages by getting ordinary people interested or actively involved in politics. We label this *participatory linkage*.

The second type of party puts less effort into stimulating active involvement. Party members are not given the same attention. Indeed, in the ideal type case, there are no formal members at all. Except during election campaigns, party activities are confined to performing the duties of the public offices to which the party has been elected. Such parties are often referred to as 'rational efficient' parties (Wright 1971: 17ff.). The classic case, which hardly exists in practice today, is the 'cadre' party (Duverger 1954: 63ff.). Here, linkage is performed by representing rather than activating ordinary citizens; hence the term *representative linkage*.

In reality, the distinction between participatory and representative linkages is blurred. Every party is something of a mixture of the two. Wright's depiction of the distinction, in which different types of parties are placed along a continuum with the participatory and representative models at opposite ends, appears the most appropriate (Wright 1971: 18). However, the purpose of this study is not to categorize parties according to Wright's continuum. Rather, the two types of linkage are the point of departure for investigating the role of parties as intermediary organizations in Western Europe.

For several years there has been extensive debate about a 'linkage crisis' being experienced by political parties; that parties are losing their legitimacy and suitability as 'transmission belts' (Kirchheimer 1966: 177). Several authors have observed an increasing distrust in politics, politicians, and in political institutions, all of which are attributed to a lack of responsiveness (Ware 1979: 171ff.; Dalton 1988: 229ff.; cf. Katz and Mair 1992*a*). Although not necessarily directed at political parties, such distrust will, it is argued, affect their linkage status. Other arguments pointing to a decline in partisanship have already been investigated in the previous chapter of this volume. Yet other arguments claim that there is an ongoing substitution process, in which the traditional parties are challenged by new types of political organizations or other types of political action (Dalton and Küchler 1990).

An important indicator of the linkage status of parties is their membership strength. Obviously, some doubt can be cast on parties as participatory linkages if they do not attract members. It would indicate either that people are becoming less politically active or that they choose channels other than the parties for their activity. But party members are also relevant in the representative perspective. Although a party does not, by definition, need to have members, parties in modern democracies almost invariably do. Most modern parties are internally democratic in some degree, which means that all members have some influence within the party organization (Katz and Mair 1992*b*). Thus, the representativeness of the members of a party can make a difference in terms of how well the party represents ordinary citizens in the political system.

That the members are important if a party is to work as a participatory linkage is close to being a truism. So, first, we examine trends in party membership over the last thirty years or so, to see whether or not parties are in crisis as participatory linkages. Then, in subsequent sections, we investigate the representative linkage of parties by examining party members. In that analysis, we are interested in how well or otherwise party members reflect, or represent, the electoral public.

Membership Strength

A party which has few members would have difficulties functioning as a participatory linkage. Recent research seems to indicate that modern parties are very interested in having a large membership (Scarrow 1991; Seyd and Whiteley 1992), which might be desirable for a variety of reasons—even if only for propaganda purposes (Scarrow 1991: 118ff.). Consequently, membership is not a sufficient criterion for participatory linkage. But it is necessary. Thus, the findings in this section will not be enough to establish whether parties in Western Europe actually do work as participatory linkages. However, they will give an indication of how well equipped parties are to do so. We also need to make one further point. The 'crisis of parties' debate is based on arguments which portray recent structural and attitudinal changes as a cause of the crisis. Consequently, low membership is not enough to make the case for the crisis thesis; there must also be an observable *decline* in membership.

Before going further, however, we need to establish what we mean by a party member. As several observers have argued, it is not easy to give a general definition, as the concept of a member varies according to the party concerned (Seyd and Whiteley 1992. 13; Duverger 1954: 61–2). In most parties, it is necessary to show a certain degree of active interest to be accepted as a member, while in others there is no formal definition of a member at all. However, these differences have tended to decrease over time. Here, a party member is defined as a card-carrying member; that is, a person who is formally enrolled in a political party.

A further problem is that there are various types of formal membership within parties. For our purposes, the main distinction among membership types is between those who have directly joined the main organization of a party, and those who are members via other organizations. Most parties have 'side organizations' to appeal to particular groups—women and young people, for example (Katz and Mair 1992b). Some parties have members who are collectively affiliated via trade unions, usually to a social democratic or labour party (von Beyme 1985: 194ff.). This is referred to as corporate membership. Among the parties examined in this chapter, there are collectively affiliated members in the Labour Party in Britain, Norway, and Ireland, and, until the end of 1990, the Social Democrats in Sweden.

Those party members who have joined the main body, we call direct members; those who are members by affiliation we call indirect members (Duverger 1954: 5ff.). We examine only direct members— except where the data make it impossible to separate direct and indirect members—for several reasons. An unknown proportion of the indirect members may, in fact, be quite ambiguous in their allegiance to the party. There may be cases of indirect members who support other parties. This primarily applies to corporate members, who, even if there exists an opportunity to 'opt out', feel social pressure not to do so. Another possibility of membership without political content is among members of the 'side organizations', where some members may join primarily to enjoy non-political activities such as sport and dances (cf. Allum 1979: 142; Scarrow 1991: 343–4).

Party membership can be measured using either internal party records or survey data. Internal records have several reliability problems, especially over-reporting by the parties and multiple membership by individuals. Parties may not have the time to keep their records intact, particularly as reporting membership figures depends on the local organization. Some parties may over-report because of the good-will qualities of a vast membership. There are also cases of financial incentives to over-report (Seyd and Whiteley 1992: 14–15). Multiple membership is a possibility because some people may be a member of more than one local branch of a party. As long as the member pays the dues to each branch, the party has no incentive to keep an eye on this.

Extensive accounts of party membership using party sources have been published elsewhere (Katz and Mair 1992*a*; Katz, Mair, *et al.* 1992). The membership figures reported in Table 5.1 are based on these data. The highest membership density is found in the Nordic countries. In Norway and Finland more than 10 per cent of the electorate are party members; Denmark displays very high figures in the early 1960s, but since then shows a marked decline down to the level of most continental countries. The Swedish figures are lower, but this could be explained by the—perhaps harsh—assumption that only 20 per cent of the Social Democratic membership are individual members.[1] The only comparable membership figures outside the Nordic countries are found in Italy. In all other cases, party membership, as a proportion of the electorate, is below 10 per cent. The lowest proportions are found in Germany, the Netherlands, Ireland, and Britain.

The table discloses few clear trends. The only tendencies in any direction are the Danish decline and the late rise in party membership in Ireland. However, the increase in Ireland is an artefact, explained by the absence of figures for the large Fianna Fáil party until 1986 (Farrell 1992: 403). Apart from Denmark, then, clear tendencies are difficult to find. Even so, in all these countries except Belgium, Ireland, and Germany, membership levels were lower in the late 1980s than in the early 1960s. Clearly, there was no general increase in party membership

TABLE 5.1. *Party membership in ten West European countries 1960–89: party records*

	BE	DK	FI	GE	IR	IT	NL	NO	SV	GB
1960		21							10	
1961	8			3				16		
1962			19							
1963						13	9			
1964		19							10	9
1965	7			3				16		
1966		17	19							9
1967							6			
1968	8	16				12			8	
1969				3				15		
1970			17						8	8
1971	8	14					4			
1972			17	1		13	1			
1973		11						13	8	
1974	9									6
1975		10	15							
1976				5		10			8	
1977	9	8			1		4	14		
1978	9									
1979		8	15			10			8	5
1980				5						
1981	9	8			2		4	15		
1982					2		4		8	
1983			14	4		9				4
1984		7								
1985	9							16	8	
1986							3			
1987	9	7	13	4	5	10				3
1988		7							8	
1989					5		3	13		

Notes: Entries are party members as a percentage of the total electorate, based on membership figures supplied by the parties. The Swedish figures have been adjusted to exclude collectively enrolled members of the Social Democratic Party, assuming an individual membership of 20 per cent of the reported total membership.

Sources: Katz, Mair, *et al.* (1992); Katz and Mair (1992*b*).

in the period 1960–89. Rather, the data indicate decline, or, in some cases, stability.

The second method of measuring party membership is to use survey data. Here, the problems are related not only to the well-known

TABLE 5.2. *Party membership in fifteen West European countries, 1989: survey data*

	BE	DK	FI	GE	IR	IT	NL	NO	SV	GB
1960									18	
1961										
1962										
1963										9
1964									17	10
1965								14		
1966										
1967										
1968									11	
1969				4				14		6
1970								10		
1971							12			
1972				4			9			
1973			19					14		
1974										7
1975										
1976										
1977							8	13		
1978										
1979									11	
1980										
1981		11					9	14		
1982		16					7			
1983	5	5		8	4	7	10			7
1984										
1985								14	12	
1986							8			
1987			14							6
1988	7	13		7	4	10	7		12	6
1989	9	8		6	4	7	7	12		5
1990										
1991			11						9	

	FR	LU	GR	SP	PO
1983	4	9	8		
1988	4	11	6	3	2
1989	4	9	12	3	3

Notes: Entries are all party members as a percentage of the total electorate, based on survey data. Collectively affiliated corporate members of the Social Democratic Party (Sweden) and Labour Party (Norway and Britain) are not included in the entries except for Sweden 1960 and 1964, where collective members are impossible to separate.

Sources: *Sweden*: national election studies (all years). *Norway*: (Listhaug 1989: table 9.1 (1965–85)), national election study (1989). *Denmark*: national election study (1981), Eurobarometer, Nos. 19, 30, and 32. *Finland*: four-party Gallup survey (1973–87), national election study (1991). *Netherlands*: Van Deth and Horstman (1989: 45 (1971–82, 1986)); Eurobarometer, Nos. 19, 30, and 32. *Britain*: Crewe, Day, and Fox (1991: table 3.3; table 3.1); Eurobarometer, Nos. 30 and 32. *Germany*: national election studies (1969, 1972), Eurobarometer, Nos. 19, 30, and 32. *All other countries*: Eurobarometer, Nos. 19, 30, and 32. In years when both Eurobarometer and national survey data are available, the latter have been used.

problems of such data, but also to problems specific to estimates of party membership. First, it is likely that people who are not willing to co-operate in a survey are also less likely to be party members, and thus are over-represented in the sample loss; in other words, a risk that the proportion of members is exaggerated. The second problem concerns corporate members. They may answer 'no' to a question about party membership because they are unaware of it, they have forgotten about it, or because they do not consider themselves as real members. At the same time, however, some corporate members may answer 'yes', even if they would really prefer not to be members. Survey data, therefore, run the risk of registering a false proportion of corporate members.

Survey data about party membership are less widely available than information from party sources. In many countries, election studies have not been undertaken regularly; and when survey data do exist, questions about party membership have not always been asked. It has only been possible to accumulate time-series data covering a reasonable length of time in Sweden, Britain, the Netherlands, Germany, Finland, and Norway. The available figures appear in Table 5.2. Collective members of the social democratic and labour parties are excluded in the British, Swedish, and Norwegian figures, but this is not possible for Sweden in 1960 and 1964.[2]

The levels of membership reported in the table differ from the levels indicated by party records, but not conspicuously. Generally speaking, the levels tend to be higher when survey data are used, but this is not the case in all instances. The Danish figures deviate in both directions. As in Table 5.1, the Nordic countries stand out as having, comparatively, the highest membership level—but the lack of data in many other countries means that we should beware of drawing far-reaching conclusions. However, the levels in other countries at a number of time points are clearly lower—as in Britain, the Netherlands, and Germany.[3]

Three observations from Tables 5.1 and 5.2 deserve particular attention. The first, which must be regarded as tentative, is methodological.

It appears that the two methods of measuring party membership validate each other, although survey data may inflate the levels. Both methods indicate quite similar membership levels, and the trends over time are, more often than not, similar. The second observation concerns the general level of party membership. The highest recorded figure using party records is 21 per cent in Denmark in 1960, while the highest proportion using survey data is 19 per cent in Finland in 1973. With the exception of the Nordic countries, membership levels are generally low, varying between 5 and 10 per cent. The third observation concerns developments over time. Party membership in Western Europe has declined, or at best has been stable, over time. The data are not quite complete enough to ascertain whether decline or stability is the more correct conclusion, but it can be safely said that there has been no general increase.

This enables us to draw some initial conclusions about West European parties as linkages. There is a decline in membership in some countries, but no uniform or steep cross-national decline. The generally low membership levels and the absence of rising membership mean that the parties cannot claim to be particularly successful as participatory linkages. However, the 'crisis theories' predict a declining role for parties as traditional intermediary organizations. The corroboration of these hypotheses requires that party membership is shown to be falling. There is no clear evidence of such a decline. Political parties in Western Europe cannot be shown to be losing their grip on the public—even if this is because they had little grip in the first place.

The findings of this section indicate some, if not overwhelming, evidence against the notion of a participatory linkage crisis for political parties. But the linkage role of the parties is not yet fully examined. We now move on to consider the more lengthy, and complex, question of the role of parties as representative linkages.

Representativeness of Party Members

Studies of political representation have tended to concentrate on the representational role of elected parliamentarians (Holmberg 1974; Eulau and Wahlke 1978; Converse and Pierce 1986; Holmberg and Esaiasson 1988, 1993). There are important differences between the representational roles of parliamentarians and party members, but there are also analogies. For example, parliamentarians are elected and can be unseated by the public, which is not the case for party members, but both parliamentarians and members take part in decisions which affect the general public. Although party leaders are more prominent in determining party policy, most West European parties are internally organized according to democratic principles, giving party members some degree of influence (Katz and Mair 1992*b*). These analogies allow us to use the representativeness of party members as an indicator of how well the parties work as representative linkages. In a democratic system based on the principle of representation, and where parties are to a large extent internally organized according to the same principle, this indicator has high validity.

Representativeness is operationalized as collective correspondence between the representatives and the represented. In other words, the representativeness of the members is measured by the similarity between members and the public (Dalton 1988: 206). Our focus is on similarity in social composition and similarity in opinions. Although there is no consensus about the necessity, even the desirability, of social or opinion representativeness in the theoretical discussion on political representation, there are arguments which justify studying both.

Three main types of arguments can be mounted for social representativeness (cf. Holmberg and Esaiasson 1988: 134ff.). First, the equity argument; that is, all social groups should have an equal opportunity of being represented in important institutions. It is unfair to a group to be under-represented among party members. Secondly, there is the life experience argument, based on the assumption that representatives have a better understanding of the needs of people of the same social group, because they share similar experiences. This does not necessarily mean that such representatives hold the same opinions as the represented, but it is assumed that their actions will be based on an understanding of the situation of the represented. Thirdly, it can be argued that social representativeness is a prerequisite of opinion representativeness. This argument of course would fall if there is no correlation between the two; that is, if opinion representativeness is high while social representativeness is low, or vice versa. Later, we shall test this argument empirically.

Representativeness in terms of opinion similarity is seen by many as indispensable in a democratic system based on representation. Arguments to the contrary are based primarily on the notion of a competence gap between the representatives and the represented. For example, it can be argued that politicians are better informed than citizens, or that popular opinion is contradictory. Against this, it can be argued that increasing levels of education have led to greater political competence among people at large. As a consequence, opinion representativeness is, if anything, becoming a more relevant indicator of parties as representative linkages.

The analysis, then, takes into account social and opinion representativeness. They are combined into a two-dimensional schema, depicted in Figure 5.1 below.

Parties in cell 1 are high on opinion representativeness and low on social representativeness. Party members are of different social standing from the party's supporters but this does not prevent them from holding similar views. Their views do not reflect demographically based self-interest. We call this the *idealistic party* model. In cell 2, the parties are representative in social as well as opinion terms. We can label this the *representative party* model. Cell 3 suggests that party members are totally secluded from the environment. They have different social positions from their supporters and their opinions do not reflect those of their supporters. This is the inverse of the situation in cell 2, consequently we call this the *unrepresentative party* model. Parties in cell 4 are high on social representativeness but low on opinion representativeness. Members are recruited from the same social groups as supporters, but inside the party they entertain unrepresentative views, either because they had such views before joining the party or because, after joining, they adopt the prevailing opinions in the

	Social representativeness	
	Low	High
	1	2
High	Idealistic parties	Representative parties
Opinion representativeness		
	3	4
Low	Unrepresentative parties	Demographic parties

FIGURE 5.1 *Models of representativeness of party members*

party. Such a situation might be thought unsatisfactory, but it is consistent with some theories on representation in which descriptive similarities are crucial (Pitkin 1967: 60–91). As these parties are demographic mirror images of the public, we call this the *demographic party* model.

When evaluating these four models, we must bear in mind that indirect indicators of party responsiveness are being used. That is, we are not examining what party members actually say or do when taking part in internal party matters, such as discussing policy, appointing party officers, or nominating candidates for election. Rather, the relevance of the two kinds of representativeness depends on the assumption that they reflect the capacity of party members to respond to the needs or the views of party supporters. If empirical objections can be raised against this assumption, then the meaningfulness of the findings which follow are reduced. Both indicators, however, are logically valid. Hence, when we find that social representativeness and opinion representativeness coincide we can conclude that we have *prima facie* evidence of party responsiveness.

Analytic Strategy

In the empirical analysis we compare the social composition and the opinions of members and supporters of political parties in Western Europe. The typology outlined in Figure 5.1 provides the framework for the analysis, with each party characterized in terms of the four 'models' set out there. The analysis includes parties from fifteen West European countries: the twelve EC member states and the Nordic countries of Sweden, Norway, and Finland. The data are for the years 1988–9, with the exception of Finland, where the data are for 1991. For the Nordic countries, we use data from national election studies; for the EC countries, we use data from four Eurobarometer surveys which were merged to give a sufficient number of party members to allow for subgroup analysis.[4]

To be included in the analysis, a party had to have a minimum of thirty members in the survey data; altogether thirty-seven parties met this criterion. Hence, there is an important caveat to bear in mind when assessing our results: the analysis is biased towards relatively large parties. Many parties which are quite significant electorally, or are important in national party systems, had to be excluded because too few members appeared in the data set. A full list of the parties represented in the national parliaments during the late 1980s but not included in this study can be found in Appendix I. But we should mention the most significant omissions. Few radical left parties and no green parties are included; these parties often have the explicit ambition of improving links between the public and the political system. Liberal parties, too, are under-represented. Although liberal parties vary in their electoral significance, they often have an important strategic location in national party systems. Parties representing specific ethnic or language groups also failed to meet the criterion for inclusion, yet these parties probably play a particularly significant linkage role for the groups they claim to represent. Moreover, no party in Spain and Portugal had a total of thirty members in the merged sample. Hence no Spanish or Portuguese party appears in the subgroup analysis.

Party members are compared with supporters of the same party. For additional descriptive purposes, comparisons are also made at the national level between all party members and the entire electorate in the country. For completeness, Spain and Portugal are included in the national level tables, as the total number of party members in both countries exceeds thirty in the merged samples. Supporters are defined as those who give a positive answer to survey questions measuring party identification; that is, if there is any party they feel closer to than other parties. No distinction is made between different degrees of support. Those who claim no leaning towards any party are excluded.[5] An alternative would have been to compare members and voters of the same party. However, supporters of a party may, for various reasons—such as tactical voting—not always vote for the party they support, and some voters may not be supporters of any party. Party members, then, are assumed to represent the party's supporters but not—necessarily—the generality of the party's voters (cf. Gilljam and Holmberg 1993: 290ff.).[6]

Social Representation

Four indicators of social representativeness are used; gender, age, class, and education. Numerous studies have found that political élites are disproportionately composed of well-educated men of relatively high occupational status (Aberbach, Putnam, and Rockman 1981; Matthews 1985; Holmberg and Esaiasson 1988, 1993). However, in so far as few party members are part of the political élite in a strict sense (cf. Seyd and Whiteley 1992: 93), party members may be very different. Thus, in this section, we are interested in discrepancies in social terms between party members and party supporters. We do not take into account the direction of the discrepancies. Under- or over-representation of a group in terms of gender, age, education, and occupation is discussed, but only as descriptive information. Whether men or women, young or old, are over-represented among party members is equally important; whatever the direction of discrepancies, the party is considered to lack representativeness. The conclusions regarding social representativeness are based on the size, not the direction, of the discrepancies between representatives and the represented.

First, we consider gender. Membership representativeness at the national level, where all party members are compared with the electorate in a country, is shown in Table 5.3. The representativeness of members is measured by comparing the percentage of men and of women among members and among the electorate. The 'difference' column is the average of these differences, calculated as the sum of the percentage point differences divided by two. We then compare the 'difference' figure with the distributions in the table. The same calculation is used in Tables 5.4–5.6, 5.9, and 5.10 (see notes to Tables 5.3 and 5.4).

The data clearly indicate male predominance among party members. To be precise, men are over-represented in every country in the study. Everywhere except in Norway, the over-representation is 10 percentage points or more. In six countries (Spain, Greece, Germany, Luxembourg, Italy, and Portugal) the over-representation exceeds 20 points. Norway is a conspicuous exception with male over-representation of only 2 points. This is probably due to the deliberate efforts of Norwegian parties to increase female representation. In some parties, this includes introducing formal gender quotas for party posts as well as nominations for public elections (Skjeie 1992); even some of the parties without formal quotas operate them in practice.

In Table 5.4, we show the gender representativeness of the national parties. Here members are compared with the supporters of the same party. The pattern as we saw in the previous table is repeated and reinforced. Male predominance, often of overwhelming magnitude, is the rule. In twenty-seven of the thirty-seven parties, men are over-represented among members by 10 percentage points or more. Women are over-represented in only three parties: the Norwegian Conservative

TABLE 5.3. *Gender representativeness of party members at the national level*

	Members			Electorate			Difference
	Male	Female	N	Male	Female	N	
Sweden	70	30	311	52	48	2,845	18
Norway	52	48	274	50	50	2,190	2
Finland	64	36	164	51	49	1,472	13
France	65	35	145	48	52	4,021	17
Belgium	63	37	336	49	51	4,043	14
Netherlands	61	39	311	49	51	3,971	12
Germany	70	30	275	46	54	4,293	24
Italy	73	27	360	49	51	4,091	24
Luxembourg	78	22	110	54	46	1,202	24
Denmark	61	39	343	50	50	4,003	11
Ireland	66	34	155	50	50	4,016	16
Britain	58	42	266	48	52	4,844	10
Greece	73	27	337	48	52	4,000	25
Spain	76	24	91	48	52	4,018	28
Portugal	72	28	79	48	52	4,000	24

Notes: Entries are percentages of men and women among party members and in the electorate. Members are included in the 'electorate' column. The 'difference' column shows the average difference between the proportion of men and women among party members and the electorate, calculated as the difference between the proportion of men among members and the electorate plus the difference in the proportion of women among members and the electorate divided by two. For a discussion of this method of describing the degree of correspondence between subgroups, see Holmberg and Esaiasson (1988: 137).

Sources: Swedish Election Study (1988); Norwegian Election Study (1989); Finnish Election Study (1991); Eurobarometer, Nos. 30, 31, 31A, and 32 merged.

TABLE 5.4. *Gender representativeness of party members at the party level*

	Members			Supporters			Difference
	Male	Female	N	Male	Female	N	
Sweden							
Social Democratic	67	33	144	52	48	1,117	15
Centre	63	37	68	53	47	260	10
Conservative	57	43	56	50	40	365	3
Norway							
Labour	60	40	78	49	51	615	11
Christian People's	37	63	40	43	57	162	6
Centre	60	40	30	50	50	111	10
Conservative	46	54	70	50	40	404	4
Finland							
Social Democratic	61	39	33	56	44	286	5
Centre	68	32	50	51	49	249	17
Conservative	54	45	35	51	49	234	3
France							
Communist	55	35	48	54	46	176	11
Socialist	74	26	42	49	51	1,069	25
Gaullist (RPR)	66	34	32	49	51	444	17
Belgium							
Socialist (Fr.)	59	31	65	53	49	389	16
Socialist (Fl.)	55	35	40	57	43	189	8
Liberal	70	30	30	55	45	194	15
Christian Democratic (Fl.)	68	32	9	51	49	296	17

Political Linkage

TABLE 5.4. *Cont.*

	Members			Supporters			Difference
	Male	Female	N	Male	Female	N	
Netherlands							
Labour	55	45	89	51	49	1,013	4
Christian Democratic	61	39	107	45	55	913	16
Liberal	75	25	32	57	43	453	18
Italy							
Communist	75	25	116	56	44	554	19
Socialist	77	23	47	55	45	396	22
Christian Democratic	69	31	122	46	54	801	23
Luxembourg							
Socialist	80	20	30	62	38	187	18
Christian Socials	77	23	47	60	40	248	17
Denmark							
Social Democratic	65	35	137	50	50	774	15
Conservative	65	35	65	52	48	467	13
Liberal (Venstre)	59	41	118	54	46	350	5
Ireland							
Fine Gael	63	37	43	52	48	408	11
Fianna Fáil	71	29	79	55	45	800	16
Britain							
Labour	58	42	74	53	47	834	5
Conservative	59	41	120	50	50	1,112	9

TABLE 5.4. *Cont.*

	Members			Supporters			Difference
	Male	Female	N	Male	Female	N	
Greece							
Communist	82	18	62	58	42	286	24
Pasok	79	21	108	49	51	959	30
New Democracy	62	38	122	52	48	948	10
Germany							
Social Democratic	65	35	110	49	51	1,043	16
Christian Democratic (CDU/CSU)	73	27	109	53	47	960	20

Notes: Entries are the percentages of men and women among party members and party supporters. Members are included in the 'supporters' column. In Sweden the question about party membership includes a follow-up question about which party the respondent is a member of. In other countries party membership is measured by party sympathy or (in Finland and Norway) party vote. Supporters are defined as respondents who indicated some degree of party preference or party sympathy. In Norway and Finland, supporters are based on party vote. The 'difference' column contains the average difference between members and supporters. For the calculation of the difference figure, see notes to Table 5.3.

Sources: see Table 5.3.

TABLE 5.5. *Age representativeness of party members at the national level*

	Members	Electorate	Difference
Sweden			
18–30	12	25	
31–60	56	52	13
61–80	32	23	
N	311	2,845	
Norway			
18–34	13	26	
35–64	56	53	13
65–	31	21	
N	274	2,190	
Finland			
18–30	10	25	
31–60	70	58	15
61–75	20	17	
N	164	1,472	
France			
18–30	26	29	
31–60	50	50	3
61–80	24	21	
N	14	3,789	
Belgium			
18–30	21	30	
31–60	60	50	10
61–80	19	20	
N	333	3,863	

	Members	Electorate	Difference
Luxembourg			
18–30	12	26	
31–60	70	57	14
61–80	18	17	
N	110	1,130	
Denmark			
18–30	11	29	
31–60	58	49	18
61–80	31	22	
N	419	3,793	
Ireland			
18–30	23	30	
31–60	61	51	10
61–80	16	19	
N	147	3,602	
Britain			
18–30	17	28	
31–60	54	48	11
61–80	29	24	
N	257	4,597	
Greece			
18–30	26	26	
31–60	60	53	7
61–80	14	21	
N	334	3,740	

TABLE 5.5. *Cont.*

	Members	Electorate	Difference		Members	Electorate	Difference
Netherlands				Spain			
18–30	14	31		18–30	22	31	
31–60	52	49	17	31–60	61	47	14
61–80	34	20		61–80	17	22	
N	299	3,754		*N*	88	3,669	
Germany				Portugal			
18–30	12	25		18–30	24	31	
31–60	64	51	13	31–60	59	48	11
61–80	24	24		61–80	17	21	
N	261	4,016		*N*	78	3,719	
Italy							
18–30	20	28					
31–60	62	53	9				
61–80	18	19					
N	354	3,839					

Notes: Entries are the percentage of young, middle-aged, and old among party members and the electorate. The 'difference' figure is calculated as in Table 5.3.

Sources: See Table 5.3.

Party, the Norwegian Christian People's Party, and the Swedish Conservatives. Five parties display rather lower male over-representation of
5 percentage points or less; one conservative party (Finland), one liberal
(Danish Venstre), and three socialist parties (PvdA in the Netherlands,
the British Labour Party, and the Finnish Social Democrats).[7] But over
all, male domination is the rule, at least outside Scandinavia. This
applies irrespective of ideological character.

To examine discrepancies by age, we divided the samples into three
age categories: young (18–30 years), middle-aged (31–60 years) and
old (61–80 years).[8] The representativeness of party members at the
national level, comparing members with the electorate at large, is
shown in Table 5.5. On this measure, the most representative party
members are found in quite diverse countries. France, Greece, and Italy
have the most representative members; that is, the smallest average
differences between members and the electorate. The largest discrepancies are found in Denmark, the Netherlands, and Finland. No country
displays an average difference of more than 20 percentage points.

The oldest age group is the best represented, with differences of 5
points or less in ten of the fifteen countries. In most countries, the
direction of the differences tends to over-represent old people, but in
southern Europe they are rather under-represented. That old people are
under-represented among members in Spain and Portugal is not surprising as democratic parties were not established there until the mid-
1970s. Bearing this in mind, the discrepancy of some 4–5 percentage
points is remarkably small. Among the middle-aged, the size of the
percentage differences are more diverse, but wherever differences are
found (more than 5 points in every country except Sweden, Norway,
France, and the Netherlands), they invariably indicate over-representation among the members. The youngest age group is the most poorly
represented. Those aged 18–30 years are under-represented in every
country except Greece, and in eight countries the differences exceed 10
percentage points. The general picture at the national level, then, is that
the middle-aged are over-represented and the young under-represented
among party members while the oldest age group is, on the whole,
relatively well represented.

The age representativeness of the parties, comparing members and
supporters of the same party, shows the same general pattern. The
details are presented in Appendix 5.2, but we can readily summarize
the major patterns. The young are under-represented among the members in thirty-two of the thirty-seven parties, while the middle-aged are

over-represented in thirty parties. However, the parties are split down the middle with regard to the oldest group. One might have expected to find the oldest age group particularly well represented among the traditional socialist mass parties, which could still have members recruited during the days when these parties really did fit the Duvergerian mass party model. But, in fact, the old are under-represented in several such parties, notably the British Labour Party and the German Social Democrats. Most of the discrepancies, however, are very small.

In terms of overall age representativeness—the average percentage point difference between members and supporters—it is difficult to find clear ideological patterns. Among the parties with small average differences, however, we find most of the Christian Democratic parties (Italy, Belgium, and Germany), but the Christian Democratic Appeal in the Netherlands displays much larger discrepancies. Among the parties on the left, those with low age representativeness dominate; for example, the French Socialist Party, the Dutch Labour Party, and the German Social Democrats. But there are also counter-examples: the Communists in Greece, the Socialists in Luxembourg, and the Labour Party in Norway.

The data do not allow us to introduce any refined measure of social class. Instead, we distinguish between the working class and all other groups, by collapsing all occupational codes which can be categorized as working class. This group is then compared with the rest of the sample within the active workforce.[9] The national figures are shown in Table 5.6.

The working class is under-represented among party members in every country except Sweden, Italy, and Portugal. In more than half of the fifteen countries, however, the differences are 5 percentage points or less, and in Sweden and Italy the proportion of the working class among members and the electorate is identical. The largest differences appear in Britain and Ireland.

The class representativeness of the parties, shown in Table 5.7, reveals much the same pattern. Workers are under-represented among members in thirty-one parties. The exceptions occur exclusively among socialist parties: the Social Democrats in Sweden, Denmark, and Finland, the Socialist Party in France and in Belgium (French-speaking), and the Italian Communist Party. In the remaining parties, the discrepancies tend to be larger among non-socialist than socialist parties, but this rule is not without exceptions.

It is important to remember when we look at the representativeness of

TABLE 5.6. *Class representativeness of party members at the national level*

	Members	N	Electorate	N	Difference
Sweden	38	299	38	2,180	0
Norway	30	248	41	1,949	11
Finland	28	164	40	1,472	12
France	31	84	44	1,948	13
Belgium	42	192	46	1,915	4
Netherlands	26	138	34	1,880	8
Germany	29	161	42	2,037	13
Italy	32	234	32	1,809	0
Luxembourg	34	74	37	587	3
Denmark	31	267	44	2,357	13
Ireland	27	99	41	1,701	14
Britain	27	146	44	2,566	17
Greece	18	228	22	1,860	4
Spain	37	48	48	1,511	11
Portugal	50	52	49	2,148	1

Notes: Entries are percentages of working class among all party members and the electorate. The 'difference' column shows the difference in percentage working class among party members and the electorate.

Sources: See Table 5.3.

party members, that the comparison is not with the general public but with the supporters of the party. The under-representation of the working-class is thus a relevant finding even among parties with a predominantly middle-class following. Among supporters of the British Conservative Party, for example, 29 per cent are working class, but there is something less than half that proportion among the members. This under-representation is even more surprising in the British Labour Party, where the discrepancy is 21 percentage points, a level surpassed—among socialist parties—only by the Flemish-speaking Socialist Party in Belgium. The size of these discrepancies is extreme and in fact not typical of other socialist parties with a working-class tradition. In Sweden, Norway, Denmark, Germany, and Greece the working-class is still well repre-sented among members of the social democratic or socialist parties, and also among the communist parties of Italy and Greece.

The education variable is problematic. It was not possible to find exactly comparable data for all fifteen countries in the data sources used. In the Nordic data, we used education level, operationalized as the proportions with low, medium, and high education. Low education means compulsory education only, medium means some education in

TABLE 5.7. *Class representativeness of party members at the party level*

	Members	*N*	Supporters	*N*	Difference
Sweden					
Social Democratic	60	139	57	1,084	3
Centre	29	66	36	253	7
Conservative	6	53	16	328	10
Norway					
Labour	52	73	53	571	1
Christian People's	25	32	33	148	8
Centre	28	29	34	102	6
Conservative	9	64	22	301	13
Finland					
Social Democratic	57	33	48	286	9
Centre	16	50	36	249	20
Conservative	17	35	32	234	15
France					
Communist	36	33	51	93	15
Socialist	48	21	46	571	2
Republican (RPR)	25	20	35	201	10
Belgium					
Socialist (Fr.)	61	44	55	196	6
Socialist (Fl.)	30	23	53	105	23
Liberal	23	22	25	99	?
Christian Democratic (Fl.)	26	34	35	127	9
Netherlands					
Labour	32	37	41	485	9
Christian Democratic	28	36	39	338	11
Liberal	10	21	27	228	17
Italy					
Communist	46	74	44	263	2
Socialist	27	30	38	189	11
Christian Democratic	21	78	28	339	7
Luxembourg					
Socialist	37	19	44	107	7
Christian Social	29	31	31	124	2
Denmark					
Social Democratic	71	70	68	404	3
Conservative	17	35	21	275	4
Liberal	15	73	24	206	9
Ireland					
Fine Gael	15	26	25	208	10
Fianna Fáil	24	49	34	363	10

TABLE 5.7. *Cont.*

	Members	N	Supporters	N	Difference
Britain					
Labour	28	46	49	420	21
Conservative	14	57	29	568	15
Greece					
Communist	20	41	23	155	3
Pasok	20	86	22	470	2
New Democracy	16	85	18	468	2
Germany					
Social Democratic	36	76	44	540	8
Christian Democratic					
(CDU/CSU)	19	54	30	452	11

Notes: Entries are percentages of working class among party members and supporters. The 'difference' column shows the difference in percentage of working class among members and supporters.

Sources: See Table 5.3.

addition to the compulsory level, and the highly educated include those with upper secondary education—roughly equivalent to British 'A levels' or German *Abitur*—and the university educated. In the remaining countries, where all the data are from Eurobarometer surveys, educational level is operationalized as school-leaving age. It goes without saying, then, that there are comparability problems here. It is impossible to compare directly the education level measure used in the Nordic countries with the school-leaving age in the other countries. Moreover, leaving school at a particular age can mean different levels of education in countries with different educational systems. Thus, education is not included when we summarize social representativeness in this section, nor in our final summary. However, a look at social representativeness in terms of education yields some valuable descriptive information. The educational representativeness of party members at the national level appears in Table 5.8.

In the 'crisis of parties' debate, in which claims are made about weakening attachments to political parties, education is regarded as an important independent variable. The reasoning is that as levels of education rise, so does political competence, hence there is less need for parties as vehicles for political expression and participation. If this is true, we would expect the people who are most attached to parties—the members—to have attained a lower level of education than the party's

TABLE 5.8. *Educational representativeness of party members at the national level*

	Members	N	Electorate	N	Difference
GROUP A					
France	17.7	129	17.1	3,623	0.6
Belgium	18.0	315	17.6	3,570	0.4
Netherlands	18.2	282	17.9	3.375	0.3
Germany	17.5	285	16.6	3,790	0.9
Italy	16.4	329	15.9	3,567	0.5
Luxembourg	17.8	109	17.4	1,076	0.4
Denmark	18.8	399	18.8	3,473	0 0
Ireland	16.8	145	16.5	3,552	0.3
Britain	17.4	254	16.5	4,587	0.9
Greece	16.9	309	16.4	3,585	0.5
Spain	17.1	77	15.8	3,440	1.3
Portugal	16.7	75	15.2	3,586	1.5
GROUP B					
Sweden		308		2,665	
Low	52		44		
Medium	21		26		8
High	27		30		
Norway		271		2,168	
Low	25		19		
Medium	47		54		7
High	28		27		
Finland		164		1,467	
Low	59		57		
Medium	27		26		3
High	14		17		

Notes: Entries for Group A are average age of leaving school; for Group B are percentages with low, medium, and high levels of education. The 'difference' column shows the difference between members and supporters for Group A in years, for Group B as average percentages. The 'difference' figure is calculated as in Table 5.3.

Sources. See Table 5.3.

supporters in general. But there are also several theories of political participation which treat education as an individual resource that predisposes people towards membership of organizations such as political parties (Listhaug 1989: 191).

The data here are largely in line with the second argument, which predicts that party members have a higher educational level than other citizens. At the national level, except in the Nordic countries, party members are, on average, more highly educated than the electorate at large right across Western Europe. The differences, however, are often quite small. Only in Spain and Portugal is there a difference of more than one full year in 'age left school' between party members and the electorate. In Sweden and Norway, however, the less educated are over-represented, while in Finland there is quite close correspondence between the electorate and party members. The corresponding figures for the individual parties are shown in Table 5.9.

The general pattern found in the national figures is confirmed. In eight of these thirty-seven parties—six of them in the Nordic countries—members are less educated than supporters. But the differences are generally very small. Of the twenty-seven parties in the EC countries, in only four is the difference in the average age of leaving school one full year or more; in no case does the difference reach two full years. The parties showing the largest discrepancies are the French Republicans, British Labour, Italian Christian Democrats, and the Greek Communists. Perhaps a few more radical left parties would have been in this group had they had enough members to be included in the study. Such parties are often looked upon as intellectual rather than working-class parties. The differences of 0.4 and 0.5 years in the French and Italian communist parties, however, work against such assumptions.[10]

Even though any conclusions based on Table 5.9 must be drawn with care, these findings do not corroborate the prediction of an inverse relationship between education and attachment to political parties. The results are more in line with Listhaug's Norwegian study, in which he concludes that 'more support is given to the traditional view of education as an individual resource which promotes organizational membership and involvement' (Listhaug 1989: 199).

Ranking Social Representativeness

Which parties are, socially, the most representative? In Table 5.10, we summarize the social representativeness of all thirty-seven parties and rank order them from the most representative to the least representative. The table is based on the relative size of the percentage differences between members and supporters on three indicators—gender, age, and

TABLE 5.9. *Educational representativeness of party members at the party level*

	Members	N	Supporters	N	Difference
GROUP A					
France					
Communist	17.1	46	16.7	166	0.4
Socialist	17.4	39	17.3	983	0.1
Gaullist (RPR)	19.0	29	17.3	404	1.7
Belgium					
Socialist (Fr.)	17.1	62	16.8	362	0.3
Socialist (Fl.)	18.0	39	17.5	180	0.5
Liberal	18.7	30	18.3	166	0.4
Christian Democratic (Fl.)	18.2	60	17.8	259	0.4
Netherlands					
Labour	18.1	83	17.5	904	0.6
Christian Democratic	18.0	101	17.7	832	0.3
Liberal	19.5	29	18.8	380	0.7
Germany					
Social Democratic	16.9	104	16.5	948	0.4
Christian Democratic					
(CDU/CSU)	17.8	101	16.9	902	0.9
Italy					
Communist	15.9	106	15.6	494	0.3
Socialist	16.2	44	15.8	362	0.4
Christian Democratic	16.8	114	15.6	784	1.2
Luxembourg					
Socialist	17.0	30	17.4	174	0.4
Christian Social	17.7	47	17.2	233	0.5
Denmark					
Social Democratic	18.0	134	17.8	724	0.2
Conservative	19.3	57	19.1	416	0.2
Liberal (Venstre)	18.7	110	18.8	319	0.1
Ireland					
Fine Gael	17.0	41	17.0	390	0.0
Fianna Fáil	16.6	76	16.3	743	0.3
Britain					
Labour	18.0	67	16.3	787	1.7
Conservative	17.3	120	16.6	1,077	0.7
Greece					
Communist	18.1	57	17.1	258	1.0
Pasok	16.0	107	16.0	901	0.0
New Democracy	16.8	109	16.5	860	0.3

TABLE 5.9. *Cont.*

	Members	N	Supporters	N	Difference
GROUP B					
Sweden					
Social Democratic		142		1,113	5
Low	64		59		
Medium	22		23		
High	14		18		
Centre		68		259	16
Low	69		53		
Medium	18		25		
High	13		22		
Conservative		55		364	9
Low	20		25		
Medium	24		28		
High	56		47		
Finland					
Social Democratic		33		285	5
Low	73		71		
Medium	15		20		
High	12		9		
Centre		50		249	8
Low	68		66		
Medium	28		22		
High	4		12		
Conservative		35		233	12
Low	37		36		
Medium	43		32		
High	20		32		
Norway					
Labour		77		612	15
Low	44		29		
Medium	52		56		
High	4		15		
Christian People's		39		160	10
Low	39		29		
Medium	41		49		
High	20		22		
Centre		30		111	2
Low	20		22		
Medium	67		67		
High	13		11		

TABLE 5.9. *Cont.*

	Members	N	Supporters	N	Difference
Conservative		70		403	7
Low	10		10		
Medium	37		44		
High	53		46		

Notes: See notes to Table 5.8.

Sources: See Table 5.3.

occupation. Education is not included because of the comparability problems. The percentage differences between members and supporters for each party on the three variables were compared, and the parties ranked according to the relative size of those differences. The ranking figures for the three variables were then added together to provide a measure of the overall social representativeness of the parties. The ranking of the parties on this summary measure appears in the fourth 'final ranking' column.

The socially most representative party is New Democracy in Greece, followed by the Norwegian Labour Party, the Christian Social Party in Luxembourg, and the Centre Party in Norway and Sweden. At the other extreme, we find two Dutch parties. The liberal VVD stands out by some distance as the least representative of all the parties analysed, and the Christian Democratic Appeal is second from bottom. The position of these two is conspicuous but not untypical in the Netherlands: no Dutch party appears in the upper ranks, and even the Labour Party is placed towards the middle level of social representativeness.

Otherwise, there are few clear patterns, neither geographically nor in terms of party types or ideological character. Socialist and non-socialist parties appear at both ends of the table. There are countries where the relative degree of representativeness follows the left–right continuum, with the left-wing parties the most representative; Norway and the Netherlands follow this pattern, and Finland is a borderline case. But this is the exception rather than the rule. In Britain, Germany, and Luxembourg, the pattern is exactly the opposite: the right-wing parties are the most socially representative. In Italy and Greece it is the party farthest to the right—among those analysed–which is the most representative. The pattern is similar in Belgium, where the non-socialist parties are more representative than the socialist parties.

Political Linkage

TABLE 5.10. *Social representativeness of members of West European political parties*

Party	Rank order			
	Gender	Age	Class	Final ranking
New Democracy (Greece)	11	6	2	19
Labour (Norway)	14	9	1	24
Christian Socials (Luxembourg)	25	6	2	33
Centre (Norway)	11	12	12	35
Centre (Sweden)	11	12	14	37
Liberal (Denmark)	5	16	19	40
Liberal (Belgium–Fl.)	18	23	2	43
Social Democratic (Denmark)	18	18	8	44
Communist (Greece)	35	1	8	44
Social Democratic (Sweden)	18	18	8	44
Christian Democratic (Belgium–Fl.)	25	1	19	45
Social Democratic (Finland)	5	21	19	45
Fine Gael (Ireland)	14	9	23	46
Christian Democratic (Italy)	34	3	14	51
Conservative (Denmark)	17	23	11	51
Socialist (Luxembourg)	29	8	14	51
Christian People's (Norway)	8	28	17	53
Fianna Fáil (Ireland)	21	9	23	53
Communist (Italy)	31	21	2	54
Conservative (Sweden)	1	31	23	55
Labour (Netherlands)	3	33	19	55
Communist (France)	14	15	31	60
Pasok (Greece)	37	23	2	62
Christian Democratic (CDU/CSU) (Germany)	32	3	27	62
Centre (Finland)	25	3	35	63
Conservative (Britain)	10	23	31	64
Republican (RPR) (France)	25	16	23	64
Socialist (Belgium–Fr.)	21	31	12	64
Socialist (Belgium–Fl.)	9	18	37	64
Conservative (Finland)	1	33	31	65
Labour (Britain)	5	27	36	68
Conservative (Norway)	3	37	30	70
Socialist (France)	36	33	2	71
Social Democratic (Germany)	21	33	17	71
Socialist (Italy)	33	12	27	72

TABLE 5.10. *Cont.*

Party	Rank order			
	Gender	Age	Class	Final ranking
Christian Democratic				
(Netherlands)	21	28	27	76
Liberal (Netherlands)	29	28	34	91

Notes: The figures are based on Tables 5.4, 5.7, and Appendix 5.2. The party with the highest representativeness (i.e. smallest percentage difference between members and supporters) on each variable has been given the ranking figure 1 on that variable, and so on down to 37. Parties with the same percentage difference on a variable have been given the same ranking figure. The ranking figures on all three variables for each party have been added and entered in the 'final ranking' column.

The final ranking hides considerable variation in the ranking of the parties on the three variables. That a party is representative on one variable does not mean that it is necessarily representative on the others. In fact, the opposite is sometimes the case: in Sweden and Finland, for example, the Conservative Party tops the rank order on gender but is far down the ranking on age and class. A rank correlation analysis shows a weak inverse relationship between age and gender, an inverse and even weaker relationship between class and gender, and no correlation at all between class and age.[11]

As we have made clear, there are some problems about the data used for the analysis of social representativeness. But the overall differences among the thirty-seven parties in fifteen countries indicate that the members of political parties in Western Europe are, on the whole, not socially representative of party supporters. Party members tend to be disproportionally male, middle-aged, and middle-class. They also tend to be better educated, even if the discrepancy is smaller here. In fact, party members display remarkable similarities to political élites as described in other studies. This suggests that the parties have failed to involve ordinary citizens in their organizations—an additional liability for parties as participatory linkages.

The findings on social representativeness are also relevant to the party campaign strategies. One campaign role for party members is to work as 'megaphones' or 'opinion leaders', to spread the party's political message among the electorate (Lazarsfeld, Berelson, and Gaudet 1968: 49 ff., 151 ff.). On this evidence, it would seem to be no easy task: members are expected to communicate with people who are likely to have very different life-styles from their own, and with whom they are unlikely to mix socially (cf. Seyd and Whiteley 1992: 40). If a party needs its members to explain party policies to women, young people, and working-class electors, it might stand a better chance of doing so effectively if it has more women, young people, and workers among its members.

We noted earlier that there is no consensus about the necessity, or desirability, of social representativeness. It can be argued that men can represent the views of women, older people can represent younger people, and that people from the middle class can represent the working-class. But if one subscribes to any of the arguments for social representativeness we set out earlier, the situation is not satisfactory. If, on the one hand, similarity in social composition is considered a prerequisite for representation, the results are, on the whole, disappointing. On the other hand, if opinion representativeness is considered the crucial aspect, these results are of secondary importance. It is to opinion representation that we now turn.

Ideological Representation

The second dimension in Figure 5.1 is opinion representativeness. To analyse this dimension, we use data on left–right self-placement, derived from respondents being asked to place themselves on a scale from 1 to 10 (in Sweden 0 to 10); low numbers indicate a position to the left and high numbers a position to the right.[12] This measure obviously taps something different from opinions on specific issues. It can be argued that self-positioning on a left–right scale can hide a lot of information which could have been revealed by issue questions. For example, a socialist may well be far out to the left in principle, but more pragmatic on many specific issues. Still, the concept and meaning of a left–right political spectrum is well known and understood among electorates in Western Europe, which enables us to make cross-national comparisons. Moreover, ideological self-location can be taken as an aggregate of opinions on various issues coupled with a more general political outlook (Fuchs and Klingemann 1989: 207ff., 232ff.; Dalton 1988: 119, 195). The average left–right self-placement figures among members and supporters are presented in Table 5.11.

Of the thirty-seven parties in the table, no party displays a discrepancy of more than one full scale step between the location of members and the location of supporters. The biggest difference is 0.7 scale steps, a result shared by seven parties, while twenty-four parties have a difference of 0.5 scale steps or less. In five parties there is an exact correspondence in average left–right self-placement between members and supporters: Belgian Liberal Party (PVV), Norwegian Christian People's Party, Italian Christian Democrats, and the Centre Party in Sweden and in Finland. The remarkable results of the Nordic centre parties are conspicuous: these are parties with a strong tradition as popular movements which is evidently still reflected in their organizations. The Swedish and, in particular, Finnish centre parties have large memberships compared to other parties in their countries, and thus show certain similarities to traditional socialist mass parties (Katz and Mair 1992*b*). But the results for the Nordic social democratic parties—and Labour in Norway—show that a mass tradition does not guarantee a relatively high degree of ideological representativeness.

Empirical studies of the representativeness of parliamentarians have tended to come up with two types of patterns. In many studies, the élites of all parties has been found to be further to the left than their voters (Converse and Pierce 1986; Schmitt 1984; Barnes 1977; Holmberg 1974). There are also studies which show the élites of left-wing parties to the left of their voters and the élites of right-wing parties to the right of their voters. Such findings have been presented by Holmberg in his study on political representation in Sweden—what he calls the 'élite conflict model' (Holmberg and Esaiasson 1988: 93ff., 105). Our findings fit this model. Members of parties on the left (communist, socialist, or labour parties) place themselves further to the left than their supporters, while members of non-socialist parties tend to place themselves to the right of their supporters. The tendency is clearer, without exception, among conservative rather than liberal or Christian democratic parties. Even so, it merits repeating that the ideological differences between members and supporters are mostly very small. But they are systematic.[13]

There are two findings to note in this analysis. First, the differences in average left–right self-placement between members and supporters can only be interpreted as relatively small. In Holmberg and Esaiasson's 1985 study of Swedish parliamentarians, the average difference in left–right self-placement between voters and legislators was 0.61; here it is 0.41. Furthermore, of the five parties analysed by Holmberg, two (the Left Party Communists and the Centre Party) were found to have differences larger than those reported in Table 5.11 (Holmberg and Esaiasson 1988: 105). Secondly, there is a systematic pattern in which

TABLE 5.11. *Ideological representativeness of party members in thirty-seven parties*

	Members	N	Supporters	N	Difference
Sweden					
Social Democratic	3.0	140	3.7	1,023	0.7
Centre	6.0	63	6.0	239	0.0
Conservative	8.4	51	7.8	340	0.6
Norway					
Labour	3.9	72	4.4	581	0.5
Christian People's	6.1	36	6.1	154	0.0
Centre	5.6	28	5.7	101	0.1
Conservative	8.1	69	7.5	393	0.6
Finland					
Social Democratic	3.6	33	4.3	286	0.7
Centre	6.4	50	6.4	249	0.0
Conservative	8.3	35	7.8	234	0.5
France					
Communist	1.9	47	2.4	168	0.5
Socialist	2.6	43	3.3	1,063	0.7
Republican (RPR)	8.0	31	7.6	440	0.4
Belgium					
Socialist (Fr.)	2.8	59	3.4	338	0.6
Socialist (Fl.)	3.3	39	4.0	178	0.7
Liberal	6.3	27	6.3	101	0.0
Christian Democratic (Fl.)	6.9	68	6.8	280	0.1
Netherlands					
Labour	2.9	86	3.6	967	0.7
Christian Democratic	7.0	107	6.6	886	0.4
Liberal	7.2	31	6.9	445	0.3
Italy					
Communist	1.8	116	2.3	541	0.5
Socialist	3.5	47	3.9	383	0.4
Christian Democratic	5.9	119	5.9	800	0.0
Luxembourg					
Socialist	3.6	28	4.3	82	0.7
Christian Social	7.4	45	7.2	228	0.2
Denmark					
Social Democratic	4.8	138	4.9	752	0.1
Conservative	8.7	66	8.0	458	0.7
Liberal	7.9	120	7.6	348	0.3
Ireland					
Fine Gael	7.1	43	6.8	368	0.3
Fianna Fáil	7.3	78	7.1	639	0.2

TABLE 5.11. *Cont.*

	Members	N	Supporters	N	Difference
Britain					
Labour	3.1	69	3.7	777	0.6
Conservative	8.1	124	7.5	1,079	0.6
Greece					
Communist	1.8	62	2.3	283	0.5
Pasok	4.1	105	4.5	930	0.4
New Democracy	8.7	121	8.3	922	0.4
Germany					
Social Democratic	3.5	109	4.1	995	0.6
Christian Democratic					
(CDU/CSU)	7.5	109	7.0	933	0.5

Notes: Entries are average self-placements on a left right self-placement scale running from 1 (extreme left) to 10 (extreme right) among party members and supporters. In the Swedish data, the scale runs from 0 (left) to 10 (right). The higher the figure, the further to the right are members or supporters. The 'difference' column gives the difference in scale scores between party members and supporters. Members are included in the 'supporters' column.

Sources: See Table 5.3.

party members are more ideologically polarized than non-card-carrying party supporters. The polarization can be given positive as well as slightly more negative interpretations. On the one hand, it could indicate that members have a clearer concept of party ideology, which could help in presenting the electorate with clear policy alternatives. On the other hand, it could mean that the party leaderships are under pressure from the members to pursue more radical policies than are supported outside the party organization. Socialist parties could be under pressure to increase public spending, and conservative parties under pressure to cut it, while party supporters take a less radical stance on the issue. Certainly, according to these data, the ideological differences between socialists and conservatives are smaller among electorates than among party members.

Differences of this sort could easily put a strain on party organizations. The leaderships may or may not agree with their radical members, but probably they will be aware of the more pragmatic sentiments outside the party. They then have to face a trade-off between alienating members and alienating supporters—and, ultimately, voters. The party systems could thus be subjected to centrifugal forces at the membership level, something which is not reflected among the electorate (cf. Sartori 1976). Given that they interpret the situation as sketched here, most party leaderships would probably consider the wrath and perhaps departure of members preferable to suffering serious electoral losses (Wellhofer and Hennessey 1974: 297ff.). This might lead to the ideologically more extreme members trying to compel the leadership to change the party organization in order to reduce party democracy, thus rendering the rank-and-file members less influential (cf. McKenzie 1982: 195; Pierre 1986: 63ff.). The fact that the discrepancies between members and supporters are quite small, however, suggests that we should guard against over-interpreting membership polarization.

The overall result of this section is a matter of judgement. If, on the one hand, we emphasize the observation that party members are ideologically more extreme than party supporters, then party members have to be placed, collectively, towards the low end of the opinion representativeness dimension. If, on the other hand, the generally small differences in left–right placement between members and supporters are emphasized, then we can place members towards the high end of the dimension.

Party Representativeness

We can now summarize the results from our analysis of social representativeness and opinion representativeness. To get an impression of the overall representativeness of the thirty-seven West European parties analysed here, we order our findings according to the four-fold table in Figure 5.1. The findings reported in Table 5.10 and Table 5.11 have been summarized as a two-dimensional graph, visualized in Figure 5.2. Social representativeness is shown on the horizontal axis, with each of the thirty-seven parties placed along this axis according to its final ranking in Table 5.10. Opinion representativeness is shown on the vertical axis; the parties are placed according to the numerical differences in average left–right self-placement between members and supporters as shown in Table 5.11. The scales along both dimensions have been reversed in order to fit the four-fold table in Figure 5.1. The lines drawn in the figure represent the mean scores of all parties along each of the two dimensions, and have been used as the borderlines between the four cells.[14]

We can see that there is little systematic ordering in the positions of

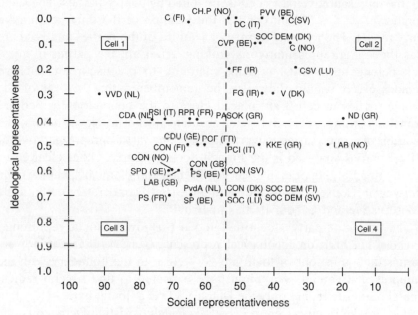

FIGURE 5.2 *Representatives of West European party members*

Notes: Ideological representativeness is based on Table 5.11. The parties are placed along the Y-axis according to the respective sizes of the differences between members and supporters in average left–right self-placement. Social representativeness is based on Table 5.10. The parties are placed along the X-axis according to the sums of their respective rank orderings on gender, age, and class from the final column in the table. The boundaries separating the cells are drawn according to the mean scores for all parties along each dimension.

the parties along the two axes. A correlation analysis does not disclose any particular relationship between social representativeness and opinion representativeness: a party's degree of social representativeness says little about its opinion representativeness and vice versa.[15] One argument for social representativeness, that it is a prerequisite for opinion representativeness, is thus refuted. This finding is consistent with Holmberg's analysis of the representativeness of Swedish parliamentarians (Holmberg and Esaiasson 1988: 150).

A few parties in the figure stand out as particularly representative; that is, they fall clearly into cell 2. They are the Centre Party in Sweden and in Norway, and the Christian Social Party in Luxembourg. The Danish Social Democrats and Liberals (Venstre), the Belgian Liberals (PVV), and Fine Gael in Ireland also end up comfortably in cell 2. In all, the representative party cell is inhabited by twelve parties. The same number of parties fall into cell 3, the location of the unrepresentative party model. The fact that as many as a third of the parties analysed are classified as unrepresentative is striking. After all, the parties in question belong to political systems claiming to practise representative democracy. It should, however, be remembered that several of the twelve parties in cell 3 are placed close to the boundaries, which are drawn according to relative—not absolute—criteria. Nevertheless, the position of some parties is worth noting. The most unrepresentative of all the parties analysed is the French Socialist Party. Other clear cases are the two Belgian Socialist parties (French and Flemish speaking), the Norwegian Conservatives, the German Social Democrats, and both the Conservative and Labour Parties in Britain.

The 'idealistic party', identified in cell 1 as low on social representativeness but high on ideological representativeness, characterizes six parties, although four of them are very close to the boundary with the unrepresentative cell. We might have expected to find several radical liberal parties here, but only the Dutch VVD is a liberal party. The other parties are the Finnish Centre Party, the Dutch Christian Democrats, the French Republicans, and the Socialist Party in Italy and in Greece. The demographic party located in cell 4—high on social representativeness but low on ideological representativeness—largely characterizes left-wing parties. These might be referred to as 'vanguard parties' in so far as their members and supporters are socially similar, but, as we found earlier, members are further to the left than supporters.

In three of the thirteen countries represented in Figure 5.2, all parties are positioned in the same cell. In Ireland, both of the parties analysed are in cell 2. Both Germany and Britain have parties which appear exclusively in the unrepresentative cell. In all the other countries the parties are located in various cells but not in any systematic way.

However, there are some patterns to be found among the ideological families. The parties of the left are strikingly unrepresentative. Of the sixteen communist and socialist parties, only the Danish Social Democratic Party can be classified as a representative party. Seven are classified as unrepresentative, six as demographic, and two as idealistic. Thus some doubt can be cast on the tag 'popular movement' often attributed to, and cherished by, many socialist and communist parties. Several of them, at least compared to the other parties analysed, are not particularly representative at all. Others are, at best, representative in the 'vanguard' sense—that is, if the more radical views of the members eventually catch on among the party's supporters. The conservative parties also tend to be unrepresentative. In this party family, four of these seven parties are classed as unrepresentative and only one, New Democracy in Greece, as representative.

There are three—but smaller—ideological families which are generally more representative. Of the six Christian democratic parties, four are found in the representative cell. However, the large and politically important Christian democratic parties in Germany and in the Netherlands appear in the idealistic and unrepresentative cells respectively. Two other party families which appear as representative are the centre and liberal parties. Among the three centre or agrarian parties analysed, all of which are in the Nordic countries, two belong to the representative party model. They are the Centre Party in Sweden and in Norway; the Finnish Centre Party is in the idealistic cell. The situation is similar for the three liberal parties: the Belgian PVV and Danish Venstre are classed as representative, the Dutch VVD as idealistic.

Conclusion

The analysis in this chapter is based on the conception of political parties as participatory and/or representative linkages between the public and their governments. The main purpose has been to investigate how the parties match up to their linkage role. Some findings are rather discouraging. The general level of party membership is relatively low. Party members are not, strictly speaking, socially representative. And ideologically, party members tend to be somewhat more extreme than party supporters. Two of these findings, however, can also be given a more encouraging interpretation. First, there is no sharp overall drop in party membership; if the parties are not doing well as participatory linkages, they are at least not doing much worse at the end of the 1980s than they were at the beginning of the 1960s. And, secondly, the ideologically extreme members do not differ greatly from their party's supporters. The overall conclusion regarding ideological representativeness is very much one of judgement: if the emphasis is on the numerically small differences between members and supporters there is cause for some optimism, but if the systematic radicalism among party members is emphasized then more caution is called for.

Although there must be a question mark about how well the parties are functioning as participatory linkages, there is no evidence of an acute crisis. In terms of representativeness, it was argued that if the lack of social representativeness were to coincide with low opinion representativeness there would be *prima facie* evidence of a lack of responsiveness and, thus, a potential linkage problem. There are some parties which display a lack of representativeness on both dimensions—notably several socialist parties—but it would be stretching our findings to conclude that this observation adequately describes West European parties in general. There seems to be a rather general lack of social representativeness, but this is not the case for opinion representativeness.

The results of our analysis in this chapter should be treated with some caution. With the exception of membership strength, the lack of data has precluded longitudinal analysis, and several important parties have been excluded from the analysis. Thus, the overall conclusion has to be of careful negation rather than conclusive assertion: it is some exaggeration to portray parties in Western Europe as in a deep crisis of representativeness.

APPENDIX 5.1

Parties not included in the study which were represented in national parliaments at the time of the surveys used in the analysis (1988–9; 1991 in Finland)

Sweden: Left Party Communists, Liberals, Green Party.

Norway: Socialist Left Party, Progress Party.

Finland: Swedish People's Party, Popular Democrats, Christian League, Rural Party, Green Party, Democratic Alternative.

France: Gaullists (RPR), Left Radicals (MRG), National Front, Union for French Democracy (UDF).

Belgium: People's Union (VU), Francophone Democratic Front (FDF), Christian Socialists (PSC/Fr.), Francophone Liberals (PRL), Greens, Flemish Bloc.

Netherlands: Political Reformed Party (SGP), Reformed Political Union (GPV), Pacifist Socialist Party, Democrats '66, Radical Political Party, Reformed Political Federation.

Germany: Free Democrats, Green Party.

Italy: Republicans (PRI), Liberals (PLI), Social Democrats (PSDI), Social

Movement (MSI), Radicals (PR), Proletarian Democracy (DP), Greens, various regional parties.

Luxembourg: Communists, Liberals, Greens, Communist Action, Green Left.

Denmark: Radical Liberals, Socialist People's Party, Christian People's Party, Centre Democrats, Progress Party.

Ireland: Labour, Workers' Party, Democratic Socialists, Greens, Progressive Democrats.

Britain: Liberal Democrats, Social Democrats, Scottish Nationalists, Welsh Nationalists.

Greece: Communist Party (interior).

Spain and Portugal: No party had a total of thirty members in the merged Eurobarometer data.

APPENDIX 5.2 *Age representativeness of party members at the party level*

	Members	Supporters	Difference
SWEDEN			
Social Democratic			
18–30	15	23	
31–60	61	49	12
61–80	24	28	
N	146	1,117	
Centre Party			
18–30	9	16	
31–60	51	53	9
61–80	40	31	
N	68	260	
Conservatives			
18–30	9	26	
31–60	54	52	17
61–80	37	22	
N	56	365	
NORWAY			
Labour			
18–34	22	30	
35–64	56	52	8
65+	22	18	
N	78	615	
Christian People's			
18–34	10	22	
35–64	43	47	16
65+	47	31	
N	40	162	
Centre Party			
18–34	17	26	
35–64	66	62	9
65+	17	12	
N	30	111	
Conservative			
18–34	21	42	
35–64	63	46	21
65+	16	12	
N	70	404	
FINLAND			
Social Democratic			
18–30	3	16	
31–60	73	63	13
61–75	24	21	
N	33	286	

APPENDIX 5.2 *Cont.*

	Members	Supporters	Difference
Centre Party			
18–30	20	24	
31–60	60	59	4
61–75	20	17	
N	50	249	
Conservatives			
18–30	9	22	
31–60	85	67	18
61–75	6	11	
N	35	234	
GERMANY			
Social Democratic			
18–30	12	23	
31–60	71	53	18
61–80	17	24	
N	104	1,010	
Christian Democratic (CDU/CSU)			
18–30	11	13	
31–60	55	57	4
61–80	34	30	
N	105	910	
ITALY			
Communist			
18–30	13	26	
31–60	65	54	13
61 80	22	20	
N	115	534	
Socialist			
18–30	19	22	
31–60	68	59	9
61 80	13	19	
N	47	381	
Christian Democratic			
18–30	24	20	
31–60	54	54	4
61–80	22	26	
N	110	800	
LUXEMBOURG			
Socialist			
18–30	17	23	
31–60	70	63	7
61–80	13	14	
N	30	184	

APPENDIX 5.2 *Cont.*

	Members	Supporters	Difference
Christian Socials			
18–30	9	14	
31–60	68	62	6
61–80	23	24	
N	47	242	
DENMARK			
Social Democratic			
18–30	10	20	
31–60	67	55	12
61–80	23	25	
N	137	755	
Conservative			
18–30	13	27	
31–60	56	46	14
61–80	31	27	
N	61	450	
Liberal (Venstre)			
18–30	10	21	
31–60	49	46	11
61–80	41	33	
N	116	344	
FRANCE			
Communist			
18–30	31	29	
31–60	58	50	10
61–80	11	21	
N	48	167	
Socialist			
18–30	21	26	
31–60	43	56	18
61–80	36	18	
N	44	1,030	
Gaullist (RPR)			
18–30	14	20	
31–60	62	51	11
61–80	24	29	
N	29	422	
BELGIUM			
Socialist (Fr.)			
18–30	19	29	
31–60	60	52	17
61–80	12	19	
N	64	380	

APPENDIX 5.2 *Cont.*

	Members	Supporters	Difference
Socialist (Fl.)			
18–30	18	25	
31–60	69	57	12
61–80	13	18	
N	39	186	
Liberals			
18–30	17	31	
31–60	70	58	14
61–80	13	11	
N	30	187	
Christian Socials (Fl.)			
18–30	21	21	
31–60	53	50	3
61–80	26	29	
N	60	285	
NETHERLANDS			
Labour			
18–30	9	27	
31–60	59	52	18
61–80	32	21	
N	85	965	
Christian Democratic			
18–30	10	21	
31–60	44	49	16
61–80	46	30	
N	103	862	
Liberal			
18–30	17	33	
31–60	53	53	16
61–80	30	14	
N	30	433	
IRELAND			
Fine Gael			
18–30	19	20	
31–60	66	58	8
61–80	15	22	
	41	393	
Fianna Fáil			
18–30	18	21	
31–60	62	54	8
61–80	20	25	
N	74	745	

APPENDIX 5.2 Cont.

	Members	Supporters	Difference
BRITAIN			
Labour			
18–30	20	26	
31–60	63	48	15
61–80	17	26	
N	71	793	
Conservative			
18–30	9	23	
31–60	52	48	14
61–80	39	29	
N	117	1,073	
GREECE			
Communist			
18–30	28	26	
31–60	57	56	3
61–80	15	18	
N	60	277	
Pasok			
18–30	17	23	
31–60	67	53	14
61–80	16	24	
N	108	913	
New Democracy			
18–30	24	22	
31–60	63	59	6
61–80	13	19	
N	121	903	

Notes: Entries are the percentage of the young, middle-aged, and old among party members and supporters. The 'difference' columm shows the average difference in the proportions of young, middle-aged, and old among party members and supporters, calculated as the sum of the difference in the percentage in each group divided by two.

Sources: Swedish Election Study (1988); Norwegian Election Study (1989); Finnish Election Study (1991); Eurobarometer, Nos. 30, 31, 31A, and 32 merged.

NOTES

1. In the 1985 Swedish Election Study, 46 per cent of the Social Democrats in the sample reported that they were collectively affiliated to the party. Another 8.7 per cent reported that they were both individually and collectively affiliated (Holmberg, Gilljam, and Oskarson 1988: 320). Social Democrat membership records have normally included all members, without separating individually and collectively affiliated members. According to the latest published figures, in 1974, about three-quarters of party members were collectively affiliated. If the women's organization is excluded from the membership total, the proportion of collective members is around 80 per cent (Pierre and Widfeldt 1992: 792 ff.).

2. In Ireland, the survey data do not discriminate between collective and individual members. Respondents have been asked only whether or not they are members of a political party.

3. The sharp decline in the Swedish figures between 1964 and 1968 is because collectively affiliated members of the Social Democratic Party cannot be separated from individual members before 1968.

4. For the three Nordic countries, the data are from the 1988 National Election Study in Sweden, the 1989 Election Study in Norway, and the 1991 Election Study in Finland. For the twelve EC countries, the data are from Eurobarometer, Nos. 30 (November 1988), 31 (March 1989), 31a (June–July 1989), and 32 (June 1989). With the exception of Eurobarometer, No. 19 (1983), the question on party membership was not asked until the November 1988 survey. Owing to internal sample loss, some of the parties in the study do not fit the criterion of thirty members on every variable. None the less, they are included in all tables and analyses.

5. Except in the national figures where the members are compared with the total national electorate.

6. In Sweden, for example, it is well known that some Social Democrats vote for the Left Party, formerly called Left Party Communists, to ensure that it passes the 4 per cent threshold for parliamentary representation. This phenomenon is sometimes referred to as 'Comrade Four Per Cent'.

7. The comparison is between party members and the total number of supporters of a party, not with reference to an 'ideal' gender division of 50–50. As can be seen in the table, the male over-representation of 5 points in the British Labour Party means that 58 per cent of the members are male compared to 53 per cent of the supporters.

8. In Norway and Finland it has not been possible to follow these guidelines strictly, but the deviations are not substantively important. The age categories for these countries appear in the table. Respondents below 18 and above 80 years of age have been omitted in all countries except Norway, where there is no upper limit.

9. This was considered the only way to achieve comparability, as the occupational codes vary among the different data sources. In the Eurobarometer data, codes 9, 11, and 12 were collapsed into a working-class category.

10. In a membership survey conducted in 1974, the Swedish Left Party Communists

(now renamed the Left Party) had 55 per cent workers among its members (Hermansson 1988: 145).

11. The rank correlations between the variables are (Spearman's rho): age–gender −0.40 ($p = 0.01$); class–gender −0.32 ($p = 0.06$); class–age 0.15 ($p = 0.39$).

12. The slightly different scale used in Sweden is not a problem since our conclusions are based on the relative differences between party members and supporters.

13. Here the well-known law of curvilinear disparity of opinion among different levels within parties springs to mind (May 1973). May postulates that the intermediate level of party activists is more extreme than either rank-and-file members or the party élite. But this study cannot be taken as a test of May's law. May's distinctions between different levels are not consistent with the distinctions used here. The data allow us only to identify those who answer 'yes' to a question about party membership. We have assumed that the members in our samples are not members of party élites. But among sub-élite members, May makes an important distinction between passive members and activists. The available data do not allow us to use that distinction. Note that in a comprehensive study of the British Labour Party, Seyd and Whiteley find some evidence that members are more to the left than Labour voters, but the differences are, on the whole, not substantial (Seyd and Whiteley 1992: 52 ff.). They find no dramatic differences between rank-and-file members and party activists (p. 217).

14. The mean rank figure for social representativeness is 54.3. The mean scale step difference in left–right self-placement is 0.41. The corresponding median scores are 53 and 0.5 respectively. It should be borne in mind that the borders separating the four cells in the figure are not set to absolute criteria, but to relative differences between the parties.

15. A rank correlation analysis (Spearman's rho) based on the rank ordering of the parties along the two axes results in a coefficient of 0.31 ($p = 0.06$). The Pearson's r coefficient based on the parties' scores on the two dimensions is 0.27 ($p = 0.10$).

6

Party Positions and Voter Orientations

HANS-DIETER KLINGEMANN

Have the citizens of modern representative democracies been abandoned by their political parties? Have the parties entered an era of crisis, in which their traditional functions are no longer performed? These questions relate to the larger theoretical framework presented in the introductory chapter. That parties no longer function properly is the general point of departure of most theories which claim that there is a 'challenge' to representative democracy, even that representative democracy is in a state of 'crisis'. According to these theories, political parties are not responding adequately to the demands of citizens. If true, this would severely undermine the core mechanism of the representative political system in which political parties are the major connecting link.

What patterns are there in the policy positions of major political parties across Western Europe? Do the election programmes of particular types of parties—communists, social democrats, liberals, and so forth—reflect the preferences of their supporters among the various electorates? More specifically, to what extent have the parties' election programmes moved or been synchronized with movements in the preferences of their own supporters? Are there differences in the degree to which particular types of parties cling to a particular set of ideological and policy positions, in contrast to other parties which are more willing to relax such positions in an effort to court broader electoral support?

This analysis would not have seen the light of day without the subtle prodding and determined help of Richard I. Hofferbert, friend and scholar.

The match between the policy positions of voters and of parties is central to the operation of a representative democratic system. Moreover, the movement of parties has been centre stage in the various efforts to build a formal theory of electoral competition (Downs 1957; Robertson 1976; Strom 1990*a*). In this chapter, we analyse recently available data which allow an initial mapping of party–voter congruence and the proclivity of different types of parties to move across the dominant left–right dimension of electoral competition in modern society. In particular, we examine standardized measures of party positions, as expressed in election programmes, for five 'families' of political parties (communist, social democratic, Christian democratic, liberal, and conservative) in twelve European countries for elections during the 1970s and the 1980s.[1] We also examine similarly standardized measures of the left–right position of those portions of electorates which identify themselves as supporters of the respective parties in each election and country. Specifically, the comparison is between the left–right position of parties as derived from content analysing election programmes and the left–right orientations of party supporters, as recorded in mass surveys.[2]

The long-standing debate about the purposes of parties assigns to them functions which are presumed to be essential for defining societal goals: the linkage of voters to political institutions, the representation of individuals and groups, and the conduct of government (Wright 1971). Parties are seen as key mechanisms for interest articulation and aggregation, thus making possible more or less rational choices by policy-motivated electors engaged in selecting those who subsequently govern and make binding decisions (Almond 1960). Competing parties present voters with alternative conceptions of future government action, expressed in the form of policy proposals. Parties also recruit and nominate the candidates for office by which the winning sets of policy options are to be enacted and implemented (Klingemann, Hofferbert, and Budge 1994).

Both aspects—the electoral and the governing function on the one hand, and the ideological or policy function on the other—have been stressed to varying degrees by different authors. Thus, for Epstein (1967), parties are just seeking votes for a labelled candidate. Schlesinger (1965), too, sees them as dominated by their lust for office. Neumann (1956: 396), representing a broader view, stresses that parties are 'brokers of ideas, constantly clarifying, systematizing, and expounding the party's doctrine'. Whatever aspect is stressed, however, parties give content and structure to the processes of competition which are essential, by definition, to a representative democracy.

Most of the early taxonomic literature on party functions was content with illustrative examples, selected to enrich our understanding of the taxonomy rather than to test hypotheses which it might suggest (e.g. Duverger 1954). The publication of Anthony Downs's (1957) *An Economic Theory of Democracy*, however, moved the debate on parties away from party types to focus on party tactics. Downs's rich theoretical discussion stimulated decades of effort to develop a formal theory of party behaviour—theory which would go beyond the specifics of particular parties in particular countries at particular times. All of this work strives to arrive at the transcendent rules governing the means by which parties select, articulate, and aggregate the demands of citizens in the contest for their votes.

Each competing party brings to the electoral arena a degree of established support among the electorate—its traditional adherents. It also brings a history of conceptions of government action which is recognized as the standing ideological orientation of the party and its loyal supporters. This institutional identity is affirmed both by past actions and by past and current programmatic commitments. Current programmatic commitments, however, may vary in their congruence with a party's historical identity. Those who lead the parties adapt current policy commitments both to that which will affirm the loyalty of long-standing adherents and to that which will accommodate the party to current societal and/or electoral advantage.

Most scholarly literature on the behaviour of political parties is speculative and formal in nature. While clear progress has been made in adjusting theory to the potential for empirical testing (e.g. Harmel and Janda 1994), few theoretical expositions provide a clear or realistic estimate of the type of information which would make for an ideal test of key hypotheses. It is often the case in the progress of inquiry that there is an inverse relationship between the elegance and complexity of theory on the one hand, and the quality and quantity of empirical evidence on the other. Indeed, the low likelihood of empirical tests seems to liberate the creative energies of formal theorists. And as new evidence becomes available, there is an interim gap between data analysis and theoretical revision. Such is the situation in current research on party programmes and voter preferences.

The present research is not theory testing in the sense that it addresses particular hypotheses derived from a set of coherent theoretical statements. Rather, it is more in the order of mapping. This mapping process, however, is by no means atheoretical. It takes as a point of departure the concern, among nearly all relevant theoretical exercises, with the formal position of parties *vis-à-vis* the actual or estimated positions of electorates. Moreover, the mapping process is accommodated to one of the central simplifying assumptions of most formal theory: the assumption of a single, central dimension along which voters and parties may be placed and move—a single dimension which captures the dominant structure of both the policy orientations of voters and the policy positions of parties.

Left–Right Party Positions

In this chapter, we report on the investigation of the congruence between the left–right positions of forty-eight political parties, classified by party family, in twelve countries over seventy-four elections and the left–right self-placement of electors who declare themselves to be supporters of those parties. The question, then, is: What are the patterns of congruence over time between, on the one hand, the left–right content of the election programmes of parties belonging to a particular ideological family, and, on the other hand, the left–right self-placement of those voters who support parties of that ideological family?

Parties differ in terms of general political positions or ideologies. Their ideologies, in turn, take their inspiration from major conflicts within modern society. These ideologies represent blueprints of alternative problem priorities and alternative strategies for resolving societies' problems. They embody images of the good society, and they describe the chief means for the construction and maintenance of such a society.

The hypothesis of a decline in attachment to political parties rests, basically, on the assumption that the 'old' blueprints for problem solving are outmoded. They are no longer relevant to modern society. As a consequence, voters turn away from these traditional parties and, thus, in turn, the distance between the policy outlooks of parties and voters grows increasingly larger over the course of time.

Two criteria were used in selecting the parties to include in the analysis. First, parties had to belong to one of the traditional party families. This criterion is central to our major research question: Is it true, as many critics claim, that the 'old' political parties are out of touch—that they have lost their capacity to formulate meaningful policy alternatives in response to their voters' demands? The second criterion was the relative importance of the parties. To be included, a party had to have won 5 per cent of the votes of the national electorate at least once during the period under consideration.[3]

The party families used in this analyses—all members of the 'old' party systems of Europe—are:

— communist parties;
— social democratic parties;
— Christian democratic parties;
— liberal parties;
— conservative parties.[4]

Measuring Party Positions

An intriguing question is how to define and measure a country's major policy dimension. Most of the better scholarship uses subjective and qualitative judgement (see, for example, Castles 1982; Schmidt 1989). Our analysis proceeds from the time honoured assumption that representative democracies are party democracies (Schattschneider 1942). That is, party élites define the policy agenda, the issues involved, and what can be done about them. Thus, it is reasonable to turn to what is, in effect, a natural source of evidence about the patterns of political discourse among the major collective political actors. Specifically, election programmes in each of the twelve countries under study were content analysed. An international team of scholars classified each sentence of each document into one of fifty-four discrete categories of policy themes. Only items relating to domestic policy issues are used in this analysis. The percentage of sentences devoted to each theme is our fundamental datum.[5]

The quantitative results of the content analyses were then subjected to country-by-country factor analyses.[6] This procedure gives maximum weight to country-specific cleavage structures, in the hope, of course, that they will be similar enough to warrant us assuming cross-national comparability. A look at Table 6.1 confirms our expectation. Thus, the risk that cross-national comparisons cannot be made is overcome by the reality of a relatively similar problem agenda across modern West European societies.

TABLE 6.1. *The left–right dimension in domestic policy*

Classification categories	Sweden	Denmark	Norway	Britain	Ireland	Germany	Netherlands	Belgium	Luxembourg	France	Italy	Spain
Freedom and human rights	0.665	0.353	0.583	0.396	−0.305	0.815	−0.063	0.194	−0.133	0.575	0.129	−0.615
Democracy	−0.229	−0.396	−0.471	0.201	−0.708	−0.029	−0.650	0.235	−0.270	−0.391	−0.343	−0.741
Decentralization	−0.063	0.353	−0.491	0.221	−0.400	0.534	0.130	−0.439	0.476	0.005	−0.495	0.617
Centralization	0.137	−0.004	0.246	0.370	−0.598	0.357	0.192	0.118	0.541	−0.86	−0.198	−0.328
Capitalist economy	0.846	0.820	0.829	0.768	0.077	0.566	0.670	0.834	0.239	0.770	−0.056	0.804
Limitation of the welfare state	0.399	0.625	0.644	0.505	0.458	0.422	0.009	0.619	0.374	0.052	−0.020	0.785
Socialist economy	−0.697	−0.419	−0.606	−0.805	−0.670	−0.180	0.033	−0.507	−0.149	−0.831	−0.748	−0.292
Expansion of the welfare state	−0.672	−0.728	−0.792	−0.655	−0.117	−0.787	−0.478	−0.248	−0.762	−0.661	−0.670	−0.571
Environmental protection	−0.327	−0.000	−0.430	0.313	−0.91	−0.115	−0.684	−0.212	0.548	−0.259	−0.310	−0.249
Social conservatism	0.431	0.343	0.353	0.679	0.634	−0.036	0.714	0.380	−0.92	0.776	0.603	0.241
Multiculturalism	0.167	−0.186	0.547	0.386	0.124	0.037	0.733	−0.421	0.789	−0.714	0.295	−0.174
Variance explained	24.0	21.1	32.4	27.4	20.1	20.4	24.3	18.8	21.3	30.8	18.0	29.5

Notes: Entries are correlations between variables and first principal component of factor analyses run separately for each country. The variables are derived from content analysis of the election programmes of political parties. Portugal and Greece are not included due to lack of party manifestos data.

Source: Party Manifestos Research Group (see n. 5).

The specific position of the election programmes of each party—in left–right terms—is the score on the first (unrotated) factor, derived from an analysis for each country of the domestic policy positions summarized in the table. This table indicates the categories used to classify the items in the party programmes and their factor loadings. Clearly, the loadings of the variables accords with common conceptions of the left–right dimension. The comparability in the array of issue areas across countries, in spite of having been separately analysed, is remarkable. Free market themes (capitalist economy) and themes related to social conservatism receive the highest positive loadings, anchoring the 'right' end of the factor. The variables identifying 'left' positions include, most commonly, the welfare state and issues related to a socialist economy.

In order to produce a scale which is comparable in range and magnitude with that extracted from survey data, the factor scores derived for the dimension presented in Table 6.1 were transformed to correspond to a comparable 10-point left–right scale for voters.[7]

Positioning and Movement of Party Families

The mean scores for each party family, for both the 1970s and the 1980s, and across the two decades, are presented in Table 6.2. The specific numbers represent positions on a 10-point scale, as described above. The smaller the number, the more to the left is the mean for the party family. The larger the number, the more to the right is the mean for the party family. The distribution of the means is displayed in Figure 6.1.

With the possible exception of the centrist position of the Christian

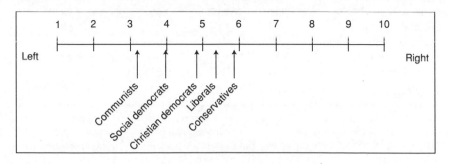

FIGURE 6.1. *Mean left–right position of party election programmes*

democrats—to the left of the liberals—there are no surprises in this distribution. The parties are located where most informed observers would place them (cf. Castles and Mair 1984; Huber and Inglehart 1994). And even the location of the Christian democrats would not surprise most scholars of comparative politics. Although strong Christian democratic parties rarely share centre stage with a seriously challenging conservative competitor, the West European Christian parties are noted more for their firmness in defending the traditional values of family and culture than for a firm stance in favour of the market rather than the state in economic matters. This is particularly true for the social Christian wings of the Christian democratic parties, whose origins go back to the social teachings of the Catholic Church of the late nineteenth century (see Irving 1979).[8]

In Table 6.2, we present the left–right position of party election programmes by party families and by decade. The table is interesting not only for confirming the expected spatial location of each party family, but also for the evidence of movement during the politically volatile 1970s and 1980s.

Several other observations are stimulated by Table 6.2. First, the general ordering of the parties, as indicated by their means over the two decades, also holds for each of the time periods. While there is indeed movement, across the board, the party families neither diverge

TABLE 6.2. *The left–right position of party election programmes by party families and by decade*

Party family (Nos. of observations)	Mean left–right score			Rightward movement
	20 years	1970s	1980s	
Communists (33)	3.25	3.17	3.35	0.18
Social democrats (73)	3.97	3.68	4.26	0.58
Christian democrats (53)	4.81	4.61	5.02	0.41
Liberals (59)	5.35	5.15	5.57	0.42
Conservatives (38)	5.88	5.47	6.21	0.74
Total (256)	4.65	4.39	4.92	0.53

Notes: Entries are the means of transformed factor scores (first principal component; unrotated factor matrix) of the domestic policy content of party election programmes, transformed to fit the 1–10 left–right scale of party supporters. The party families are arrayed from mean left to mean right score.

Source: See Table 6.1.

nor converge noticeably from the 1970s to the 1980s. In other words, there is a stable structure to the ideological positioning of West European parties and elections over the period.

That the structure is generally constant, however, should not detract from the second observation: the universal movement to the right, on average, by all party families during the 1980s. With a twenty-year mean of 4.65 (on the 10-point scale), an average movement of over half a scale-point is worthy of more than passing notice. It is likewise noteworthy that such movement is detectable for every party family. That the communists moved the least is testimony to their determination, if not to their survival instincts. Unquestionably the first decades of the post-war period were devoted to building and reinforcing the welfare state (Flora 1986*a*; 1986*b*; Klingemann, Hofferbert, and Budge 1994), thus policy moved leftwards. But the 1980s was clearly a decade of hesitation, reassessment, and perhaps consolidation—at least by the party élites responsible for articulating the positions taken in election programmes.

Where were the voters in this process? More particularly, how were the orientations of the voters aligned with each of the respective party families and how did they move over the two decades?

Voters' Left–Right Orientations

The left–right dimension, which has often been demonstrated to be familiar to voters as a political schema (Fuchs and Klingemann 1989), allows citizens to orient themselves in a complex political world. On the one hand, it is a means for reducing political complexity. On the other hand, it acts as a code in the system of political communication. Citizens in West European countries have no difficulty expressing their own policy positions in left–right terms. And likewise, they are usually able to locate political parties along the same dimension. The detail and differentiation of policy positions can be generalized in the public mind by relating them to 'left' or 'right,' thus simplifying political orientation.

Political parties exploit this simplification process and seek to communicate with voters in this fashion in order to gain support in the competitive context of elections. Here, too, left–right signals serve to encode and send messages regarding issues which might otherwise have been perceived as diverse and disconnected (Popkin 1991; Sniderman 1993).

Measuring Voters' Left–Right Orientations

In this study, the left–right positions of citizens are measured by a 10-point self-placement scale.[9] In most countries, as seen in Table 6.3, recognition of the left–right dimension is well above 85 per cent. In the countries examined here, it is lowest in Spain (75 per cent), a relatively new member of the community of democracies, and Belgium (77.7 per cent), a country in which linguistic and regional issues have over-whelmed most other concerns and so are not readily expressed in left–right terms. The distribution of mean self-placement within party families, displayed in Table 6.3, is on the same scale as the earlier display of party programme distributions.

It is evident from the table that, in terms of their means on the left–right scale, the twelve countries divide into two groups. A centre-left

TABLE 6.3. *Recognition of the left–right schema and mean left–right self-placement in twelve West European countries*

	Mean recognition of the left–right schema (%)	Mean self-placement on the left–right scale	
Spain	75.0	4.49	Left
Italy	84.1	4.61	↑
Sweden	95.4	4.93	I
France	87.3	5.04	I
Denmark	90.7	5.64	I
Norway	84.6	5.65	I
Netherlands	93.6	5.68	I
Luxembourg	85.6	5.68	I
Germany	89.4	5.68	I
Britain	90.1	5.72	I
Belgium	77.7	5.78	↓
Ireland	86.0	6.15	Right

Notes: Entries are based on responses to the following question: 'In political matters people talk of "the left" and "the right". How do you place your views on a scale from 1 to 10, when 1 means "left" and 10 means "right"?' The countries are arrayed by mean left–right self-placement.

Sources: European Community Study (1973); Eurobarometer, Nos. 2–10, 10A, 11–31, 31A, and 32–4; Norwegian election surveys; Swedish election surveys.

orientation is characteristic of Spain (4.5), Italy (4.6), Sweden (4.9), and France (5.0). There is a sizeable communist party in each of these countries' party systems, unlike the other countries which are characterized by more centre-right orientations. Irish voters anchor the right pole of the scale.

As interesting as these cross-national differences might be, however, the central concern here is not differences between countries but, rather, more general patterns of party and voter positioning. Our focus is on the voter–party connection. Thus, we need to assess the congruence between the general left–right orientation of party supporters and the comparable positions of the parties they support.

Positioning and Movement of Party Supporters

The left–right positions of groups of party supporters display a clear pattern, as seen in Table 6.4 and, graphically, in Figure 6.2.[10] The overall pattern is obvious. Party supporters array themselves along the left–right dimension from the communists on the left to the conservatives on the right, with the social democrats, the liberals, and the Christian democrats in between—in that order. The pattern is striking in its conformity to both common expectations and to the array found with the left–right emphases in party programmes (see Figure 6.1). The only difference in ordering is the positioning of liberal and Christian democratic supporters—perhaps more in line with common stereotypes,

TABLE 6.4. *Left–right orientations of party supporters by party family and by decade*

Party family (Nos. of observations)	Mean left–right score			Movement	
	20 years	1970s	1980s		
Communists (33)	2.84	2.83	2.86	0.03	⇒ R
Social democrats (73)	4.19	4.25	4.13	0.12	L ⇐
Liberals (59)	6.09	6.05	6.12	0.07	⇒ R
Christian democrats (53)	6.63	6.70	6.55	0.15	L ⇐
Conservatives (38)	7.04	7.00	7.08	0.08	⇒ R
Total (256)	5.38	5.36	5.40	0.04	⇒ R

Notes: Parties are arrayed from mean left to mean right scores.

Sources: See Table 6.3.

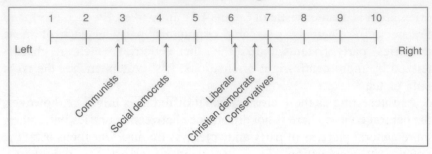

FIGURE 6.2. *Mean left–right orientation of party supporters*

which would put the liberals somewhat to the left of the Christian democrats. To the extent that we can have confidence in the comparability of the scales for the party programmes and party supporters (and we suggest trusting them quite a long way), except for supporters of communist parties, voters are generally rather to the right of the parties they support. There is a dynamic to this difference which we look at in more detail in the next section.

The ordering of groups of party supporters from communists to conservatives, as with the party programmatic positions, is stable from the 1970s through the 1980s. The average range between the left-most and the right-most party is 4.2 scale points. However, there are considerable differences between countries, with the largest average distance in Sweden (4.6 scale points) and the smallest in Ireland where, on average, the range reaches only 1.7 scale points.

The biggest difference between two neighbouring party families is the 1.9 between social democrats and liberals. The most proximate pair of party supporters are the Christian democrats and the conservatives, separated on average by only 0.4 scale points. Considering that most party systems have either a Christian democratic or a conservative party, and rarely both (of any comparable magnitude), this means that, on average, Christian democratic and conservative supporters occupy virtually all of the available space on the right (other than that taken up by various protest parties not dealt with here).

In contrast to the movement in party programmes between the 1970s and the 1980s, there was little inter-decade shifting in the mean left–right orientations of voters attached to specific party families. Supporters of communist, liberal, and conservative parties moved slightly to the right. Social democrats and Christian democrats moved rather to the left. Thus the pattern is one of even more overall stability than found in the programmatic pronouncements of the parties.

The analysis and discussion so far should give a fairly clear picture of the differentiation between the left–right orientations of the election programmes of the various party families. Likewise, we have a clear picture of the general left–right location of supporters of those party families. Now we need to turn our attention to the match between these two sets of information, that is, to the congruence between the orientation of the parties and the voters who support them.

Congruence of Party and Voter Orientations

Are the programmatic orientations of political parties in modern democracies congruent with the orientations of their core supporters? It is precisely this question which is addressed by Table 6.5. And the answer is virtually an unequivocal 'Yes.'

In the previous two sections we spelled out the measures for,

TABLE 6.5. *Correlation of parties and voters'*
left–right positions by country

Country (Nos. of observations)	Correlation (r)
Spain (9)	0.92
Sweden (28)	0.86
France (17)	0.85
Denmark (35)	0.85
Norway (20)	0.83
Netherlands (18)	0.71
Luxembourg (20)	0.66
Britain (15)	0.58
Belgium–Walloon (19)	0.54
Germany (15)	0.45
Belgium–Flemish (21)	0.44
Italy (15)	0.40
Ireland (23)	(0.26)
Mean (255)	0.64

Notes: Countries are arrayed by strength of correlation. The data for Italy exclude the MSI–DN (neo-fascists); if included, r rises to 0.63. Correlations in parentheses are not significant at the 0.05 level.

Sources: See Tables 6.1 and 6.3.

respectively, party positions and voter orientations along the dominant—left–right—dimension of modern politics. A mean correlation
of 0.64 is a dramatic affirmation of the congruence of parties and
voters in modern democracies. Bear in mind that the units yielding
the correlations in Table 6.5 are party programmes in particular elections. Thus, for example, the data for Germany's three traditional
parties cover five elections, yielding fifteen observations. The variables
correlated for these observations are the left–right positions of party
programmes and the mean orientations of survey respondents expressing support for each party. Again, the dominant message of Table 6.5
affirms the congruence of parties and their supporters. We should note
that this affirmation is a serious challenge to those who would claim
that there is a crisis in party performance, or a breakdown of the
connection between parties and their respective publics.

It is perhaps, in a sense, particularly impressive that, of the countries
studied here, the result for Spain, the most recent entry on the list of
democracies points to the tightness of the connection between parties
and voters. The Irish deviation says simply that the dominant concern of
political life is not the left–right dimension around which political
competition is organized elsewhere. In this case, as is the case in
Belgium, some of the basic questions of nation-building are still
unresolved. However, our purpose here is not to explain exceptions
but, rather, to identify general patterns. The intriguing exceptions may
be left to others whose concerns are more particularistic.

Comparisons across Party Families

Table 6.5 tells us, unequivocally, that the left–right position of parties is
generally quite well matched to that of their supporters. And it shows
the broad variation in this match across countries, suggesting, in fact,
little obvious patterning to cross-national variation in the degree of
congruence. Concealed within the national correlations, however, are
possible differences across party families. Those differences are the
subject of Table 6.6.

In the previous sections, we spelled out the tactics employed to
measure the left–right orientations of parties and their supporters. We
also indicated the manner in which these two measures were standardized to a common metric. The numbers in Table 6.6 are based on the
absolute distance between those two metrics. Thus, for example, on the

TABLE 6.6. *Distances and patterns of convergence of parties and voters by party family*

Party family (Nos. of observations)	Mean distance			Convergence
	Both periods	1970s	1980s	
Communists (33)	0.84	0.85	0.82	0.03
Social democrats (73)	0.85	0.97	0.73	0.24
Liberals (59)	0.96	1.11	0.80	0.31
Conservatives (38)	1.26	1.54	1.04	0.50
Christian democrats (53)	1.83	2.11	1.53	0.58
Total (256)	1.14	1.30	0.97	0.33

Note: Party families are arrayed from lowest to highest convergence.

10-point scales for Christian democratic parties and voters, the mean difference between them, across the whole period, is 1.83, with the parties being closer to the centre (that is, less right-wing) than their supporters. The two centre columns report that distance for all the elections held in the 1970s and the 1980s. And the last column indicates the extent of convergence; that is, we have subtracted the distance score for the 1980s from the score for the 1970s. Note that convergence is the pattern for all party families, a point to which we return later.

Two messages are conveyed by Table 6.6, and they must be carefully distinguished. The first concerns mean absolute differences between parties and voters, both within party families and at two time periods. The second message concerns differences between party families in the direction and magnitude of convergence.

The array of party families by the degree of distance between their programmes and their voters is almost a match of their relative right-to-left positions, with some qualification in the case of the Christian democrats—in this instance ranking higher than the conservatives. But generally, the more right-wing party families have been most distant from their voters. Likewise, the programmes of the communists and social democrats achieve the closest match to their loyalists. As to the parties of the right, this is a glass either half empty or half full. As we shall see below (Table 6.7), when we examine the direction of the divergence for the respective pairs of parties and voters, it will be clear that the programmes of the Christian and conservative parties moderate the positions which would be adopted if their voters held full sway over party pronouncements.

The degree of distance also says that the leadership of the Christian and conservative parties—who draw up the party's programme—is perhaps more willing to risk offending party loyalists in the pursuit of electoral success than the leadership of the parties of the left. This finding suggests that, at elections, the parties of the left give higher priority to being in close agreement with their supporters while parties of the right give higher priority to the median voter. Thus, the two possible points of reference which Downs's spatial theory of party competition spells out are of differing importance for parties of the left and parties of the right. Parties of the left—and their adherents—are ideologically more visionary, if not utopian, than their competitors on the right. In pursuit of such visionary goals, parties of the left either follow or carry along with them a comparable degree of ideological enthusiasm from their supporters. Voters of the right have no comparably reliable institutional organs articulating their case. The moderating which is done is done mostly by parties of the right, perhaps in pursuit of electoral victory at the expense of ideological purity.

Contrary to the jeremiads among modern critics of party, there is no evidence whatever of divergence between parties and their followers. Quite the contrary: the mean distance of every party family from their voters was less in the 1980s than in the preceding decade. Further, the greater the mean distance at the outset, the more pronounced the convergence. It is a monotonic function. The Christian democrats, whose average distance from their voters in the 1970s was 2.11, reduced it by 0.58. Much the same happened, in descending order, with the conservatives (0.50), the liberals (0.31), and the social democrats (0.24).

The communists, on the other hand, were the most congruent with their supporters across both decades, although they still had ample room to manoeuvre in a possible effort to draw even closer to their voters. But, as perhaps the most visionary of all the party families, they were also the most rigorous in maintaining their positions, with a convergence of only 0.03—by far the least of all the party families.

For all the clarity of its double message, Table 6.6 does not convey a sufficiently clear picture of the location of parties and voters, as contrasted to the distance between them. We have advanced the view that the more right-wing parties moderate their voters' views. However, a clearer view of the role of the various party families, *vis-à-vis* their supporters is required. We can sharpen that view.

In Table 6.7 we classify election programmes, by party family, in terms of whether the parties or the voters are more 'extreme'. Thus, if the supporters of the communists are further to the left than the party's programme in a given election, the case is classified under the first column in the table. Similarly, if supporters of a conservative party are to the right of their party's programme, that was also classified under the first column, 'Party supporters more "extreme"'. Where the left party is to the left of its supporters or the right party is to the right of its supporters, then the entry is in the column headed 'Party election programmes more "extreme"'. The party families are arrayed in Table 6.7 in terms of this positioning of election programmes as against party supporters towards the extreme or towards the middle of the left–right dimension, irrespective of the magnitude of the difference between parties and voters.

Overall, 71 per cent of the parties' programmes are more 'moderate' than are the parties' supporters. The generalization applies to all party families, save for the communists. Furthermore, a comparison between Table 6.7 and Table 6.6 reveals clearly that the relatively greater distance of the right-wing parties from their respective supporters is almost entirely in the direction of party moderation. Only 2 per cent of the Christian democratic and 11 per cent of the conservative party families' programmes are to the right of the mean among their

TABLE 6.7. *' Extremism' of party supporters and party election programmes by party family*

Party family (Nos. of observations)	Party supporters more 'extreme' (%)	Party election programmes more 'extreme' (%)
Communists (33)	36	64
Social democrats (73)	53	47
Liberals (59)	78	22
Conservatives (38)	89	11
Christian democrats (53)	98	2
Total (256)	71	29

Note: Party families are arrayed according to the extent to which the election programmes are more 'extreme'.

loyalists. This contrasts with nearly two-thirds of the communist programmes, which are to the left of their supporters' mean positions.

The data in Table 6.7 contrast, in a subtle manner, with rather long-standing evidence regarding parties and their followers. Over a generation ago, McClosky and his colleagues (McClosky, Hoffmann, and O'Hara 1960) showed that, at least in the United States, party activists were generally nearer the poles—that is, more ideological—than were their followers in the electorate. This result also holds for Sweden, as Holmberg (1991) has demonstrated. The present findings, from the vantage point of the left–right orientation of party programmes compared to the orientation of voters, suggest rather the reverse.

During the 1970s and 1980s, then, parties of the right were generally more centrist than their voters. In this sense, these parties moderate the ideological struggle. Downs gives us reasons for this behaviour, if not for the relative stubbornness of left-wing parties. Evidently, the partisan search for the median voter has been largely a task performed by the right.

Conclusion

Two questions were posed at the outset of this chapter. Have the citizens of modern representative democracies been abandoned by their political parties? Have the parties entered an era of crisis, in which their traditional linkage functions are no longer performed? Our answer to both questions is a rather firm 'no'.

A systematic examination of these questions has been made possible by the unique combination of two types of data. First, a massive archive of the programmes of political parties, coded in such a manner as to allow for reliable comparisons, over parties, countries, and time. Secondly, systematically assembled surveys of mass publics in a dozen countries of Western Europe. These data provide material for comparing the positions of parties and the orientations of voters along a standardized left–right scale.

The first finding of importance regarding the functioning of the parties was that they share a common dimension along which the major issues are arrayed. In all twelve countries, the left–right dimension is central and comparable in its issue content (Table 6.1). Furthermore, this dimension distinguishes the various party families comparably, and in such a manner as to ensure that meaningful choices have been presented to the electorates of contemporary representative democracies. This array has been maintained over time, allowing us to compare developments during the 1970s to the 1980s.

All this is not to suggest, however, that the policy positions of the parties have been stagnant. The inter-decade comparisons also show movement, modestly to the right on the left–right dimension. The degree of movement has not reduced the array of choice available to voters but, rather, has expanded it. While the mean positions of all party families moved somewhat rightwards from the 1970s to the 1980s, the more right-wing the party family, the greater the degree of movement to the right—without, however, suggesting any dramatic abandonment of the generally centrist orientation of most of the parties (see Table 6.2).

The neat positioning of party families along the left–right scale is matched by the distribution of left–right self-placement among those groups of voters who express support for each of the party families. Somewhat surprisingly, voters' orientations tend to be spread rather wider along the left–right dimension than the positions of the parties. The distance between party positions and voters' orientations becomes steadily wider as one moves to the right along the scale. That is, the communists match most closely the positions of their supporters, with the conservatives most distant. Depending on the stance one takes, this can be seen as either a failure of the right-wing parties to represent accurately the political orientations of their voters, or it can be seen as the parties of the right acting to reach the median voters and thus moderate the more extreme views of their supporters. The parties, in the main, tend to be more centrist than their supporters.

This, too, however, is not a stagnant situation. Those writers who see a rising crisis of party performance in modern societies seem to be suggesting that the secular trend is for the parties to be ever further from their supporters. Our research demonstrates the opposite. While, indeed, there is a pattern of the absolute distances between parties and voters becoming steadily larger as one moves to the right of the scale, the inter-decade analysis shows a pattern of convergence between parties and voters. Those very parties which were most distant from their voters in the earlier period were the ones that moved most vigorously toward their supporters (see Tables 6.6 and 6.7).

In sum, the positions of the parties match rather well the orientations of their supporters. To the extent that there is change, it is in the direction of ever more accurate representation of popular wishes by those collective élites who define the purpose and direct the actions of political parties in modern representative democracies.

NOTES

1. The selection of countries is restricted to Western Europe and to the availability of longitudinal data derived from party election programmes and cross-sectional surveys containing the left–right self-anchoring scale. The following twelve countries are included in the analysis: Belgium, Denmark, France, Germany, Britain, Ireland, Italy, Luxembourg, the Netherlands, Norway, Spain, and Sweden. Recognizing the *de facto* 'division' of Belgium, we display most of the results for the Walloon and Flemish regions separately.

   The time period covered and number of elections in each country is as follows: Belgium (Walloon), November 1971–December 1987, 7 elections; Belgium (Flemish), November 1971–December 1987, 7 elections; Denmark, December 1973–May 1988, 8 elections; France, March 1973–June 1988, 5 elections; Germany, November 1972–January 1987, 5 elections; Britain, June 1970–June 1987, 6 elections; Ireland, February 1973–June 1989, 7 elections; Italy, May 1972–June 1987, 5 elections; Luxembourg, December 1969–June 1989, 5 elections; Netherlands, November 1972–September 1989, 6 elections; Norway, September 1973–September 1989, 5 elections; Spain, October 1982–October 1989, 3 elections; Sweden, September 1968–September 1988, 8 elections.

   Data are not available for the British election of February 1970, the Danish elections of September 1987 and May 1989, and the Swedish election of September 1970. Thus, the total number of elections analysed is seventy-four. For the comparisons over time, we have summarized all elections from 1968 to 1980 (the 1970s) and from 1981 to 1989 (the 1980s).

2. Party supporters are identified by the question: 'If there were a general election tomorrow which party would you support?' The analysis is limited to those 18 years and older.

3. Altogether fifty-three parties qualified, but five had to be excluded because of missing data. Thus the total number of parties in the analysis is forty-eight. The traditional party families were classified principally by their membership in one of the international party organizations and by consulting major works on party families. We used two authoritative reference books for the classification (Hobday 1986; Day 1988) as well as Oberndörfer (1978) and Rühle and Veen (1979).

Social democrats:	Socialist International; Confederation of Socialist Parties in the EC (Paterson and Thomas 1977).
Christian democrats:	Christian Democrat International; Christian Democrat Union; European People's Party (Irving 1979).
Liberals:	Liberal International; Federation of Liberal Parties; Democratic and Reform Parties of the EC (Kirchner 1988).

| *Conservatives*: | International Democrat Union; European Democrat Union (Girvin 1988). |
| *Communists*: | There is no comparable international party organization for the communist parties (Rühle and Veen 1979). |

By concentrating on the traditional party families for theoretical reasons we have thus excluded regional parties (the Belgish Parti Wallon and De Volksunie); protest parties (the Danish Fremskridtspartiet, the Norwegian Fremskrittspartiet and the Aktiouns-Komite 5/6 Pension fir Jiddfereen of Luxembourg); extremist right parties (the Movimento Socialista Italiano-Destra Nationale and the French Front Nationale); the new left-liberal or ecology parties (the German Die Grünen and the Dutch Democraten '66); and the agrarian parties (the Norwegian Senterpartiet and the Swedish Centerpartiet). All these parties have met the 5 per cent criteria. The five parties excluded because of missing data were: Fédération Nationale des Républicains Indépendents, France; Partido Comunista de Espana, Union del Centro Democratico, Spain; Parti Social Démocrate/Sozialdemokratesche Partei, Luxembourg; Social Democratic Party, Britain.

4. The party families used in this analysis are composed as follows:

Communist:	Socialistisk Folkeparti, Denmark; Parti Communiste Français; Partito Comunista Italiano; Parti Communiste Luxembourgeois/Kommunistesch Partei vu Letzebuerg; Sosialistisk Venstreparti, Norway; Vänsterpartiet, Sweden (6).
Social democratic:	Parti Socialiste, Belgium (Walloon); Belgische Socialistische Partij, Belgium (Flemish); Socialdemokratiet, Denmark, Parti Socialiste, France, Sozialdemokratische Partei Deutschlands; Labour Party, Britain; Labour Party, Ireland; Partito Socialista Italiano; Parti Ouvrier Socialiste Luxembourgeoise/Letzeburger Sozialistisch Arbechterpartei; Partij van der Arbeid, the Netherlands; Det Norske Arbeiderparti; Partido Socialista Obrero Espagnol; Sveriges Socialdemokratiska Arbetareparti (13).
Christian democratic:	Parti Social Chrétien, Belgium (Walloon); Christelijke Volkspartij, Belgium (Flemish); Centrum Demokraterne, Denmark; Mouvement Républicain Populaire, France; Christlich Demokratische Union/Christlich Soziale Union, Germany; Fine Gael, Ireland; Democrazia Cristiana, Italy; Parti Chrétien Social/Chrestlech Sozial Volekspartei, Luxembourg; Christen Democratische Appel, the Netherlands; Kristelig Folkepart, Norway (10).
Liberal:	Parti Réformateur Libéral, Walloon Belgium; Partij voor Vrijheid en Vooruitgang, Flemish Belgium; Det Radikale Venstre, Venstre, Denmark; Union pour la Démocratie Française; Freie Demokratische Partei, Deutschland; Liberal Party, Great Britain; Progressive

Democratic Party, Ireland; Parti Démocratique/Demok-
ratesch Partei, Luxembourg; Volkspartij voor Vrijheid
en Democratie, Netherlands; Centro Democrático y
Social, Spain; Folkpartiet Liberalerna, Sweden (12).

Conservative: Konservative Folkeparti, Denmark; Gaullists, France;
Conservative Party, Britain; Fianna Fáil, Ireland;
Hoyre, Norway; Partido Popular, Spain; Moderata Sam-
lingspartiet, Sweden (7).

5. The original idea of assembling such documents, developing a coding scheme, and
actually coding the data up to 1990 rests with the Manifesto Research Group of the
ECPR, headed by Ian Budge. Two major publications have resulted from research
on these data: Budge, Robertson, and Hearl (1987), and Laver and Budge (1992).
The data used for these publications are available through all major academic data
archives. Since 1990, the Science Centre, Berlin has enlarged and completed the
data collection for projects undertaken in its Research Unit on Institutions and
Social Change. Publications growing out of the expanded data collection include:
Klingemann, Hofferbert, and Budge (1994); Hofferbert and Budge (1992); Hofferbert and Klingemann (1990); Volkens (1995 forthcoming).

6. The factor analysis uses an aggregated version of the classification scheme of
domestic policy categories. The categories are grouped as follows:

Polity themes: freedom and human rights; democracy; decentralization;
centralization
Economy themes: capitalist economy; socialist economy
Society themes: expansion of the welfare state; limitation of the welfare state;
environmental protection; social conservatism; multicultur-
alism; environmental protection.

The country-specific factor analysis is based on party election programme data
for the entire post-war period to ensure the statistical robustness of the results.
Details are as follows: Belgium, 1946–87, 15 elections, 13 parties, 89 programmes;
Denmark, 1945–84, 17 elections, 11 parties, 140 programmes; France, 1958–88, 9
elections, 9 parties, 33 programmes; Germany, 1949–87, 11 elections, 4 parties, 35
programmes; Britain, 1945–87, 13 elections, 4 parties, 39 programmes; Ireland,
1948–89, 14 elections, 6 parties, 45 programmes; Italy, 1948–87, 11 elections; 10
parties, 78 programmes; Luxembourg, 1948–89, 11 elections, 6 parties, 44 programmes; Netherlands, 1946–89, 14 elections, 12 parties, 72 programmes; Norway,
1945–89, 12 elections, 8 parties, 74 programmes; Spain, 1977–89, 5 parties, 5
elections, 18 programmes; Sweden, 1944–88, 15 parties, 6 elections, 76 programmes.

7. The transformation of factor scores followed three steps. First, the range of the
factor scores representing the left–right positions of party election programmes and
the range of the mean left–right orientations of the groups of party supporters were
calculated. Secondly, the party supporter range was then divided by the range for
the party election programmes; that is, the party-programme range is expressed as a
fraction of the party-supporter range. Thirdly, the factor scores of the party election
programmes were multiplied by this fraction. To bring the new standardized score
up to positive numbers, the minimum value of the new scores is added. To move

the scale to the minimum value of the groups of party supporters, the minimum value of the groups of party supporters is added also. By this procedure, scale values were generated for party election programmes which can be compared to the scores generated by the means of the 10-point left–right self-anchoring scale for groups of party supporters.

8. A closer comparison of the country-specific rank order of the parties of the traditional party families in the countries under consideration shows a very high degree of agreement between party locations as determined by mean factor scores and the expert ratings. Comparison is possible for forty-four parties; Luxembourg is not included in the expert ratings reported by Castles and Mair (1984) or Huber and Inglehart (1994). In only six cases (14 per cent) is the rank order in dispute. This can be regarded as another validation of the left–right interpretation of the first principal component of our factor analysis.

9. With the exception of Norway and Sweden, all the data are from the Eurobarometer surveys. The Norwegian data were kindly supplied by Ola Listhaug, the Swedish by Sören Holmberg. The scales used for these two countries differed. In Norway, 7-point and 9-point scales were used; in Sweden 11-point scales. These scale values were transformed and projected on to a 10-point scale.

10. For all countries for which Eurobarometer data were available, the mean left–right orientations of groups of party supporters were generated by aggregating observations over election periods. A total of 372 surveys (approximately 40,000 respondents) were processed for this analysis. More detailed information about technical procedures is available on request.

7

Relationships between Citizens and Political Parties

ROBERTO BIORCIO AND RENATO MANNHEIMER

The formation of the main political parties in Western Europe is connected with cleavages going back to the nineteenth century or to even earlier periods: between centre and periphery, church and state, industry and agriculture, and workers and entrepreneurs. Our perception of the main European parties is, for the most part, determined by the 'transnational' dimension of the left–right axis, which is essentially related to the class cleavage. Thus, the major West European parties have during their history tied themselves both materially and symbolically to those interests that are directly or indirectly connected with the type of cleavage which provided the basis for their foundation.

Today, the situation has changed considerably. Various processes are undermining the foundations of consolidated systems of representation and bringing into question traditional political divisions and the type of demands that citizens make on the political system. In the present period, we are witnessing the cumulative effects of a series of concomitant phenomena: the collapse of the regimes of 'real socialism' and the end of the cold war; the crisis in several sectors of European industry and rising unemployment; the greatly increased and more visible immigration from Eastern Europe and the Third World; the crisis affecting the welfare state. Furthermore, the process of European integration is making economic competition more intense, leading to the re-emergence of questions concerning the redefinition and/or safeguarding of national identity.

The aim of the analysis in this chapter is to further our understanding of the relationship between citizens and political parties in the five most populated countries in the European Community and to identify its specific dynamics. The transformation of this relationship may be examined from different angles related to its different poles, with the parties at one end and citizens at the other.

With regard to parties, the transformation has, since the beginning of the 1980s, been affecting two fundamental aspects of their activity: the capacity to transmit social demands and the capacity to foster identification, solidarity, and consensus.[1] As for citizens, it may be assumed that the growth in cognitive resources and the changing needs found in large sectors of society are raising questions about the traditional form of the 'representation contract'. Moreover, these questions seem to have arisen quite independently of more specific concerns about the political class and institutional systems in various countries.

The assumption we look at more closely is that the process of modernization in West European societies is leading to a dislocation of the party–citizen linkage. The way these changes affect the relationship between parties and citizens, however, varies from country to country, depending on the type of political party, the role it plays in the system of interest intermediation, and the political traditions prevailing in different national contexts.

Linkage between Citizens and Parties

The linkage between citizens and political parties is often viewed as a one-dimensional variable whose intensity and variations through time and space can be measured. In the representative model of democracy, casting one's vote is a crucial, and usually exclusive, moment in which political élites obtain a general mandate.[2] The party–citizen relationship, however, is very complex and we need to understand its various modalities. Rather than the strength of the relationship, it is more illuminating in many cases to try to grasp its specific configurations in different national contexts and how they may evolve.

Our starting-point is that the party–citizen relationship, as it has come about in the history of each country and in its connection with different political forces, forms a complex system that permits, at the same time, the expression of a collective identity and the intermediation of specific interests. A schematic typology based on two basic dimensions of analysis serves to illustrate this point. The first dimension relates to the classic concept of a citizen's identification with a political party as a collective subject; here we find the *affective* aspect of the party–citizen relationship. The second is the role of interest intermediation which is attributed to political parties.[3] This dimension forms the *rational–instrumental* aspect of citizens' orientation towards parties; attributing to a party the precise role of intermediation establishes a specific link between the party and its voters. This linkage varies in strength and duration. If citizens regard a political party as having the capacity to act effectively on what they consider to be important issues, they implicitly acknowledge the existence of a link. This form of linkage may not even have any affective value or stimulate any form of identification.

In order to understand the significance of the changes in the party–citizen relationship, a more complex analytical grid is required. It is obtained by combining the dimension of identification with the dimension of interest intermediation (see Figure 7.1). Although the resulting typology is only a very schematic representation of the relationship, it is useful for interpreting ongoing processes in various national cases.

The integrated relationship does not necessarily imply a particularly strong connection but, rather, a situation in which the two central aspects of the party citizen linkage are positively integrated; this is the representation pact that has historically characterized the relationship between electors and the most important mass parties in Europe. The cohesion between the two dimensions of the relationship has been ensured largely by the particular role played by ideology, both in forming the identity of individual parties and as a cognitive and value-sifting filter for the orientation of voters. We define voters who display such a relationship with a political party as (politically) integrated.

This kind of harmonious linkage between identification with the party and interest intermediation has been undermined by the process of modernization taking place in European societies. The contours of those social groups which were considered the primary reference point

		Interest intermediation	
		No	Yes
	Strong	Identifying	Integrated
Identification with party voted for			
	Weak	De-aligned	Pragmatic

FIGURE 7.1. *Typology of the relationship between citizens and parties*

for the promotion of issues linked to traditional cleavages are less clearly defined today. A more complex social organization means that individuals often find themselves in a wide range of situations requiring loyalty to various different social groups. Moreover, the ability of parties to mediate on even traditional issues in a clear fashion has been weakened by the general trend of their transformation into catch-all parties, which are increasingly independent of particular interests and social reference points. This evolution of political parties clearly runs counter to the trend which is emerging among citizens of attaching more importance to participation in politics which is issue oriented rather than ideologically oriented.

The change affecting the integrated form of party–citizen linkage is promoting the development of the other types of relationship. The spread of dealignment among citizens may be an indication that both of the fundamental aspects of the relationship are in crisis.[4] It may also indicate—at least—a potential transformation in the relationship between citizens and parties to make room for forms of intermediation on new bases, thus giving rise to support for neo-populist and single-issue parties. We define as 'de-aligned' voters involved in this type of relationship.

It is, however, possible that the transformation in the classical party–citizen relationship is leading simply to a disassociation of its two aspects. All that survives in the relationship is an attachment to a party without necessarily attributing to it any capacity to handle effectively issues held to be important. This is a situation that can be defined as 'schizophrenic': the attachment to the symbolism of the party remains but there is no genuine regard for its capacity to handle what are considered to be the most important issues. Voters with this kind of relationship to a party we define as 'identifying'.

In the pragmatic relationship, on the contrary, there is no, or only a very weak, feeling of attachment to—or identification with—a party. The relationship with the party voted for is based on the capacity attributed to it to deal effectively with issues held to be important. The spread of this kind of relationship among a national electorate, or among particular sectors of society, may mark the existence of a specific phase in the transformation of the political system.

Analytic Strategy

We carried out an empirical analysis of the state of the relationship between citizens and parties, using data from Eurobarometer, No. 31 (Spring 1989), for the five countries—France, Germany, Britain, Spain, and Italy—which account for more than four-fifths of the total population in the European Community. However, before moving on from the theoretical scheme to the empirical analysis, certain points need to be clarified. First of all, an individual citizen may have links of a different nature and intensity with more than one party. We focused our attention on what voters have indicated is the most important linkage in the relationship with the party for which they have voted or to which they felt 'closest'. The question on the 'closeness to the party voted for', a constant item in the Eurobarometer surveys, is used in our analysis as an indicator of identification with a party.[5] To simplify the analysis, a distinction has been made between those who declare themselves 'very close' or 'fairly close' to a party and all others.

Measuring the efficacy of a party in mediating interests is more complicated. While a precise link between forms of social belonging and a consistent set of interests has grown weaker, the expression of social demands is increasingly taking on the form of support, at the level of individual opinion, for specific issues. In this perspective, a measurement instrument has been elaborated which is useful for revealing a possible relationship between citizens and political parties based on the intermediation of interests perceived as relevant by individuals.[6] Respondents were asked to choose priorities from a set of issues to be placed on the political agenda. They were then asked to indicate which party is most effective[7] in dealing with each of the three problems held to be the most important. Lastly, they named the party they intended to vote for.[8]

In this way it is possible to construct an indirect indicator of respondents' assessment of the capacity of a party to act effectively on the most important issues. The highest point on the scale is where there is the most effective representation regarding the most important issues and the lowest where there is none at all.[9] In order to simplify the analysis, we divided this variable into two: a party is considered capable of representing interests if a voter considers it to be effective in handling at least two of the three issues held to be the most important.[10]

We are interested in the relationship between the party and the voter. Attributing to various parties the capacity to manage issues effectively

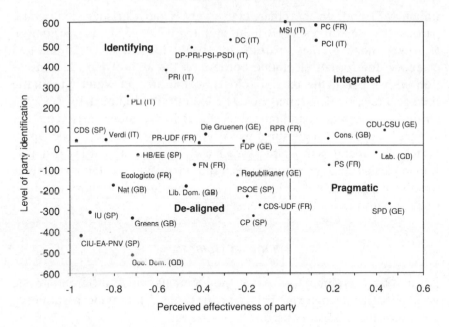

FIGURE 7.2. *Political parties and the type of linkage with voters*
Source: Eurobarometer, No. 31.

may be an indication of satisfaction with the party system, but it cannot be taken as pointing to a specific link between the party and the voter. So the two indicators—party identification and party effectiveness—are used to estimate the distribution of the four types of party–citizen linkage outlined in Figure 7.1.

The technique of correspondence analysis enables us to represent within a two-dimensional space the affinities between the parties in the five European countries examined here and the various types of relationships established with citizens.[11] The dimensions produced by the analysis, displayed in Figure 7.2, are much as expected. The first dimension (the horizontal axis) refers to the capacity of parties to take effective action on issues. The second dimension (the vertical axis) is based on levels of party identification.

It is easy to identify the party areas in which the different forms of linkage are predominant. The position of parties is clearly influenced, first, by their national context and, secondly, by their ideological characteristics. The traditionally integrated linkage marks, on the one hand, the electorate of communist parties (French and Italian) and the

Italian MSI and, on the other, conservative and Christian democratic parties (Conservatives in Britain and the CDU–CSU in Germany). However, none of these parties are firmly located in the integrated category: the former electorate borders on the area of pure identification with a party, the latter is closer to the area in which pragmatic linkage prevails. This area, in turn, is entirely occupied by socialist parties—of Germany and France, and the British Labour Party. The 'de-aligned' category, suggesting weak voter–party linkage, is occupied largely by liberal-democratic, green and 'new right' parties. Finally, Italian parties clearly predominate in the 'identifying' category whereas Spanish parties tend to be located in the 'de-aligned' category in which linkage with parties is at its weakest.

National Contexts

Let us take a preliminary look at the elements which differentiate the various national contexts. The data in Table 7.1 provide a summary picture of the indicators used in our analysis.

It can be seen that 'identification with a political party' is much more common in Italy than in the other countries, and is particularly low in Spain. In contrast, perceptions that parties can represent interests is much higher in Germany and Britain, rather lower in France, and very low in Italy and Spain. By combining the two indicators, which point to different aspects of the relationship between citizens and parties, we obtain a more precise picture of national differences. The distribution of the four types of relationship, or linkage, in these countries is set out in Table 7.2.

The table makes it quite clear that only about one-sixth of citizens have an integrated relationship with a political party. That is, a relationship in which identification with a party corresponds to the perception

TABLE 7.1. *Interest intermediation and closeness to a party*

	Italy	France	Britain	Germany	Spain
Interest intermediation	27.7	35.4	51.3	59.7	20.5
Closeness to a party	37.7	22.4	28.6	27.6	11.6
N	988	973	945	994	969

Notes: Entries are percentages.

Source: Eurobarometer, No. 31.

TABLE 7.2. *Typology of relationship with a party*

	Integrated	Identifying	Pragmatic	De-aligned	N
France	13.3	8.8	22.1	55.8	973
Britain	21.2	7.0	30.1	41.7	945
Germany	21.9	5.1	37.8	35.2	994
Italy	18.3	19.0	9.4	53.3	988
Spain	5.1	6.4	15.4	73.1	969
% of total	16.0	9.2	23.2	51.6	9,869

Note: Entries are row percentages.

Source: Eurobarometer, No. 31.

that it is effective in interest intermediation. The number of citizens who indicate no significant relationship in terms of either identification or interest mediation—the de-aligned—is much higher. More than half of the sample expressed no significant linkage to the party voted for, either in terms of identification or specific interest intermediation. The largest proportion of de-aligned voters are found in Spain. In France and Italy, citizens without close links to parties account for more than half the voters. In Germany and Britain, on the other hand, de-aligned voters are much less common. About one-third of the respondents in the sample indicate a relationship with a party through only one of the dimensions considered; that is, either identification with a party or interest intermediation. These respondents are pragmatic voters.

Thus, notable differences show up between the five countries. Certain similarities can be seen between France, Germany, and Britain, whereas there are wide differences between Italy and Spain. Italy stands out for the high proportion of identifying voters: those who feel close to a political party but do not attribute to it any specific capacity to transmit social demands. In the other four countries, such an attitude is found only on the marginal fringes of the electorate. This situation derives from the historically important role of political subcultures, especially those with a Catholic or socialist–communist background, in ensuring strong participation in the major mass parties. By contrast, the pragmatic type of relationship is relatively widespread in the other four countries, probably because citizens, although not feeling close to any party in particular, attribute to the party they vote for a specific capacity to represent the most important issues. The very low levels of identification with a party in Spain can clearly be put down to the recent formation of the party system.

Types of Political Parties

As we noted earlier, the form of the party–citizen relationship may be markedly influenced by the type of political party that is taken as a reference point. The history and ideology of various parties, together with their specific role within national political systems, may determine both the nature and the intensity of the relationship they have established with the electorate. Table 7.3 presents the proportions of the four voter types among supporters of the several parties in the five West European countries.

The traditional form of the representation contract (the integrated relationship) is found most frequently in parties with a strong ideological character: the communist parties in Italy and France, and the Italian MSI. It is also very widespread among voters for the Christian Democrats in Germany and in the British Conservative and Labour parties. A de-aligned relationship is characteristic of the green parties and, to some extent, of the liberal parties.

If European political parties are grouped according to the 'ideological families' schema proposed by Klingemann (see Chapter 6), we can show the connection between ideological types and types of voter–party relationships. This is evident in Table 7.4.

It is manifest that for the liberal parties on one side and the green and left libertarian parties on the other, the relationship with citizens is particularly weak in the various forms considered here. However, a strong relationship, comprising both identification and interest intermediation, is especially widespread among those voting for communist parties. In contrast, the pragmatic type of relationship—characterized by interest intermediation without identification—is prevalent among those voting for socialist parties.

The relationship between citizens and political parties may depend, at least in part, on the particular role that the various political forces play in different political systems. A first assumption is that a strong relationship, of the integrated or pragmatic type, is more likely among voters for parties in government, while the other types of relationship are more frequently found among voters for opposition parties. The distributions in Table 7.5 provide limited support for the assumption.

TABLE 7.3. *Relationship between vote and party indentification*

	Integrated	Identifying	Pragmatic	De-aligned	N
Italy					
PCI	42.8	16.4	13.8	27.0	151
PSI	18.2	26.4	14.0	41.3	109
PRI-PLI-PSDI	14.0	34.9	4.7	46.5	39
DC	21.4	27.6	13.6	37.4	224
MSI	34.1	25.0	13.6	27.3	43
Verdi	16.7	26.7	10.0	46.7	48
PR-DP	2.0	22.4	4.1	71.4	29
France					
PCF	29.3	20.7	20.7	29.2	49
PS	20.4	7.3	36.7	35.6	340
Ecologiste	2.1	13.8	11.7	72.3	92
UDF	10.4	10.4	25.0	54.2	89
RPR	19.1	12.2	19.8	48.9	124
Front National	6.9	13.8	24.1	55.2	27
Germany					
CDU-CSU	33.6	5.5	39.1	21.9	258
SPD	22.0	3.4	49.8	24.8	456
FDP	14.8	14.8	22.2	48.1	27
Die Grunen	21.6	10.8	17.6	50.0	67
Die Republikaner	15.6	6.7	24.4	53.3	45
Britain					
Conservative	27.9	7.9	33.8	30.5	383
Labour	27.9	6.0	41.9	24.2	291
Lib Democrat	7.1	9.0	19.4	64.5	144
Nationalist	8.3	8.3	4.2	79.2	24
Green	0.0	8.3	16.7	75.0	24
Spain					
PSOE	10.5	7.1	28.5	54.0	294
PP	9.1	6.1	31.8	53.0	120
Izquierda Unida	0.0	8.1	2.7	89.2	67
CIU EA PNV	0.0	4.4	1.1	94.4	29
CDS	0.0	20.8	0.0	79.2	85
HB/EE	0.0	19.0	14.3	66.7	27

Note: Entries are row percentages.

Source: Eurobarometer, No. 31.

TABLE 7.4. *Relationship with a party and party families*

	Integrated	Identifying	Pragmatic	De-aligned	N
Communist	33.3	16.5	12.9	37.3	255
Socialist	20.0	7.6	37.9	34.5	1,609
Liberal	9.9	13.8	17.4	58.9	251
Christian democrat	22.7	16.1	23.8	37.3	653
Conservative	23.2	9.4	29.4	38.1	705
Green–New Left	8.7	15.5	12.3	63.5	278

Note: Entries are row percentages.

Source: Eurobarometer, No. 31.

TABLE 7.5. *Relationship with a party and participation in government*

	Integrated	Identifying	Pragmatic	De-aligned	N
Government parties	21.6	12.0	29.0	37.5	2,840
Other parties	17.6	9.8	26.8	45.8	2,169

Note: Entries are row percentages.

Source: Eurobarometer, No. 31.

The only significant finding is the increase in the de-aligned relationship with regard to opposition parties. This can be read, however, as a spurious effect due to two other much more important variables: ideological connotation and party size.

It can be assumed, then, that the party–citizen relationship is stronger—especially with regard to interest intermediation—in the case of those parties which are seen as the main protagonists in a country's political life, whether in government or opposition. This assumption can be tested by analysing the importance of the different types of party–citizen relationship among the electorates of the two main parties in the national political systems and among the other parties. We can see from Table 7.6 that the de-aligned vote is much less widespread among the electorates of the main political parties. Among the electorates of the other parties, in contrast, pragmatic and integrated relationships are much more common. The identifying type of relationship is relatively more common with regard to the minor parties: large sections of the voters for these parties identify with party symbols but do not attribute to the parties a significant capacity to deal effectively with those issues held to be the most important.

TABLE 7.6. *Relationship with a party and size of political parties*

	Integrated	Identifying	Pragmatic	De-aligned	N
Italy					
Two main parties	28.6	23.0	13.1	35.4	375
Other parties	16.6	25.7	10.7	46.9	276
Germany					
Two main parties	26.3	4.2	45.8	23.7	714
Other parties	17.2	9.6	20.4	52.9	151
France					
Two main parties	20.1	8.6	32.2	39.1	464
Other parties	10.9	13.7	20.0	55.4	280
Britain					
Two main parties	27.9	7.1	37.3	27.7	674
Other parties	6.4	8.8	17.2	67.6	193
Spain					
Two main parties	10.1	6.8	29.4	53.7	414
Other parties	—	12.2	2.2	85.7	226
Total					
Two main parties	23.2	8.9	33.7	34.1	2,641
Other parties	10.4	15.2	13.5	60.9	1,126

Note. Entries are row percentages.

Table 7.6 shows that this particular linkage between voters and the two main parties exists in all the different national contexts we have examined, although with different degrees of emphasis for the reasons we noted above.

Individual Values and Ideological Orientations

We conclude our analysis by examining the effect of particular political or ideological leanings and individual values on the relationship between parties and citizens. If we look at the ideological orientation of respondents, as expressed by where they place themselves on the left–right axis, we see that the integrated relationship is clearly over-represented among respondents who are more decidedly on the left or right. This is evident in Table 7.7.

Maximum de-alignment is found, in contrast, among those respondents who, despite voting for a party, refuse, or are no longer able, to

TABLE 7.7. *Relationship with a party and left–right self-placement, by country*

	Integrated	Identifying	Pragmatic	De-aligned	N
Italy					
Left	28.8	21.1	12.4	37.8	319
Centre	15.5	19.2	9.1	56.1	340
Right	22.5	29.7	10.8	36.9	112
No reply	2.2	8.7	3.8	85.3	216
France					
Left	22.6	11.2	31.3	34.7	368
Centre	2.7	4.0	16.7	76.7	297
Right	16.6	13.5	20.2	49.7	190
No reply	3.1	4.2	6.3	86.5	117
Germany					
Left	31.9	3.8	40.6	23.6	305
Centre	12.9	5.9	40.6	40.6	362
Right	31.1	6.2	33.3	29.3	218
No reply	4.6	3.7	29.6	62.0	108
Britain					
Left	31.6	8.9	32.6	26.8	185
Centre	11.3	4.3	31.2	53.2	378
Right	31.3	10.0	28.9	29.9	282
No reply	11.0	5.0	25.0	59.0	100
Spain					
Left	8.9	11.6	22.0	57.5	365
Centre	1.9	3.3	8.4	86.5	209
Right	9.2	6.9	29.8	54.2	132
No reply	0.0	1.2	3.7	95.1	263
Total					
Left	23.6	11.6	27.2	37.6	1,578
Centre	9.7	7.5	23.1	59.7	1,607
Right	24.2	11.7	26.2	38.0	949
Not classified	3.1	4.4	10.8	81.7	735
% of total	16.0	9.2	23.2	51.6	4,869

Note: Entries are row percentages.
Source: Eurobarometer, No. 31.

relate to any position on the left–right axis. The party–citizen linkage, moreover, is notably weak among those voters who define themselves as in the centre, especially in the case of identifying and integrated relationships.

There is still, however, the difficulty of distinguishing between the effects of individual orientations and the influence of the specific

TABLE 7.8. *Relationship with parties, groups of parties, and individual orientation*

	Integrated	Identifying	Pragmatic	De-aligned	N
Communist					
Left	40.5	17.4	15.9	26.2	195
Centre	8.1	10.8	2.7	78.4	37
Right	12.5	—	12.5	75.0	8
Not classified	13.3	26.7	—	60.0	15
Socialist					
Left	26.8	9.2	38.6	25.4	933
Centre	11.5	5.3	39.7	43.4	433
Right	11.8	11.8	36.8	39.5	76
Not classified	7.7	3.0	29.6	59.8	169
Liberal					
Left	11.5	15.4	11.5	61.5	26
Centre	5.4	12.8	19.6	62.2	148
Right	16.7	15.2	16.7	51.5	66
Not classified	23.1	15.4	7.7	53.8	13
Christian democrat					
Left	12.2	21.4	9.2	57.1	98
Centre	23.0	16.3	24.7	36.0	300
Right	33.0	12.4	31.4	23.2	194
Not classified	5.1	18.6	18.6	57.6	59
Conservative					
Left	21.4	—	28.6	50.0	14
Centre	12.3	3.7	34.8	49.2	187
Right	29.4	12.1	28.3	30.2	463
Not classified	2.5	7.5	17.5	72.5	40
Ecologist new left					
Left	18.7	22.8	11.4	47.2	123
Centre	—	9.6	14.4	76.0	104
Right	—	8.3	8.3	83.3	12
Not classified	2.6	10.5	10.5	76.3	38
% of total	20.4	11.0	28.9	39.6	3,751

Note: Entries are row percentages.
Source: Eurobarometer, No. 31.

characteristics of the party which is most easily associated with a particular orientation. Individual positions on the left–right axis might only be a different way of specifying the type of party to which respondents feel linked. We would thus simply be looking again at the connection between types of party–citizen linkage and a party's ideological features already discussed above. A combination of the two types of variables—type of party and individual ideological orientation—is shown in Table 7.8.

It can be seen that whenever the ideological orientation of the party and the individual correspond, the integrated type of relationship is more common. The highest levels of integrated voters are found with communist parties among people with a left-leaning orientation, and with Christian democratic and conservative parties among people with a right-leaning orientation. The pragmatic type of relationship is widespread among voters for socialist parties, whatever their individual orientations. It is also common among voters for conservative parties who declare themselves to be in the centre, and among voters for Christian democratic parties who define themselves as on the right. The identifying type of linkage is found among voters for communist parties who do not know how to classify themselves on the left–right axis. Individual ideological factors assume a specific importance in defining the type of party–citizen linkage; their effect, however, is connected to the degree of consistency with the ideological orientation of parties and these may differ in different political areas.

In contrast, the influence of postmaterialism on the type of party–citizen relationship is very weak (data not shown). This may depend, in general, on the fact that attitudes towards the traditional parties matured and were fixed before postmaterialism became an important phenomenon in society.

Generational Differences

The configuration of the different modalities assumed by party–citizen linkage is clearly conditioned by specific national traditions and institutional arrangements. Stages in the modernization process, however, seem not to be particularly significant. We have seen that education levels and occupation do not play an important role in determining the relationship between parties and citizens (see Chapter 4). Consequently, improved levels of education and occupational status—implicit in the process of modernization—should not have any direct effect on changes in this relationship. By spreading greater cognitive competence, however, they may create the conditions in which political and social change will influence the relationship more rapidly.

A question which may be asked is whether it is possible to identify trends in the transformation of the party–citizen linkage in these five West European countries. Although no second survey for a later date is available, we shall assume—on the basis of the results provided by our analysis—that certain trends exist.

First, let us consider generational differences. It can be seen from Table 7.9 that in all countries the relationship with political parties is weaker among young people born after 1970. Among the next age group (which has completed the first phase of political socialization), the de-aligned relationship declines while the pragmatic type increases. Among the middle aged and the elderly, there is some tendency towards an increase in the integrated relationship and a decline in the de-aligned type. This phenomenon is particularly marked in Italy. In the other countries, less regular trends emerge, perhaps reflecting the different experiences of each generation during the initial phase of political socialization.

In interpreting these results, the classic life-cycle effect needs to be taken into account. This leads to an explanation in terms of, on the one hand, the relatively long time it takes for identification with a party to develop and, on the other, the possibility that many of the issues which interest young people are not adequately represented by political parties. In this way, the problem of linkage with parties can be related to the traditional processes of political socialization, which foster the development and stabilization of attitudes towards political parties during a person's lifetime. The differences between young and old people in respect of the de-aligned relationship suggest that younger people find it more difficult to establish a satisfactory relationship with a party, both in terms of identification and interest intermediation.

It can be assumed that, as with many other cognitive and value-based attitudes, the party–citizen linkage is established in the pre-adult phase: the so-called 'socialization hypothesis' put forward by Inglehart (1977). Once a specific attitude towards a party has been formed during the first phase of political socialization, it will probably persist through time and change only very slowly. In this perspective, the attitudes of young people towards parties could be viewed as an anticipation of attitudes which will gradually spread throughout the entire population. The higher degree of attachment to parties now found among the older generations may be seen as a residue of previous periods and experiences.

Evaluating the incidence of ideological factors allows us to make other predictions. We have seen that the diffusion of the integrated type

TABLE 7.9. *Relationship with a party by birth cohort*

	Integrated	Identifying	Pragmatic	De-aligned	N
Italy					
After 1970	7.9	11.9	8.9	71.3	105
1960–69	12.4	17.1	10.9	59.6	201
1940–59	18.4	19.0	11.1	51.5	318
Before 1940	24.5	22.2	7.2	46.1	362
France					
After 1970	5.3	8.4	15.8	70.5	95
1960–69	11.1	6.3	23.2	59.5	191
1940–59	15.3	9.9	25.8	49.0	354
Before 1940	14.8	9.1	19.3	56.8	333
Germany					
After 1970	11.9	2.4	26.2	59.5	41
1960–69	17.7	4.8	41.9	35.5	242
1940–59	25.2	4.0	35.2	35.5	410
Before 1940	22.1	7.1	39.6	31.2	310
Britain					
After 1970	8.9	5.4	26.8	58.9	55
1960–69	19.3	7.1	25.0	48.6	206
1940–59	20.1	8.4	31.1	40.4	374
Before 1940	26.2	5.8	32.7	35.3	305
Spain					
After 1970	4.2	4.2	14.2	77.5	120
1960–69	5.5	6.0	15.5	73.0	200
1940–59	4.3	7.0	13.3	75.4	312
Before 1940	5.8	7.0	17.5	69.7	344
Total					
After 1970	6.8	7.0	16.2	70.0	414
1960–69	13.5	8.1	24.3	54.2	1,047
1940–59	17.3	9.3	24.5	48.9	1,767
Before 1940	18.5	10.4	22.7	48.4	1,646
% of total	16.6	9.2	23.1	51.6	4,869

Note: Entries are row percentages.

Source: Eurobarometer, No. 31.

of relationship is greater if, firstly, the individual is able to identify with the left or with the right, and, secondly, if there is sufficient cohesion between this kind of individual position and the identity of the party for which they voted. Therefore, we can speculate that the decline in importance of a vision of political life dominated by the ideological polarization between left and right is making the linkage between citizens and political parties along the traditional lines of the representation pact more problematical.

There appears to be no decline in the ability of the voters in Western Europe to identify their own political position on the left–right axis. The significance attributed to this polarization, however, is no longer based on the traditional division between workers and employers (see Fuchs and Klingemann 1989), and there is a tendency to attribute other meanings to it. The cohesion which the main parties achieve with the ideological positions of a large part of the electorate diminishes to the extent that they maintain a political approach which merely reproduces the traditional divisions. The potential effect is one of de-alignment. This trend is confirmed in the studies by Schmitt and Holmberg (see Chapter 4), which show a tendency for identification with a party to be in decline in four of the five countries they investigated.[12]

Finally, various new issues have appeared on the political agenda which play an increasingly important role as focal points for political participation: the environment, crime, corruption, drugs, the inefficiency of public services, poverty, immigration, health. Attitudes on these issues cut across traditional class and party lines. Moreover, as the issues in politics have changed, a pragmatic type of linkage with parties, emphasizing the policy role of parties, may take on ever greater importance. Whether or not parties participate in government seems less relevant than perceptions of their role as important actors, in the sense of having a concrete influence on a series of issues.

Conclusion

This chapter has focused on the relationship between citizens and parties. A typology was proposed combining the affective orientation (party identification) and the instrumental orientation (interest representation) of voters which yielded four types of relationship: integrated, pragmatic, identifying, and de-aligned. We examined the empirical distribution of these types of relationships in five large West European countries using data from Eurobarometer, No. 31 (1989). As we have only one time-point, no comparisons across time are possible. But analysis by age provides a quasi-dynamic perspective.

Our results show that de-alignment between citizens and parties is the dominant type of relationship (52 per cent), followed by the pragmatic

(23 per cent), the integrated (16 per cent), and identifying (9 per cent) types of relationship. These figures seem to indicate a rather low degree of linkage between citizens and parties. However, these results have to be interpreted with care as much depends on our choice of the cutting points on the indicators used for classification.

Although the de-aligned relationship is the dominant form, it appears to be particularly widespread in the southern countries. The proportion of de-aligned voters is notably high in Spain (73 per cent) and characterizes about half the voters in France (56 per cent) and Italy (53 per cent). The proportions for Britain (42 per cent) and Germany (35 per cent) are noticeably smaller. These figures suggest particular problems in the relationship between citizens and parties in the southern countries.

To explain differences between countries and parties, we examined the role and the relative strength of the parties, as well as their ideological orientation. The role of parties—whether they are in government or in opposition—proved to be of little importance in shaping the relationship with citizens. The strength of parties and their ideological character, however, have a considerable impact. Supporters of the larger parties and voters with a clear ideological orientation showed far fewer signs of de-alignment.

Generational differences were also evident. In particular, whereas we classified 48 per cent of the voters born before 1940 as de-aligned, among voters born after 1970 this figure reaches 70 per cent. Clearly, a de-aligned relationship is much more prevalent among the young than the old. Although we have to be careful not to compound generational differences and life-cycle influences, these rather dramatic differences suggest that young voters find it more difficult to establish a settled relationship with a political party.

NOTES

1. It is especially useful for our purposes to take into account Pizzorno's (1993: 44) analytical distinction. He defines political parties as 'more or less permanent social bodies that become the point of identification and the expression of political interest intermediation'.

2. See the discussion in Chapter 1.

3. In political systems theory, a distinction is generally made between parties and other social actors in which the aggregation of social demands is attributed to

parties whereas the articulation of demands is seen to be a function of interest groups and collective movements (Von Beyme 1984; Almond and Powell 1978).

4. The time series data available from national election studies seem to confirm, for most countries, a long-term tendency for citizens' closeness to parties to decline (see Table 4.1). Exceptions are those countries in which democracy and party systems have been rebuilt in the last twenty years (Spain, Greece, and Portugal). Note, however, that the declining intensity of 'party identification' is manifested in a changing declaration of 'closeness to a party', in particular by older respondents, only after some time and only if a certain threshold level is reached.

5. The measurement of 'party identification' starting from 'closeness to the party voted for' presents evident problems and limits. It differs from that used in mainstream North American studies. For our purpose, however, we maintain that 'closeness to party voted for' provides the right indicator for this fundamental aspect of the party–citizen relationship. It is worth remembering that 'closeness to a party' cannot be compared with 'closeness' to any kind of 'issue': to state that one is close to an object like a 'party'—which is charged with history, traditions, affective and symbolic values—is totally different from expressing a favourable opinion on specific, and often contingent, issues. Closeness to the party voted for points to the existence of a type of relationship that is in most cases an affective one; in contrast, deciding which party is most effective at handling a specific problem involves a rational, evaluative choice. It is, moreover, apparent that the empirical indicators for these two dimensions can, to some extent, contaminate and condition one another. We are right to believe, however, that both indicators mainly reflect only one of the two dimensions.

6. We used this technique for an opinion poll in Italy in 1984 (Biorcio and Mannheimer 1985). The application of this technique to the twelve countries of the EC is the work of Manfred Küchler (1991).

7. The question put was: 'Which political party do you think would be best at handling . . . ?' The twelve items included in Eurobarometer No. 31 are related to both transnational problems (unemployment, price stability, arms limitation, protection of the environment), questions relating to European unity, and national issues specific to each country, The questionnaire was prepared by Manfred Kuechler (1991).

8. Where no voting intention is recorded, the party to which respondents consider themselves 'closest' is indicated.

9. Obviously we must take into account that the absence of issues particularly important to certain kinds of respondents may reduce the accuracy of the indicator. Note that the list of questions does not include issues historically associated with religious parties (abortion and state support for denominational schools), or socialist and communist parties (defending wages in particular).

10. Respondents who did not give priority to any of the issues listed have been excluded from the analysis. Also excluded are those who were reluctant to indicate the party voted for in previous elections and the one favoured for future elections. In this case, the reluctance to indicate a specific party as the best intermediator on priority issues could simply be due to a reluctance to reveal one's own political leanings.

11. For the technique of correspondence analysis, see Lebart, Morineau, and Warwick (1984).
12. Spain is an exception. Here identification with a party is increasing slightly after starting from very low levels due to the recent introduction of democracy.

8

Intermediate Organizations and Interest Representation

KEES AARTS

Political and social linkages are widely regarded as indispensable for the stability of political regimes. If such linkages deteriorate, the stability of the regime may also be at stake. In this chapter, we investigate some indicators of linkages in West European countries. We consider first the development of organizational membership in a general sense and then turn to the development of union membership, since it is the most widespread traditional form of linkage. The final section of the chapter is devoted to new social movements, which, as has been argued in the introductory chapter, potentially offer people new kinds of linkage.

The term 'linkage' refers to the various types of bonds which may exist between individual citizens, social organizations, and the political system. In some instances, these bonds are primarily organizational, as in the case of the formal and informal ties between social organizations and the political system; for example, the links between trade unions and social democratic parties. In other instances, linkage refers to more subjective, individual feelings of attachment to organizations and to the political system. It is the latter type of linkage with which we are mainly concerned.

This chapter has benefited greatly from comments by colleagues in Group 1 of the Beliefs in Government project. Tables from the Norwegian, Swedish, and German election studies were provided by Ola Listhaug, Martin Bennulf, and Dieter Fuchs, for which I thank them. Bas Denters and Ingrid Smeets of the University of Twente gave helpful comments on an earlier draft.

In the political system, social cleavages are articulated through and with the help of intermediary organizations (Easton 1965: 250–7). Accordingly, when it comes to the articulation of cleavages, linkages are indispensable for the stability of political regimes. But, as argued in the introductory chapter, the need for linkages is far from evident in classical democratic theory. Two of the best-known models of democratic government, Rousseau's direct democracy and Schumpeter's party democracy, while opposed in many respects, have one important characteristic in common: the irrelevance of linkages between citizens and the political regime. In Rousseau's case, there is no need for intermediary organizations because, in the ideal democracy, state and society merge, and intermediate organizations would only threaten the realization of the general will (Sabine 1952: 462–5). For Schumpeter, the democratic process is concentrated in the regular election of public authorities, in which intermediary organizations other than the political parties play practically no role. But somewhere between purely direct and purely representative democracy, more realistic theories of democratic politics usually encompass networks of relationships linking individual citizens, social organizations, and the political system (Dahl 1989: 215–24).

The present anxiety about linkages, in Western Europe as well as in the United States, stems from the perceived consequences of long-term social developments. The increase in material wealth, as indicated by higher personal incomes and higher consumption levels, has rendered the social cleavages based on material inequality less important. Population growth and urbanization or suburbanization have distorted traditional social structures. The rise of the mass media, especially television, has challenged the social role of traditional organizations. The increased complexity of political communication and the social mobilization set in motion by the processes of industrialization have resulted in the dissemination of political skills. According to Inglehart (1990*a*: 336–42), rising levels of education are the main indicator of this process of cognitive mobilization. The impact of cognitive mobilization is reinforced by the declining importance, in some but not all political cultures, of gender-based differences in political skills, as well as by the shift in political value priorities (Inglehart 1977: 341). The effect of these developments, which recur in many social theories, is that traditional forms of social and political linkage will become obsolete and will consequently lose their importance for the political attitudes and behaviour of citizens (Habermas 1975: *passim*).

These social changes are well documented (Lane, McKay, and Newton 1991; Inglehart 1990*a*). However, their consequences for the relationship between individual citizens and intermediate institutions are, empirically, less obvious. Presumably they all amount to a weakening of traditional ties. The theory of the mass society serves as a case in point. Bell has argued that the transport and communications revolutions of this century have made people more interdependent than ever before, but at the same time have caused growing isolation, resulting from the simultaneous decline in the importance of family and community ties and of traditional unifying values (Bell 1988: 22–3). Other examples are readily found.

To be more specific, the decline of individual linkages can be put in terms of empirical hypotheses. First, it is to be expected that adherence to traditional organizations, as measured by their membership, is declining or has declined (see Figure 1.2). Secondly, ties between adherence to these organizations and adherence to the political system, as indicated by a preference for one of the existing parties, may become weaker. These two related forms of decline in linkage may be summarized as the *mass society hypotheses* (Kornhauser 1959). If true, both cases point to linkage problems at the institutional level of society which may lead to a decline in the legitimacy of the political system.

There is a third possibility. People may still find themselves attached to intermediary organizations and also have a political preference for a specific party, but the two have grown apart ideologically. For example, union membership in most countries has traditionally been associated with voting for left-wing parties. When this association becomes weaker, a problem may arise for the legitimacy of the political system, since the ideological dimensions of the intermediary organizations and the party system no longer match. This third form of linkage development may be summarily named the '*end-of-ideology*' hypothesis (Bell 1988).

All three of these possible developments give rise to pessimistic expectations about the future of either intermediary organizations, or the party system, or both. This is a familiar theme in much of the recent literature about linkages (cf. Lawson and Merkl 1988; Streeck 1987). A more optimistic perspective is offered by Inglehart and others, who claim that the traditional dimensions of political conflict are being replaced by a new materialist–postmaterialist dimension (Inglehart 1984). Others (Klandermans, Kriesi, and Tarrow 1988; Dalton and Küchler 1990) point to the emergence of new social movements—the environmentalist movement, opposition to nuclear power, the peace movement, the women's movement, the consumer advocacy movement—which have propelled new issues on to the political agenda. The action repertoire of these movements contains not only instrumental but also expressive components (Kaase 1990), which stimulate the development of alternative linkages. Therefore, in addition to examining data about the more traditional intermediary organizations, we look at data about support for new social movements. The latter data are restricted to the 1980s.

Empirical evidence relating to the two main hypotheses are presented in this chapter. It will be argued that, contrary to what the hypotheses predict, there is no convincing evidence of a decline in linkages. There are few clear trends, and short-term fluctuations are less impressive than continuity.

Organizational Membership

The argument that the *non*political attitudes and affiliations of citizens sustain a political culture favourable to stable democracy (Almond and Verba 1989: 244–50) draws attention to the relationship between membership of social organizations and the political attitudes associated with a civic political culture. Almond and Verba have emphasized that involvement in any social organization—and even more so in political organizations—increases one's potential for political involvement, since organizational involvement means social interaction, and social interaction precedes political activity. It is an open question whether, in this argument, organizational membership stands for an expressive, ritualistic activity or for a primarily instrumental mode of social participation. The answer is probably not very important for the relationship between organizational membership and political attitudes. If the internal validity of Almond and Verba's argument is accepted, it is useful to consider, as they did, the extent and correlates of, and developments in, organizational involvement.

Apart from Almond and Verba's data, which include three European countries, four Eurobarometer surveys (for 1977, 1983, 1987, and 1990) contain a comparable question about membership in several social and political organizations.[1] The various organizations mentioned are not exactly the same, but the number of alternatives justifies the expectation that all respondents have been able to declare any organizational involvement they may have had. It should be noted in advance that the relative scarcity and uneven distribution of time points precludes any grand longitudinal generalizations based on these data.

The frequency with which membership of different organizations was mentioned in the Civic Culture data and the Eurobarometers varies between countries and over time. Since organizational membership includes membership of a football club as well as a political group, it is evidently meaningless to try constructing indicators measuring a general dimension of organizational membership. Instead, the only instructive way to look at these data in a comparative perspective is to turn the concept around and focus on non-involvement. Our comparisons are therefore based on those respondents who do not mention any kind of organizational membership, as opposed to all those who are a member of at least one organization, of whatever kind.

A similar approach is taken towards the political attitudes which presumably result from organizational involvement. The surveys used contain questions on how often the respondent discusses political and social problems with others. (See also Chapter 3 in this volume.) When respondents state that they never discuss politics with others, we can conclude that they lack political involvement. The significance of both organizational involvement and political discussion as indicators of cross-national differences in political culture was established more than thirty years ago (Almond and Verba 1989: 86).

In the next section, respondents who have not answered even one membership question affirmatively are singled out. These are the people who, according to the civic culture argument, are the most likely to lack political involvement as well. Both indicators reflect the linkage of respondents to the political system.

Organizational Involvement and Talking about Politics

The relative size of the two groups of respondents, those who are not organizationally involved and those who never talk with others about social and political problems, is shown in Table 8.1. Non-involvement here includes the absence of involvement in traditional interest groups, such as political, social, and religious groups, and trade unions. Therefore the data in this table can be seen as evidence relating to the first of the mass society hypotheses. Although the table presents data on non-involvement and non-communication, we can also interpret

TABLE 8.1. *Organizational involvement and talking about politics in nine West European countries, 1959–90*

	1959		1977		1983		1987		1990	
	(a)	(b)	(a)	(b)	(a)	(b)	(a)	(b)	(a)	(b)
Denmark	—	—	25	27	35	27	20	18	14	21
N			992		1,027		1,002		1,000	
Belgium	—	—	29	52	56	36	61	45	44	46
N			1,006		1,038		1,005		996	
Germany	59	39	47	18	43	17	65	16	43	18
N	995		999		1,049		957		1,002	
Ireland	—	—	46	46	45	34	46	40	44	43
N			997		987		997		1,022	
Netherlands	—	—	20	22	22	17	38	26	26	25
N			943		998		965		1,067	
Britain	52	29	46	36	42	37	47	30	39	30
N	963		1,053		1,027		992		1,047	
France	—	—	38	35	56	23	67	37	58	35
N			1,130		1,011		999		1,022	
Italy	71	67	54	40	64	40	70	41	62	33
N	995		1,155		1,031		1,032		1,073	
Greece	—	—	—	—	68	18	83	26	75	16
N					1,000		1,000		1,008	

Notes: Entries in column (a) are the percentage of respondents indicating no organizational involvement; in column (b) the percentage of respondents stating that they never talk about social or political problems. The percentage base is all respondents in the national samples.

Sources: Civic Culture (1959); Eurobarometer, Nos. 8, 19, 28, and 34.

these data positively as indicating levels of organizational involvement and political communication.

It is obvious that there are large cross-national as well as across-time variations in the entries here. Looking for a pattern in the cross-national variations, and interpreting the data positively, we can see that some countries may be grouped together. First, there are those countries with high levels of both organizational membership and political discussion. Denmark and the Netherlands are in this group. A second group comprises Germany, Britain, and France, where political communication is also at a high level, but organizational membership is lower. Belgium and Ireland, where both indicators are at an intermediate level, constitute a third group. Finally, there is a group of countries in which organizational membership is absolutely low, while the level of political communication varies from low to high. Italy and Greece belong to this group.

These cross-national differences in organizational membership and—but less so—in political discussion, to some extent reflect variations in economic and social developments. The relative positions of, on the one hand, the Netherlands and Denmark, and, on the other hand, Greece (and, although the data are not presented here, Spain and Portugal) point to the importance of modernization processes. However, modernization is a dynamic process, so it should also be reflected in differences over time in organizational involvement and the frequency of political discussion.

Looking at the data over time, however, some countries are consistently high or low on the indicators, but there are also considerable fluctuations. A decline in organizational membership would be consistent with our first hypothesis on declining adherence to traditional organizations and with the modernization theory set out in the introductory chapter. No evidence of such a decline is found in these data about non-involvement. We return to this point when union membership is examined.

Organizational Involvement and Mass Society

Apart from developments in organizational membership proper, it was predicted that the ties between membership of traditional social organizations and political involvement would weaken. According to mass society theory, this should show up, in the first place, in a weaker relationship between organizational involvement and political communication, and, in the second place, in a weaker relationship between adherence to the political system and both involvement and discussion. We operationalize adherence to the political system as the expression of a preference for a political party, tapped by responses from a question asking respondents which party they would vote for if a general election were held tomorrow.

The relationship between organizational involvement and political discussion is shown in Table 8.2. There is an evident, and moderately strong, positive relationship between the two measures: in every instance, people who are involved in at least one organization are more likely to talk about politics than people who have no organizational involvement.

TABLE 8.2. *Organizational involvement as a cause of talking about politics in nine West European countries, 1959–90*

	1959	1977	1983	1987	1990
Denmark					
None	—	42	40	29	34
At least one	—	22	20	15	19
Belgium					
None	—	65	45	56	54
At least one	—	47	27	32	39
Germany					
None	52	23	26	20	27
At least one	22	14	10	9	12
Ireland					
None	—	57	45	50	50
At least one	—	35	25	31	37
Netherlands					
None	—	38	26	35	36
At least one	—	19	15	19	21
Britain					
None	58	46	50	36	38
At least one	21	28	28	25	25
France					
None	—	47	29	42	41
At least one	—	28	15	26	26
Italy					
None	73	53	27	47	40
At least one	51	26	14	29	21
Greece					
None	—	—	23	29	18
At least one	—	—	6	13	10

Notes: Entries are percentages of respondents never discussing social or political problem with others. The percentage base for the first row are respondents who are not members of any social organization; for the second row, respondents who are members of at least one social organization.

Sources: Civic Culture (1959); Eurobarometer, Nos. 8, 19, 28, and 34.

This positive relationship does not vary cross-nationally and neither has it substantially changed over time. In other words, there is no indication that modernization processes have had an impact on the relationship between organizational involvement and talking about politics, as the second mass society hypothesis would lead one to believe.

TABLE 8.3. *Organizational involvement and expressed political preference in nine West European countries, 1959–90*

	1959	1977	1983	1987	1990
Denmark					
None	—	28	28	39	30
At least one	—	18	22	30	27
Belgium					
None	—	59	49	55	43
At least one	—	41	35	39	41
Germany					
None	31	26	17	19	26
At least one	24	20	11	16	21
Ireland					
None	—	28	36	37	28
At least one	—	20	32	33	31
Netherlands					
None	—	26	17	30	20
At least one	—	14	11	18	13
Britain					
None	17	21	10	20	24
At least one	11	18	9	15	21
France					
None	—	28	20	26	39
At least one	—	17	9	18	32
Italy					
None	45	32	35	45	47
At least one	36	22	22	31	40
Greece					
None	—	—	39	52	33
At least one	—	—	26	33	27

Notes: Entries in the first row are percentages of respondents who do not express a preference for an existing political party among those not organizationally involved at all. Entries in the second row are percentages of respondents who do not express a preference for an existing political party among those involved in at least one organization. For the size of national samples, see Table 8.1. The Italian codes in 1983 do not allow for a separate category 'no preference'. The figures are the results when the category 'other party' (which apparently includes 'no preference') is regarded as the 'no preference' category.

Sources: Civic Culture (1959); Eurobarometer, Nos. 8, 19, 28, and 34.

The direct relationship between organizational membership and party preference is shown in Table 8.3.[2] Here, the association between the two variables is weaker than that found in Table 8.2. None the less it is

TABLE 8.4. *Involvement, communication, and expressed preference in Germany, Britain, and Italy, 1959–90*

	Organizational involvement	Political communication	Expressed preference
Organizational involvement			
1959	—	0.13 (7.30)	0.07 (3.66)
1977	—	0.13 (7.55)	0.04 (2.25)
1983	—	0.16 (8.99)	0.04 (2.38)
1987	—	0.10 (5.61)	0.06 (3.44)
1990	—	0.15 (8.24)	0.07 (3.90)
Political communication			
1959	—	—	0.11 (5.62)
1977	—	—	0.14 (7.90)
1983	—	—	n.s.
1987	—	—	0.07 (3.90)
1990	—	—	0.10 (5.59)
Age			
1959	n.s.	−0.05 (−2.73)	—
1977	−0.06 (−3.10)	n.s.	—
1983	n.s.	−0.09 (−4.72)	—
1987	0.07 (3.70)	−0.05 (−2.51)	—
1990	n.s.	n.s.	—
Sex			
1959	−0.33 (−18.42)	−0.18 (−10.03)	—
1977	−0.28 (−15.97)	−0.17 (−9.66)	—
1983	−0.13 (−7.61)	n.s.	—
1987	−0.10 (−5.24)	−0.16 (−9.20)	—
1990	−0.14 (−7.74)	−0.12 (−8.84)	—
Education			
1959	0.11 (6.03)	0.17 (9.71)	—
1977	0.04 (2.32)	0.17 (9.65)	—
1983	0.16 (9.20)	0.14 (7.55)	—
1987	0.17 (8.80)	0.13 (6.46)	—
1990	0.16 (8.61)	0.16 (8.84)	—
Dummy 1: Britain			
1959	0.15 (7.69)	0.31 (15.68)	0.28 (13.23)
1977	0.08 (4.04)	0.07 (3.54)	0.07 (4.13)
1983	0.24 (11.81)	−0.20 (−11.63)	n.s.
1987	0.24 (11.62)	0.10 (5.03)	0.22 (10.21)
1990	0.26 (12.50)	n.s.	0.23 (10.91)

TABLE 8.4. *Cont.*

	Organizational involvement	Political communication	Expressed preference
Dummy 2: Germany			
1959	0.15 (7.49)	0.26 (13.19)	0.14 (6.45)
1977	0.07 (3.73)	0.23 (11.92)	n.s.
1983	0.21 (10.42)	n.s.	−0.05 (−2.87)
1987	0.04 (2.07)	0.25 (12.40)	0.24 (11.18)
1990	0.18 (9.07)	0.12 (8.81)	0.20 (9.84)
R^2			
1959	0.15	0.22	0.11
1977	0.09	0.14	0.03
1983	0.10	0.11	0.00
1987	0.08	0.12	0.07
1990	0.09	0.09	0.08

Notes: Entries are beta values and *t*-values; R^2 coefficients. Constants have been omitted. See n. 3 for details of the regression models. All respondents in the national samples for Britain, Germany, and Italy are included. The number of cases are respectively: 2,753, 3,028, 2,940, and 2,955.

Sources: Civic Culture (1959); Eurobarometer, Nos. 8, 19, 28, and 34.

clearly present and positive. This means that in all the countries investigated, regardless of their national political culture, membership of social or political organizations increases the probability that the respondent has a preference for a political party. Again, it is not possible to detect clear differences over time in the data—although this may, of course, be attributed to the limited number of time points.

Thus far, then, little or no evidence for the mass society hypotheses has been found. The bivariate relationships assumed in the theory do exist, but there is no evidence of change in the relationships, as the theory predicts. Apart from cross-national variation, only some fluctuation over time is found. But bivariate relationships may be just too simple to catch the decline of linkages. A causal model taking into account the correlates of organizational involvement and political communication allows us to explore more complex changes.

The variables most often associated with social and political involvement are education and gender (Almond and Verba 1989). More highly educated respondents are considered to be better equipped with social and political resources than the less educated, and in most societies men are traditionally more active in political life than women. The age of the respondent can be added as a third factor, since organizational membership and political communication often increase with age, although it is not clear beforehand whether age is linearly related to organizational involvement and political communication.

For three countries, Germany, Britain, and Italy, data are available from the 1959 Civic Culture study and from the four Eurobarometer surveys. The data for these countries were pooled for each of the five surveys, and three regression equations estimated in which countries are entered as dummy variables.[3] The results are presented in Table 8.4.

It is clear from Table 8.4 that the relationships between the three dependent variables are consistently positive. With the exception of 1983, when it was not significant, the effect of political communication on expressed preference is stronger than the effect of organizational membership on expressed preference. None the less, organizational membership is always positively related to political communication. Of the three individual background variables, age is the least significant, which may be attributed to its curvilinear relationship with the dependent variables. As expected, education has a consistently positive effect on both organizational membership and political communication, while the effect of gender clearly has become less important over the years, but is still considerable. Here, pooling the data from the three countries may, in fact, have obscured the culturally specific decline of gender-based differences in political skills (Inglehart 1977). The coefficients for the dummy variables show that national differences are always present, although they are not always equally strong. Generally, the regression models show a moderate and sometimes poor fit to the data, as indicated by the low R^2 coefficient which points to the neglect of other important relationships in explaining the dependent variables. Even so, our findings from this multivariate model do not alter our earlier conclusion: the hypothesized relationships exist and differ between countries, but they do not show systematic variation through time.

The relationships found thus far are consistently positive. But apart from considerable cross-national variation, there are no systematic tendencies through time. The introduction of relevant background variables did not alter this conclusion. As we shall see next, this conclusion by and large also holds when we examine more closely developments in one prime example of an intermediary organization: the trade union.

Union Membership

Organizational membership or non-membership, as operationalized in the previous section, may be just too general or too diverse to capture the concept of linkage adequately. Therefore we look at trade-union membership as a specific instance of linkage to a traditional intermediary institution. Moreover, since union membership is often associated with a specific ideological outlook, it allows us to test the end-of-ideology hypothesis which anticipates a growing mismatch between intermediary organizations and the party system.

The association between union membership and ideological outlook may, however, at least at the individual level, be blurred by the structure of the union system. National union systems vary along several dimensions. Union density (the proportion of union members among the workforce) is one dimension. The membership figures set out in Table 8.5 give an impression of the cross-national and longitudinal variations on this dimension.

As is evident from these figures, there is considerable cross-national variation. The Scandinavian countries (Denmark, Norway, and Sweden) are characterized by high rates of union membership. Germany, Italy, Britain, and the Netherlands have moderately high proportions of union members among the workforce, while low levels of unionization are found in France and—although the data are not presented in the table[4]—Portugal, Spain, and Greece. In other words, union density

TABLE 8.5. *Union density rates in eight West European countries, 1950–85*

	1950	1960	1970	1980	1985
Denmark	58	63	64	80	82
Norway	50	63	63	63	63
Sweden	68	73	73	88	92
Germany	35	38	38	41	39
Netherlands	43	42	40	35	29
Britain	44	44	49	53	45
France	21	19	21	17	15
Italy	50	35	38	54	51

Note: Entries are percentages of trade-union members based on all wage and salary earners in and out of employment, including retired workers.

Source: Visser (1990: 34).

declines as we go from the north of Europe to the south, with Italy being an exception. There is also considerable over-time variation. Although the relative ranking of the countries is quite stable, between 1950 and 1985 unionization levels dropped in the Netherlands and France, rose in the Scandinavian countries and Germany, and remained broadly stable over the period in Britain and Italy.

Visser (1990) has suggested a two-dimensional classification of union systems according to their horizontal and vertical integration. Horizontally, the most integrated are the representative, unified, and concentrated union systems of Sweden and Germany. At the other end of the continuum are the divided and conflict-ridden systems of France and Italy until about 1970. Weakly integrated are the Norwegian, Danish, British, and Dutch systems. Vertical integration, which refers to the level of centralization of the union confederations, is highest in Britain, France, and Italy, and is much lower in Norway, Sweden, and the Netherlands.

Religion is a major source of divisions in the union systems in many West European countries, but not in the Scandinavian countries, Britain, Ireland, and Greece. Occupational status is important in Scandinavia, Germany, the Netherlands, Italy, and France. Finally, in many countries union confederations are—formally or informally—aligned to political parties of the left (von Beyme 1985).

All these specificities of union systems call for great care in any cross-national comparison of union membership. None the less, we do not expect such specificities to rebut the general tendencies associated with membership of a workers' or employees' intermediary organization. These are, first, an above average adherence to the party system, indicated by stating a preference for an existing party, and, secondly, an above average preference for parties of the political left.

A total of thirty-seven data sets are used for the analysis in this section. Twenty-eight of these are national election studies from Norway, Sweden, and Germany, which stand out for their availability over a relatively long period of time. Of the other nine data sets, four come from the USIA-XX studies which provide information on Germany and Britain in the 1950s and the early 1960s. The remaining five data sets are Eurobarometer surveys for 1973, 1976, 1985, 1989, and 1990, which cover the EC member states.

Union Membership and Mass Society

As was already clear from Table 8.5, it would be more than premature to speak of a decline in union membership in Europe. It is possible that the number of people eligible for union membership, those in the workforce, has declined, but that is a different issue.

Individual linkage to the trade-union system, as part of the intermediary structure of society, and to the party system supposedly leads to a positive relationship between union membership and stating a preference for a political party. According to the mass society hypotheses, this relationship should have weakened over recent decades. Table 8.6 shows the relevant data. In two instances, the data were collected around the time of national elections—Germany in October 1976, and Ireland in June 1989—which may have had the effect of reducing the proportion of respondents without a party preference (see n. 2).

The association between stating a party preference and union membership is generally comparable to the association with organizational membership (see Table 8.3). The direction is again in most cases consistent with our theoretical predictions: union members more often state a party preference than non-members. Exceptions are found in the British, Belgian, and especially the Danish data. In the case of Denmark, the extremely high level of unionization not only among blue-collar workers but also among white-collar employees may serve as an explanation. In all the other countries, the relationship is clearly positive, thus validating the underlying assumption of the analysis. But the findings also show that there is no visible over-time development in the data. This again clashes with the core of the mass society hypotheses, which predict directional change rather than fluctuation.

Union Membership and the End of Ideology

While the likelihood that union members state a party preference has not apparently declined, it may still be the case that the kind of parties they prefer has changed. Historical tradition suggests that union members disproportionally prefer parties of the left (socialist, social-democratic, and communist parties), since both trade unions and left-wing parties originate from the same nineteenth-century labour movement. As a result of the variety in union systems, cross-national variation in

TABLE 8.6. *Union membership and expressed political preference in nine West European countries, 1955–90*

	1955		1964		1973		1976		1985		1989		1990	
	(a)	(b)	(a)	(b)	(a)	(b)	(a)	(b)	(a)	(b)	(a)	(b)	(a)	(b)
Denmark	—	—	—	—	19	18	—	—	22	17	12	11	27	26
N					443				506		556		540	
Belgium	—	—	—	—	33	53	27	31	41	44	31	30	26	44
N					381		499		385		340		400	
Germany	31	43	22	34	24	30	12	14	15	19	12	18	18	27
N	835		574		768		485		465		621		471	
Ireland	—	—	—	—	22	28	20	26	27	39	10	12	21	37
N					410		446		278		361		341	
Netherlands	—	—	—	—	18	24	17	24	13	22	3	6	5	12
N					221		462		328		366		458	
Britain	9	10	8	16	21	19	20	23	8	14	11	10	16	27
N	722		536		714		608		472		412		488	
France	—	—	—	—	16	28	10	18	6	17	9	21	20	34
N					647		686		357		406		449	
Italy	—	—	—	—	21	30	20	36	16	41	20	28	28	51
N					557		527		323		336		320	
Greece	—	—	—	—	—	—	—	—	42	42	15	19	30	39
N									188		331		243	

Notes: Entries in column (a) are percentages among union members who indicate no party preference; those in column (b) are percentages among non-members who indicate no party preference. N includes only respondents in employment. The 1955 data are from the USIA-XX studies; Nos. 3, 5, and 6 (Germany) and 5 and 6 (Britain) have been pooled. In 1973, for coding reasons, the sample base was narrowed to respondents who were head of household. Danish data on union membership for 1976 have been omitted as they appear to be unreliable.

Sources: USIA-XX studies (3, 5, 6, 16); European Community Study (1973); Eurobarometer, Nos. 6, 23, 31*a*, and 34.

this association is to be expected. What is interesting, however, are the longitudinal developments in this relationship.

One obvious problem with this kind of analysis is determining which political parties are to be labelled as socialist, social-democratic, or communist. It is difficult to find any objective standards for the ideological position of parties. It is possible to rely on judgements by expert informants (Castles and Mair 1984; Laver and Schofield 1991) but we prefer to use the notion of party families (von Beyme 1985: 29–31; Chapter 6 above). Parties which were identified as belonging to

TABLE 8.7. *Union membership and left-wing party preferences, 1955–90*

	1955 (a) (b)	1964 (a) (b)	1973 (a) (b)	1976 (a) (b)	1985 (a) (b)	1989 (a) (b)	1990 (a) (b)
Denmark	– –	– –	49 36	– –	65 39	56 26	57 35
N			362		399	491	396
Belgium	– –	– –	33 19	43 16	42 29	34 27	34 25
N			214	356	223	237	256
Germany	62 28	70 30	67 42	75 33	66 44	57 46	57 40
N	504	391	552	420	381	519	358
Ireland	– –	– –	46 24	28 14	18 14	33 12	27 16
N			306	337	190	319	236
Netherlands	– –	– –	37 27	48 27	68 43	58 42	36 32
N			173	364	266	346	413
Britain	69 41	68 42	52 32	42 20	52 37	57 31	62 43
N	653	468	572	474	418	370	377
France	– –	– –	66 43	78 44	62 42	63 43	72 51
N			490	579	305	327	302
Italy	– –	– –	69 42	55 46	51 52	57 41	52 43
N			406	362	215	252	186
Greece					87 83	38 46	41 43
N					109	272	154

Notes: Entries in column (*a*) are percentages among union members who express a preference for a left party; in column (*b*) are percentages among non-members who express a preference for a left party. Only respondents who are in employment and express a party preference are included. USIA-XX studies 3, 5, and 6 (Germany) and 5 and 6 (Britain) for 1955 have been pooled. In 1973, for coding reasons, the sample base was narrowed to respondents who were head of household. Danish data on union membership for 1976 have been omitted as they appear to be unreliable.

Sources: USIA-XX studies (3, 5, 6, 16); European Community Study (1973); Eurobarometer, Nos. 6, 23, 31*a*, and 34.

the left-wing family were, first, member parties of the Socialist International and, secondly, communist parties which, until 1990, counted as Soviet-recognized (Day and Degenhardt 1984). In addition, several other parties which may be regarded as leftist, such as Pasok in Greece, were included.[5]

Of course, parties of the left are not always and everywhere equally successful, but the overall impression from Table 8.7 is very clear. In all instances, supporters of left-wing parties are much more numerous among union members than among non-union members. Again, this result corroborates the starting point for this analysis. In most countries, it is hard to see a real departure from this point. But here the relatively limited time-span of less than twenty years for most countries may lead to the wrong conclusions. When earlier decades are taken into consideration, which was possible with the British and German data, it appears that, at least in the German case, the overrepresentation of union members among Social Democratic voters has declined since 1976. The British data show no such trend.

The German case suggests, however, that the end-of-ideology hypothesis—and *a fortiori* the decline of linkage to intermediate organizations—may apply to the entire period following the Second World War rather than merely to the twenty years or so before 1990. For some countries, data are available over a longer period of time which may give more insight into long-term processes. Table 8.8 presents data from the national election studies of Germany, Norway, and Sweden, covering two union systems which are quite different from most other systems in Western Europe. For both Norway and Sweden, we do not look just at union membership in general. Unionization in these countries, as in Denmark, is also widespread among white-collar workers, so it makes little sense to draw conclusions from the proportion of union members voting for left-wing parties. Instead, we look at party preference among members of the largest, mainly blue-collar trade-union confederations, the Landesorganisasjon (LO) in Norway and the Landesorganisationen (LO) in Sweden (see also Visser 1989).

The ratio of the two percentages in each entry (for example, 88/49 in Norway 1957) can be regarded as a measure of association between union membership and voting behaviour. A ratio of 1.00 would indicate complete similarity in voting behaviour among union members and non-members; ratios higher than 1.00 point to a positive association between union membership and voting for left-wing parties. In Sweden the ratio of the two percentages has dropped from 2.21 in 1956 to 1.82 in 1991, and in Germany from 1.97 in 1965 to 1.38 in 1990. A decline of this sort, however, is not found in Norway. This can also be seen in Figure 8.1, which summarizes the data from Table 8.7 and Table 8.8 for Britain, Germany, Norway, and Sweden from the 1950s onwards.

In Figure 8.1, the ratio of left-voting union members to left-voting non-members is at all time points higher than one, indicating a persistent ideological linkage between union membership and left-wing voting. It can also be seen that the Swedish and German curves tend to decline. The British and Norwegian curves, however, have held rather steady. These differences can be related to the structure of the

TABLE 8.8. *Union membership and left-wing party preferences: Norway, Sweden, and Germany, 1956–91*

	Norway (a)	(b)	Sweden (a)	(b)	Germany (a)	(b)
1956			84	38		
			(937)			
1957	88	49				
	(1,023)					
1960			91	33		
			(798)			
1964			83	38		
			(1,495)			
1965	81	43			69	35
	(1,436)				(957)	
1968			84	36		
			(1,302)			
1969	80	45			67	44
	(1,359)				(960)	
1970			84	37		
			(678)			
1972					71	50
					(1,719)	
1973	75	39	78	31		
	(1,085)		(1,141)			
1976			72	36	62	38
			(1,408)		(1,713)	
1977	71	43				
	(1,376)					
1979			76	34		
			(1,587)			
1980					61	46
					(1,239)	
1981	67	33				
	(1,226)					
1982			77	39		
			(1,562)			
1983					60	44
					(1,394)	
1985	75	36	72	36		
	(1,636)		(1,628)			
1987					62	40
					(1,702)	
1988			72	38		
			(1,560)			
1989	73	38				
	(1,819)					
1990					55	40
					(1,856)	
1991			60	33		
			(1,530)			

Notes: Entries in column (a) are, for Norway, percentages of members of LO intending to vote for DBA, NKP, or SV; for Sweden, percentages of members of LO intending to vote for SSA or VK; for Germany, percentages of union members intending to vote for SPD. Entries in column (b) are corresponding percentages among non-members. See n. 5 for details of parties. The percentage base for Norway and Germany is all respondents belonging or not belonging to a union who express a vote intention; for Sweden, the percentage base is all members of the various unions who express a vote intention.

Source: national election studies.

Political Linkage

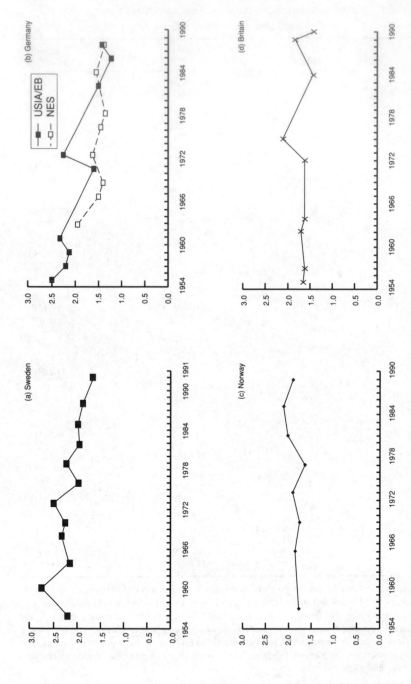

FIGURE 8.1. *Union membership and left-wing party preferences: ratios of union members to other respondents, 1954–90*
Sources: Tables 8.7 and 8.8.

union systems of, on the one hand, Germany and Sweden, and, on the other hand, Britain and Norway. Recall that the German and Swedish systems are horizontally highly integrated; as a result, they may be more vulnerable to a decline of ideological loyalty than the more pluralist union systems of Britain and Norway. In all four countries, union density has at least remained stable since the 1960s (see Table 8.5).

The data on union membership, then, generally fail to confirm the central hypotheses of this chapter. And this becomes even clearer once the time horizon is expanded. The mass society hypotheses are not supported by data comparing union members with other employees. To be sure, the assumption underlying the second hypothesis, which implies that union members are generally more likely to state a preference for a political party, is confirmed. So too is the similar assumption underlying the end of ideology hypothesis. But it is difficult to infer any general development from the data. Only in Sweden and Germany, for which data are available over a longer period than for most of the other countries, may some support be found for the end-of-ideology thesis. But the data for Britain and Norway, which also cover a longer period, provide no support for the hypothesis. For the other countries, it would be light-headed to read any trends into the data presented here.

New Social Movements

The rise of a number of social movements in the Western world in the 1970s and 1980s led to major research efforts; the results were reviewed in the introductory chapter. Participation in the grass-roots activities associated with new social movements are examined elsewhere (Volume iv, Chapter 15). For the argument in this chapter, however, an important question arises from the emergence of new social movements: what consequences does mass participation in these movements have for traditional intermediary organizations and for traditional parties? As new social movements can, on the one hand, be regarded as challenging organizations, then participation could be the result of tensions between participants and the old intermediary system. If this is the case, participation in new social movements would amount to protest *against* the intermediary system. On the other hand, new social movements can be regarded as new intermediary organizations which provide participants with an outlet for immanent grievances, thus contributing to support for the social and political system. This would amount to protest *within* the system (Dalton, Kuechler, and Bürklin 1990: 3–6).

Which of these two explanations is correct can only be determined by comparing adherence to the political system among supporters of new social movements and the population at large. Again, the mass society hypotheses and the end-of-ideology hypothesis serve as guidelines. When new social movements are considered as organizations which challenge the political system, we would expect to find that a dispro-portionately high percentage of their supporters do not have a party preference. Similarly, we would expect to find among them no ideolo-gical leaning towards one of the traditional poles of the party system. This point has been stated very clearly by Dalton, Küchler, and Bürklin (1990: 10–12): 'the ideology of these movements is the major factor distinguishing them from other traditional European leftist movements and their own historical predecessors.' Of course, it might be argued that the ideology of the supporters of new social movements is expressed in particular value orientations rather than party preference. But that kind of argument, although it may be valid, goes beyond the scope of this chapter.

During the first half of the 1980s, the ecology movement, the anti-nuclear movement, the anti-war movement, and the women's move-ment flourished in the number of their supporters as well as in public attention. These movements are widely regarded as prime examples of new social movements. Comparative survey evidence before this surge of support is limited to some questions about the ecology movement and the women's liberation movement in Eurobarometer, No. 8 (1977), which will be disregarded here. The main comparative data sets are Eurobarometer, Nos. 17, 21, 25, and 31*a*, for 1982, 1984, 1986, and 1989 respectively. Data on all four of these time points are available only for Germany, the Netherlands, Britain, France, and Italy. Our analyses are restricted accordingly.

Before going any further, however, a cautionary note about the comparability of this section with the previous two sections. Adher-ence to unions and, more generally, to social and political organizations can be defined by fairly clear membership criteria, for example 'paying union dues'. In the case of new social movements, because they are not formal organizations (although they may in part consist of formal organizations), there is no such clear distinction between members and non-members. Membership of new social movements is of a psychological, rather than formal, nature (Kriesi 1988: 42–6). This implies different ideas about what counts as membership. So instead of membership in the strict sense, a combined membership and support indicator is used to distinguish ardent supporters of the movements from other respondents, based on two questions about support for, and membership of, the ecology movement, the anti-nuclear movement, and the anti-war movement (Fuchs and Rucht 1994; Hofrichter and Schmitt 1991). In the analysis here, the activists and potential activists of new social movements are treated as their 'members'. These are the members, or would-be members, who are either strong or moderate supporters.[6]

New Social Movements and Mass Society

The proportions of activists and potential activists for the three new social movements are depicted in Table 8.9. Clearly, Germany stands out with high and even increasing levels of support throughout the 1980s. There is no indication here that 'in West Germany, N[ew] S[ocial] M[ovements] do not rest on such broad sympathy bases and mobilization potentials as in some other West European countries' (Schmitt-Beck 1992: 369). The Netherlands also show an increase in support for all three movements in 1989. The rise of the environment as a political issue is reflected in higher levels of support for the ecology movement in all five countries in 1989. But four time points over a period of seven years is not a sound basis upon which to infer trends in any direction.

The relationship between support for new social movements and adherence to the party system is shown in Table 8.10.[7] In all countries except Germany, activists or potential activists in new social movements more often tend to state a party preference than other respondents. In Germany, however, activists or potential activists are more likely to state no preference, so Germany again appears to be the deviant case. During the 1980s, however, this relationship changed, so that by 1989 the same pattern is found in Germany as in the other countries. We might interpret this pattern as evidence that German supporters of new social movements are not particularly opposed to political parties (Hofrichter and Schmitt 1991). In a comparative perspective, however, the conclusion must be that German supporters

TABLE 8.9. *Support for new social movements in five West European countries, 1982–9*

	Ecology movement				Anti-nuclear movement				Anti-war movement			
	1982	1984	1986	1989	1982	1984	1986	1989	1982	1984	1986	1989
Germany	33	31	29	41	31	23	26	40	47	43	44	49
N	1,170	849	865	1,079	1,178	829	849	1,075	1,219	868	889	1,088
Netherlands	32	31	32	44	17	16	15	20	23	24	19	24
N	1,200	973	977	936	1,193	992	985	941	1,203	996	984	948
Britain	22	18	20	30	24	10	15	15	26	14	16	17
N	989	984	941	854	1,061	993	1,000	896	1,065	1,006	1,007	905
France	15	11	11	13	8	4	4	7	14	9	10	10
N	1,169	983	964	1,027	1,163	971	947	1,005	1,164	975	961	1,012
Italy	31	21	19	20	17	11	11	11	34	19	19	16
N	1,217	1,003	1,042	983	1,156	984	1,013	966	1,241	1,003	1,042	979

Notes: Entries are percentages of respondents classified as activists or potential activists for each of three new social movements. The percentage base is all respondents in the sample with valid scores on the 'support' indicator. See n. 6 for details of the support indicator.

Sources: Eurobarometer, Nos. 17, 21, 25, and 31a.

TABLE 8.10. *Support for three new social movements and expressed political preference in five West European countries, 1982–9*

	Ecology movement				Anti-nuclear movement				Anti-war movement			
	1982	1984	1986	1989	1982	1984	1986	1989	1982	1984	1986	1989
Germany												
(a)	28	16	19	13	26	19	16	15	26	17	18	13
(b)	21	12	12	18	22	11	13	15	23	11	13	18
Netherlands												
(a)	21	15	13	7	16	12	14	7	16	16	14	5
(b)	19	17	15	7	21	17	14	7	21	17	14	8
Britain												
(a)	16	13	9	5	18	10	11	7	16	9	12	5
(b)	19	16	15	11	18	16	16	19	18	17	16	10
France												
(a)	19	10	11	11	20	8	14	16	18	16	8	11
(b)	28	17	20	24	27	16	20	22	28	16	21	23
Italy												
(a)	40	24	31	19	36	20	31	17	35	23	28	16
(b)	31	33	40	29	39	32	39	28	42	33	40	29

Notes: Entries in row (*a*) are percentage of activists or potential activists of the movement expressing no preference for an existing political party; in row (*b*) the corresponding percentage among other respondents. The percentage base is all respondents with valid scores on the 'support' indicator (see Table 8.9).

Sources: Eurobarometer, Nos. 17, 21, 25, and 31a.

of new social movements are more averse to political parties than 'members' of new social movements in other West European countries. So, coming back to the alternative interpretations of new social movements, it seems most likely that participation in new social movements is participation within, not against, the political system.

New Social Movements and the End of Ideology

In many West European countries, the rise of new social movements has been accompanied by the rise of new political parties. The best example is the German Die Grünen, which has been electorally quite successful since the early 1980s. Similar parties with radical environmental programmes have been established in practically all EC member states. Since the issues of the new social movements are usually associated with left-wing ideology in which government intervention is important, green parties are also generally regarded as left-wing parties (Inglehart 1990*b*). Moreover, in some countries, existing left-wing parties have successfully integrated the environmental issue into their own programme; for example, the Dutch Communists, Pacifist Socialists, and Radicals eventually merged into a new Green Left party.

A final test for the end-of-ideology hypothesis consists in comparing the party preferences of activists and potential activists in the new social movements with the preferences of other respondents. According to the hypothesis, the party preferences of supporters, if they state one at all, would not fit within the dominant left–right ideological framework. Again, it leaves open the possibility that supporters of new social movements are distinguished by their value priorities. But without further assumptions, and strange as it may sound, the hypothesis suggests that supporters of new social movements are *not* more likely to prefer parties of the left or green parties than any other party. The results of the analysis for the three new social movements are presented in Table 8.11.[8]

The table shows that it is not useful to speak of the end of ideology in the context of new social movements. The proportion of supporters of new social movements who vote for parties of the left and green parties is as disproportionately high compared with other respondents as in the case of trade-union members. This overrepresentation of left-wing and green voters is found in all five countries, for all three movements, and at practically all time points. In 1989, when the green parties were well

TABLE 8.11. *Support for new social movements and party preferences in five West European countries, 1982–9*

	1982 (a)	(b)	1984 (a)	(b)	1986 (a)	(b)	1989 (a)	(b)
Ecology movement								
Germany	74	38	76	45	79	48	75	42
N	896		733		741		908	
Netherlands	55	39	60	43	59	48	58	46
N	962		815		839		871	
Britain	62	56	44	43	49	45	55	43
N	811		831		809		772	
France	82	59	71	49	68	51	77	59
N	861		825		777		801	
Italy	58	44	62	49	53	55	66	55
N	739		693		648		720	
Anti-nuclear movement								
Germany	75	37	83	45	86	47	76	43
N	908		723		730		913	
Netherlands	76	37	79	42	86	45	72	46
N	953		828		844		874	
Britain	70	54	69	40	71	42	73	44
N	870		836		850		813	
France	80	62	65	51	79	52	77	60
N	857		818		759		787	
Italy	69	44	77	49	71	53	63	57
N	710		681		628		709	
Anti-war movement								
Germany	65	36	68	43	71	47	72	41
N	924		750		756		918	
Netherlands	74	35	77	39	83	44	74	44
N	962		831		843		880	
Britain	75	51	65	40	70	43	72	44
N	876		848		856		823	
France	77	61	67	51	77	50	76	60
N	856		822		771		789	
Italy	55	44	71	48	62	53	60	57
N	753		693		650		717	

Notes: Entries in column (*a*) are percentages of activists and potential activists in the ecology, anti-nuclear, and anti-war movements expressing a preference for a party of the left or an ecological party; in column (*b*) are the corresponding percentages among other respondents. The percentage base is all respondents expressing a political preference who also have a valid score on the 'support' indicator.

Sources: Eurobarometer, Nos. 17, 21, 25, and 31*a*.

established in all five countries, the overrepresentation is found both for traditional left-wing parties and for green parties (data not shown here). The only exceptions were among supporters of the ecology movements in Britain and France, who were less likely to vote for the traditional left than other respondents, and supporters of the anti-nuclear movement in France. This poses the question of whether the ideology of (potential) activists in new social movements can meaningfully be regarded as a defining characteristic of the movements (Hofrichter and Schmitt 1991).

Taking into account all the reservations about comparing support for new social movements with membership of traditional intermediary organizations, we have not found weaker than average ties between these supporters and the party system. On the contrary, supporters of new social movements are generally more likely to state a party preference than the average respondent. The only exceptions are found in Germany in the early 1980s. There is also no support for the hypothesis that (potential) activists in new social movements are ideologically different from other people. As might be expected, they are usually more likely to prefer left-wing or green parties. In this respect, they are not all that different from union members in preferring left-wing parties. This is not to say that supporters of new social movements do not have a distinct political orientation. What we do find, however, is that their party preferences fit well within the traditional framework.

Conclusions

In this chapter we have investigated evidence about the development of individual linkage to intermediary organizations in Western Europe, a constant source of anxiety among social scientists for at least thirty years. Based on a number of well-documented social changes, largely pessimistic prognoses have been arrived at about the decline of linkage to the traditional intermediary system, resulting in problems for the legitimacy of the political system. To test these general predictions, we posed three empirical hypotheses which were investigated for three forms of linkage: membership or non-membership of social and political organizations in general, trade-union membership, and support for new social movements. The first two hypotheses—the *mass society hypotheses*—predict that membership of traditional social and political organizations is declining, and that membership of intermediary organizations is gradually becoming disconnected from support for the party system. We applied these two hypotheses to all three forms of linkage. The third hypothesis—the *end-of-ideology hypothesis*—predicts that membership of intermediary organizations and political preference are growing apart ideologically. This hypothesis was applied to union membership and to support for new social movements.

Although the rationale underlying the hypotheses is broadly confirmed, there is generally little evidence for trends in either of the predicted directions. Cross-national variation and trendless fluctuations account for most of the differences found. Only data on union membership from 1954 onwards suggest that there may be some truth in the end-of-ideology hypothesis, if longer time spans are considered. This was apparently the case in Germany and Sweden, but this result can also be attributed to the inflexibility of the German and Swedish union systems. Germany also appeared to be exceptional in the case of support for new social movements. Whereas in other countries activists and potential activists in these movements have always been more likely to state a preference for one of the political parties, activism in new social movements in Germany was associated with a lack of political integration of this kind during most of the 1980s. At the same time, the German Greens were one of the first successful radical ecological parties in Western Europe. This seems contradictory.

However, in the case of both trade unions and new social movements, the institutional structure of the intermediary system can provide a clue to this paradox. The adaptation of intermediary institutions to long-term social developments has been much more effective than was foreseen by several social scientists. But examining the adaptability of these institutions requires a different mode of analysis from that adopted in this chapter, which is based on data from upwards of 110,000 survey interviews.

The research presented in this chapter has several limitations. There are too few time points to be confident about trends; the very notion of membership of intermediary organizations makes for definitional problems. Moreover, in some instances, the analyses are elementary, even crude, and thus may not capture the reasoning of the theories which gave rise to this research. At the same time, this kind of empirical evidence often lacks theoretical exposition. However plausible the theoretical grounds for anticipating a decline in political linkage consequent on long-term socio-economic developments, we found no evidence for a general decline in individual linkages to the intermediary system.

NOTES

1. In determining which countries and which surveys should be analysed in this chapter, the general rule was to include countries where data for two or more time points are available and to use surveys which include at least two countries. Hence, Spain and Portugal are not included in the tables. Luxembourg and Northern Ireland are excluded because of small sample sizes. The national election studies of Germany, Sweden, and Norway were included in the section on union membership for their longitudinal perspective.

2. We add some cautionary notes about Table 8.3, which also apply to Tables 8.4, 8.6, and 8.10. These tables are based on whether or not respondents state a party preference. The cross-national and across-time variation in the percentage of respondents indicating no such preference is considerable, as the entries in Table 8.3 show. This variation may have been caused by quite different factors. First, stating no party preference may be a valid indicator for not having a preference; this is the assumption underlying our second hypothesis. Secondly, stating no party preference may be partly caused by cultural factors; for example, a taboo on talking about politics in a face-to-face interview while in reality the respondent does have a preference. Finally, answering the question on party choice may have been influenced by the proximity of (national) elections when campaigning activities and media attention to politics are higher than usual.

   A comparison of the survey data with turnout data (non-voters and non-valid votes) shows that the variation in the percentage of respondents stating no party preference is high in both cases (Volkens, Schnapp, and Lass 1991). Nevertheless, the survey data practically always show higher percentages of respondents with no stated party preference. Many people seem to make up their mind only at election time. The largest discrepancy occurred in Belgium, where almost half the respondents indicated no party preference, while, largely as a result of compulsory voting, the post-war low in valid votes at a general election was 83 per cent in 1968 (see Hill 1974). There is, however, no conclusive evidence that the survey data are generally unreliable.

   Disturbance also occurs when the fieldwork for one or more of the surveys is conducted at a time of (national) elections. In this case, the increase in political communication will induce more people to state a party preference when prompted, a phenomenon familiar to pollsters. Checks were carried out on whether in any country national elections were held less than a month before or after the fieldwork (Volkens, Schnapp, and Lass 1991). For the surveys used in this section, this is the case with the German election of March 1983, the Danish election of September 1987, and the Belgian election of December 1987. Table 9.3 shows that only in the German case might the election have induced more people to express a party preference. The other two cases would rather lead to the opposite conclusion.

3. The equations for each survey are:

$$Y_1 = a_1 + b_1 Y_2 + b_2 Y_3 + b_3 D_1 + b_4 D_2 + e_1$$
$$Y_2 = a_2 + b_5 Y_3 + b_6 X_1 + b_7 X_2 + b_8 X_3 + b_9 D_1 + b_{10} D_2 + e_2$$
$$Y_3 = a_3 + b_{11} X_1 + b_{12} X_2 + b_{13} X_3 + b_{14} D_1 + b_{15} D_2 + e_3$$

in which Y_1 = expressed party preference (yes or no); Y_2 = political communication; Y_3 = organizational involvement; X_1 = age; X_2 = sex; X_3 = education; D_1 = dummy variable for Britain; D_2 = dummy variable for Germany.

The variables were coded as follows: age from '18–30 years' (1) to '61 years and over' (5); sex is 'male' (1), 'female' (2); education (operationalized as school-leaving age) from 'up to 16 years' (1) to '22 years and over, or still studying' (4); political communication from 'never' (zero) to 'at least sometimes' (1); organizational involvement from 'none' (zero) to 'at least one' (1); expressed preference from 'no party preference' (zero) to 'preference for existing party' (1). Two dummy variables for the three countries were added. To assess the difference that country makes in these analyses, the dummy variables distinguishing, respectively, Britain from Germany and Italy, and Germany from Britain and Italy are sufficient; there is no need for a third variable distinguishing Italy from Germany and Britain. The cases were not weighted.

4. There are no reliable figures for union membership in Spain, Portugal, and Greece: cf. Visser 1990; Lane and Ersson 1991; Lane, McKay, and Newton 1991.

5. The resulting parties for each country are: for Denmark, Social Democratic, Socialist People's, Communist; for Sweden, Social Democratic, Communist; for Norway, Labour, Communist, Left Socialist; for Belgium, Socialist (PSB and BSP), Communist (PCB and KPB); for Germany, Social Democratic, Communist; for Ireland, Labour, Communist, coalition of Labour and Fine Gael, Workers', for the Netherlands, Labour, Pacifist Socialist, Radical, Communist (the latter three merged into the Green Left in 1989); for Britain, Labour, Communist, Social Democratic; for France, Socialist, Left Socialist, Communist; for Italy, Socialist, Social Democratic, Communist, Democratic Proletarian; for Greece, Pasok, Communist (exterior and interior).

6. The precise categories of this combined indicator are: *activists* and *potential activists*, would-be members who are simultaneously strong or moderate supporters or did not answer the support question; *sympathizers*, non-members (or no answer on the membership question) who strongly or moderately support the movement; *weak opponents*, non-members (or no answer on the membership question) who moderately oppose the movement (or did not answer the support question); *strong opponents*, non-members (or no answer on the membership question) who strongly oppose the movement. Missing values were assigned to (1) those who failed to answer both questions; (2) members and would-be members who moderately or strongly opposed the movement.

7. The low percentage of respondents stating no party preference in the Netherlands in 1986 may have been influenced by proximate national elections. See n. 2.

8. For the five countries, in addition to the parties mentioned in n. 5, the following parties are considered as carriers of new politics: in Germany, Green, Alternative List; in the Netherlands, Green Left, D66; in Britain, Ecology; in France, Left Radicals (MRG), Ecologist; in Italy, Radicals, Green (Day and Degenhardt 1984).

PART III
The Political System

9

The Dynamics of Trust in Politicians

OLA LISTHAUG

In this chapter we examine trends in support for politicians in Western Europe. We are thinking here of politicians as leaders of parties and office holders in government. The focus is not on particular politicians, such as the prime minister or the president, or the leader of a specific party, but on trust in politicians in general. Within a typology of political support, our concern is neither with specific support nor with its most diffuse aspects, like support for elections or democracy, but rather with trust in the political system at the intermediate level. Because our interest is directed at change over time, preferably for a period spanning decades rather than years, the analysis is confined to four West European countries: Denmark, Norway, Sweden, and the Netherlands. For these countries we have been able to find a series of survey data which are reasonably adequate to answer research questions. Data for these countries are, in our judgement, functionally

Data are from the Danish, Dutch, Norwegian, and Swedish election studies, and were collected by Ole Borre and associates, Cees van der Eijk and associates, Henry Valen and associates, and Sören Holmberg and associates, respectively. The data sets were made available by the Danish Data Archives, the Steinmetz Archive, the Norwegian Social Science Data Services, and the Swedish Social Science Data Service. Neither the original principal investigators nor the data archives bear any responsibility for our use and interpretation of these data. Svein Åge Relling and Thor Thøring contributed excellent research assistance. Kees Aarts kindly helped with analysis of data from the 1989 Dutch Election Study. The preparation of this chapter benefited from co-operation with Arthur Miller while I held a Fulbright fellowship at the Department of Political Science, University of Iowa. The support of research funds from the Norwegian Research Council for Science and the Humanities and the University of Trondheim is appreciated.

equivalent, which allows us to compare the dynamics of trust over time.

The scholarly and non-scholarly literature abounds with allegations that mass publics are losing confidence in politicians and many aspects of the political system. Such concerns are also the basis for this chapter. First, we review some of the arguments for the decline of trust and give an overview of where trust should be placed within the hierarchy of political support. In the following section we discuss the data used, with particular emphasis on the question of dimensionality and the issue of comparability across nations and over time. Next follows a description of the main trends in support from the late 1960s and early 1970s through the 1980s. We then present findings from the analysis of independent variables which explore explanations for patterns. This part focuses on sociological as well as political explanations. In the final section we draw out the main conclusions and put the empirical findings in wider perspective.

Explanations for the decline in trust in politicians are sought in a multitude of political and social factors. Some of the explanations propose a long-term—almost secular—decline, leading to pessimistic prospects for achieving high levels of support in advanced democracies. Competing theories are more inclined to explain variations in trust by factors which are germane to the workings of the regular political process, principally in the functioning of the party system, the alternation of government between 'ins' and 'outs', and how well government is perceived to be solving current problems. Prominent among theories predicting a long-term decline of trust are explanations based on 'new politics' arguments, which see the rising competence of the electorate and changing issue orientations among the mass publics as a threat to political legitimacy and confidence.

The new politics argument can be divided into two parts. The first stresses that rising educational levels, especially at university level, increases the potential for cognitive competence which encourages political action and protest. Furthermore, enhanced political resources and skills among citizens will make them functionally independent of political parties. As parties constitute a principal institution for the integration of individuals into the political system, growing political independence, or anti-party feelings, in the electorate would have negative consequences for levels of political trust. The new politics arguments also contend that the issue agenda of the mass publics of the economically advanced countries is increasingly dominated by questions which are not reflected in current political priorities. This will alienate citizens holding political values which do not agree with the goals of their governments. The question of 'new' versus 'old' values is frequently formulated as the conflict between materialist and post-materialist value priorities (Inglehart 1977, 1990a), with the latter issue preferences more strongly represented among groups which are not part of the political establishment.

The political overtones of the new politics argument are rather radical, breaking with conventional leftist views on some points— most openly in the weight given to non-economic conflicts and the marginal role ascribed to the working-class in advancing radical social change. The 'overload' hypothesis, on the other hand, represents a conservative or free-market position, although coinciding arguments have been raised from the left as well, as noted by both Birch (1984) and Weil (1989). The roots of the argument can be found in the enormous expansion, in all countries, of the role of government. This development can be measured in the growth of the public sector, the emergence of a welfare state, and in the numerous other arrangements by which government behaviour affects the lives of citizens.

One consequence of the growth of government and state is the increase in the public's expectations about government to a level where these cannot be met. This is seen as of paramount importance for political legitimacy for it is in the domain of unfulfilled expectations that political cynicism will thrive. This argument resembles the J-curve theory of revolutions advanced by Davis (1962) which claims that revolutions will occur when objective improvements in living conditions slow down such that expectations of further improvement become frustrated. It is not surprising that the overload argument emerged in the 1970s since this was a period when the economic growth of the post-war period weakened and the expansion of social services came to a halt, or the level of provision was reduced, in a number of countries. It might be appropriate to note that most countries, including the four studied here, have been trying, during the 1980s, to balance government budgets and to contain public sector outlays. The overload thesis is relevant for most of the period covered by our time-series data.

A final explanation for long-term trends in trust is suggested by the idea that there is a negativity bias in political perceptions (Lau 1982, 1985), such that negative information about political objects receives more attention than positive information. If we assume that the mass media are biased towards reporting negative news, and that citizens rely more on the media as a source of political knowledge than before, this would constitute a factor which might contribute to a continuous decline in trust. The effects of media-driven negativity would be even stronger if we add the assumption that political information in the media has become even more negative over recent decades. However, blaming the media for a decline in political trust rests on a set of assumptions which are not easily verified, although important empirical studies have demonstrated that the mass media have a stronger influence on the attitudes and behaviour of citizens than claimed by the earlier wisdom (Iyengar and Kinder 1987; Asp 1986).

Explanations for variations in trust levels should also be investigated over a shorter time span as some models maintain that trust in politicians is determined by factors of a cyclical nature. Such explanations are less pessimistic than the implications of the secular hypotheses, as the same factors which might erode confidence are also likely to rebuild trust in government. Secular forces can be both socio-demographic and political in nature, whereas the cyclical forces are clearly political. A key aspect is the linkage of citizens to government. In a broad sense, this can be denoted by such factors as popular assessments of the way governments are managing the economy, the degree of issue representation, the in–out dynamics of elections, and more general evaluations of incumbents.

The way a government handles the economy might evoke positive as well as negative evaluations from citizens which might enhance or reduce trust. We expect the impact of economic evaluations on more generalized attitudes of trust to be weaker than their impact on the popularity of specific office holders or the governing party. It should take much larger negative economic assessments to weaken the attitudes of citizens towards the political system rather than particular incumbents. How blame and excuses are attributed most likely form an important nexus between economic evaluations and their impact on the political process (McGraw 1990). In contrast to the gloomy predictions of the overload thesis, we expect the impact of economic evaluations to exhibit cycles depending on how the economy performs. In short, the impact of economic factors on trust in government should be put in a broader and more balanced frame than the arguments of the overload thesis would suggest.

The importance of issues or policy distance was advocated in early work by Arthur Miller (1974). He saw political cynicism developing primarily among citizens who prefer policy positions which differ from those implemented by the government. The relevance of policy distance for the growth of cynicism suggests that the outcome of elections is crucial. In a polity where there are conflicting issue positions among the public, popular elections normally determine who will be winners or losers. When the issue positions of the winners are established as public policies, those with opposing issue positions might become politically alienated. This should also hold for the outcome of elections more generally: people identifying with the winning parties should, in general, become more trusting than those on the losing side.

According to Miller and Listhaug (1990), political institutions are important here. The rules governing the formation of parties and the chances of parties achieving representation vary between political systems. If, over a long time, significant groups are excluded from political representation, negative attitudes towards government might accumulate among members of such groups. A political system with some degree of flexibility makes it possible for those groups to form parties and achieve representation, thereby entering the stream of viable politics. This argument points to the potential advantages of multiparty systems as contrasted to two-party systems. However, as discussed by Weil (1989), the level of party fragmentation and, especially, the structure of opposition will be decisive for the level of political support in a multiparty system. Analysing time-series data from the United States, Italy, Spain, Germany, France, and Britain revealed that polarization, fragmentation, oversized or minority governments, and unstable executives, all depress support levels (Weil 1989: 697). These findings point to a critical aspect of democracy: how to give citizens who are excluded from political power a legitimate chance of having their voices heard and give them a reasonable chance of replacing unpopular incumbents.

Demographic variables are not seen as major determinants of trust. Short-term shifts in trust levels among different social groups are most likely explained by other factors, probably by how strongly group members are affected, favourably or unfavourably, by specific public policies or by the outcome of elections. The persistence of substantial differences in trust levels over a long period might mark the accumulation of political inequalities which alienate certain groups from the political mainstream. Abramson's studies (1977, 1983) of the link between race and trust provide major examples of this process.

To explain variations in political trust between blacks and whites in the United States, Abramson considers the social deprivation and the political reality models. The social deprivation mechanism mainly works through levels of individual self-confidence; deprived individuals tend to have low self-confidence, leading to low efficacy and political cynicism. But this explanation does little to explain shifts in trust across time. While blacks remained underprivileged for the period covered by Abramson's data, they were actually more trusting than whites in the late 1950s and most of the 1960s. But an important shift occurred in the summer of 1967 when the racial unrest which hit several cities indicated that American blacks had become less satisfied with their environment; thereafter black youth generally became more cynical than whites. Abramson relates the shift to the halting of progress for blacks: the decade from the mid-1950s to the mid-1960s had been a period of political progress, from the landmark decision in *Brown* v. *Board of Education* in 1954 to the 1965 Voting Rights Act, but, as Lyndon Johnson deferred his Great Society reforms to concentrate on the Vietnam war, fewer gains were achieved after 1965 (Miller 1974; Abramson 1977). Abramson argues that this political reality explanation is the most promising way to explain racial and other subcultural differences.

One implication of Abramson's theory has been tested recently by Howell and Fagan (1988), who compared racial differences in trust among the American electorate with trust differences by race from a survey of New Orleans, a city with a black mayor and administration. The national political environment following the re-election of Ronald Reagan was much more negative for blacks than the environment in New Orleans, where blacks had been in power for eight years. According to the political reality model, blacks should be less trusting than whites in the national setting but more trusting in the local setting. This hypothesis is nicely supported by the data as the correlation between trust and race is 0.22 at the national level and −0.49 in the black-run city (Howell and Fagan 1988: table 1). Moreover, this pattern is explained by shifts among blacks; whites have about the same trust levels locally as in the nation generally (Howell and Fagan 1988: 345).

The generalization of this reasoning to demographic variables besides race would depend on how strongly the political system bears on members of a demographic group, and if, and how, they respond in political terms. American blacks constitute a group which has been strongly affected by government policies. Blacks have also, more than most groups, been extremely homogeneous in their voting behaviour, which might have added to their propensity to be uniformly affected by, and responsive to, the outcomes of elections.

Strong arguments, then, have been raised as to which causes and processes should lead to a decline of political support in advanced industrial societies. The new politics arguments predict that important social groups which are numerically on the rise will become politically alienated. The overload thesis sees the growth of the responsibilities of government and state as a source of distrust, especially in times of slower economic growth and cutbacks in the public sector. The greater impact of the media on political cognition and behaviour is seen as a source of increasing political negativism among citizens.

In contrast to these predictions, we expect representative democracy to have the capacity to respond to the problems confronting the political system. The responsiveness of the system might well be decisive if the sources of political strain actually lead to a decline of political support among citizens. A first test of these predictions is to look at the trends in trust to see if there is a downward movement over time in the four countries examined here. But before doing that, we need to discuss the problems of measurement. How trust should be measured, and how trust levels across nations can be compared, is not straightforward.

Data and Measurement

The data for all four countries are taken from their national election studies. However, although these studies have a common heritage in being descended from the American National Election Studies of the University of Michigan, there is great variation in the political support items, both in the item wording and the continuity of the items over two or more elections. This creates problems for comparisons across nations and over time. We have included items that make some reference to output support as contrasted to input support; the wording of the items is given in the Appendix to this chapter.

The distinction between feelings of personal political competence among citizens and their assessments of how the political system responds is fundamental to much of the research on political support or political alienation: 'people may feel alienated because they feel powerless to influence [make inputs to] government or because they feel the outputs of government are unresponsive to their wishes or needs' (House and Mason 1975: 125). In theory, generalized trust in

TABLE 9.1. *Factor analysis of political trust items in four countries*

	Factor 1	Factor 2	Factor 3
Norway 1973			
Voting	0.55	0.07	−0.05
Relevance	0.51	−0.05	0.06
Complex	0.55	0.07	−0.06
Difference	0.37	0.04	0.12
Leaders trusted	0.03	0.48	0.10
Waste taxes	0.08	0.55	0.05
Leaders smart	−0.01	0.52	−0.03
Only votes	0.41	0.37	0.30
Don't care	0.49	0.50	0.15
Lose touch	0.38	0.39	0.23
Party promises	0.45	0.41	0.20
Extra government power	0.29	0.17	0.15
Voting important	0.11	0.08	0.63
Elections matter	0.00	0.06	0.55
Denmark 1971			
Complex	0.12	0.69	
Knows too little	0.05	0.42	
Don't care	0.60	0.17	
Make right decisions	0.32	−0.09	
No principles	0.36	0.16	
Waste taxes	0.57	0.19	
Sweden 1968			
Voting	0.31	0.62	0.08
Complex	0.10	0.80	0.05
Difference	−0.15	0.24	0.77
Party representation	0.23	−0.05	0.70
Relevance	0.22	0.64	0.14
Lose touch	0.73	0.09	0.00
Voting important	0.52	−0.10	0.49
Party promises	0.62	0.31	0.09
Only votes	0.63	0.37	0.10
Don't care	0.74	0.34	0.06
Netherlands 1981			
Promises more than deliver	0.14	0.61	
Personal interest	0.38	0.56	
MP because of friends	0.31	0.55	
Don't care	0.66	0.28	
Only votes	0.73	0.32	
No say	0.65	0.25	
Voting doesn't matter	0.26	0.17	

TABLE 9.1. *Cont.*

	Factor 1	Factor 2	Factor 3
Party promises	0.24	0.47	
Decisions in secret	0.34	0.44	
Waste taxes	0.27	0.40	

Note: Entries are factor loadings from varimax rotation.

Source: national election surveys.

politicians should belong to the output dimension. To verify this empirically, and to establish a basis for constructing indices of trust in politicians, we performed a factor analysis for the four countries, using data from surveys with the most political support items. The results for one election in each country are presented in Table 9.1. We also performed a factor analysis covering all elections (with the exception of the Netherlands) where support items were included in the survey. With minor exceptions, which we shall return to, these solutions are compatible with the results shown in Table 9.1.

The solution for Norway yields three factors. The items most easily classified as input support or internal efficacy ('voting', 'relevance', 'complex', 'difference') load only on the first factor. The three items tapping trust in politicians ('politicians trusted', 'waste taxes', 'politicians smart') load exclusively on the second factor. The external efficacy items ('only votes', 'don't care', 'lose touch', 'party promises') load on both the first and second factors, while 'voting important' and 'elections matter' load on the third factor. The item 'extra government power' shows the weakest pattern and does not seem to fit the recovered dimensions. This might be because the item does not directly relate to the processes and institutions of electoral democracy (Listhaug 1989: 223–4). Overall, the factor analysis for Norway demonstrates that a person's feeling of political competence or internal efficacy has to be differentiated from the various aspects of output support.

In the Swedish case, three of the four internal efficacy items ('voting', 'relevance', 'complex') load most strongly on the second factor, while the fourth ('difference') loads on the third factor. All external efficacy items with the exception of 'party representation' load on the first factor. The item 'voting important' has about the same loading on factor one and factor three. It is striking that factor three is defined by three items which, in contrast to the other items, are all formulated in a reverse direction such that agreement with the statements yields an efficacious or supportive response. This, in conjunction with the findings from Norway, where the two items similarly directed ('voting important', 'elections matter') define the third factor, suggests a form effect in the survey responses depending on the ordering of the agreement—disagreement statement.

An alternative, but less likely, interpretation is that the reversed items tap a separate dimension of political support. Some of the survey items forming the basis of the political support measures were formulated in the 1950s. Survey researchers of that period were very much aware of problems relating to acquiescence, following controversies about the use of agree–disagree questions for the *F*-scale in *The Authoritarian Personality* (Adorno *et al.* 1950). The 1956 American election study included an experiment to investigate the particular problem of acquiescence in some of the statements in the *F*-scale. Ten items were employed, five in the traditional format where 'agree' tapped the authoritarian position, and five items which were reversed, meaning that 'disagree' designated the authoritarian position. The results of this experiment could not be more revealing: the correlations between the two halves of the items were negative, and the relationship between education and authoritarianism was reversed such that college-educated individuals seemed to be more authoritarian than the poorly educated. The authors (Campbell *et al.* 1960: 513) go on to explain their contradictory findings:

The tendency for poorly educated people to be uncritical of sweeping statements and to be 'suggestible' where inadequate frames of reference are available has long been recognized . . . It is interesting to note in this regard that sophisticated respondents with more differentiated perceptions find it difficult to accept such strong statements whether formulated in an 'authoritarian' direction or reversed. Thus there is a clear tendency to 'disagree' at higher levels of education which approaches that of the 'acquiescence' effect demonstrable among the less educated.

Still, despite these rather dramatic findings, the format of the efficacy items was kept, and more items were added in the same form to the American election studies as well as to other national election studies and surveys of political phenomena.

One reason why the possible acquiescence effect from using efficacy items ordered in the same direction did not lead to more scepticism about the measures may be found in the relationship between the items (or the scales resulting from combining the items) and other variables. Indeed, it seems reasonable to expect efficacy to be driven by education and to be positively related to other political resources and cognitive capabilities. If the 'true' relationship between education and efficacy is positive, the bias introduced in the standard formats might inflate the correlations. While it seems plausible to expect input support to depend on education and related variables, anticipating a similar relationship between output support and education or other demographic variables is not warranted. In the case of output support, it is more likely that the political aspects of demographic factors would be crucial in determining trust.

Only Wright (1975) has reported a study of the acquiescence problem in relation to political support. He administered the four standard efficacy items in their conventional agree—disagree form in the pre-election wave of the 1986 American election survey, but administered a forced choice version for the post-election survey. His main conclusion is that the acquiescence effect is negligible. None the less, the possibility of an acquiescence bias in the data should lead us to be especially careful when examining the social correlates of trust in government as low status groups and individuals with low cognitive capacity may be especially vulnerable to such effects. However, for the investigation of trends over time, which is our main focus here, acquiescence effects will constitute a smaller problem as we can assume that the measurement error introduced by acquiescence will be constant over time. In reporting the static correlations for the background variables, we place more confidence in the Norwegian data since the index in that case is based on forced choice items.

The factor analysis for Denmark is based on only five items. The factor solution gives two factors, with the two internal efficacy items loading on the second factor and the remaining items on the first factor. We have replicated this pattern for the elections from 1973 to 1981. The tendency of 'make right decisions' and 'no principles' to load more weakly on the first factor than either 'don't care' or 'no principles' is confirmed. The solution in 1977 is less clear than for the other years. But, in general, the Danish results confirm the tenability of the distinction between input and output support.

The Dutch election studies include several political trust questions. Unfortunately for the dimensional analysis, only 'voting doesn't matter' taps input support, which virtually precludes input support from defining a separate dimension in the factor analysis. However, as shown in Table 9.1, that item has weak loadings on both dimensions in the Netherlands, hinting at the relevance for the distinction even here. The pattern of the Dutch results points to the possibility of some carry-over effects in creating the factors. The items which load most strongly on the second factor were all asked in one sequence of the questionnaire, and so were the three items loading most strongly on the first factor, suggesting that respondents were predisposed to use the answer to the first item as a cue for the answers to the next items, so artificially inflating the correlations between the items. Even with this caveat in mind, the results from the three Scandinavian countries should be quite reliable as the input and output items were administered in the same sequence in the questionnaires.

In sum, the dimensional analyses provide evidence for the usefulness of the distinction between citizens' assessments of their personal ability to act politically and the propensity to form attitudes towards various aspects of the political system, such as confidence in politicians and parties. It is striking that, in general, assessments of politicians and parties are not very different. This is most probably explained by the fact that politicians in these countries are closely aligned with their parties.

For much of the analysis reported below we rely on a trust index. As not all items are available for the entire time spans, the choice of items for constructing the index is somewhat pragmatic. So the items comprising the trust index for each country vary. Thus the values on the indices should not be compared across nations. All the indices were constructed by adding dichotomous versions of the items. A high value indicates the trusting position on all measures. The items which go into the index are, for Norway, 'politicians trusted', 'waste taxes', 'politicians smart'; for Sweden, 'don't care', 'only votes'; for Denmark, 'make right decisions', 'no principles', 'don't care', 'waste taxes'; for the Netherlands, 'don't care', 'only votes'.[1] Before we proceed with these measures, a look at the trends for the individual items gives a detailed picture of how trust has developed over the period.

Trends in Trust Levels

Has trust in politicians declined or increased over the twenty years or so covered by our time-series data? For reasons already indicated, we

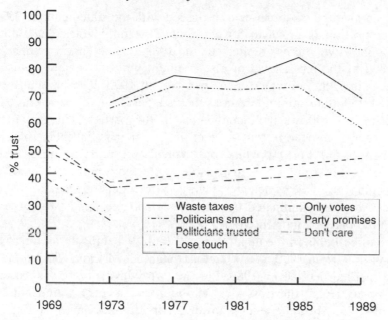

FIGURE 9.1. *Trends in political trust: Norway, 1969–89*

Source: Norwegian election surveys.

cannot make strong statements about differences in trust levels
between nations. Nevertheless, since some of the items have a wording
and form which seem reasonably close, we can comment on cross-
national differences for these items.

The trend for Norway is set out in Figure 9.1. Four of the trust
questions were asked in a Likert format, but were included only in
1969 and 1973. Two of these ('don't care', 'only votes') were replicated
in 1989. The forced choice trust items were introduced in 1973 and
have been kept in the studies since then. For the Likert questions we
follow the convention in the figures, reporting the percentage who
disagree with the statements, or, where the form is reversed, those
who agree. With the forced choice items, we code as trusting those
who say that most politicians, or politicians by and large, can be trusted,
those who say that politicians are smart people who know what they are
doing, and those who say that people in government waste very little or
some taxes. On all items, missing data are excluded from the computation of percentages.

In Norway we observe a dramatic decline in trust from 1969 to 1973.
The trend is parallel for all four items in the lower half of the graph. In

1969, an average of 45 per cent disagreed with the statements; in 1973, this proportion is down to 30 per cent. For 'only votes' and 'don't care'—the two items replicated in 1989—some improvement is recorded as the mean level of disagreement with the statements is 44 per cent in 1989 compared to 36 per cent in 1973. The parallel trend lines for the items are important as they suggest that voters' confidence in politicians follows their confidence in the parties. The two items 'don't care' and 'lose touch' refer to politicians in their roles as members of the Storting, while 'only votes' and 'party promises' refer to parties. This result seems reasonable as elected representatives in the Norwegian political system have very little independence from their parties; they are nominated by the parties and are under strong party discipline on all important votes.

The three items in the upper part of Figure 9.1 indicate an improvement in trust from 1973 to 1977, a fairly stable level from 1977 to 1985, and a marked decline by 1989. For the two items 'politicians trusted' and 'waste taxes', the trust level is about the same or slightly higher than in 1973, while the level is lower for 'politicians smart'. Using the trend for all items covering the period 1973–89, the level of trust in 1989 seems to be only somewhat higher than in 1973. In assessing the trend in Norway, we should note the cyclical pattern; trust declined from 1969 to 1973, then improved again in 1977 and basically remained constant for the next three elections, before falling back in 1989.

The trend for trust in politicians in the Swedish case, shown in Figure 9.2, is easy to summarize as both items demonstrate a fairly strong downward trend for the period. In 1968, 60 per cent of Swedish citizens disagreed with the statement that parties are only interested in people's votes; by 1988 only 32 per cent disagreed, a decline of almost 50 per cent. Similarly, but slightly weaker, disagreement with the 'don't care' item declined from 51 per cent in 1968 to 32 per cent in 1988. While no cycle is recorded for the period, we should note that since 1979 trust levels in Sweden have declined only marginally. Preliminary data from the 1991 election (not shown here) indicate an additional marginal decline in trust.[2]

The pattern for Denmark, Figure 9.3, is close to what we found for Norway. All items indicate a decline of trust from 1971 to 1973, with a further decline in 1975. After that, an improvement is observed. With the exception of 'make right decisions', support levels reach at least their 1971 values. Not much would be changed if we were to look at more recent data: Goul Andersen (1992) reports a further improvement

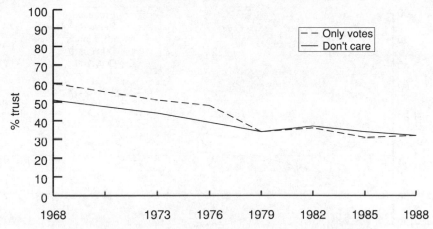

FIGURE 9.2. *Trends in political trust: Sweden, 1968–88*
Source: Swedish election surveys.

in trust on 'waste taxes' from 1979 to the late 1980s, with a small decline in 1991, while 'don't care' shows a decline in trust after 1984.

In the Dutch case, Figure 9.4, the two items 'don't care' and 'only votes' are covered in all elections from 1971 to 1989. The remaining items start in 1977. As measured by 'don't care' and 'only votes', trust levels in the Netherlands were at a low in 1971–2 with 42 per cent and 35 per cent, respectively, disagreeing with the two statements. In 1977

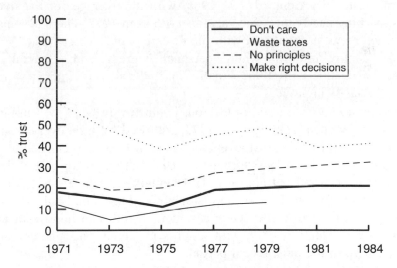

FIGURE 9.3. *Trends in political trust: Denmark, 1971–84*
Source: Danish election surveys.

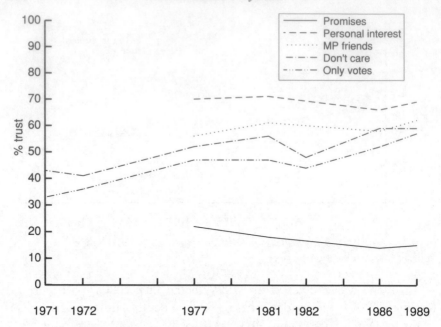

FIGURE 9.4. *Trends in political trust: Netherlands, 1971–89*
Source: Dutch election surveys.

an improvement of about 10 percentage points is recorded as now an
average of 50 per cent disagree with the two statements. We note a
pattern of stability from 1977 to 1986, with the average for the five
items reaching nearly the same value in 1986 as in 1977. There is some
difference between the items, with 'don't care', 'only votes', and 'MP
friends' edging upwards while 'personal interest' and, especially,
'promises' decline until 1986. Finally, in 1989, all trust indicators in
the Netherlands improve.

There is no uniform trend in the four countries. In Norway, trust in
politicians declined from 1969 to 1973, followed by a recovery from
1973 to 1985, before the trust levels fell again in 1989. Sweden shows a
long-term decline from 1968 through to 1988, but the major part of the
fall in trust occurred before 1979. In Denmark trust levels fell from
1971 to 1973, followed by an improvement in the second half of the
1970s and early 1980s. The Dutch case demonstrates an improvement
in trust from 1971–2 to 1977, with stability in the next decade, and an
improvement in the most recent period.

The variations in these trends question the usefulness of overarching
explanatory models, especially those which predict a ubiquitous decline

in trust. Before we reject the hypothesis of decline, however, a few caveats should be borne in mind. First, and most important, our time-series data start at a point when much of the volatility which character-ized electoral politics in the late 1960s and, especially, the 1970s, had already begun. Thus the possibility that trust had already deteriorated by the beginning of the time series presented here should be considered. The longer time series from the United States suggests that trust levels there declined at a comparable point in time, and that the recovery observed in the early 1980s did not bring trust back to earlier levels (Miller and Borelli 1987). Secondly, as most of the indicators of trust were presented to respondents in an agree—disagree format, which is susceptible to measurement error, the steadily increasing level of educa-tion among the citizenry could have led to an increase of trust over time as the acquiescence effect is weakened. This interpretation questions the assumption of constant measurement error in the indicators and makes the interpretation of trends in the data even more problematic.

To conclude this section, we comment on the differences in trust levels between the four countries. However, as already noted, we have to be extremely cautious in making cross-national judgements about trust differentials as identical questions were not asked in the four countries. An exception can be made for two items that are formulated in identical, or near-identical, wording. These items, 'don't care' and 'only votes' (but 'only votes' was not asked in Denmark), allow us to compare trust levels. Looking at the percentage of the mass public which disagrees with these statements, we find that at the start of the period Swedish people were the most trusting, followed by the Norwe-gians, the Dutch, and the Danes. At the end of the period, we find that the Dutch are the most trusting, followed by the Norwegians, the Swedes, and the Danes. While the drop in trust levels among the Swedish public is dramatic, they have not quite reached the distrust levels we find in Denmark. Political confidence in the Danish case has recovered somewhat from the widespread dissatisfactions of the first part of the 1970s, but not enough for Denmark to climb in the ranking of the four countries.

Social and Political Explanations

Can the trends and variations in trust levels be explained by social and political factors? Earlier we outlined some arguments about the possible causes of variations in trust levels, and in this section we present findings from empirical analyses which shed some light on these explanations. We have relied primarily on independent variables which are available for all four countries. This somewhat limits the analyses. With the data at hand we can investigate two major arguments about the development of distrust: that distrust tends to accumulate in specific social groups; that shifts in the political and ideological leanings of incumbent governments can influence support levels. The analysis is based on the mean for the trust index among relevant social and political subgroups in each country. To summarize the statistical information we report the eta coefficients in Table 9.2; the size of the coefficient gives an impression of the strength of the relationships.

The demographic analysis for Norway is rather more reliable than for the other countries as we do not have to struggle with the methodological problems created by the agree–disagree scales. The demographic correlates of trust in Norway are not very impressive. In general, young people are more trusting than older people. The variation of trust by gender and education is weak and inconsistent. In 1973, those at the

TABLE 9.2. *Trust by socio-demographic groups in four countries*

Norway	1973	1977	1981	1985	1989		
Age	0.09	0.08	0.09	0.04	0.10		
Sex	0.02	0.04	0.01	0.07	0.05		
Education	0.08	0.02	0.04	0.09	0.08		
Sweden	1968	1973	1976	1979	1982	1985	1988
Age	0.12	0.06	0.10	0.12	0.08	0.09	0.10
Sex	0.12	0.15	0.16	0.10	0.08	0.10	0.03
Education	0.12	0.06	0.05	0.05	0.07	0.06	0.18
Denmark	1971	1973	1975	1977	1979		
Age	0.08	0.07	0.06	0.10	0.15		
Sex	0.04	0.13	0.07	0.04	0.06		
Education	0.22	0.19	0.19	0.15	0.19		
Netherlands	1971	1972	1977	1981	1982	1986	1989
Age	0.04	0.07	0.08	0.10	0.14	0.18	0.17
Sex	0.07	0.12	0.09	0.08	0.05	0.04	0.01
Education	0.20	0.20	0.25	0.27	0.31	0.24	0.23

Note: Entries are eta coefficients.

Source: national election surveys.

highest educational level are less trusting than the less educated, but the difference is narrow (data not shown here). This is the only piece of evidence which supports the 'new politics' contention that distrust develops among the highly educated. However, a more detailed analysis investigating the possibility that distrust develops among young people with high education (not shown here) is not supported in the Norwegian case. Thus the weak, although consistent, social correlates of trust in Norway demonstrate that shifts in trust levels are not strongly related to the integration or alienation of social groups. A similar observation is also broadly valid for Sweden, Denmark, and the Netherlands. In general, the correlations in those three countries are somewhat stronger, possibly influenced by measurement error. The conclusion that shifts in trust levels are largely unrelated to demographic variables has only one noticeable exception: the improvement in trust in the Netherlands is weakest among those aged 50 and older.

The outcomes of elections shift the fortunes of partisan groups. We contend that the evolution of political distances—by party, ideology, and policy positions—which are decided in voting contests will affect political trust levels among citizens. In general, we expect voters who are politically close to the incumbent party to be more trusting than those aligned with the losing side. A change of government at an election provides the potential for an increase in trust levels among supporters of the winning parties. At the same time, a change of government holds the potential to alienate losers. This mechanism would predict some equilibrium in political support levels as the gains among the winners are offset by the decline among the losers. The equilibrium is not guaranteed, however, as the realization of the incumbents' advantage may depend on how effectively the winning party utilizes government power to implement its programme promises.

To further complicate the issue, there is a methodological problem about when to measure incumbency shift. Most survey data are collected in post-election surveys: should those who vote for a party which loses incumbency be classified as 'ins' or 'outs'? There is no clear-cut answer to this question. The argument for counting them as 'ins' would be that their attitudes have been nurtured by their party having been in power for some time, while those voting for the opposition parties probably have seen fewer of their political positions represented in government policies. On the other hand, voters who see their party winning an election might anticipate that government will become more receptive to their policy positions, while the supporters of losing incumbents might develop more cynical attitudes in the anticipation that the government will now turn against their interests. In examining the data, we are open to both interpretations.[3]

In assessing the effects of political distance on trust we rely on two variables, vote and ideological self-placement. Unfortunately, ideological self-placement is not available for Denmark. A further problem is that in some electoral periods, two or more governments have been based on different party coalitions. Norway neatly illustrates this problem. In the four-year term preceding the 1973 election, three politically distinct cabinets were in power: in 1969–71 a majority coalition of the Liberals, the Centre Party, the Christians, and the Conservatives; in 1971–2, a minority Labour government; and in 1972–3, a minority government of the three centrist parties led by the Christian People's Party. After the 1973 election, Labour formed a minority government until 1981, followed by a minority Conservative government which was converted to a majority government of the three major bourgeois parties in 1983. At the 1985 election this became a minority government and had to give way to a minority Labour government in 1986. After the 1989 election, the three bourgeois parties continued their minority regime in a Conservative-led government.

In Table 9.3, we show the mean values for the trust index among party supporters in Norway. The parties are displayed as running from the far left to the far right. In 1973, Conservative voters and, especially, supporters of the newly emerged right-wing Progressive Party were the most cynical in Norway. That trust levels were about equally as high among voters for the centrist parties and Labour probably reflect that these parties had been in government during the most recent period. As Labour took control of government in 1973, and stayed in power for eight years, we expect political trust levels among Labour voters to increase. And this is what we see in the data. However, trust recovers among voters for the non-socialist parties as well. In 1981, following the defeat of Labour, trust levels are fairly stable among the supporters of Labour and the Socialist Left Party, while among supporters of non-socialist parties, trust is rising, reaching a peak in 1985. But trust levels among socialist voters are somewhat lower. Indeed, a comparison of the trust ratings for the major government parties in 1977 and 1985 is instructive. In 1977, Labour was returned to power in a very close election. In 1985, the Conservative-led coalition was barely elected to continue in government, and had become dependent on a fourth party—

TABLE 9.3. *Trust by vote and left–right self-placement: Norway, 1973–89*

	1973	1977	1981	1985	1989
Party vote					
Socialist Left	5.1	5.4	5.3	5.3	5.3
Labour	5.3	5.6	5.6	5.4	5.3
Liberals	5.2	5.5	5.2	5.4	5.3
New People's	5.3	5.4	—	—	—
Christian People's	5.2	5.4	5.5	5.7	5.2
Centre	5.2	5.3	5.5	5.5	5.2
Conservatives	4.9	5.1	5.3	5.6	5.0
Progressive	4.3	4.8	4.9	5.3	4.6
Left–right self-placement					
1 left	4.6	4.9	5.0	5.2	4.9
2	5.2	5.4	5.3	5.4	5.4
3	5.3	5.5	5.4	5.2	5.4
4	5.1	5.7	5.5	5.4	5.5
5	5.1	5.4	5.4	5.4	5.1
6	4.9	5.4	5.4	5.4	5.1
7	4.6	5.3	5.3	5.6	4.9
8		5.1	5.2	5.6	5.1
9		4.9	4.8	5.5	4.9
10 right				5.5	4.5

Notes: Entries are mean values for the trust index. The index ranges from 3 to 6. High value is trusting. Where no data are shown, either the party did not stand for election or the party had fewer than ten respondents in the sample. Left–right self-placement was measured on a seven-point scale in 1972, a nine-point scale in 1977 and 1981, and a ten-point scale in 1985 and 1989.

Source: Norwegian election surveys.

the Progressives—in the Storting. In 1977, the mean trust rating among Conservative voters was lower than that among Labour voters, 5.1 as against 5.6. In 1985 the pattern was reversed: now Conservative voters had a 5.6 trust rating as compared to 5.4 for Labour voters. In other words, the failure to form a stable government leads to lower trust.

On the other hand, incumbency shifts probably played a role in the decline of trust after 1985. Trust levels for Labour and the Socialist Left stayed about constant from 1985 to 1989 but a sharp drop is recorded for the coalition parties, reflecting the failure of these parties to form an effective government, despite a non-socialist majority in the Storting. The pattern for the three parties which stayed out of the cabinet in this period, the Socialist Left, the Liberals, and the Progressive Party is quite interesting. In general, trust levels among voters for the Socialist

Left follow those among Labour supporters, reflecting the position of the Socialist Left as a backing party for Labour governments. The pattern for the Liberals also follows that of the socialist parties, reflecting the shift of the Liberal Party from its traditional position in the non-socialist bloc to a more socialist-leaning position in recent elections. Finally, voters for the Progressive Party are consistently less trusting (except in 1985, when they tied with the Socialist Left) although there is a clear movement to a more trusting position among Progressive voters; in 1985 they are much less distinctively cynical than in 1973. Following the breakdown of the non-socialist coalition government in 1989, however, trust levels decline sharply. Progressive voters, then, followed the trend among the non-socialist bloc even though the party played a role in returning Labour to power.

The shift over time of trust levels by left–right self-placement, shown in the lower half of Table 9.3, further substantiates the role of incumbency for the dynamics of political trust. Governments do not usually accommodate the most extreme ideological positions, but steer a course on the centre-left or centre-right. Thus we expect some alienation effects among citizens who locate themselves on the political fringes. And this is what we generally see. In 1973 and 1977 trust was highest on the centre-left. In 1985 the pattern was reversed, with trust levels generally higher on the right side of the ideological spectrum. Indeed, the only election when the identifiers furthest to the right are not noticeably less trusting than those with more centrist leanings was in 1985. In 1989 trust levels were maintained among the centre-left while those on the right showed quite considerable losses in trust. These empirical patterns add to the findings for voting, supporting the notion that political confidence is partly driven by the political distance between government and the governed.

Sweden was long considered the pre-eminent example of political stability in Western Europe. Party structure, voter alignments, and the political basis of government have shown a higher continuity in the post-war period than in almost any multiparty system. The strong continuity in Swedish politics has primarily been determined by the strength of the Social Democratic Party. Except for the period 1976–82, and again after the upheavals of the 1991 election, the Social Democrats have held power in Swedish society for the entire post-war period. This makes a strong case for expecting supporters of the non-socialist parties to become cynical about politics. On the other hand, did the non-socialist victories in 1976 and 1979 ease the cynicism of bourgeois voters?

Looking at the data in Table 9.4, we clearly find no increase in trust on the non-socialist side in Sweden in 1979. But we do observe a slightly weaker decline than among Social Democrats. Following the return of the Social Democrats to power in 1982, we find a stability of trust among Social Democrat voters, while trust declines among the non-socialists. In 1988, the connection with party is weakened, with socialist voters only marginally more trusting than voters for the bourgeois parties.

The pattern of trust by left–right self-placement adds to these findings. The decline in trust after 1982 has been rather stronger on the right than on the left, showing some indication of an incumbency effect in the Swedish case. The 1976–82 non-socialist government was fragile, with the original three-party cabinet collapsing after two years.

TABLE 9.4. *Trust by vote and left–right self-placement: Sweden, 1968–88*

	1968	1973	1976	1979	1982	1985	1988
Party vote							
Communist	1.3	0.8	0.8	0.8	0.9	0.8	0.8
Social Democrats	1.2	1.1	1.0	0.7	0.8	0.8	0.7
Centre	1.0	0.8	0.7	0.6	0.7	0.5	0.7
Liberal	1.1	0.9	0.9	0.8	0.7	0.6	0.7
Conservative	1.1	0.9	0.8	0.8	0.7	0.6	0.6
Christian	0.7	0.7	0.5	(0.4)	0.6	—	0.5
Environmentalists	—	—	—	—	—	0.8	0.6
Left–right self-placement							
0 left	1.1	0.9	0.9	0.5	0.7	0.6	0.7
1	1.4	1.0	1.1	0.8	0.8	0.8	0.8
2	1.3	1.1	1.1	0.8	0.9	0.9	1.0
3	1.3	1.1	1.1	0.8	0.9	0.9	0.8
4	1.3	1.0	1.0	0.7	0.8	0.8	0.9
5	1.0	0.9	0.8	0.5	0.6	0.5	0.5
6	1.1	1.0	0.9	0.7	0.7	0.7	0.7
7	1.1	0.9	0.9	0.7	0.8	0.5	0.5
8	1.0	0.9	0.8	0.7	0.7	0.6	0.6
9	1.0	0.9	0.7	1.0	0.8	0.7	0.6
10 right	1.0	0.9	0.8	0.6	0.6	0.4	0.6

Notes: See notes to Table 9.3. Observations in parentheses are based on 10 to 19 people. The trust index ranges from 0 to 2.

Source: Swedish election surveys.

The Liberals continued in a minority government on their own in the third year of the electoral term. The second three-party government, following the narrow non-socialist victory in 1979, was replaced by a minority government of the Centre Party and the Liberal Party in 1981. In other words, the strong internal contradictions of the non-socialist alternative in Sweden could account for the failure of trust levels to increase among non-socialist voters. This stands in contrast to what was achieved by the non-socialist government in Norway 1981–5, which enjoyed relative success in its first years. But the breakdown came here too, accompanied by a strong decline of political trust among supporters of the non-socialist parties in 1989.

Denmark in the 1970s was known for high voter volatility, frequent elections, and weak governments. Minority governments may be better than their reputation (see Strom 1990b). The Social Democrat governments of 1971–3 and 1975–82 had little opportunity to implement strong policy programmes. The reliance of Danish governments in this period—as before and after—on a distinctive set of compromises with parties not in the cabinet, and across the left–right divide, lead us to predict that incumbency effects on political trust will be weak or non-existent in the Danish case. This is largely supported by the data in Table 9.5. The recovery of trust after 1975 is not markedly stronger among supporters of the incumbent parties, but seems to be across the

TABLE 9.5. *Trust by vote: Denmark, 1971–9*

	1971	1973	1975	1977	1979
Party vote					
Communist	—	(7.3)	6.7	8.4	8.5
Left Socialist	—	—	(8.7)	(11.2)	10.2
Socialist People's	8.1	8.5	7.9	9.8	9.9
Social Democrats	9.6	8.9	8.3	10.2	10.2
Radical Liberals	10.5	9.2	9.5	10.1	10.2
Centre Democrats	—	8.3	—	10.3	9.8
Liberal	10.2	9.6	9.7	9.8	10.2
Conservative	10.9	8.7	9.3	10.4	9.7
Progressive	—	7.6	7.4	7.9	8.2
Justice	(8.8)	(7.9)	9.1	10.0	8.4
Christian People's	(9.8)	(7.9)	8.6	9.9	10.9

Notes: See notes to Tables 9.3 and 9.4. The trust index ranges from 4 to 20. Left–right self-placement is not available for Denmark.

Source: Danish election surveys.

board, although the improvement is slightly stronger among Social Democratic voters. Note also that we do not find partisan groups which are becoming distinctively more cynical.

The Netherlands is similar to Denmark in the high number of parties contesting elections and a complex, often extremely difficult, process of government formation. Dutch governments have frequently been coalitions of two to five parties, sometimes oversized and cutting across ideological divides. In the period 1967–72, governments were formed by the major religious parties and the Liberals. From 1973 to 1977, the Labour Party dominated a coalition government in partnership with the Catholic People's Party, the Anti-Revolutionary Party, the Radicals, and Democrats '66. After 1977, the main government alternative has been a coalition of the Christian Democratic Appeal and the Liberals. The exception is the short-lived coalition of the Christian Democrats, Labour, and D'66 in 1981–2.

As expected, looking at Table 9.6, we find that the period of Labour dominance, 1973–7, was accompanied by a marked increase in trust among the party's supporters. Changes in trust levels among supporters of the separate religious parties cannot be examined since they merged in the Christian Democratic Appeal in 1977. Trust levels among Christian Democrats in 1977 were only marginally higher than for supporters of the three largest religious parties (Catholic People's, Anti-Revolutionary, and Christian Historical Union) in 1972. Liberal voters also become more trusting, but less so than Labour supporters. During the Christian Democrat–Liberal coalition of 1977–81, trust grew weakly among their followers while trust levels among Labour voters declined. The oversized coalition in 1981–2 did not, apparently, benefit its constituency as trust declined among both Labour and Christian Democrat voters. Trust levels among D'66 supporters, on the other hand, increased from 3.0 to 3.3.

During the Christian Democrat–Liberal coalition of 1982–6, trust increased somewhat more among their voters than among Labour supporters. These shifts are by no means dramatic, but they demonstrate that the relationship between trust and party was reversed between 1977 and 1986. The data for 1989 are more mixed, with a less clear incumbency effect. This pattern is further substantiated when we look at shifts across left–right self-placement. In 1977, following a period of centre-left governments, trust levels were highest among those locating themselves on the centre-left. In 1986, after a period of centre-right governments, trust levels were relatively highest on the

TABLE 9.6. *Trust by vote and left–right self-placement:*
Netherlands, 1971–89

	1971	1972	1977	1981	1982	1986	1989
Party vote							
Labour	2.7	2.7	3.2	3.0	2.8	2.9	3.0
Pacifist Socialists	2.9	(2.5)	—	3.2	2.9	(3.1)	—
Communists	2.5	2.4	(2.7)	2.8	(2.5)	—	—
Democrats '66	2.9	2.7	3.1	3.0	3.3	3.2	3.3
Green Left	—	—	—	—	—	—	3.3
Radicals	2.7	3.1	3.3	3.4	(3.5)	(2.9)	—
Democratic Socialists '70	2.8	3.0	—	—	—	—	—
Catholic People's	2.8	2.8	—	—	—	—	—
Reformed Political Union	(2.8)	(3.0)	(2.9)	(3.3)	—	(3.6)	3.5
Political Reformed	2.6	2.7	—	3.1	2.8	(3.5)	3.1
Liberals	2.9	2.9	3.1	3.2	3.1	3.4	3.3
Boerenpartij	(2.3)	(2.4)	—	—	—	—	—
Anti-Revolutionary	2.9	3.1	—	—	—	—	—
Christian Historical Union	2.8	2.8	—	—	—	—	—
Reformed Political Federation	—	—	—	—	—	—	(3.5)
Christian Democrats	—	—	2.9	3.2	3.0	3.2	3.3
Left–right self-placement							
1 left			2.9	2.8	2.6	2.6	2.8
2			3.1	3.2	3.0	3.0	3.2
3			3.3	3.2	2.9	3.1	3.2
4			3.2	3.1	3.0	3.0	3.3
5			3.0	2.9	2.8	3.1	3.1
6			3.0	3.1	3.0	3.1	3.3
7			3.0	3.1	3.1	3.4	3.3
8			3.0	3.1	3.1	3.3	3.2
9			2.9	3.1	2.9	3.4	3.5
10 right			3.0	3.1	3.0	3.1	3.1

Notes: See notes to Tables 9.3 and 9.4. The trust index ranges from 2 to 4.

Source: Dutch election surveys.

centre-right. As for vote, the trust pattern by left–right self-placement becomes less distinct in 1989. In all, then, these data show that the relationship between trust and left–right self-placement shifts according to which party bloc is incumbent.

Some of our findings have pointed to a possible link between the performance of parties in government and the dynamics of political trust among the mass public. The analysis by vote and by left–right self-placement, however, provides only an indirect empirical test of this relationship. Unfortunately, the surveys do not contain many data that can be used to address these questions more directly. A notable exception is the 1985 Swedish survey which includes two questions asking respondents to evaluate the performance, in government, of the bourgeois parties in 1976 82 and the Social Democrats in 1982 5. In addition, respondents were asked to assess the hypothetical performance of the two party blocs if they came to power after the 1985 election. Performance was evaluated using an eleven-point scale running from −5 to +5 with 0 as a neutral evaluation. The tables are not shown here but the results are readily summarized.

Not unexpectedly, the Social Democrat government of 1982–5 receives the higher score, with an average of 1.21 on the scale compared to −0.75 for the bourgeois parties. Moreover, the Social Democrat advantage holds up even in evaluations of future performance; the respective means on the scale are 1.19 and 0.10. Furthermore, examining evaluations of government performance by vote, we find that supporters of the three bourgeois parties are consistently more negative in their assessment of the bourgeois parties' ability to govern than are Social Democrat and Communist voters in their assessment of a Social Democrat government. The average evaluation of the past performance of the non-socialist governments is 1.09 among bourgeois voters compared to 2.89 for the Social Democrat government by socialist voters. Assessments of the hypothetical performance of their 'own' parties are similar: the average is 2.34 for bourgeois voters and 3.03 for socialist voters. Bourgeois voters are also less negative towards Social Democrat governments than are socialist supporters in their assessments of bourgeois governments.

It remains to be demonstrated, however, that there is an empirical relationship between evaluation and trust. This is done in Table 9.7, where we report the average value of the trust index by performance evaluation among supporters of the two political blocs. For past evaluations, we find that trust increases as performance evaluations become more positive. The pattern for bourgeois performance is slightly irregular, showing that those with the most positive evaluation have the lowest level of trust. This aberration can be taken lightly as the number of cases in this group is very small. The relationship for the Social Democrats is quite linear, but reaching a ceiling effect at +3. The relationship between trust and future evaluations is strong and monotonic for both groups. In sum, we find that satisfaction with the performance of one's own party, past or future, builds political trust.

The Political System

Table 9.7. *Trust and evaluation of party performance in government by supporters of major political blocs in Sweden, 1985*

	Negative	Neutral	Positive				
	−5 to −1	0	+1	+2	+3	+4	+5
Past evaluations by supporters of							
Bourgeois parties 1976–82	0.52	0.48	0.61	0.56	0.57	0.72	0.36
N	102	116	49	81	94	47	22
Social Democrats 1982–5	—	0.50	0.59	0.74	0.84	0.85	0.88
N	5	34	54	87	139	95	88
Future evaluations by supporters of							
Bourgeois parties	0.32	0.39	0.44	0.57	0.59	0.62	0.70
N	25	36	71	99	182	73	33
Social Democrats	—	0.58	0.69	0.81	0.81	0.84	0.84
N	6	33	48	72	127	110	99

Notes: Entries are mean values for the trust index (range 0–2). High value is trusting. The number of cases is shown in parentheses. Respondents were asked (in the pre-election survey) to assess, on an eleven-point scale from −5 to +5, the performance of parties in government. The evaluation of bourgeois parties includes only voters for the Centre Party, the Liberal Party, and the Conservative Party. Evaluation of the Social Democrat Party includes voters for the Communist Party.

Source: Swedish Election Study (1985).

That non-socialist voters in Sweden in 1985 show relatively weak belief in the ability of the bourgeois parties to govern suggests why the outcome of the 1976 and 1979 elections was unable to stem the long-term decline of trust in Sweden.

Our discussion of performance assessments has not referred to particular policy domains. The economy constitutes a domain where the publics' assessments are assumed to be significant for voting behaviour, the evaluation of parties and leaders, and, we anticipate, for trust in government. The basic hypothesis is that negative assessments of the economy weaken trust while positive evaluations lead to a more trusting attitude. Time-series data are available for Norway and Sweden, but not for Denmark and the Netherlands. However, the Norwegian and Swedish data have indicators that cover both the personal and sociotropic aspects of economic evaluations,[4] so we can observe whether personal or collective judgements have the greatest impact on trust.

The findings for Norway are presented in Table 9.8. The table reports a percentage difference index for trust, calculated as the percentage with trusting responses on all indicators minus the percentage with no trusting responses.[5] The results for Norway demonstrate that those who think that their future personal finances will become worse or who fear unemployment are, invariably, the least trusting. Similarly, those who say that the Norwegian economy has become worse over the previous year have the lowest trust levels in 1985 and 1989. The differences are not big but they are unmistakably consistent across time.

An interesting aspect of the observed patterns is the asymmetry in the

TABLE 9.8. *Trust and evaluations of economic performance:*
Norway, 1973–89

	1973	1977	1981	1985	1989
Future personal finances					
Better	46	59	47	61	39
	(15)	(24)	(24)	(30)	(31)
Same	40	58	57	62	41
	(64)	(54)	(54)	(55)	(47)
Worse	9	38	43	43	20
	(22)	(22)	(22)	(15)	(22)
N	939	1,411	1,394	1,795	1,909
Future personal unemployment					
No fear of unemployment	37	55	52	61	38
	(83)	(73)	(70)	(72)	(52)
Some chance of unemployment	39	58	55	58	41
	(10)	(15)	(16)	(13)	(16)
Fears unemployment	−2	46	48	51	33
	(7)	(12)	(14)	(15)	(32)
N	978	1,426	1,350	1,660	1,769
Past national economy					
Better	—	—	—	60	40
				(56)	(31)
Same	—	—	—	61	38
				(34)	(24)
Worse	—	—	—	45	30
				(11)	(45)
N	—	—	—	1,720	1,877

Note: Entries are values on the percentage trust index which is calculated as the difference between the percentage with trusting answers to all trust questions minus the percentage with no trusting answer. The figure in parentheses is the proportion giving a particular category of assessments. Missing data have been excluded.

Source: Norwegian election surveys.

impact of economic evaluations. Individuals with positive evaluations are not more trusting than those who think that the economic situation will remain the same. If economic evaluations drive the trust trend, it would be enough to examine the increase or reduction in the proportion with negative assessments. This proportion is shown in parentheses in the table. On the item about future personal finances, the group with negative expectations is of almost identical size across time, with 22 per cent expecting their personal situation to become worse in all years except 1985, when 15 per cent are pessimistic about the future. The proportion with a negative view on employment increased marginally from 1973 to 1977, but stayed about constant through 1985. From 1985 to 1989 the proportion fearing unemployment doubled, from 15 to 32 per cent. The largest change in trust levels in Norway occurred in the improvement between 1973 and 1977 and the decline between 1985 and 1989. It is only for the latter year that one of the personal indicators— fear of unemployment—contributed to the decline in trust. But even then, the decline in trust was largely independent of unemployment evaluations. In fact, the steepest decline in trust was among those who reported no fear of becoming unemployed! Increased pessimism about the national economy is also observed in 1989 when negative assessments jumped from 11 to 45 per cent. But again the decline in trust was at least equally strong among optimists, pessimists, and neutrals.

The Swedish results, shown in Table 9.9, look much like those for Norway in that economic evaluations—personal and collective— showed a consistent impact on trust. But Sweden showed no consistent asymmetry of negative and positive effects. Note also that the trend in economic evaluations cannot contribute much to explaining shifts in trust levels as the latter have been on an almost secular downward path (see Figure 9.2) while economic assessments have shifted back and forth and, if anything, showed an improvement from the 1970s to the end of the 1980s.

Economic evaluations are substantially intercorrelated. The bivariate analysis does not allow us to conclude which economic dimension is of greatest importance for trust. The question of relative effects is important for the distinction between collective and personal judgements: does trust suffer most from perceived private economic problems, or from citizens' assessments about the economic predicament of the country? Multivariate analysis allows us to get some measure of the relative impact of these effects. In Tables 9.10 and 9.11 we report the main results from a regression analysis.[6]

TABLE 9.9. *Trust and evaluations of economic performance:*
Sweden, 1973–88

	1973	1976	1982	1985	1988
Past personal finances					
Better		8	−19	−24	−25
	—	(13)	(21)	(31)	(37)
Same		−7	−31	−41	−41
	—	(48)	(40)	(42)	(41)
Worse		−23	−27	−42	−45
	—	(39)	(39)	(27)	(22)
N	—	2,316	2,497	2,464	2,337
Future national economy					
Much better	26	18	0		
	(4)	(2)	(1)	—	—
Somewhat better	11	−3	−19		
	(36)	(32)	(32)	—	—
Same	−10	−13	−32		
	(33)	(40)	(29)	—	—
Somewhat worse	−22	−12	−30		
	(23)	(23)	(32)	—	—
Much worse	−33	−60	−32		
	(4)	(3)	(7)	—	—
N	2,110	2,294	2,395	—	—
Past national economy					
Better				−15	−27
	—	—	—	(28)	(65)
Same				−34	−44
	—	—	—	(30)	(22)
Worse				−49	−55
	—	—	—	(43)	(13)
N	—	—	—	2,335	2,207

Notes: See notes to Table 9.8.

Source: Swedish election surveys.

All the economic performance items have the correct negative signs.
The net impact of the various indicators are, however, modest. In
Norway, the effects of the personal items are slightly stronger than
the one sociotropic item which was included in 1985 and 1989. In
Sweden, the opposite is true as evaluations of both past and future
national economic performance are more strongly related to trust than
expectations about future private finances. The verdict—in the case of

TABLE 9.10. *Trust and economic performance evaluations in Norway: multivariate analysis, 1973–89*

	1973		1977		1981		1985		1989	
	b	beta	*b*	beta	*b*	beta	*b*	beta	*b*	beta
Future personal finances	−0.30	−0.19**	−0.11	−0.09**	−0.04	−0.03	−0.06	−0.06	−0.07	−0.06*
Future personal unemployment	−0.30	−0.17**	−0.06	−0.05	−0.03	−0.02	−0.07	−0.07*	−0.03	−0.03
Past national economy	—	—	—	—	—	—	−0.03	−0.03	−0.05	−0.05

$*p < 0.05$ $**p < 0.01$

Notes: The independent variables include the economic items, age, education, gender, vote (dummy), and left—right self-placement (dummies). The dependent variable was the trust index (high value is trusting). The economic items are coded with high value = negative evaluations.

Source: See Table 9.8.

TABLE 9.11. *Trust and economic performance evaluations in Sweden: multivariate analysis, 1973–88*

	1973		1976		1982		1985		1988	
	b	beta	b	beta	b	beta	b	beta	b	beta
Future personal finances			−0.11	−0.09**	−0.02	−0.02	−0.05	−0.05*	−0.05	−0.05
Future national economy	−0.14	−0.14**	−0.10	−0.11**	−0.04	−0.04	—	—	—	—
Past national economy	—	—	—		—		−0.12	−0.12**	−0.09	−0.07**

$*p < 0.05 **p < 0.01$

Notes: See notes to Table 9.10.

Source: See Table 9.9.

these two countries—thus makes for a tie in the contest between the influence of private and collective judgements on the trust of citizens in their government.

Conclusion

At the beginning of this chapter we reviewed some of the explanations put forward to account for the dynamics of political trust in democracies. Some of the theories present a bleak outlook for the development of trust as they contend that factors related to the long-term developments of society and politics in advanced industrial countries will exert growing pressure on the relationship between citizens and political élites. In contrast to these rather gloomy predictions, the diverse empirical trends in Norway, Sweden, Denmark, and the Netherlands do not justify such a uniformly pessimistic—nor an excessively optimistic—picture of developments in political trust. The empirical analysis has not left us with firm evidence about which factors are crucial to explain variations in trust levels. But some of the shifts in trust within partisan and ideological groups point to the relevance of alternation in government, the role of incumbency, and the performance of parties in government for the development and maintenance of positive mass attitudes towards government.

Before closing the case, we again point to the limitations of this study. The three Scandinavian countries together with the Netherlands constitute a fairly homogenous set of countries, which makes generalization to a more heterogeneous group of nation states problematic. The imperfections of any study which has to rely on secondary data should also be evident. In an analysis which attempts to be both diachronic and cross-national, there are several difficulties about finding identical, or at least comparable, measurements of concepts. Further research to expand the data base, over time and across countries, is needed before we can fully grasp the dynamics of political trust.

Political trust constitutes an important aspect of the democratic orientations of mass publics. Trust is directed at the actors in the system without identifying a specific person or party. In this sense, it is a fairly general attitude. Trust in the institutions of government is at an even more general level. A decline in confidence in institutions is potentially more serious than a weakening of political trust. Hence in the next chapter, we examine developments in confidence in institutions during the 1980s.

APPENDIX
Wording of the Trust Items

Norway

Voting: Voting is the only way that people like me can have any say about how government runs things.

Relevance: What's happening in politics is rarely of relevance for me.

Complex: Sometimes politics is so complicated that ordinary citizens cannot understand what's going on.

Difference: It is difficult to see the important differences between the parties.

Politicians trusted: Do you think that most of our politicians can be trusted, or that politicians by and large can be trusted, or that hardly any can be trusted?

Waste taxes: Do you think that people in government waste a lot of the money we pay in taxes, waste some of it, or they don't waste very much of it?

Politicians smart: Do you think that almost all the politicians are smart people who usually know what they are doing, or do you think that quite a few of them don't know what they are doing?

Only votes: Parties are interested in people's votes but not in their opinions.

Don't care: Those people that are in the Storting and run things don't pay much attention to what ordinary citizens think and believe.

Lose touch: Those representatives that we elect to the Storting lose touch with the people pretty quickly.

Party promises: One can never trust a party to keep its promises.

Extra government power: The real power in the nation lies outside the Storting and the cabinet.

Voting important: By voting in the elections one can really influence the governing of the country.

Elections matter: Elections play a decisive role for the outcome of political decisions in the country.

A more detailed presentation of political support items and how they relate to their American source is given for the Norwegian case in Listhaug (1989: ch. 10). A full overview of the items classified according to dimensions is presented in Miller, Miller, and Schneider (1980).

Sweden

Voting: Voting is the only way that people like me can have any say about how government runs things.

Complex: Frequently politics is so complicated that one cannot understand what's going on.

Difference: It is never difficult to see the important differences between the parties.

Party representation: There is at least one party that always seeks to fight for my interests.

Relevance: What's happening in politics is rarely of relevance for me.

Lose touch: Those members of the Riksdagen that we elect lose touch with ordinary people pretty quickly.

Voting important: By voting one can really influence the governing of the country.

Party promises: One can never trust any party to keep its promises.

Only votes: The parties are only interested in people's votes not in their opinions.

Don't care: Those people that are in the Riksdagen and run things don't pay much attention to what ordinary people think.

Denmark

Complex: Sometimes politics is so complex that people like me can't understand what's going on.

Knows too little: I know so little about politics that I really shouldn't vote.

Don't care: In general politicians care too little about the opinions of the voters.

Make right decisions: In general one may trust our political leaders to make the right decisions for the country.

No principles: People who want to make their way to the political top have to give up most of their principles.

Waste taxes: The politicians waste too much of the taxpayer's money.

The Netherlands

Promises: Politicians consciously promise more than they can deliver.

Personal interest: Cabinet ministers and vice-ministers are first of all looking after their personal interests.

MP because of friends: One becomes a member of parliament because of one's friends rather than because of skill and ability.

Don't care: Members of parliament don't care much about the opinions of people like me.

Only votes: The political parties are only interested in my vote and not in my opinion.

No say: People like me don't have any say about what the government does.

Voting doesn't matter: So many people vote in the election that it does not matter whether I vote or not.

Party promises: Political parties promise much, but don't deliver.

Decisions in secret: Too many political decisions are made in secret in the Netherlands.

Waste taxes: Quite a bit of the taxpayer's money is spent wrongly by the government.

NOTES

1. Details on the construction of the trust index are available from the author.
2. For additional analyses of trust trends in Sweden, see Holmberg (1984: 56–60), and Gilljam and Holmberg (1990, 113–18).
3. Of course, some of the conflicting expectations following from these arguments can be resolved by comparing data, when available, from pre- and post-election surveys.
4. See Kinder and Kiewiet (1979) for an elaboration of this distinction.
5. The full wording of the economic items in the Norwegian and Swedish election surveys is available from the author.
6. Full documentation of the multivariate analysis is available from the author.

10

Confidence in Political and Private Institutions

OLA LISTHAUG AND MATTI WIBERG

In this chapter we examine patterns in the public's confidence in major institutions in Western Europe during the decade of the 1980s. We first address some conceptual and theoretical issues about the measurement of confidence in institutions and introduce the data source for the study. We then go on to present evidence for the main trends in confidence from 1981 to 1990. Identifying trends when we have only two time points is, of course, hazardous. But a reading of the 'crisis' literature of the 1970s, reviewed in Chapter 1 and noted again in Chapter 9, would lead us to expect a decline of confidence in institutions during the 1980s. Finally, we explore variations in levels of confidence in several institutions and investigate factors which can account for shifts in confidence.

Assessments of beliefs in government are most informative when they are addressed in a form which makes comparisons possible. This is so because it is extremely difficult, if not impossible, to set absolute standards for what should be considered high or low confidence. In lieu of unequivocal benchmarks, comparisons of confidence levels over time, between countries, and between different types of institutions— and particularly between government and non-governmental institu-

The data analysed in this chapter are from the 1981 and 1990 European Values Survey conducted by the European Value Systems Study Group and were made available by the Norwegian Social Science Data Services. Beate Huseby and Svein Åge Relling contributed excellent research assistance. We appreciate the critical comments of William L. Miller.

tions—are likely to enhance our understanding of the public's confidence in political institutions. Thus the focus here is deliberately on institutions, not on the actors which occupy a given institution at a particular time.

Much has been written about the need to distinguish between institutions and institutional actors as it is assumed that people might lose confidence in the actors while at the same time remaining confident about the institution itself. A good example is the controversy between Miller and Citrin on how to explain the decline in trust in government in the United States in the 1960s and early 1970s. Whereas Miller (1974) saw the drop in trust levels as a sign that American political institutions were in trouble, Citrin (1974) was inclined to dismiss this as a mere reflection of dissatisfactions with particular incumbents.

The focus on institutions raises the question of whether low confidence, or a decline in confidence levels, should be seen as a threat to legitimacy. The concept of legitimacy moves the analytical focus beyond support for particular parties, politicians, incumbents, or maybe even institutions. But the analysis of confidence in institutions is at least a step towards measuring legitimacy. The reason we hesitate to go further is that the legitimacy of democracy must be evaluated relative to other forms of government (Linz 1988). Our study here introduces a series of relative appraisals, but it does not make direct comparisons with competing political systems. A low level of confidence in political institutions should be read as an indicator that something is going wrong, but it does not necessarily reflect a threat to the legitimacy of the system. To repeat a point which is central to this volume: legitimacy would be threatened only if the public was losing trust and, at the same time, showed support for alternatives to existing institutions (see Chapter 1).

Confidence in institutions might also be termed a middle-range indicator of support (Niemi, Mueller, and Smith 1989: 93), lying between support for specific social and political actors and the overarching principles of society like democracy and capitalism. Arguments have also been raised that distrust is not all bad; a sound scepticism, or realistic cynicism, rather than a blind faith in institutions might be considered appropriate for a democratic polity (Wiberg 1986). The latter argument is generally advanced by writers who emphasize the importance of constitutional arrangements which protect citizens from being abused by the power of government, and includes political philosophers and theorists like Hume, Locke, Madison, and Mill

(Parry 1976: 133–42). Indeed, distrust of others is a basic tenet of political theory, starting with Machiavelli's *The Prince*: 'men will always do badly by you unless they are forced to be virtuous' (Machiavelli 1975: 127).

It is thus a fundamental problem of constitutional design to ensure that all powerful political actors operating within institutions have incentives not to misuse the confidence of other actors. The constitutionalist, or contract theory approach (Rogowski 1974: 51–2), puts the focus on mechanisms which ensure that the power of institutions will be used only for the purpose specified. According to this view, distrust is more or less to be expected when individuals transfer authority to corporate actors and thus surrender some of their control over private life. It is indeed rational to be a bit cynical under such circumstances. This view can be contrasted to a political culture approach (Almond and Verba 1963; Easton 1965), which is inclined to see trust in institutions as a relatively stable characteristic of society, reflecting the socialization of citizens into its dominant norms. The norms are seen as enduring traits which make it meaningful to label societies according to the most prevalent norms. But this view of institutions is unnecessarily static as it tends to exclude factors which might contribute to a change in the confidence levels of the mass public. Furthermore, the constitutionalist view might seem unrealistically rigorous as the public's trust in institutions is seen as deriving from the same kind of processes as the game of an assembly of founding fathers designing an optimal constitution (Buchanan 1991).

It is sometimes argued that the question of whether high confidence is good or bad is primarily normative, so it cannot be answered by empirical analysis (Kaase 1988). But it is also possible to see this as an empirical issue; for example, to investigate whether there is a relationship between a decline of confidence levels and political and societal malfunctioning, or even the breakdown of regimes. If one finds over time that societies with low confidence levels do not register a noticeably weak political performance, one could conclude that the analysis of confidence in institutions is, at best, of only academic interest.

The hypothesis of a rational scepticism can be investigated at the micro-level by correlating indicators which facilitate individual rationality with measures of trust or confidence. Core indicators of rationality would be tapped by measures of political involvement like political interest, information, and education. Much empirical research has been directed at the analysis of the impact of education on trust, which is somewhat unfortunate as this indicator bears only an indirect relationship to the appropriate theoretical concepts. Döring (1990, 1992), for example, working with the same data as we use, has argued that higher education may not breed cynicism towards all types of institutions. While he contends that the higher educated will show an overall inclination towards low confidence in institutions, they might 'place confidence in those institutions that criticize or punish rulers in case of breach of trust: the judiciary, the press, and—possibly—parliament' (Döring 1992: 128). It seems that Döring singles out institutions which have the potential to defend individual liberties.

It should be seen as something of a paradox, however, that parliament in most countries has been a key actor in expanding the power of corporate actors—by way of social and economic legislation—which has strongly limited personal freedom. If the basic hypothesis that education has a negative impact on confidence in institutions has any merit, it is difficult to see that we should make an exception for parliament—and we see that Döring expresses some doubt here. Thus the test of a rational basis for confidence in institutions should not be limited to an assessment of the impact of education. If true, we should expect low trust to be most prevalent among citizens who satisfy the requirements of ideal citizens: the highly informed and the politically involved.

Support for institutions depends on the attitudes and values of individuals. Which attitudes and values are important, and the strength of the relationships, will vary across institutions. It is obvious that support for the church will be strongly related to the strength of people's religious beliefs. Confidence in business, or as phrased here, major companies, will depend on ideological orientations. A weakening of religious beliefs in the population can undermine confidence in the church. Similarly, a radicalization of the masses in traditional left–right terms can erode the public's confidence in major companies. Confidence will also depend on the deeds of institutions. The performance criterion might not be equally important for all institutions, and will also vary in its particular meaning across institutions. As the economic role of government has expanded in all sectors, it is likely that mass support for public institutions—parliament included—becomes increasingly sensitive to performance evaluations.

In sum, the public character of political institutions makes them particularly dependent on support from all groups of citizens. Political

institutions constitute a framework which lasts beyond the time and day
of particular incumbents. On the other hand, political institutions are
not completely insulated from social and political life. We expect
confidence to depend on the political distance between government
and the governed, and on how well political institutions solve the
problems they are designed to address. If this holds true, then the
dynamics of confidence in institutions will not be dramatically different from the dynamics of political trust examined in Chapter 9 (see also
Miller and Listhaug 1990).

Data

Our data are from two surveys conducted by the European Value
Systems Study Group (EVSSG). The EVSSG consists of scholars
from a large number of countries who are interested in the study of
long-term value change. The survey is a broad study of value systems,
covering religion, family, work, and politics. Interviews with representative samples of the population 18 years and older were carried out in
1981 (Norway in 1982, Iceland in 1984), and in 1990. The 1990 survey
replicated the main part of the questionnaire from the 1981 survey. In
both waves, the survey included a question which tapped confidence in
ten major institutions: the church, the armed forces, the education
system, the legal system, the press, trade unions, the police, parliament, the civil service, and major companies.[1] In 1990 the list was
expanded to include the social security system, along with the European
Community, NATO, and the Nordic Council in the relevant countries.
These institutions were added to the questionnaire after the ten original
institutions, and are not analysed here. This chapter is restricted to an
analysis of the main results for fourteen nations in Western Europe.
Data for Finland are included for 1981 only, and Portugal was part of
the study only in 1990.

Trends in Confidence

With ten institutions, fourteen nations, and two time points, there is an
obvious need to simplify the analysis. We do this by focusing on the
major trends across Western Europe and by comparing the trends for
private and public institutions. In Table 10.1 we report the percentage

who say they have confidence in the institutions named.[2] We have created a European average by summing the percentages across all countries and dividing by the number of countries, giving each country equal weight.

The distributions demonstrate that there is no general trend either in the direction of declining or increasing confidence in institutions. Three institutions show a decline of confidence in the order of three percentage points or more: the church (-4), the armed forces (-8), and the legal system (-7). Two institutions show a positive trend across Western Europe: the education system $(+3)$ and major companies $(+9)$. The positive trend for major companies is the most pervasive as this increases in all countries except Britain, where it declines marginally from 50 per cent to 48 per cent. The increase in support for business was extraordinarily strong in Italy $(+29)$, France $(+18)$, the Netherlands $(+14)$, Sweden $(+11)$, and Spain $(+10)$. Thus our results do not verify a key finding in Lipset and Schneider's (1983) detailed study—that, in the United States, confidence in institutions moved in tandem across different types of institutions. On the contrary, support for institutions in Western Europe, both within and across the public–private sector divide, seems to move more independently than suggested by the American data.

To simplify the analysis we need some form of data reduction. Data reduction can be achieved pragmatically or empirically. The pragmatic approach was used by Rose (1984) in a study based on data from some of the countries in the first wave of the survey. He classified six institutions as belonging to government (the armed forces, the education system, the legal system, the police, parliament, and the civil service), and four as non-governmental (the church, the press, the trade unions, and major companies). In some of the countries, however, and clearly so in Scandinavia, the allocation of the church to the private sphere is questionable since these countries all have Lutheran state churches. However, although still formally a part of the state, the church in Scandinavia has long had considerable independence from government. Moreover, this autonomy has probably grown in recent decades. When people are asked to evaluate the church, we will assume that they are more likely to think of the religious role of the clergy rather than the state functions of the church. If this is true, it justifies allocating the church to the private sphere.

Alternatively, an empirical reduction can be achieved by factor analysing the ratings of the ten institutions (Listhaug 1984). We

TABLE 10.1. *Confidence in institutions in fourteen West European countries, 1981 and 1990*

	Church	Armed forces	Education system	Legal system	Press	Trade unions	Police	Parliament	Civil service	Major companies	N (unweighted, min.)
Denmark											
1981	48	40	65	80	30	52	85	—	47	34	853
1990	47	46	81	79	31	46	89	42	51	38	978
Norway											
1982	50	68	80	84	41	56	89	78	58	45	1,035
1990	45	65	79	75	43	59	88	59	44	53	1,221
Sweden											
1981	39	61	62	73	27	49	80	47	46	42	1,115
1990	38	49	70	56	33	40	74	47	44	53	949
Finland											
1981	49	71	83	84	34	56	88	65	53	45	983
Iceland											
1984	69	—	69	69	16	46	74	56	48	34	910
1990	68	—	80	67	20	51	85	53	46	40	675
Belgium											
1981	65	43	79	58	35	33	64	39	47	44	972
1990	49	33	74	45	44	37	51	43	42	50	2,741
Germany											
1981	44	53	43	67	31	38	70	52	33	34	1,292
1990	40	40	54	65	34	36	70	51	39	38	2,093
Ireland											
1981	79	76	68	58	44	37	86	53	55	50	1,190
1990	72	61	73	47	36	43	86	50	59	52	992

TABLE 10.1. *Cont.*

	Church	Armed forces	Education system	Legal system	Press	Trade unions	Police	Parliament	Civil service	Major companies	N (unweighted, min.)
Netherlands											
1981	40	43	73	65	28	39	73	45	45	35	1,173
1990	32	32	65	63	36	53	73	54	46	49	996
Britain											
1981	47	82	60	66	29	25	86	40	48	50	1,173
1990	43	81	47	54	14	26	77	46	44	48	1,436
France											
1981	54	55	57	57	33	40	64	56	53	49	1,031
1990	50	56	66	58	38	32	67	48	49	67	902
Italy											
1981	58	56	54	43	31	29	65	30	27	33	1,348
1990	63	48	49	32	39	34	67	32	27	62	2,003
Spain											
1981	49	63	52	50	48	33	64	49	40	39	2,216
1990	53	42	62	45	51	40	58	43	37	49	2,565
Portugal											
1990	57	47	51	41	36	29	44	34	32	45	1,148
Europe											
1981	54	58	64	64	33	40	75	50	45	41	
1990	50	50	67	57	35	41	74	48	44	50	
Diff.	−4	−8	+3	−7	+2	+1	−1	−2	−1	+9	

Notes: The data were based on the following question: 'Please look at this card and tell me, for each item listed, how much confidence you have in them. Is it a great deal, quite a lot, not very much, or none at all?' Entries are the percentage saying 'a great deal' or 'quite a lot'. The estimates are based on weighted data, when appropriate. The countries are given equal weights in computing the European averages. Finland and Portugal are excluded from the European average as they were surveyed at only one time point. The question on confidence in parliament was not asked in Denmark in 1981; the question on confidence in the armed forces was not asked in Iceland as it does not have a regular national defence force. Thus Denmark is excluded from computing the mean for confidence in parliament, and Iceland is excluded from the mean for the armed forces.

Source: European Values Survey (1981, 1990).

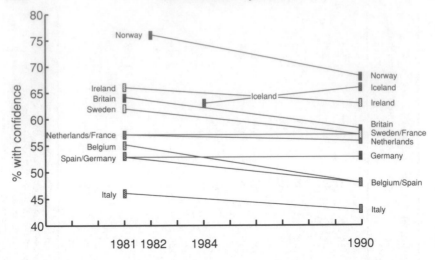

FIGURE 10.1. *Confidence in government institutions, 1981–90*

Notes: Entries are the average percentages who have confidence in the armed forces, the education system, the legal system, the police, the parliament, and the civil service. Armed forces are excluded for Iceland.

Source: Table 10.1.

performed a series of factor analyses using varimax rotation. The results for the several countries are fairly similar, with the most prevalent tendency for what we can term 'the institutions of order'—the armed forces, the legal system, the police, and, somewhat less distinctly, the church—to load on the second factor in a two-factor solution.[3] This underlines the need to make a distinction within state institutions, a point we return to in various parts of the discussion. We start by analysing the trust differential between state and private institutions.

Is it still true, as Rose concluded (1984: 180), based on the 1981 data, that 'people are more likely to trust government than private sector institutions'? The trend lines for the individual countries are set out in Figures 10.1 and 10.2. They show that, in general, confidence in government institutions is either stable or in modest decline while confidence in private institutions is either stable or weakly rising.

The most marked decline of confidence in government institutions is found in Norway where the confidence level, on average, fell from 76 to 68 per cent. Similar but rather less steep falls are observed in Belgium (55 to 48 per cent), Sweden (62 to 57 per cent), and Britain (64 to 58 per cent). In Denmark, however, which is not included in Figure 11.1 since we lack time-series data for confidence in parliament, there was an

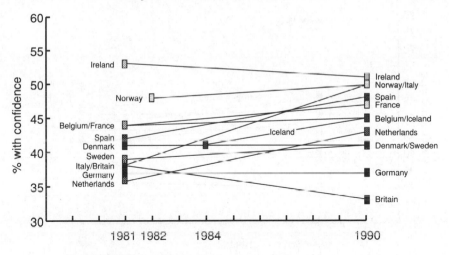

FIGURE 10.2. *Confidence in private institutions, 1981–90*

Notes: Entries are the average percentages saying that they have confidence in the church, the press, the trade unions, and major companies.

Source: Table 10.1.

improvement in confidence in government institutions (excluding the missing data for parliament). As to confidence in private institutions, the most marked improvement is found in Italy where confidence rose from 38 to 50 per cent. Improvements, but of lower magnitude, are also found in the Netherlands (36 to 43 per cent), and Spain (42 to 48 per cent). We should note that the major factor in rising confidence in the private sector is accounted for by the strengthening of public sentiments about major companies.

Having looked at the mean levels of confidence in public and private institutions, we can calculate the confidence gap between the institutions in the two sectors during the 1980s. The gap narrows in Norway from 28 to 18 per cent, Sweden (23 to 16 per cent), Belgium (11 to 3 per cent), the Netherlands (21 to 13 per cent), Spain (11 per cent to zero), and Italy (8 per cent to −7 per cent). The remaining countries show a fairly constant confidence gap over the period. With the exception of Italy, where the public has the highest degree of confidence in private institutions, and Spain, where there is no difference, confidence in government was still higher than in private institutions in 1990.

Even so, government institutions lost some comparative edge during the 1980s. The primary factor here is the tendency on the government side, although not perfectly consistent, towards declining confidence in

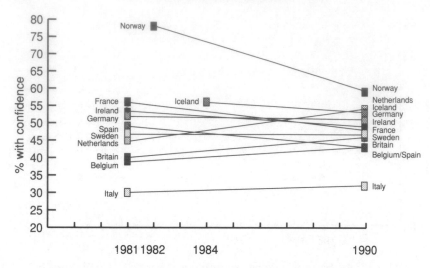

FIGURE 10.3. *Confidence in parliament, 1981–90*

Source: Table 10.1.

the order institutions. As we can see from Figure 10.3 (see also Table 10.1), a key democratic institution like parliament experiences virtually no change in confidence. A notably sharp decline is recorded for Norway with a fall of 19 percentage points, and a somewhat more modest decline is found in France (−8 points) and Spain (−6 points), but an improvement is observed in the Netherlands (+9 points), Britain (+6 points), and Belgium (+4 points). We should note, too, the relative stability in the rank order of the countries at the two time points. Thus despite the marked decline in support for government institutions in Norway, confidence in the Storting still remains at the top of the rankings.

The confidence of Norwegians in their political institutions—and especially in parliament—was extremely favourable at the start of the 1980s, so the effect of the decline during the 1980s was to bring Norway more into line with the European average.[4] Norway also shows very high confidence in private institutions, giving the country the number one ranking in overall confidence in institutions at both time points. The extreme position at the other end is occupied by Italy, which records the lowest level of confidence in public institutions—including parliament—in both years. Finland in 1981 and Portugal in 1990 show quite different levels of confidence in government institutions: Portugal is near the bottom and Finland is near the top.[5]

It is beyond the scope of this chapter to investigate the causes of shifts in confidence levels for separate institutions in each country. Such efforts would anyway be speculative as the effects of particular events cannot be explored systematically with only two time points. A *post facto* interpretation of the almost universal increase in support for major companies would probably emphasize that the 1990 survey was conducted close to the high mark of the euphoria following the breakdown of the socialist regimes in the Soviet Union and Eastern Europe. It is likely that the mass public's assessments of market principles, as well as private business, improved under the influence of these major events. This speculation aside, despite our resolve not to dwell on specific events to explain particular differences, we pause to consider the case of Italy. As a demonstrable outlier on confidence in government, this case warrants some comment.

The weak showing of Italy comes as no surprise. It has been almost a ritual for political scientists as well as journalists to characterize Italy as a polity in deep trouble. This has subsequently been borne out by the decimation of the political class with the exposure of political scandals and the upheavals in the party system at the 1994 elections. One aspect of Italian political life—prior to the collapse of the 'old system'— which regularly met with much negative comment was the frequency of weak coalition governments, often with only minority support in parliament. Although Strom has done much to rehabilitate minority governments as efficient policy instruments, he is unflattering about the Italian case: 'With the possible exception of the French Fourth Republic, the feebleness and malaise associated with minority governments appear nowhere better demonstrated than in the history of post-Fascist Italy' (Strom 1990*b*: 132–3).

Not all commentators have taken the same critical view of Italian politics. LaPalombara (1987), in particular, dismissed much of the 'crisis' interpretation of Italian political life, using the idea of politics as *spettacolo*—as a show or drama—which is not taken too seriously by citizens. But the recent developments in Italy seriously question LaPalombara's dissenting opinion, particularly in view of the 19 to 1 majority approving of anti-corruption electoral reform in the 1991 referendums—clearly a blow to the widespread *clientilismo* of the parties. The Italian case also demonstrates that beliefs about government have consequences for the conduct of politics, and that real problems for democracy could be signalled by negative survey findings about confidence in institutions.

The Impact of Government Performance

The case of Italy raises the question of the functioning of institutions which are crucial to maintaining the public's faith in them. It is worthwhile, then, to move the analysis beyond the description of a single case to see if there is some relationship between levels of confidence in institutions and measures of political and economic performance. Two types of performance measures seem important. First, as our discussion of Italy suggests, the instability or fragmentation of the government might undermine confidence levels among the mass public. Secondly, we postulate that favourable economic conditions will breed confidence in public institutions and, conversely, that negative economic circumstances will undermine confidence. The small number of cases we can examine—fourteen at maximum—limits the analysis, and only very strong relationships can be discerned in a statistically meaningful way.

With these caveats in mind, we analysed variables related to the two groups of measures. Three indicators of government structure were used. The first measures the number of governments in the previous decade; the first time point is in the 1970s, the second in the 1980s. The second variable is the duration of governments relative to the maximum for the life of a government during the same period, measured as a percentage (Lane, McKay, and Newton 1991: 117). This variable is reversed to bring the interpretation in line with the other measures. The third indicator in this group is the number of governments in the decade preceding the two time points—that is, in the 1970s and 1980s, respectively. Economic performance is tapped by two measures of unemployment: the OECD standardized rate and the commonly used definition in each country. The latter, which is available for all countries, has a somewhat lower cross-national comparability than the former. The third measure is inflation, which is tapped by the standard inflation rate for the year preceding the year of the surveys. Note that these are different years for Norway and Iceland.

We expect all relationships to be negative since we postulate that both government instability and weak economic performance undermine confidence in public institutions. The results from a bivariate analysis are presented in Table 10.2.

Of the twenty-four correlations, nineteen have the predicted sign. Three of the five positive signs relate to inflation, which seems to be much less important for confidence than unemployment, where all

TABLE 10.2. *Macro characteristics of countries and confidence in public institutions, 1981 and 1990*

Macro characteristics	Confidence in government		Confidence in parliament	
	1981	1990	1981	1990
Number of governments in previous decade	0.09	−0.42	−0.11	−0.49
Duration of governments relative to maximum (reversed)	−0.13	−0.29	−0.15	−0.43
Number of parties in government in previous decade	−0.29	−0.18	−0.23	0.10
Unemployment in previous year (standardized rate)	−0.56	−0.11	−0.53	−0.15
Unemployment in previous year (commonly used definition)	−0.44	−0.27	−0.44	−0.30
Inflation rate in previous year	0.08	0.08	0.10	−0.11

Notes: Entries are correlation coefficients. The countries listed in Table 10.1 are included unless excluded because of missing data. Confidence in government is the average percentage saying they have confidence in the armed forces, the education system, the police, parliament, and the civil service. The index is calculated without parliament for Denmark in 1981 and without armed forces for Iceland in both years. The sources for the independent variables are Lane, McKay, and Newton (1991: Tables 6.11 and 6.12) for government structure, and *OECD Economic Outlook*, July 1983, No. 33; December 1985, No. 38; and June 1992, No. 51, for economic indicators. The EVSSG data for Norway were collected in 1982 and for Iceland in 1984.

coefficients—to varying degrees—are negative. Only one coefficient obtains statistical significance at the conventionally accepted level. Although the small number of cases virtually precludes an elaborate statistical analysis of the material, an inspection of scatter plots is helpful for understanding and clarifying the relationships. As many of the patterns look fairly similar, we present just some of the few plots, using confidence in parliament as the dependent variable.

In Figure 10.4 confidence in parliament in 1990 is plotted against the stability of government as measured by the number of governments in the 1980s. Incidentally, this is the strongest negative relationship from Table 10.2, yielding a correlation of −0.49. Italy is on the extreme end of both variables, with the lowest level of confidence and the highest degree of government instability. We also note that Norway has a higher confidence level than we would expect from its level of government instability. Britain and Portugal, on the other hand, show lower than expected confidence levels.

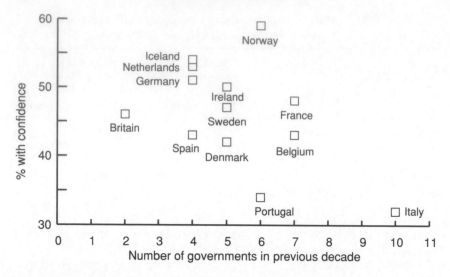

FIGURE 10.4. *Confidence in parliament in 1990 by government instability*
Note: See Table 10.2 for a discussion of variables.

Table 10.2 shows that the correlation between confidence in parliament in 1990 and the unemployment rate in the preceding year was −0.30. This is slightly lower than the average for the eight correlations by unemployment reported in the table. This relatively weak negative impact of the unemployment rate on confidence in parliament comes out clearly in Figure 10.5.

Norway is again somewhat higher in confidence than expected, while Italy and, especially, Portugal demonstrate comparatively lower levels of confidence than the levels of unemployment would lead us to expect. The negative correlation between confidence and unemployment suggests that changes in unemployment levels should explain some of the change in confidence levels in these countries. Figure 10.6, however, shows that not much can be accounted for by this factor.

Again, the drop in confidence in the Norwegian parliament is much out of line with what we would expect if unemployment is a decisive factor. We should add that the removal of Italy from the plots—and from the computation of correlations—would considerably weaken the observed relationships.

Overall, we must conclude that the analysis of performance indicators has not produced definitive answers. At best it has hinted that the structure of government, primarily instability in government, and weak

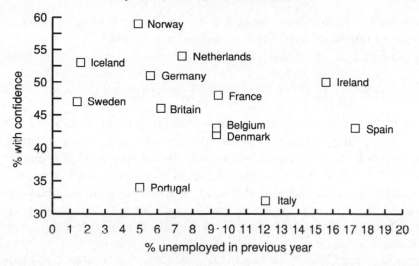

FIGURE 10.5. *Confidence in parliament in 1990 by unemployment rate in previous year*

Notes: See Table 10.2 for a discussion of variables. The unemployment measure is the commonly used definition.

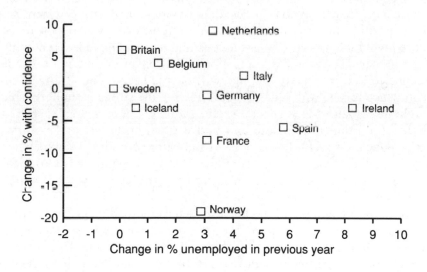

FIGURE 10.6. *Change in confidence in parliament by change in unemployment*

Notes: See Table 10.2 for a discussion of variables. The unemployment measure is the commonly used definition.

economic performance—notably unemployment—might have a negative impact on confidence in public institutions.

Individual-Level Correlates of Confidence in Institutions

The rationale for investigating individual factors which correlate with confidence in governments is that the results can be used to predict long-term trends in confidence. For example, if education is negatively correlated with confidence, and education levels among the population increase over time, this would lead us to predict that confidence would decline. Such predictions are of course speculative, as a host of factors are likely to influence confidence. A further difficulty arises from the variation across institutions of the impact of different factors (Lipset and Schneider 1983). It is thus important to examine institutions separately, or at least distinguish between the institutions of government and private institutions.

Before examining the data, we outline the hypotheses which can be linked to the factors we analyse. We have included three demographic variables: sex, age, and education. A person's sex is unlikely to have a general impact on confidence, but we assume that men show more confidence in the armed forces than women, and that women are more positive towards the church. We might also expect men to be more favourable towards labour unions and major companies, reflecting their higher labour force participation and stronger orientation towards economic life. It is likely that age will have a fairly general impact on confidence levels, with older people showing the stronger support. This might be explained by a general socialization effect as ageing is seen to increase attachment to institutions and weaken critical attitudes. Similarly, education might be seen as an indicator of political competence which stimulates a critical scepticism towards institutions. Political interest is an even more direct measure of cognitive competence which could have a comparable effect in stimulating a critical attitude towards institutions. Ideology and values also determine confidence in institutions. Religion, tapped here by the strength of the religious dogmas in which an individual believes, is obviously related to confidence in the church such that stronger believers are likely to have more confidence in the church. But religion might also play a positive role for confidence in a broader sense, especially confidence in order institutions, whereas religion is unlikely to promote confidence in secular institutions such as the press, the labour unions, and major companies.

Among the factors influencing voting behaviour and political evaluations at the mass level the consistently most important is left–right ideology. Various hypotheses have been put forward for how political ideology relates to confidence in government (see Miller and Listhaug 1993). One line of reasoning suggests that there is a direct relationship between ideological position and confidence. Individuals on the far left are assumed to be generically sceptical about the existing institutions of society, which are often portrayed as repressive or unable to represent the real interests of the masses. Among those on the far right, a negative attitude towards government is seen as derived from an assumed belief that government in any form is bad, as government tends to restrict personal freedom and market competition. This latter contention assumes that those on the right are bearers of libertarian values. In contradiction to this, some scholars (Miller and Listhaug 1993) argue that conservatives would develop a fundamental allegiance to political institutions. Left–right ideology might also be related to confidence in non-governmental institutions. For example, support for the church is more likely to be found on the right than on the left, and confidence in labour unions should be more prevalent on the left than on the right.

While left–right ideology has long been a dominant cleavage in the politics of the industrialized democracies, a major school of research argues that postmaterialism and other forms of 'new politics' are becoming increasingly prominent in the mass politics of advanced democracies (Inglehart 1977, 1990a). The emergence of 'new politics' has also been related to political distrust as citizens who hold postmaterialist values are sceptical about the political institutions of current society because these institutions embody values and interests associated with the 'old' materialism (Jennings, Van Deth, *et al.* 1989). But postmaterialist values might also have a negative impact on institutions more broadly, particularly those representing the materialist and authoritarian values of yesteryear.

Finally, we include two variables tapping subjective life satisfaction. The idea is simply that there exists a positive spill-over from personal life satisfaction to institutions such that dissatisfied individuals become less confident in institutions; for example, by blaming them for their own problems.

We tested the impact of these various factors by running a series of regression models for each of the ten institutions. The results are shown in Tables 10.3 and 10.4. All the countries in the first wave of the European Values Survey were included, and data for the United States

The Political System

TABLE 10.3. *Multivariate analysis of confidence in institutions, 1981*

	Parliament		Church		Armed forces		Education system	
	Beta	B	Beta	B	Beta	B	Beta	B
Sex	−0.02	−0.04	−0.06	−0.12	0.01	0.01	−0.01	−0.02
Age	0.09	0.04	0.13	0.07	0.13	0.07	0.04	0.02
Education	0.03	0.04	−0.03	−0.04	−0.05	−0.06	−0.03	−0.03
Political interests	0.09	0.07	0.01	0.01	0.00	0.00	−0.03	−0.02
Religious dogmas	0.12	0.04	0.51	0.21	0.24	0.09	0.16	0.05
Extreme left	−0.05	−0.17	−0.09	−0.36	−0.11	−0.39	−0.03	−0.11
Moderate left	−0.01	−0.02	−0.07	−0.19	−0.09	−0.23	−0.01	−0.02
Moderate right	0.01	0.03	0.03	0.08	0.04	0.08	−0.03	−0.07
Extreme right	0.03	0.10	0.02	0.07	0.04	0.16	−0.01	−0.02
Materialist	−0.01	−0.02	0.02	0.06	−0.01	−0.03	−0.02	−0.05
Postmaterialist	−0.04	−0.11	−0.06	−0.20	−0.13	−0.42	−0.05	−0.13
Financial satisfaction	0.06	0.02	0.03	0.01	0.03	0.01	0.03	0.01
Life satisfaction	0.05	0.02	0.06	0.03	0.08	0.03	0.10	0.04
R^2	0.06		0.39		0.20		0.06	

Notes: All countries surveyed in the 1981 survey are included (see Table 10.1) with the addition of USA and Canada. Confidence is coded on a four-point scale with 4 as 'much confidence'. Sex is coded 1 = male, 0 = female. The age groups are: 1 = completed full-time education at age 15 or younger; 2 = completed full-time education aged 16–19; 3 = completed full-time education at age 20 or older. The political interest scale is: 1 = not interested in politics at all; 2 = interest in politics not greater than other interests; 3 = interested in politics but don't take any active part; 4 = take active interest in politics. Dogmas is the number of religious dogmas a person believes in (God, life

and Canada were added in order to strengthen the statistical basis for the analysis. Further, the data for each year were pooled—on the assumption that the impact of the factors is independent of national contexts. This assumption might not be justified in all cases, but might be reasonable to uncover the broad picture. Finally, taking into account the very large number of cases, it is obvious that ordinary significance tests and probability levels are of little value, since small coefficients will be significant at conventional levels. Hence, we do not report any tests of significance in the tables.[6]

In examining the results of the regression analysis, the first thing to note is the relatively modest explanatory power of the models. The church constitutes the main exception, with an explained variance of 39 per cent in 1981 and 37 per cent in 1990. Next come the armed forces,

TABLE 10.3. *Cont.*

Legal system		Civil service		Press		Trade unions		Police		Major companies	
Beta	B	Beta	B	Beta	B	Beta	B	Beta	B	Beta	B
−0.04	−0.06	−0.02	−0.03	−0.01	−0.01	0.02	0.04	−0.04	−0.06	0.05	0.08
0.06	0.03	0.06	0.03	0.04	0.02	−0.03	−0.01	0.11	0.05	0.04	0.02
0.01	0.01	−0.01	−0.01	0.03	0.03	−0.05	−0.06	−0.05	−0.06	0.01	0.01
0.01	0.00	0.03	0.03	0.04	0.04	0.06	0.06	0.01	0.01	0.01	0.01
0.06	0.02	0.18	0.06	0.14	0.05	0.08	0.03	0.13	0.04	0.12	0.04
−0.08	−0.29	−0.03	−0.09	−0.01	−0.02	0.05	0.16	−0.10	−0.34	−0.08	−0.26
−0.02	−0.04	−0.02	−0.04	0.01	0.03	0.07	0.16	−0.06	−0.12	−0.06	−0.14
0.02	0.05	0.00	0.00	0.01	0.02	−0.04	−0.09	0.04	0.09	0.05	0.10
0.01	0.04	0.03	0.09	0.02	0.08	−0.01	−0.03	0.03	0.10	0.06	0.18
0.04	0.08	−0.03	−0.01	−0.03	−0.07	−0.05	−0.11	0.03	0.07	0.00	0.01
−0.02	−0.06	−0.08	−0.23	−0.04	−0.11	0.02	0.05	−0.09	−0.25	−0.07	−0.20
0.05	0.02	0.03	0.06	0.00	0.00	−0.00	−0.00	0.04	0.01	0.05	0.02
0.07	0.03	0.09	0.04	0.05	0.02	0.03	0.01	0.10	0.04	0.07	0.03
0.01		0.08		0.04		0.02		0.12		0.07	

after death, a soul, the devil, hell, heaven, sin). Left–right is a ten-point scale: extreme left is 1, 2; moderate left is 3, 4; moderate right is 7, 8; extreme right is 9, 10. The materialist variable is a dummy where 1 is the materialist value combination on Inglehart's four item battery; postmaterialism is a dummy where 1 is the postmaterialist value combination on Inglehart's four-item battery. Financial satisfaction is satisfaction with financial situation of household on a ten-point scale; 1 = dissatisfied, 10 = satisfied. Life satisfaction is a ten-point scale; 1 = dissatisfied, 10 = satisfied. N = 15,355.

with 20 per cent and 12 per cent explained variance in the two respective years, followed by the police with 12 per cent and 8 per cent explained variance. The R^2 for the last of the 'order' institutions, the legal system, is only 3 per cent in both years. This is more in line with the remaining institutions. Despite the modest success of the model, the main findings are of some substantive interest.

The variable tapping religious dogmas is by far the most important factor in explaining confidence in institutions. This is true not only for the church, where the link should be obvious and constitutes the main explanation for the high explained variance, but religion is also important in explaining confidence in other institutions. It is remarkable that even secular and partly anti-religious institutions like the press and labour unions display positive signs.

TABLE 10.4. *Multivariate analysis of confidence in institutions, 1990*

	Parliament		Church		Armed forces		Education system	
	Beta	*B*	Beta	*B*	Beta	*B*	Beta	*B*
Sex	−0.01	−0.02	−0.04	−0.09	0.01	0.02	−0.01	−0.01
Age	0.07	0.03	0.15	0.08	0.07	0.03	0.05	0.02
Education	0.07	0.07	−0.04	−0.05	−0.08	−0.09	0.02	0.02
Political interests	0.14	0.11	−0.02	−0.02	0.06	0.05	−0.03	−0.03
Religious dogmas	0.07	0.02	0.49	0.20	0.15	0.05	0.05	0.02
Extreme left	−0.05	−0.16	−0.06	−0.27	−0.09	−0.33	−0.01	−0.02
Moderate left	0.01	0.01	−0.05	−0.12	−0.09	−0.20	−0.01	−0.03
Moderate right	0.03	0.07	0.03	0.07	0.04	0.10	−0.01	−0.01
Extreme right	0.01	0.05	0.04	0.15	0.05	0.17	0.01	0.02
Materialist	0.03	0.05	0.05	0.11	0.05	0.11	0.02	0.04
Postmaterialist	−0.03	−0.06	−0.05	−0.11	−0.11	−0.24	−0.04	−0.07
Financial satisfaction	0.07	0.02	0.02	0.01	0.01	0.00	0.04	0.01
Life satisfaction	0.04	0.02	0.04	0.02	0.04	0.02	0.10	0.04
R^2	0.06		0.37		0.12		0.03	

Among the demographic variables, the most consistent impact is observed for age, which has a positive effect on confidence—suggesting that socialization over the life cycle leads to attachment to the existing order. Sex has the predicted impact for confidence in the church, with women showing the strongest confidence. However, the impact of sex on confidence in the armed forces is negligible, although the sign goes in the expected direction. This finding refutes the hypothesis that women are less supportive of the military. Education is only weakly, and inconsistently, related to confidence in institutions. In general, the sign is positive, and one of the stronger effects is recorded for parliament in 1990, with a beta of 0.07.

Among the political variables, political interest shows much the same pattern as education. However, the effects are somewhat stronger and, with the exceptions of the education system in both years and the church in 1990, the signs are all positive. The effect is fairly strong for parliament, with betas of 0.09 and 0.14 in the two waves. These results suggest that the most politically informed and involved develop

TABLE 10.4. *Cont.*

Legal system		Civil service		Press		Trade unions		Police		Major companies	
Beta	B	Beta	B	Beta	B	Beta	B	Beta	B	Beta	B
−0.03	−0.05	−0.03	−0.04	0.01	0.01	−0.01	−0.01	−0.02	−0.04	0.03	0.04
0.04	0.02	0.06	0.02	−0.01	−0.00	−0.01	−0.01	0.07	0.03	−0.00	−0.00
0.08	0.08	0.01	0.01	−0.03	−0.03	0.02	0.02	−0.03	−0.03	0.00	0.00
0.09	0.07	0.06	0.05	0.04	0.03	0.07	0.05	0.08	0.06	0.01	0.01
0.04	0.01	0.10	0.03	0.02	0.01	0.03	0.01	0.12	0.04	0.04	0.01
−0.05	−0.18	−0.04	−0.13	−0.00	−0.01	0.08	0.29	−0.07	−0.24	−0.07	−0.24
−0.01	−0.02	−0.01	−0.01	0.01	0.03	0.10	0.21	−0.03	−0.06	−0.05	−0.11
0.03	0.05	0.00	0.00	0.00	0.00	−0.06	−0.12	0.03	0.06	0.05	0.10
0.00	0.02	0.00	0.01	0.01	0.02	−0.04	−0.16	0.02	0.07	0.05	0.17
0.03	0.06	0.03	0.06	−0.01	−0.01	0.01	0.01	0.04	0.08	0.03	0.06
−0.04	−0.09	−0.05	−0.10	0.02	0.04	−0.01	−0.02	−0.08	−0.15	−0.07	−0.13
0.04	0.01	0.05	0.02	0.03	0.01	−0.00	−0.00	0.04	0.01	0.08	0.03
0.06	0.03	0.07	0.03	−0.00	−0.00	0.04	0.02	0.11	0.04	0.03	0.01
0.03		0.04		0.01		0.03		0.08		0.04	

Notes: See Table10.3 for details of variables. $N = 20{,}250$.

an allegiance to democratic institutions, thus refuting the thesis that cognitive competence breeds distrust in these institutions.

Left–right ideology was coded as a series of dummy variables to allow for curvilinearity. The empirical results, however, demonstrate that ideology has a fairly linear impact on confidence in institutions: the highest confidence levels are on the right and the lowest on the left. The major exception is, of course, found for labour unions where the signs are reversed. The sign for postmaterialist value orientations is negative, and has a particularly notable impact on confidence in the armed forces and the police. The impact of postmaterialism on other institutions, however, is much weaker. This finding suggests that the anti-authoritarian dimension in postmaterialism is the stronger ingredient in determining confidence in institutions. Finally, there is some positive impact—albeit tenuous—of subjective satisfactions, particularly overall life satisfaction, on confidence levels.

The most interesting result from the micro-level analysis is the positive relationship between confidence in institutions and traditional values. A long-term shift in value priorities can thus have some relevance for mass support for institutions, but most directly and strongly for allegiance to the order institutions in society. Religious beliefs appear to have a particularly important role here.

Conclusion

The data from the two European Values Surveys do not demonstrate that there has been a widespread decline in the public's confidence in institutions during the 1980s. There is some decline in confidence in order institutions, but confidence in other political institutions is either stable, as in the case of the civil service and parliament, or, as with the education system, has become stronger. The most consistent improvement in confidence is recorded for major companies. However, the positive confidence gap in favour of government institutions as compared to private institutions has declined somewhat over the decade. Since we began this study by stressing the difficulties of setting absolute standards for what should be considered high or low confidence, this relative decline should at least be read as a discreet warning for the popular standing of government institutions in Western Europe in the early 1990s.

Our finding that not all confidence levels move in tandem—not even within the two main classes of institutions—should direct attention to the possibility that an individual might be attached to the political and social system through some, but not necessarily all, institutions. Inter-institutional linkages might therefore be important for determining overall confidence in the political order.

At the macro level, confidence in government—including parliament—is negatively related to government instability and unemployment. With the relatively few cases we have been able to examine over two time points it is not demonstrated conclusively that shifts in performance levels according to these two indicators can explain much of the shifts in confidence. But the analysis has not weakened this line of argument. The micro-level analysis has produced some tentative evidence that decline in support for—especially—order institutions could be due to a weakening of traditional belief systems, principally of religious beliefs. The modernization factor, particularly in its secularizing aspects, could thus undermine confidence levels in the longer run. Finally, we have not found empirical support for the idea of an informed scepticism or cynicism, as indicators of political competence, mostly promoting confidence in institutions.

NOTES

1. See the notes to Table 10.1 for the wording of the questions in the survey.
2. The percentages are based on weighted data, where appropriate. For the 1981 data, the weights correct for the oversampling of youth aged 18–24. In the 1990 data we rely on the demographic weights if the national sample has been found to have too large deviations from the population. Note that results from the 1981 survey, which have been available from the data archives for a long time, are sometimes analysed using a more elaborate weighting scheme or not weighted at all. We ran a series of analyses using various forms of weighting as well as unweighted data. In general we find that the analyses produce consistent results, so the main conclusions do not depend on weighting procedures.
3. The relevant tables can be obtained from the authors.
4. The marked decline of confidence in government in Norway, especially for parliament, raises the question: why was Norway not an exception in 1990? We performed a series of analyses in search of explanations. We found the decline of confidence in parliament only weakly related to social structural variables. Political explanations, however, are more promising. One major explanation for shifts in confidence in government is to relate trust to the political distance between government and the governed: in times of the left's control of government those on the left become more trusting, while right-leaning citizens become disenchanted, and vice versa if the right comes to power. As we found in Chapter 9, this interactive model has some merit in explaining the development of political trust in Norway, Sweden, Denmark, the Netherlands, and the United States from the 1960s to the 1980s.

   But this kind of explanation cannot normally account for changes in overall confidence levels as the gains in one political camp should be offset by losses in the other. In 1981–2, Norway was governed by a minority Conservative government and there was a solid non-socialist majority in the Storting. In 1990, a minority government of the Conservative, Centre, and Christian People's parties was in power following a minority Labour government 1986–9. If our assessment is restricted to the political complexion of the governments in the period immediately preceding the two surveys, we might expect improving confidence among voters on the centre-right. But changes in confidence by left–right self-placement show an almost linear relationship between the decline of confidence and ideological position, with those on the extreme left showing virtually no decline and those on the right demonstrating a marked decline. Thus changes in the ideological character of government—in a traditional proximity sense—offer a poor explanation. The relationship by party is more promising for the conventional wisdom as we find that voters for the Centre and Christian People's parties show a very weak decline in confidence whereas the drop in confidence among voters for the other major parties, on the left and the right, was considerable. These latter findings suggest that the deadlock in Norwegian politics during the second half of the 1980s and 1990 produced a situation with no winners, as governments from both camps were unable to govern effectively, thus alienating both their own and the opposition's supporters. This could well be part of the explanation of the decline in confidence in the Storting 1982–90. Tables relevant to this analysis can be obtained from the authors.

5. Other data for Finland in 1992, which have reasonable comparability, indicate a marked decline in confidence in parliament from 1981. The figure is as low as 32 per cent. It is tempting to interpret the fall in confidence by pointing to the dramatic downturn in the Finnish economy due to both the general depression in Western Europe and the collapse of Finland's trade with Eastern Europe. See *Kaleva*, 4 April 1992.

6. The documentation of the national data is uneven, and some problems remain on measurement accuracy. None the less, the overall results can be judged to be of satisfactory quality.

11

Support for the Democratic System

DIETER FUCHS, GIOVANNA GUIDOROSSI, AND PALLE SVENSSON

On and off during the last two decades, scepticism has been voiced about the condition of Western democracies. One of the first, and major, expressions of this scepticism was the appearance of crisis theories in the mid-1970s (Habermas 1973; Brittan 1975; Crozier, Huntington, and Watanuki 1975; King 1975). Although quite different reasons were advanced for the supposed crisis, these theories largely converged in their diagnosis (Offe 1979; Birch 1984; Svensson 1988). They agreed in identifying 'government overload', due to the increasing demands of citizens, as a problem which would lead to the erosion of legitimacy in representative democracies. In the longer term, this erosion of legitimacy would result in problems about maintaining the democratic system. Only when this occurs does it make sense to regard these problems as constituting a crisis of representative democracy. However, the development of Western democracies since the mid-1970s has not provided much reason to continue assuming that there is a crisis. Representative democracy as a form of government in these countries has, so far, not been threatened.

This obvious stability at the system level, however, does not exclude the possibility that a slow process of legitimacy erosion began in the mid-1970s. This process could lead either to future problems in maintaining representative democracies, or might have no impact at all at the systemic level, because there is no credible alternative. Although the available evidence for several countries does not seem to support the idea of the erosion of legitimacy, the empirical base is still too narrow for a definitive answer.

In the literature on developments in modern representative

democracies, there has been a dearth of analyses attempting to clarify the question of the erosion of legitimacy across countries and over time. It is this kind of analysis which is our concern in this chapter. However, instead of the term 'legitimacy', we follow Easton's tradition and use his term 'support' for the democratic system. The term has a broader meaning and is more appropriate to our concerns.

The perspective from which scepticism about the condition of Western democracies was voiced changed considerably during the 1980s. Unlike the crisis theories, the problem was seen less as the general overload of governments caused by citizens' demands but, rather, as a lack of government responsiveness to certain demands. According to a number of critical analyses, new political priorities have emerged as a result of societal and individual modernization processes. Above all, demands for more self-fulfilment and political participation have increased (see Chapter 1). The demand for greater political participation is usually connected to the expectation of being able to influence more effectively—in the interests of citizens—the decisions taken by the government and the administrative system. In other words, the realization of a basic democratic norm is encouraged (Cohen 1971; Dahl 1989).

According to the critical analyses noted above, the representative institutional systems of Western democracies are unable to process these new demands adequately for structural reasons. If this lack of responsiveness is structurally rooted, then the dissatisfactions it generates cannot be compensated for by exchanging governing parties through the electoral process. In which case, the central mechanism of representative democracies for neutralizing dissatisfactions no longer functions. A likely consequence is that citizens will become dissatisfied with the system of representative democracy itself. This would inevitably lead to the question of structural alternatives.

For most critics, these structural alternatives do not include the replacement of the representative system by a completely different political system. Instead, the alternatives involve the introduction into the existing institutional framework of more or less radical elements of direct democracy. This represents the second difference to the crisis theories: the problem is no longer the preservation of representative democracy but, rather, its enrichment through forms of direct democracy. In some Western democracies, at least, such reform proposals find favour among citizens and thus pose a credible alternative. It is this generalized dissatisfaction with representative democracy among citizens, as postulated by critics, together with proposals for limited structural reform, which constitute what was described in the introductory chapter as a *challenge* to representative democracy.

For completely different reasons, and to a very different extent, the crisis hypothesis and the challenge hypothesis see the representative democracies of Western societies as being in jeopardy. However, the question addressed in our analysis is not which of these two hypotheses is theoretically more plausible, nor which one better describes reality. Rather, we question whether there is a threat at all. In tackling this question we refer to an assumption which is part of both hypotheses and poses a necessary condition for a threat to representative democracy.

According to the two hypotheses, the citizens of representative democracies must have become increasingly dissatisfied. The source of this dissatisfaction is not just their respective governments but the very structure of the democratic system. We call this extension of dissatisfaction to the system level a generalization process. Because such a generalization can only be thought of as a long-term process, both with regard to individual citizens and to the citizen body in aggregate, we hypothesize a trend which can be tested empirically. Accordingly, we assume initially a decline in support for the democratic system—an assumption which was discussed in Chapter 1 (see Figure 1.2, hypothesis 9). The specific democratic systems under analysis are the representative democracies of Western Europe and our time span covers the period from 1976 to 1991. The data base for the analysis is drawn from the Eurobarometer survey series.

The analysis proceeds in several steps. The first step includes a discussion of the concept of political support and its operationalization. In the second step, we examine trends in political support in each country and across Western Europe as a whole. The third step compares levels of political support between West European countries. Then, finally, the trend and the level of political support in each country are considered in order to make a more accurate estimation of the state of democracy in these countries. We conclude with a summary and discussion of the main empirical results.

The Concept of Political Support

The concept of political support, in its general meaning, 'refers to the way in which a person evaluatively orients himself to a [political] object through . . . his attitude' (Easton 1975: 436). This evaluation can be positive or negative to a greater or lesser degree. With regard to the term political support, there is strong support in the positive case and low support in the negative case.[1]

The concept of political support can be further differentiated by interrelating different categories of political objects and different modes of evaluation (Fuchs 1993*a*). We can use Parsons's (1951) universal orientations towards all objects to differentiate the evaluative modes. Depending on whether an individual sees an object from an expressive, a moral, or an instrumental perspective, and experiences the object in the light of these standards, attitudes towards this object will be different. Which standard of orientation towards which object is adopted by an individual is partly determined culturally and partly depends on subjective decisions. Within the framework of our question, however, differentiation at the level of evaluative modes is only of secondary importance.

We start out from the hypothesis that a decline in support for the democratic system has taken place, irrespective of which evaluative mode played a role in that decline. The concept of political support on which our empirical analysis is based requires only a general evaluation of the democratic system, leaving open the question of which one of the three different evaluative modes underlies support. Instead, for our purpose, differentiation among the objects of the political system is the more relevant question. Here, it is essential to differentiate between the structural level and the actor level.

Both the crisis hypothesis and the challenge hypothesis are based on the performance deficits of Western democracies. These performance deficits are understood to be mainly that the state responds inadequately to citizens' demands in general and to certain demands in particular. The way of handling such performance deficits is to assign responsibility to the ruling parties and to vote them out at the next election. The citizen dissatisfaction generated by the performance deficits thereby remains at the actor level of the political system, and is thus neutral on the question of the system's maintenance. However, the matter looks quite different when the performance deficits are not only assigned to the decision-making actors but also to the system *per se*, including the institutional structures. This process of generalization—expanding and shifting of responsibilities—is affected by a number of factors. Here we note only the most important.

The first factor refers to the dissatisfaction itself: the stronger the intensity and the longer its duration the more likely it is that a generalization will take place. The second factor refers to a precondition for an effective government/opposition mechanism. This can only function if those who are dissatisfied assume that at least one opposition party might perform better than the ruling party or parties and that this opposition party has a real chance of participating in the government in the foreseeable future. To the extent that this is not the case, the probability that the dissatisfaction will remain at the actor level declines.

The third and most important factor is the extent to which the institutional structure of the political system has been legitimized. Such legitimization is based on fundamental values, such as freedom and justice, but also on democracy in the sense of government by the people. A country's democratic system has been sucessfully legitimized to the extent that its citizens believe that the structural arrangements correspond with the fundamental values. Under the conditions of stable democracy, citizens learn during the primary socialization processes that the institutional structure and the values correspond with each other in their country and, thus, they develop strong support for the system, or 'legitimacy beliefs'. These constitute the much-cited 'reservoir of good will' (Easton 1975: 444), which, at least for a while, leads citizens to accept performance deficits.

The effectiveness of the reservoir of good will, and the related barrier to performance deficits being generalized to the system level, depends—in theoretical terms—on how deeply system support (legitimacy beliefs) is rooted in the personality of every individual through the primary socialization. If one assumes, as Easton does, that processes of psychological identification[2] are essential, then one has to assume that the effectiveness of those barriers is also relatively high in the later life of these individuals. In contrast, if one assumes that the legitimization of a system is to be understood mainly as a cognitively-dominated socialization process, then the ensuing experiences of individuals with the operation of the system are far more important. In the first case, in the face of continuous performance deficits, we would expect a relatively slow generalization of dissatisfaction to the system level; in the latter case, we would expect a relatively rapid generalization.[3] Which of the two theoretical ideas is more appropriate need not be discussed further, because we take it for granted that a generalization of citizens' dissatisfactions to the system level has taken place.

Hitherto, we have spoken of the structure of the political system in general. But now we have to make a further distinction. According to Easton (1965: 266), the structure of a political system can be defined as a 'regularized pattern of behaviour and expectations' or, more simply, as the rules of the game. They constitute what Easton calls the political regime. In most Western democracies, the most important rules of the game are laid down in the constitution and can, due to this legal codification, also be regarded as the formal structure of the political system. However, if one is interested in describing and explaining real political phenomena, then restricting the rules of the game to the written constitution is inadequate. The 'constitutions in operation' (Lane and Ersson 1991: 194) must be also taken into consideration. The constitutions in operation, or the constitutional reality, is essentially determined by the informal structure of the political system. This informal structure is constituted in the rules of the game which have developed from political practice, and have become a matter of fact in the interaction between parties and between politicians. Although the formal structure provides the frame for the development of the informal rules of the game, and also controls them to a certain extent, it does not determine them completely.

Some of the most common indicators for describing democracies refer to this informal structure. This includes, for example, the fragmentation and polarization of party systems (Sartori 1976).[4] Fragmentation refers to the number of parties, and polarization to the ideological distance between them. It can be assumed that the parties' reciprocal expectations of behaviour and their patterns of interaction differ depending on how many parties there are in the party system and how strong is the ideological polarization between them. These different patterns of interaction become obvious mainly through their consequences. For example, it could be shown that party systems under conditions of polarized pluralism systematically impede a change of government and, at the same time, lead to unstable government coalitions (Sartori 1976; Powell 1987).

Moreover, the different patterns of interaction within party systems have systematic effects on the 'electoral control' exercised by citizens. Such interactions influence, among other things, the clarity of responsibility for government action as well as the clarity of alternatives with which the voters are confronted during an election campaign (Powell 1989). According to Weil (1989), it is mainly these informal rules of the game in a democracy, and their consequences, which represent the most important determinants of the legitimacy beliefs of citizens in Western democracies.

We do not want to go into further detail on the informal structure of democracy. Our explanation only illustrates that it is useful, even necessary, to distinguish between the formal and the informal structure of a democratic system. In the hierarchy of the objects of a political system, the informal structure lies between the level of the formal institutional structure and the level of individual actors. In relation to our question, this means, above all, that a generalization of citizen dissatisfaction to the informal structure of democracy does not necessarily extend to the formal structure. That further generalization requires yet additional conditions, one of them certainly being the existence of a credible alternative system.

The various objects of the political system have been discussed from a theoretical perspective and, thus, objectively determined in a certain sense. The question, however, is how the informal structure can be constituted as an attitudinal object at the subjective level of the citizens. In the nature of things, it is more difficult to identify the informal rules of the game than the formal, constitutional rules. In the end, the citizens can only identify the informal rules through their perceived consequences. At this stage, consistently perceived performance deficits are no longer assigned to individual actors but they are not yet assigned to the formal structure of democracy. Rather, the deficits are assigned to the pattern of interaction between the actors in the political system.

The cognitive explicitness of this attitudinal object is not decisive for our approach. However, what is decisive is that a somewhat systematic and consistent pattern is seen in the interaction of the actors—without them necessarily recognizing it as such. So the subjective complement of the informal structure, as we have defined it theoretically, is that an interaction pattern among the political actors is assumed and, moreover, that the performance deficits are attributed to that pattern of interaction. We assume that individual citizens are alert to this interaction pattern according to different degrees of cognitive clarity. Our empirical analyses largely use one indicator which we judge measures such a generalized attitude towards the democratic system on the part of citizens. And in this case, the system represents the pattern of interaction between the political actors—or the informal rules of the game.

Operationalizing Political Support

The empirical analysis relies, principally, on the Eurobarometer indicator about the functioning of democracy, although we also use two other indicators measuring attitudes towards democracy. The exact wording of the Eurobarometer question is: 'On the whole, are you very satisfied, fairly satisfied, not very satisfied or not at all satisfied with the way democracy works (in your country)?' Exactly the same question has been asked in almost all Eurobarometer surveys since 1976. There are no comparable indicators covering a similar time span nor covering as many countries as the Eurobarometer series. Even more to the point, we regard this indicator as measuring what it should measure: system support at a relatively low level of generalization.

As with almost all attempts at measuring generalized support for the political system, the theoretical status of this indicator is not uncontroversial. Some critics regard it as an indicator of specific support in Easton's sense (Schmitt 1983: 365; Merkl 1988: 29), while others classify it as an indicator of diffuse support (Weil 1989: 690; Widmaier 1990: 23). There is also room for confusion between diffuse and specific support (Kaase 1985, 1992*b*) due to Easton's lack of conceptual clarity: the criteria developed by Easton do not distinguish adequately between the two types of support (Fuchs 1989, 1993*a*). Thus, a discussion about whether the indicator measures specific or diffuse support does not take us forward: the important question is whether or not the indicator refers to a generalized attitude towards the political system. It is support, after all, which is decisive when it comes to maintaining the democratic system.

We agree with Muller, Jukam, and Seligson (1982: 246) that an indicator of system support must fulfil two basic conditions: first, that the attitudinal object refers, without doubt, to the system; secondly, that it is possible to give a different evaluation of that object. If both conditions are fulfilled, then it can be assumed that the indicator captures the attitude of citizens towards the political system. That is, analytically, the determinants and consequences of the attitude should be separated from the definition of the attitude. The second of the conditions is fulfilled by presenting the four response categories for the question (see below). The first of the conditions is fulfilled because the attitudinal object of the indicator is democracy in the respondent's own country. The validity of the indicator depends, first, on the fact that the respondents have any understanding at all of that object and, secondly, that this understanding corresponds also with the term 'the democratic system'. In our view, both can be assumed without difficulty. For citizens of West European countries, the term democracy should not be at all difficult to grasp; all have been living in a democracy for a long time, and instruction in what democracy means—if only to a rudimentary level of understanding—is part of the educational socialization process. We can demonstrate this point empirically in the case of Germany.

In a number of surveys conducted by the Allensbach Institute, respondents were presented with a list of various characteristics generally considered to be defining properties of democracy. They were asked to mark which characteristics, in their opinion, a country must have to count as a democracy. There are three time points for West Germany and one for East Germany. In Table 11.1 we show those characteristics which, on average, over the three time points, more than 75 per cent of West German respondents indicated to be necessary features of a democracy. In addition, the table gives the percentages among East German respondents in 1990.

The results from the surveys are remarkable. Almost by common

TABLE 11.1. *Meaning of democracy in Germany*

	West Germany				East Germany
	1978	1986	1990	Average	1990
Freedom of expression/freedom of the press	85	89	91	88	92
Equality before the law	84	87	86	86	88
The choice between several parties	78	84	87	83	85
Periodic free and secret elections	74	80	83	79	84
Freedom to travel	79	79	78	79	76
Freedom of religion	78	73	79	77	83
Every vote counts equally at elections	72	79	80	77	70

Notes: Entries are percentages. The question wording is: 'In your opinion what is most important in a democracy; which characteristics from the list must a country definitely have in order to count as a democracy?'

Source: Noelle-Neumann and Köcher (1993).

consent, the citizens of both West and East Germany consider several basic rights and some aspects of the competitive party system as the constitutive characteristics of a democracy. Indeed, the responses reproduce almost exactly the basic institutions of a polyarchy which, according to Dahl (1989), are the necessary requirements for a democratic system. Comparable results have also been found for the Netherlands (see Chapter 13).

According to this evidence, then, citizens understand democracy as they should understand it. In other words, we find that an indicator whose attitudinal object is democracy does, indeed, refer to the democratic system in the manner which we set out theoretically. In addition, the Eurobarometer indicator refers not to democracy as such in one's own country but, rather, to the *functioning* of democracy in one's own country. Thus we can assume that the question does not tap the constitutional norm but, rather, the constitutional reality or the 'constitution in operation'. In terms of our earlier discussion, the attitudinal object is the informal structure of the political system which lies between the formal structure and the actors in the political system.[5]

Thus, we assume that the Eurobarometer indicator measures generalized support for the democratic system, and that it refers to the informal structure of democracy. If the hypothesis of a decline in support for the democratic system is correct, then it should be possible to confirm the hypothesis empirically on the basis of this indicator.

Trends in Support

According to the theoretical framework developed in the introductory chapter, and the first section of this chapter, we can expect a decline in support for the democratic system in modern societies. The countries of Western Europe are obvious cases for testing such expectations. The Eurobarometer data allow us to examine developments in several of these countries over the period 1976–91.[6]

When asked about the way democracy works in their country, respondents could answer—from 1976 and onwards—'very satisfied', 'fairly satisfied', 'not very satisfied', and 'not at all satisfied'. The first two categories were combined in order to obtain a single expression of satisfaction. In Figure 11.1 we show the general trend in satisfaction among the citizens of the member states of the European Community.

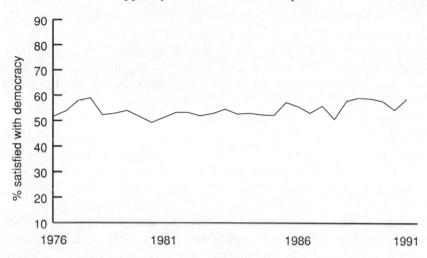

FIGURE 11.1 *Trends in satisfaction with democracy in Western Europe, 1976–91*

Notes: The data base is the total population. The data are pooled and weighted by population size. EC-12 consists of Belgium, Britain, Denmark, France, Germany, Greece, Ireland, Italy, Luxembourg, Netherlands, Portugal, and Spain. Northern Ireland is entered as a separate case.

Sources: Eurobarometer, Nos. 6–35.

The curve shown in the figure relates to the twelve countries of the European Community, with the data for each country pooled and weighted by population size. However, the simple curve conceals some details about the data. In the first place, the measure is not based on exactly the same countries for the entire period. Data for Greece have been available since 1980, for Spain and Portugal only since 1985, and for East Germany only at the last time point (spring 1991). However, when we calculated the trend in satisfaction with democracy for the nine 'old' EC countries—that is, excluding Greece, Spain, Portugal, and East Germany—the results were virtually identical. Thus, the changing basis of the measure has no substantive implications for our analysis. The second detail is that Northern Ireland is entered as a separate case. The conditions for the functioning of democracy in the province, particularly over the last twenty-five years, are very different from mainland Britain—a point we come back to in the analysis.[7]

The first impression given by the trend line in Figure 11.1 is of relatively high stability.[8] The proportion of those satisfied varies fairly evenly around a little over 50 per cent. The exact mean value is 57 per cent (see Table 11.4). The lowest value for the entire time series is 49 per cent (autumn 1980); the highest is 59 per cent (autumn 1989). With only one exception, a majority of the population of the European Community is satisfied with democracy over the entire period.

However, we cannot conclude from the trend lines in Figure 11.1 whether the general tendency is towards an increase or a decline in satisfaction with democracy. To clarify this question, a linear regression with time as the dependent variable was carried out. The results, presented in Table 11.2, yield a positive and statistically significant coefficient, clearly indicating an overall increase in satisfaction with democracy. This result stands in clear contrast to the expectations derived from the theoretical arguments. That is, there has *not* been a general decline in support for the democratic system in Western Europe, even at the relatively low system level measured by the Eurobarometer indicator. Rather, there has been a significant, if not particularly marked, increase in satisfaction with democracy.

Trends among Subgroups

A generalization of citizen dissatisfaction to the structure of democracy is the result of a prolonged process which neither influences all subgroups of the population simultaneously nor influences them to the same extent. So we test the hypothesis of declining support for the democratic system among selected subgroups. The subgroups are selected on theoretical grounds, guided by Inglehart's theory of cultural change which played a major role in delineating the specific issues addressed in this volume (see Chapter 1).

According to Inglehart (1990: 6), two fundamental changes are taking place at the individual level of the citizen which impact on their political attitudes and behaviours. One is evaluative and involves the value change towards postmaterialism. The other change is cognitive and involves an increase in personal skills, which Inglehart also calls 'cognitive mobilization'. Within the framework outlined in our introductory chapter (see Figure 1.1), both changes are understood as the essential components of individual modernization. In theoretical terms, it is precisely these changes which lead to the development of new demands on the political decision-making processes. Therefore, two of the subgroups we examine consist of postmaterialists and the highly 'cognitively mobilized'. A third subgroup consists of younger citizens. According to Inglehart, young people are still in their formative years and, thus, most receptive to new social developments: 'When basic cultural change does occur, it will take place more readily among younger groups . . . than among older ones, resulting in inter-generational differences' (Inglehart 1990*a*: 19).

Postmaterialists are identified using the common index distinguishing between materialists, postmaterialists, and people of mixed value orientation. Those who are highly 'cognitive mobilized' are identified as people of high educational level. To deal with the problem of different national education systems, the highly educated are those who have completed their education at the age of 20 or more.[9] Younger citizens are respondents aged 18–24. If it is mainly among these three subgroups that the new and different political demands have developed—and to which the parties respond inadequately—then the postulated decline in support for the democratic system should be most evident here.

However, Inglehart himself is not entirely clear on this question. Indeed, the question of support for the democratic system among citizens in general and postmaterialists in particular hardly features in his later study *Culture Shift in Advanced Industrial Society* (1990*a*). In contrast, *The Silent Revolution* (1977) discusses this point several times, but, even then, his observations are not consistent. On the one hand, Inglehart (1977: 143) states that political dissatisfaction is not inherent in postmaterialist values, and that political dissatisfaction among postmaterialists differs considerably from country to country. But, on the other hand, he observes: 'Yet, the global tendency is clear: Dissatisfaction [with the functioning of democracy] is most prevalent among the postmaterialists'; and 'distrust for the current political power holders does tend to be generalized into distrust for other institutions and other levels of the political system' (Inglehart 1977: 143, 307).

In a detailed analysis of Inglehart's work, Gabriel (1986: 117ff.) finally concludes that, according to Inglehart, postmaterialists are relatively distant not only from governments and their actions but also from the political system. Distance from the political system arises from the lack of congruity between postmaterialist values and the values and rules institutionalized in the structure of the system. From the postmaterialists' perspective, this incongruity is due, for example, to the mechanisms of party competition—which, in centring on competition between particular group interests—neglects collective goods. Other sources of incongruity are the representative structures of interest mediation in the political decision-making processes. As representative structures, they cannot satisfy postmaterialist desires for more participation in political decision-making.

In Figure 11.2 we show the trends in satisfaction with democracy in Western Europe among the three subgroups. The units on the two axes are identical with those in Figure 11.1 and all later figures. This allows us to compare the trends in satisfaction with democracy shown in the several figures. Comparing the trends among the subgroups with those for the entire population, it becomes obvious that the subgroup variations are rather larger. The reason, at least in part, might be the fewer cases.

More important for our question, however, is the impression of an upwards trend towards satisfaction with democracy among the three subgroups. In order to clarify the position, regression analyses were again carried out. The results are reported in Table 11.2.

These results confirm the impression already given in Figure 11.2: all three subgroups show positive and very strong regression coefficients. In all three cases the standardized regression coefficient (beta) is 0.72 or higher which means that at least 51 per cent of the variance is

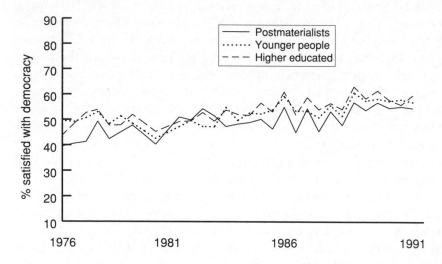

FIGURE 11.2. *Trends in satisfaction with democracy among selected subgroups in Western Europe, 1976–91*

Notes and sources: see Figure 11.1.

TABLE 11.2. *Trends of satisfaction with democracy among selected subgroups, 1976–91*

	B	Beta	R^2	Sign.	t-statistic
Total population	0.02	0.42	0.18	0.02	2.49
Postmaterialists	0.07	0.75	0.57	0.00	6.16
Younger people	0.06	0.72	0.51	0.00	5.55
Higher educated	0.07	0.79	0.62	0.00	6.89

Note: Linear regression on time.

Sources: Eurobarometer, Nos. 6–35.

explained. Moreover, the regression coefficients for all three subgroups are highly significant. Thus, we can conclude that among postmateri-alists, young people, and the more highly educated—or more cogni-tively mobilized—there is a distinct tendency towards increasing satisfaction with democracy.

Returning to our hypothesis about declining support for the demo-cratic system, the results of the trend analyses must be classed as a surprise. According to Figure 11.1, there is not the postulated trend for the entire population but, rather, a slight but significant upwards tendency. In the case of the three subgroups among whom, in particu-lar, we expected to find declining support, we find exactly the opposite: that is, increasing support for the democratic system.

Country Trends

So far, the hypothesis about declining support for the democratic system has been tested for Western Europe taken as a whole. For two reasons, we now turn to test the hypothesis in the separate countries. First, the condition of democracy in each country may be very different, both in relation to the general position across Western Europe and relative to each other. Secondly, the general hypothesis about declining support for democracy takes on a rather different character when applied to differences between countries. We start by describing the trends in satisfaction with democracy in each country, and then examine levels of satisfaction with democracy in these countries.

In Figure 11.3 we present the trends in satisfaction with democracy for three groups of West European countries. As the groupings—north-ern, central, and southern Europe—are for the purposes of clarity, the

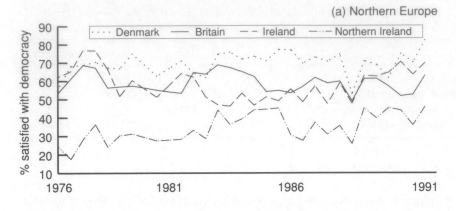

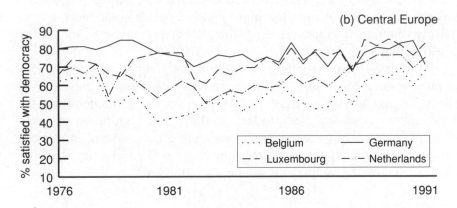

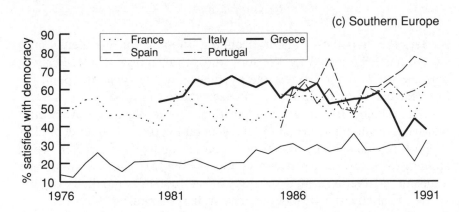

FIGURE 11.3. *Trends in satisfaction with democracy, 1976–91*

Sources: Eurobarometer, Nos. 6–135.

separation of the countries is rather arbitrary. Ireland and Britain (with Northern Ireland as a separate case) are classed as northern European countries, together with Denmark, while France is included with the countries of southern Europe. However, these three categories are not derived from any theoretical assumptions.

It is quite evident from the three figures that the overall picture of stability across Western Europe conceals very different country-specific developments. The differences relate to both the degree of (in)stability and to the size and the directions of changes. Clearly, then, the overall picture of stability across Western Europe is the effect both of country-specific fluctuations which are generally larger for individual countries than for these countries as a whole and of changes in opposite directions which tend to neutralize each other.

Even so, four patterns may be identified. The first is of small fluctuations and a clear trend, as in Italy which shows a tendency towards increasing satisfaction with democracy. The second pattern is of small fluctuations but no clear trend; in Germany, for example, after a decline in the early 1980s, satisfaction with democracy shows no obvious trend. A third pattern reveals large fluctuations combined with a clear trend—which is either towards increasing satisfaction such as in Northern Ireland, or declining satisfaction during the late 1970s but increasing satisfaction during the 1980s such as in Belgium. Finally, the fourth pattern is one of large fluctuations without any clear trend such as in France.

None the less, despite being able to detect these four patterns, the overall picture is still confusing. Above all, the strong short-term fluctuations in several countries make interpretation difficult. To obtain a more precise basis for drawing any conclusions about long-term trends, we carried out a regression analysis for each country. The results are shown in Table 11.3.

Looking first at the signs of the regression coefficients (B and beta), we see that there are four countries with a negative trend and nine with a positive trend. But if we look at the levels of significance, then we are justified in speaking of a real trend in only seven of the thirteen countries. That is, a negative trend in Greece, and a positive trend in Luxembourg, the Netherlands, Italy, Portugal, and Northern Ireland. France is a borderline case: according to the F-test, the increase in satisfaction with democracy is statistically significant (at the 10 per cent level) but the t-value is below 2.0. However, it is not clear that we can speak of a linear trend in Greece and Portugal. In the case of

TABLE 11.3. *Trends in satisfaction with democracy in thirteen West European countries, 1976–91*

	B	Beta	R^2	Sig.	t-statistic
Denmark	0.03	0.28	0.08	0.12	1.58
Belgium	0.04	0.26	0.07	0.15	1.47
Britain	−0.02	−0.20	0.04	0.29	−1.07
Germany	−0.03	−0.29	0.09	0.11	−1.64
Ireland	−0.02	−0.14	0.02	0.45	−0.76
Northern Ireland	0.10	0.65	0.43	0.00	4.64
Luxembourg	0.06	0.52	0.27	0.00	3.31
Netherlands	0.06	0.39	0.15	0.03	2.30
France	0.04	0.33	0.11	0.07	1.87
Italy	0.08	0.76	0.58	0.00	6.39
Greece	−0.14	−0.63	0.39	0.00	−3.68
Spain	0.06	0.24	0.06	0.44	0.81
Portugal	0.30	0.58	0.33	0.04	2.34

Note: Linear regression on time.

Sources: Eurobarometer, Nos. 6–35.

Greece, we are dealing with a shorter time span (1980–91), which, for the most part, was characterized by stability in satisfaction with democracy but with a dramatic decline concentrated on 1989–91. This undoubtedly resulted from the revelation of widespread scandals in Greek politics connected with allegations of corruption against the prime minister and the ruling Socialist Party. In the case of Portugal, the time span is limited to 1985–91 during which period there were enormous fluctuations. At the end of 1987, 76 per cent of the population was satisfied with democracy; by the end of 1988, this figure had fallen to 46 per cent; it then grew again to reach 77 per cent at the end of 1990. Thus, although the trends for Greece and Portugal are statistically significant, they can also be seen as a statistical artefact of large variations within a relatively short period rather than a real long-term trend.

The analysis of trends in support of the democratic system in each country reveals a fairly mixed picture as between decline, increase, and stability. There was an increase in Luxembourg, the Netherlands, Italy, and Northern Ireland. In Denmark, Belgium, Spain, Britain, and Ireland, satisfaction must be considered stable. This may also be the case in Norway; although only four data-points are available, they were taken at different time points between 1977 and 1989 and show only minor variations. France is an ambiguous case; and Greece and Portugal cannot be clearly assigned to any of the three categories. In terms, then, of the general hypothesis about declining support for the democratic system, we conclude that the broad picture is one of stability along with a slight tendency towards increasing support.

Levels of Support

One of the most obvious features of Figure 11.3 is that the average level around which fluctuations take place varies considerably from one country to another. This becomes clear in Table 11.4 which shows the mean values of satisfaction with democracy. All the available data-points for each country are included in the calculation of the mean values. Despite the limitations of the data in the case of Greece, Spain, Portugal, and Norway, we assume that at least a rough comparison between all fourteen countries is possible.

The countries are arranged in the table according to the average level

TABLE 11.4. *Levels of satisfaction with democracy in fourteen West European countries*

Countries	Mean (1976–91)		Time frame	Cases
Norway	86	High support	1977–89	4
Germany	77		1976–91	28
Luxembourg	73		1976–91	28
Denmark	70		1976–91	29
Netherlands	64	Medium support	1976–91	29
Portugal	63		1985–91	13
Britain	59		1976–91	29
Ireland	58		1976–91	30
Spain	58		1985–91	13
Greece	56		1980–91	22
Belgium	56		1976–91	29
France	51		1976–91	29
Northern Ireland	35	Low support	1976–91	29
Italy	24		1976–91	29
EC-12	57		1976–91	338

Notes: Entries are percentage satisfied with democracy. For the EC-12 countries, see Figure 11.1.

Sources: Eurobarometer, Nos. 6–35. The data for Norway were provided by Ola Listhaug.

of satisfaction with democracy. Norway shows the highest value with 86 per cent and Italy the lowest with 24 per cent. This difference is striking, although less confusing when we consider all the countries. Taking the 50 per cent threshold as a criterion, then a majority of people in twelve of the fourteen countries is satisfied with democracy. The average falls below this threshold in only two countries, although France is a marginal case. However, with the 66 per cent threshold as our criterion, then four countries show overwhelming support for the democratic system. According to these two criteria, support is high in Norway, Germany, Luxembourg, and Denmark (67 per cent or higher), low in Italy and Northern Ireland (50 per cent or lower), and at a medium level in the remaining countries (51–66 per cent).

The stability of representative democracy depends not just on the trend in satisfaction but also on the level of satisfaction. There is no objective criterion by which to determine how widespread satisfaction must be before we can talk of a stable democracy. However, it is implausible to assume that a democracy is in jeopardy if a majority of citizens are content with the system. According to the data shown in Table 11.4, this is clearly the case in eleven of the fourteen countries. France is just above the 50 per cent threshold. Remember that the question on which these data are based refers to the reality of democracy in the respondents' own country, not to democracy as a type of government. Thus, in terms of the level of satisfaction with democracy, we cannot talk of a threat to democracy in most of the countries of Western Europe.

This generally positive picture does not, none the less, alter the fact that there are considerable differences between these countries. What are the reasons for these differences? We do not attempt to provide a systematic explanation but we can suggest some possible reasons. Therefore, our discussion in the next section has only heuristic implications for further research.

Cross-National Differences

In order to identify possible reasons for the different levels of satisfaction with democracy, we divided the hierarchy of countries shown in Table 11.4 into two groups. The lower half runs from Spain through to Italy. In this group, we see common aspects between three pairs of countries. The first pair comprises Spain and Greece; the second, France and Italy; and Belgium and Ireland make up the third pair.

In the case of Spain and Greece, they are both relatively young democracies which were established after a long period of dictatorship. Dahl (1989: 315) emphasizes that the chances of stabilizing a democracy are, among other things, a function of the duration of the democracy. Only the existence of democratic institutions over a fairly long time allows people to gain positive experiences with the functioning of these institutions. Such positive experiences are, in turn, a source for the successful legitimization of a democracy among its citizens. However, while this duration factor helps to explain the relatively low level of satisfaction with democracy in Spain and Greece, it does not seem plausible in the case of Portugal. Although Portugal is a young democracy, satisfaction with democracy is more widespread there than in such a well established democracy as Britain. But in this case, we can point to the rapid and relatively continuous upswing in the Portuguese economy; as we know from the case of West Germany, there is a feedback effect from economic development to the legitimacy of democracy. That such a feedback might have happened in Portugal as well becomes obvious in the considerable and significant increase in satisfaction with democracy in Portugal during the period under analysis (see Table 11.3).

The common characteristic of the second pair is the structure of the party system. Italy and France are usually considered the best examples of polarized pluralism, in which the essential elements are high party fragmentation and strong polarization between the parties. We explained earlier, in our conceptual discussion of political support, that both aspects have a systematic impact on the level of system support. Thus, the low levels of satisfaction in France and Italy are not surprising. However, against that background, the highly significant increase in satisfaction with democracy in Italy and the significant increase in France between 1976 and 1991 (see Table 11.3) seems remarkable. But this development corresponds to structural changes in the party system. In particular, the strength of the communist parties—a major factor in the strong polarization of both party systems—steadily declined over the period. Thus, according to this consideration, as the degree of polarization in the party systems declined, so we would expect satisfaction with democracy to increase.

It is, perhaps, paradoxical that Italy has recently carried out structural reforms in its political regime despite the positive trend in satisfaction with democracy. Against the background of long-standing mistrust by citizens of the political élite, the relatively sudden and massive publicity given to widespread corruption among the Italian political élite must have played an important role in this increase. However, although there was a positive trend in satisfaction with democracy for the period 1976–91, it was still only a minority (31 per cent) who were satisfied with the functioning of democracy in Italy by the end of this period. Thus, despite demonstrating the strongest upwards trend over the entire time span, Italy still ranks at the bottom of the country hierarchy.

As for the third pair—Belgium and Northern Ireland—the political community is divided in both countries. In Belgium the division is between the Dutch-speaking Flemings and the French-speaking Walloons; in Northern Ireland, between the nationalist and unionist communities. However, whereas Belgium has accommodated the divisions by extensive revisions of the constitution, there is virtually a situation of civil war in Northern Ireland—which also involves a large-scale presence by the British army. Under such circumstances, despite the formal existence of democratic institutions, it is difficult to speak of the successful functioning of democracy. Easton (1965), in particular, has argued that the subjective feeling of the citizens of a country that they belong to a united political community is a precondition for the formation of a legitimate regime. We can, thus, probably assume that the relatively low level of satisfaction with democracy in Belgium and Northern Ireland has something to do with the severity of the divisions in the political community.

We have identified three possible ways of accounting for the differences between the higher and lower levels of satisfaction with democracy among these West European countries: the age of the democratic system; the structure of the party system; and the homogeneity of the political community. What effects these factors have on support for the political system, either separately or in combination, remains to be clarified in other analyses.

Support and Party Preference

In the representative democracies of Western Europe, political parties are the most important collective actors representing citizens' interests in the political decision-making processes. The manner in which they represent these interests depends decisively on whether the party is in or out of government. This difference may also have an impact on citizens' subjective perceptions. Citizens whose party is in power certainly have the feeling that their interests are considered in political decision-making, in contrast to citizens whose party is in opposition. Moreover, psychologically, supporters of a party which is in power are likely to see the functioning of democracy in their country in a more positive light than those whose party is not in government. That this is indeed the case is borne out in Table 11.5.

In all countries, as expected, supporters of governing parties are more satisfied with the way democracy works in their country than supporters of opposition parties.[10] Even so, in eight of these countries 50 per cent and more of opposition party supporters are satisfied; in three countries this figure exceeds 66 per cent. Evidently, then, party preference does not completely determine satisfaction with democracy but gives rise to a more or less broad variance around a mean value. The variance is rather low in Germany, Luxembourg, and Denmark—one reason why

TABLE 11.5. *Satisfaction with democracy and party preferences*

	Preference for a		Difference
	Government party (satisfied with democracy)	Opposition party (satisfied with democracy)	
Denmark	85.5	68.9	16.6
Norway	—	—	—
Belgium	69.5	57.6	11.9
Britain	86.1	48.6	32.5
Germany	97.5	81.3	16.2
Ireland	68.2	58.0	10.2
Northern Ireland	—	—	—
Luxembourg	82.6	70.0	12.6
Netherlands	91.2	67.9	23.3
France	79.3	57.1	22.2
Italy	34.9	14.4	20.5
Greece	82.7	38.7	44.0
Spain	79.2	40.9	38.3
Portugal	82.5	50.7	31.8

Notes: Party preference is a dichotomized variable: preference for a governing or opposition party. No party in Northern Ireland can be identified as a governing or opposition party. Relevant data are not available for Norway.

Source: Eurobarometer, No. 31*a*.

they are top-ranking in satisfaction with democracy. We do not have parallel data for Norway, but the very high level of satisfaction with democracy among the population at large (see Table 11.4) suggests that satisfaction is high among the clientele of both governing and opposition parties. Thus, among all the countries under analysis, Norway, Germany, Luxembourg, and Denmark form a group characterized by high popular satisfaction with democracy and relatively narrow differences in satisfaction between the supporters of governing and opposition parties.

There are strikingly large differences in the three younger democracies: between 30 and 40 per cent in both Portugal and Spain, 44 per cent in Greece. This is not surprising, bearing in mind our earlier discussion about the relevance of the duration of a democratic system: trust in the functioning of democratic mechanisms depends upon citizens having had positive experiences with those mechanisms over a long period of time. In particular, they need to have had experience with relatively easy changes of government. This group, however, includes Britain with a satisfaction gap of 32.5 per cent between supporters of the governing and opposition parties. In this case, the reasons might lie in the striking ideological polarization between the Conservative and Labour parties, and perhaps also the long period during which Labour has been excluded from government.

In all, then, in every country for which it is possible to distinguish between supporters of governing and opposition parties, we see a difference between the two groups in the level of satisfaction with democracy. In most of the countries, however, a majority of the supporters of opposition parties are also satisfied with the functioning of democracy in their country. Thus, according to these criteria, it is not reasonable to conclude that there is a legitimacy problem in Western European democracies. However, it is worth noting that the four countries at the top of the rank ordering—both by satisfaction with democracy and by the proximity of both groups of party supporters— are not only older democracies but also societies with a very high standard of living. In contrast, the countries with large differences between supporters of governing and opposition parties are all younger democracies with a comparatively low standard of living. Finally, we should note the special position of Italy among the fourteen countries cited in Table 11.5. It is the only country which has a clear minority, even among supporters of the governing parties, who are satisfied with democracy in their country. This highlights the widespread and profound dissatisfaction with the political system among Italian citizens. From this perspective, the recent structural reforms to the Italian political system are no accident.

We conclude this section by reflecting again on the status of the Eurobarometer indicator. Party preference is often used as a criterion for validating an indicator which should measure generalized support for the political system. If we had employed this procedure, the validation of the Eurobarometer indicator would have failed in Britain, the Netherlands, France, Italy, Greece, Spain, and Portugal, where there is a 20 percentage point difference in levels of satisfaction between supporters of governing and opposition parties (see Table 11.5). However, we believe that this validation strategy is not appropriate.

In the first place, there is little reason for citizens whose party is in power to believe that democratic mechanisms are not functioning as they should, particularly when the mechanisms work to their advantage. Secondly, preference for a governing or an opposition party may be the very reason for high or low satisfaction with democracy. However, this does not alter the fact that satisfaction with democracy is an attitude towards the democratic system—irrespective of what is influencing that attitude. The important point is that the respondent understands the attitudinal object as it is theoretically intended. We dealt with this point earlier when discussing the operationalization of the concept of political support. Thirdly, the validation strategy using party preference leads to a paradoxical result. If we applied the strategy consistently, then an indicator such as that referring to the idea of democracy would emerge as a good indicator simply because it hardly correlates at all with party preference. However, we used the indicator 'satisfaction with democracy'—rather than the 'idea of democracy'—as our principal indicator because it refers to a certain institutionalized form of democracy in a particular country. This, it seems to us, is the appropriate indicator—theoretically and empirically—when addressing the question of the stability of democracy.

Support for Democracy as a Value

The indicator 'satisfaction with the way democracy works [in your country]' refers to the informal structure and measures support at a low level of generalization. But, as we know, there are all manner of ways in which a democratic system, in practice, may fail to live up to democratic principles; for example, as in Italy, the more or less permanent exclusion from power of a major opposition party despite the emphasis on elections as a mechanism for dealing with citizen dissatisfaction. But citizens may be prepared to live with the deficiencies of a democratic system because they are committed to democracy as an idea, or as a principle according to which government should be conducted. Moreover, critics who are dissatisfied with the way democracy works in their country may not see a promising alternative system of government. In other words, dissatisfaction with the way a democracy works may be mitigated by support expressed at a higher level of generalization.

The Eurobarometer survey No. 31*a* contains two further questions about democracy which allow us to make this jump from a low to a high level of generalized support. The first asks respondents whether they are in favour or against the idea of democracy 'in principle'. The second asks respondents to decide between 'democracy is the best form of government' and 'dictatorship can be positive', with a third option of indifference between democracy and dictatorship. The important point here is that the questions do not refer to the functioning of democracy in any particular country but to more abstract notions of democracy as such; that is, the object of the attitude is not the functioning of a particular system of democracy but the very idea of democracy. In Table 11.6 we show the extent of support for such notions in twelve West European countries.

The message of this analysis is straightforward: in all the countries, over 90 per cent of respondents—indeed, over 95 per cent in most countries—support the idea of democracy. Interestingly, the highest level of support is found in Greece and Portugal, two countries which only recently emerged from a long experience with dictatorship. Unquestionably, then, in-principle commitment to the idea of democracy is almost universal in Western Europe. Support for democracy as a form of government is somewhat lower, but even so, with the exceptions of Ireland and Northern Ireland, exceeds 70 per cent. In so far as this indicator measures *active* support for a democratic form of government—and is therefore rather closer to satisfaction with the functioning of democracy—this gap is not suprising. We can only presume that the two exceptions reflect the failure to resolve 'the Irish question'.

What do these results tell us about the question of legitimacy and stability in the contemporary democracies of Western Europe? These democratic systems have been justified to their citizens by the political

TABLE 11.6. *Support for democracy*

	Idea of democracy	Democracy as a form of government
Denmark	97.5	92.8
Belgium	92.9	76.4
Germany	95.9	82.2
Britain	95.3	77.4
Ireland	93.3	64.9
Luxembourg	98.2	82.5
Netherlands	97.5	84.9
Northern Ireland	95.4	65.3
France	94.8	78.0
Italy	92.9	74.0
Greece	98.7	92.2
Spain	95.5	77.8
Portugal	98.5	84.2

Notes: Entries are percentages. The wording of the first question is: 'Let us consider the idea of democracy, without thinking of existing democracies. In principle, are you for or against the idea of democracy? Are you for very much, for to some extent, against to some extent, against very much?' The wording of the second question is: 'Which of the following opinions about different forms of government is closest to your own? (1) In any case, democracy is the best form of government, whatever the circumstance may be. (2) In certain cases a dictatorship can be positive. (3) For someone like me it doesn't make any difference whether we have a democracy or a dictatorship.' Comparable data are not available for Norway.

Source: Eurobarometer, No. 31a.

élites on the grounds of the idea of democracy and the values related to that idea. To the extent that the citizens of a particular democracy accept these justifications their legitimacy is secured. Legitimacy is generally defined as the extent to which a political order is rightful; and democracy is legitimate if the citizens are convinced that the institutional mechanisms of government embody these values. Put another way, democracy as a value is the standard by which democracy as a structure of institutions is evaluated by the citizens. The prerequisite of a successful legitimation process is the acceptance by the citizens of the values by which it is legitimized. The commonly accepted political values used for the evaluation of political structures are the most important elements in the culture of a political system. If one follows through this conceptional difference between structure and culture, then a political system is more legitimate and more stable the greater the congruence between structure and culture (Almond and Powell 1978; Fuchs 1989).

The extremely high levels of agreement with the idea of democracy seen in Table 11.6 shows that the basic requirement for successful legitimation has been fulfilled in all the West European countries considered. If the citizens of these countries also see a functional deficit in the way democracy works in their country, it is presumably from the perspective of democratic ideals.

Summary and Conclusions

The crux of our analysis is an empirical test of the hypothesis that support for the democratic system is in decline. This hypothesis is the inescapable inference if it is supposed that representative democracy is being questioned as a form of government—whether represented as a challenge or a crisis. According to both variants, contemporary representative democracies are no longer, for structural reasons, in a position to respond to the changed preferences and demands of their citizens. Such a systematic lack of responsiveness leads to the generalization of dissatisfaction at the system level, which, in turn, leads to declining support for the democratic system.

The empirical test was based on the Eurobarometer indicator measuring satisfaction with the functioning of democracy in a particular country, which measures attitudes towards the democratic system at the lowest level of generalization. Thus, the hypothesis had a good chance of being confirmed: if an erosion of legitimacy is taking place, then it ought to appear, at least, at this level. In the light of our analysis, this hypothesis must be considered falsified. Indeed, in so far as there is a trend, it is towards increasing satisfaction with democracy. But this increase is not particularly noteworthy. However, the increase in satisfaction with democracy among postmaterialists, young citizens, and the well educated is decidedly noteworthy and statistically highly significant. Moreover, these are exactly the groups in the population for which the theoretical literature anticipates precisely the opposite response.

There are certainly marked differences between individual countries, but these hardly disturb the general pattern. In Table 11.7 we have combined the results of two facets of the analysis—trends and levels—of satisfaction with democracy in the several countries.

We would have to come to a very sceptical conclusion about the condition of democracy if many countries were located on the lower

TABLE 11.7. *Classification of countries by trends and levels of satisfaction with democracy*

Trends	Levels		
	High (≥ 67%)	Medium (51–60%)	Low (≤ 50%)
Increasing*	Luxembourg	Portugal Netherlands	Northern Ireland Italy
Stable	Denmark Norway Germany	France Britain Ireland Spain Belgium	
Declining*		Greece	

*$p < 0.1$

Notes: The level of satisfaction for each country is the mean percentage satisfied with democracy 1976–91. The trend for each country is the regression on time 1976–91. Only four data points are available for Norway.

right side of the nine-cell matrix. Such democracies would demonstrate both low and declining levels of satisfaction among their citizens. However, as Table 11.7 clearly shows, only Greece is in the lower part of the matrix; and no countries are located in the bottom-right cell. Moreover, in the case of Greece, although our analysis does indeed suggest a significant linear trend, this is apparent only over a relatively short period; and during that period, there is considerable fluctuation. In other words, even in Greece, there is no clear evidence of a long-term trend towards declining satisfaction. Only two of the fourteen countries are situated in the 'low level of satisfaction' category. However, although Italy and Northern Ireland show, overall, low levels of satisfaction with democracy, they also show increasing satisfaction during the period examined.

Quite clear conclusions emerge from our analysis. First, there has been no legitimation problem in the representative democracies of Western Europe since the mid-1970s. Secondly, there is currently no legitimation crisis in West European polities. And, thirdly, there is a high probability that there will be no legitimation crisis in the foreseeable future. To cling on to some sort of crisis hypothesis in spite of our findings unquestionably places the burden of proof on its proponents.

There is one final point to make. Except for the latest time points, the analyses in this chapter refer to the last twenty years or so before the collapse of the socialist systems of Central and Eastern Europe. Thus, while our findings are valid for a substantial part of the period during which Europe was riven by competing social and political systems, questions arise about their relevance for future developments. In so far as a major alternative political system has failed, the institutions of the representative democracies of Western Europe are less likely to be questioned. Yet it is no longer possible to point to a worse alternative as part of a legitimating rhetoric for representative democracies. Thus, citizens may become less concerned with democracy as better than some alternative system and more concerned with the reality of democracy measured against normative expectations. From this perspective, dissatisfaction among citizens could generalize more rapidly than has been the case so far. Even so, it will have less to do with a 'crisis of democracy' rather than fevered conjuring about the problems of democratic politics.

NOTES

1. The term political support has a positive meaning. In order to show the possibility of a negative evaluation in the definition of the term, Muller, Jukam, and Seligson (1982) call their indicator the 'political support–alienation scale'. While the concept of support was developed in the context of systems theory, the alienation concept comes from a socio-psychological tradition (Seeman 1959). Thus, the meaning of the two terms is not identical. We prefer the variation between strong and low support to characterize the evaluation continuum.
2. Processes of psychological indentification are taking place; for instance, as a transfer of affective relations from the father figure to the political authorities. See Easton and Dennis (1969).
3. Easton (1975: 445) also assumes that permanent performance deficits have repercussions on diffuse system support in the long run.
4. This also includes some of the structural indicators analysed by Lijphart (1984); e.g. the composition and stability of government cabinets.
5. We assume that, because the question is about the *functioning* of democracy, it taps an attitudinal object at a lower level in the hierarchy of objects in the political system. However, if citizens understand democracy in the sense of the basic institutions, then it is unlikely that this reduction in the level of generalization goes so far as to overstep the threshold separating the system level and the actor level.
6. The question on satisfaction with the functioning of democracy has been asked regularly in the Eurobarometer surveys since 1973, but a ten-point scale was applied in the earlier surveys which is difficult to adapt to the four-point scale applied since 1976. Hence, we concentrate on the period 1976–91.

7. In the later analysis, for convenience, we refer to Northern Ireland as a country although it is a British province.

8. The time axis has been constructed on the basis of the months when the Eurobarometer surveys were conducted. The first time point is given the value 1 and the second the value 5 because the next survey was conducted four months later. This cumulation is carried on until the last time point with a value of 173. Thus the time factor is relatively realistic. For reasons of clarity, the figures do not show all these values.

9. Inglehart defines the highly cognitive mobilized as well-educated people who, at the same time, are very interested in politics. But if one is mainly interested in cognitive abilities, the involvement of political interests, which is a motivational factor, is inappropriate. Thus, we restrict our criterion to educational level. According to Inglehart (1990: 337), this is the best substitute for cognitive mobilization.

10. The data in Table 11.5 are based only on Eurobarometer, No. 31a (1989). So it cannot be ruled out that the particular political situation at the time in the individual countries had some effect on the differences. We assume, however, that situation effects would not change the basic pattern.

12

Political Support in East–Central Europe

GÁBOR TÓKA

In this chapter we examine the relevance for the new democracies of Eastern Europe of arguments about challenges to representative democracy in Western Europe. As in several other chapters, we focus on generalized political support: we are interested in mass attitudes conventionally thought to affect the stability of political regimes. After reviewing how the theoretical arguments might be applied to development in Eastern Europe, we derive some hypotheses about support for political regimes. These hypotheses are then confronted with recent data from four East European countries. Two limitations to the study have to be made clear from the outset, however. The first is geographic: we consider only Poland, Hungary, and the two republics which, prior to 1993, constituted Czechoslovakia. For simplicity, these four countries are denoted as East–Central Europe. The second limitation is the lack of sufficiently long and densely populated time-series data to allow us to identify clear trends. Thus, in many instances, only tentative conclusions can be reached about the plausibility of our hypotheses.

Political Support in New Democracies

Economic crises are usually identified as the most serious obstacles to democratic consolidation in Eastern Europe (cf. Przeworski 1991). The argument largely parallels the theories, emerging in the 1970s, predicting a crisis of democracy in Western Europe. Observing the expansion of state intervention in economy and society, 'overload' theorists expected governments in Western democracies to suffer diminishing autonomy: as citizens expected governments to react rapidly to an ever widening range of distributive problems, so the capacity of governments to make consistent, effective, and legitimate decisions would be reduced. The difficult economic conditions of the early 1970s, together with the allegedly declining loyalty to traditional authorities—thought to arise from cultural modernization—implied growing popular dissatisfaction with the functioning of democratic regimes.

Although these 'crisis' theories soon became unfashionable, it was not entirely clear whether the predictions were wrong because the theories were wrong or because the economic conditions of the 1970s were not sufficiently unfavourable and governments were not (yet) overloaded enough. None the less, it is not surprising that both the 'overload' and the economic crisis arguments appeared so soon in discussions about democratic consolidation in Eastern Europe. The legacy of the communist regimes and the region's position in the world economy mean that adverse economic conditions and government overload exist in these countries by default.

Although the literature on East European democratization rarely refers explicitly to 'overload' arguments, the similarities are evident in Przeworski's (1991) analysis of the transition to a market economy. He starts from the assumption that the new democracies need radical economic reform to achieve economic success. However, the high social costs of economic reforms give rise to mass unrest, which—provided no slide into authoritarianism takes place—ultimately leads to a deceleration in economic reforms. According to Przeworski, the key determinant of economic success (and thus, political consolidation) lies in the initial phase of reforms. If the reforms are not radical enough, the politically inevitable concessions to popular pressures will undermine their success and so economic deprivation will become permanent.

Przeworski's model can be summarized thus: popular dissatisfaction with policy outputs → introduction of economic reforms → popular dissatisfaction with the initial results of reforms → slow down of reform → declining efficiency of economic policy decisions → popular dissatisfaction with economic policy outputs → loss of legitimacy → which leads (under certain circumstances) to serious challenges to democratic consolidation. Thus, partly due to continuous economic decline, and partly due to the vicious circle generated by government overload, we expect a decline in regime support in East–Central Europe (*hypothesis 1*). This hypothesis implies that regime support will decline and, eventually, rise with economic performance and/or its evaluation.

We assume that economic performance has a particularly high salience for East–Central European publics for several reasons. First, the economic backwardness of the region relative to its Western neighbours. Secondly, the constraints posed by economic problems on regime performance in other potentially salient domains—such as crime, defence, social equity. Thirdly, the unusually sharp decline in production which accompanied the East European transitions to democracy. Moreover, following Easton's (1965, 1975) lead, we can add that new democracies cannot rely on a previously accumulated reservoir of diffuse support. Therefore, we can expect that the level of regime support is lower in East–Central Europe than in Western Europe (*hypothesis 2*), and that it will be strongly affected by the evaluation of particular incumbents (*hypothesis 3*).

On the grounds of various arguments, we have to modify the hypothesis about a decline in regime support due to economic decline (see hypothesis 1). We might expect citizens to express substantially greater satisfaction with the new democracies than would be expected on account of economic conditions. Either citizens blame the previous regime for economic failures, or they judge the new political system from the vantage point of a previous, even less popular, authoritarian regime. Weil (1989: 695) speaks of a 'honeymoon period' which can sometimes serve as a functional equivalent to a previously accumulated reservoir of regime support, thereby inhibiting the conversion of economic hardship into a 'deeper legitimacy crisis'. He adds that citizens 'may extend credit to an unproven regime or make an "advance payment" to the reservoir' of regime support on the basis of taking foreign democracies as models—provided there is a foreign democracy which is both held in high esteem and believed to be a comparable case. That is, a model which really can be followed (Weil 1989: 699–700). McDonough, Barnes, and Pina (1986: 736–7) suggest that 'in polities such as Spain . . . , where regime change has occurred within the living memory of most citizens, the public is likely to distinguish between types of political systems, and not just among different incumbents . . . [An] overarching sense of legitimacy may decay, rather than accumulate, over time as the "common enemy" (e.g. Francoism) recedes into the past.'

In both formulations, it is precisely the novelty of the democratic regime which adds to its initial legitimacy. In other words, these arguments assume that new democracies have a support reservoir to lose in the case of poor performance. Moreover, both Weil and

McDonough *et al.* apparently assume that Spaniards supported democracy throughout a rather long period (at least for a decade). But the East European literature talks about an erosion of the initial euphoria within a period of one or two years after the installation of democracy, and an equally rapid growth of disenchantment with democracy (cf. Simon 1992). Note, however, that both Weil and McDonough *et al.* anticipated that the 'system honeymoon' could only have a short-term effect in East Central Europe—not least because the different role and behaviour of the armed forces meant that the revival of the previous authoritarian regime ceased to be a credible scenario much sooner than in Spain. Furthermore, the level of assistance and capital investment from established democracies probably maintained the credibility of foreign models in Spain, but hardly in East–Central Europe. Thus, earlier scholarly work suggests that an initially high level of regime support was followed by a rapid increase of political dissatisfaction in East–Central Europe (*hypothesis 4*). The theoretical rationale behind the hypothesis is that although the new democracies have not accumulated a reservoir of regime support, they may be initially credited a certain reservoir of regime support—provided either that the revival of the previous authoritarian regime is a credible threat, or that there are some credible foreign models to follow.

The functioning of democratic institutions may also cancel out the effects of bread and butter issues on regime support. In Chapters 9–11, it is suggested that democratic systems have inbuilt mechanisms for recovering popular support. In line with these arguments, *hypothesis 5* states that the alternation of government and opposition—the prime example of such mechanisms—boosts regime support (cf. Widmaier 1990). For this to happen, dissatisfaction with the incumbent government must be converted into a shift in popular preferences followed by the installation of an alternative government. This process does not imply that the supporters of the new governing parties will be any more satisfied with the new government than were supporters of the parties forming the previous government. What hypothesis 5 assumes is a causal link between a change in the ratio of government and opposition supporters on the one hand, and the alternation of government and opposition on the other.

Certainly not all changes in the partisan composition of East–Central European governments in the 1990–3 period implied a change in this ratio. The first three (December 1990, December 1991, June–July 1992) out of four changes in Poland were carried out without a clear popular mandate for the new (usually minority) government. The reshuffle in Slovakia in Spring 1991 actually narrowed the partisan basis of the government; the same applies to the January 1992 change in Hungary when one of the coalition partners left the government. The July 1992 change in the Czech Republic was caused by the stunning electoral defeat of what had previously been the majority government party, but only involved its exclusion from the legislature and a reallocation of the portfolios among its former coalition partners. A clear link between changes in government and in the ratio of government vs. opposition supporters accompanied only the September 1993 change in the Polish government and the July 1992 change of the Slovak government. Thus, we expect that these two straight alternations of government and opposition were much more likely to boost regime support than the other five changes in the partisan composition of governments; the early 1992 changes in Hungary and Slovakia might actually have depressed regime support.

Finally, a conventional assumption of democratic theory is that, because people have a voice in the political process, satisfaction with democratic systems is greater than evaluations of policy outputs and economic conditions alone would justify. If so, then satisfaction with the functioning of the political system should be correlated with party preference. However, it is not particularly interesting to show that people who feel represented by the governing parties are disproportionately more satisfied. Those who think that their concerns are represented by the opposition parties show a higher degree of political efficacy and satisfaction with the functioning of democracy than those who do not feel represented by any of the principal actors in the political system (*hypothesis 6*). That is, among supporters of governing parties, those who feel their concerns represented by the opposition parties as well will be more satisfied with the political system. Alternatively, among people dissatisfied with the government or the economy, or whatever, those who feel that their concerns are not represented by any party will be less satisfied than those who feel represented by the opposition. The implication here is that regime support can increase even under severe economic conditions, provided the parties convince increasing numbers of citizens that some party speaks for their interests.

The literature on Eastern Europe's new democracies identifies several constraints on the capacity of the parties to generate support for the regime. The atomization of postcommunist societies, the high fragmentation of the party system, the low *Koalitionsfähigkeit* of some significant parties,[1] the instability and ideological heterogeneity of alternative governing coalitions—all are advanced as reasons why parties in the new democracies may be unsuccessful in convincing citizens that there is a party which expresses their concerns, or that, via a party, they have a voice in the political process (cf. Waller 1991). These considerations suggest that the effects anticipated by hypothesis 6 may not exist in East–Central Europe, although they may exist in (some) consolidated democracies.

Regime Support: Measurement, Levels, and Trends

The arguments we have outlined focused on the determinants of mass attitudes towards the democratic political system, in which we have assumed that these attitudes can affect regime stability. As our indicator of regime support we selected responses to the survey item: 'On the whole, are you very satisfied, fairly satisfied, not very satisfied, or not at all satisfied with the way democracy works in . . . (country)?' The object of evaluation is the existing democratic system as a whole, and not particular incumbents or institutions. We consider this indicator a more appropriate measure of legitimacy than support for the idea of democracy: citizens may well support some abstract ideal of democracy and still withhold support from democratic systems or institutional arrangements which they find to be imperfect realizations of that ideal. The validity of the indicator as a measure of system or regime support is discussed at length in Chapter 11.

Clearly, the notion of legitimacy implies something more than just 'satisfaction': 'It reflects the fact that in some vague or explicit way . . . [a person sees the authorities and the regime] as conforming to his own moral principles, his own sense of what is right and proper in the political sphere' (Easton 1965: 278). However, although our indicator does not encourage the expression of such feelings, neither does it prohibit their expression in the form of satisfaction and dissatisfac tion. It should also be noted that by relying on the distinction between attitudes towards particular authorities and the regime as a whole, we do not intend to match Easton's distinction between specific and diffuse support. In fact, we presume that regime support has several specific components yet remains distinct from support for political authorities. Citizens may well perceive certain policies as commitments of the regime rather than associate them only with particular incumbents: privatization, unrestricted rights to travel, religious freedom, or monetary restriction are appropriate examples in the East European context. Some citizens may also convert outrage over government performance into dissatisfaction with a system which allowed the rascals to come to power. A central assumption of our analysis, however, is that support for particular incumbents and for the regime constitute two separate dimensions of political support.

In Table 12.1 we show comparable data on 'satisfaction with the way democracy functions' among people in the four East–Central European countries and the EC member states. In 1992 at least, hypothesis 2 is emphatically supported: levels of popular support for the political system were lower in East–Central Europe than in Western Europe. During the period 1976–89, only Italians show levels of satisfaction anywhere as low as those found among Czechs and Slovaks in 1992. Satisfaction levels were even lower among Poles and Hungarians.

The trends for 1990–2 are more difficult to judge. The Central and Eastern Eurobarometer survey asked a Czechoslovak national sample in January 1990, 'Are you very satisfied, fairly satisfied, not very satisfied, or not at all satisfied with the way democracy is developing in our country?' The same item was asked again in an expanding sample of post-communist countries in October 1990, autumn 1991, and November 1992. The country means of the resulting variable are shown in Table 12.2, in the 'item 1' columns. At the time of writing, only some

TABLE 12.1. *Satisfaction with democracy in Western Europe and East–Central Europe*

Germany	77	Greece	56
Luxembourg	73	Belgium	56
Denmark	70	France	51
Netherlands	64	Italy	24
Portugal	63	Czech Republic	38
Britain	59	Slovakia	28
Ireland	58	Hungary	22
Spain	58	Poland	19

Notes: Entries are the percentage who are 'very satisfied' or 'fairly satisfied' with the way democracy functions in their country. For the EC member states, the 1976–91 average is reported. The surveys for the East–Central European countries were conducted in late September and early October 1992.

Sources: Table 11.4 and CEU (1992).

aggregate data (shown in Table 12.4) are available from the 1992 survey, so country means could not be computed.

It appears that satisfaction with the development of democracy declined markedly in both the Czech and Slovak lands of Czechoslovakia between January and October 1990, but remained virtually unchanged over the following twelve months. The Hungarian data suggest a small, although statistically significant, increase in political support between October 1990 and October 1991. Other data suggest that, all in all, support probably remained largely stable.[2] In Poland, however, a fairly significant decline in support seems to have occurred between October 1990 and October 1991, but still leaving Poles a little more satisfied with their democracy than Hungarians.[3] However, the data shown for item 2 in Table 12.2 suggest that, by September 1992, this was probably no longer the case. That is, comparing the means for 1990 and 1991 with the means for 1992, political support declined in Hungary between 1991 and September 1992, but did so even more markedly in Poland in the same period.[4]

We anticipated a secular decline in regime support in East–Central Europe (hypothesis 1). It was also noted that this proposition is consistent with the economic crisis argument only as long as the East European economies are deteriorating. With the exception of Slovakia, this was no longer the case by 1993. As we can see from item 2 in Table 12.2, increasing satisfaction with the way democracy functions was registered in Poland, the Czech Republic, and Hungary. However, even within the 1990–2 period, the monotonic decline thesis is supported only in the case of Poland. It is not the case with Hungary, where a relatively low level of satisfaction seems to have remained essentially unchanged from November 1990 up to late 1993. After the great decline in the first half of 1990, a stable level seems to have characterized the Czech Republic, too, only to be replaced by a fairly substantial rise in 1993. In Slovakia, the initial drop in political satisfaction was even sharper, but there seems to have been no change from 1990 to 1991, and a statistically significant increase of political support seems to have appeared there between October 1991 and September 1992. This seems a fairly safe conclusion when we see that by September 1992, Slovaks appear to be more satisfied with their democracy than Poles and Hungarians. In the autumn of 1991, they were apparently the least satisfied among the four countries. However, the strongest evidence against hypothesis 1 is provided by the post-1992 increase of regime support in the Czech Republic, Hungary, and Poland.

TABLE 12.2. *Trends in satisfaction with democracy in East–Central Europe*

	Item 1				Item 2			
	January 1990	October 1990	October 1991	Autumn 1992	Early 1993	Autumn 1993	April 1994
Czech Republic	3.3	2.4	2.3	2.2	2.4	2.5	—
Hungary	—	1.9	2.1	1.9	1.9	2.0	2.2
Poland	—	2.5	2.2	1.9	1.9	1.9	2.0
Slovakia	3.1	2.0	2.0	2.1	2.1	2.1	—

Notes: Entries are the country means on a scale running from 1 (not satisfied at all) to 4 (very satisfied). Item 1 is based on responses to the question: 'On the whole, are you very satisfied, fairly satisfied, not very satisfied, or not at all satisfied with the way democracy is developing in [our country]?' Item 2 is based on responses to the question: 'On the whole, are you very satisfied, fairly satisfied, not very satisfied, or not at all satisfied with the way democracy works in . . . [country]?' The third and fourth CEU surveys in Poland were conducted in August and October 1993.

Sources: Central and Eastern Eurobarometer (item 1); CEU (1992, 1993a, 1993b, 1994 (item 2)).

There are two apparent reasons why the decline thesis might be wrong. The first is that in the Czech and Slovak republics, most of the decline in regime support appears to be concentrated within a relatively short period. Considering the very high starting level of satisfaction with democracy in January 1990—just a few weeks after the November 1989 'velvet revolution'—this is consistent with hypothesis 4 about the effect of a honeymoon period. Secondly, as we shall see below, most deviations from the expected trend are anticipated by hypothesis 1: after the end of the honeymoon period, fluctuations in regime support (including the recent increases) apparently correlate with changing popular evaluations of economic conditions. Therefore, the economic crisis theory seems to be supported at the expense of overload theory.

Regime Support and Economic Conditions

We proposed that the main determinant of regime support in Eastern Europe is to be found in economic conditions. In the absence of comparable hard data on economic conditions on a monthly basis, we decided to employ only survey data to measure the independent variable. Among the possible indicators we selected evaluations of personal economic prospects, again for reasons of data availability.

In Table 12.3a we show the individual level correlations between personal economic evaluations and satisfaction with democracy, and the aggregate values of the two indicators in fourteen Central and Eastern Eurobarometer surveys carried out during 1990–2. Table 12.3b reports the respective figures for thirteen surveys sponsored by the Central European University Foundation,[5] which measured the same two variables but with slightly differently phrased items.

In each case, the individual level correlations are significant and in the expected direction. However, the existence of a causal link between economic conditions and regime support is, at first sight, contradicted by the aggregate level data. Across the fourteen observations for both variables shown in Table 12.3a, the correlation between the percentage satisfied with democracy and the percentage expecting favourable economic trends over the next twelve months is statistically insignificant and—quite unexpectedly—negative ($r = -0.18$). But if we ignore the three samples in which, at the individual level, the correlation between the two variables is conspicuously weak (the Czech Republic in January and October 1990, and Slovakia in January 1990), then across

TABLE 12.3. *Evaluation of economic situation and satisfaction with democracy*

Survey date	Percentage expecting favourable economic trends	Percentage satisfied with democracy	Correlation between the two variables
(a) ECONOMIC PROSPECTS[a]			
Czech Republic			
January 1990	9	87	0.14
October 1990	9	40	0.15
October 1991	25	35	0.24
November 1992	26	40	n.a.
Hungary			
October 1990	6	21	0.30
October 1991	22	34	0.30
November 1992	14	23	n.a.
Poland			
October 1990	31	50	0.36
October 1991	21	35	0.34
November 1992	25	37	n.a.
Slovakia			
January 1990	11	82	0.17
October 1990	12	26	0.35
October 1991	19	17	0.23
November 1992	22	24	n.a.

	Mean score on economic evaluations index	Percentage satisfied with democracy	Correlation between the two variables
(b) ECONOMIC CONDITIONS[b]			
Czech Republic			
October 1992	−0.2	39	0.36
April 1993	−0.2	47	0.44
November 1993	−0.1	53	0.48
Hungary			
September 1992	−1.7	22	0.32
January 1993	−1.8	22	0.34
December 1993	−1.8	29	0.32
April 1994	−1.2	39	0.36

TABLE 12.3. *Cont.*

Survey date	Mean score on economic evaluations index	Percentage satisfied with democracy	Correlation between the two variables
Poland			
October 1992	−1.6	19	0.35
January 1993	−1.7	20	0.27
August 1993	−1.6	22	0.36
October 1993	−1.3	26	0.30
Slovakia			
October 1992	−1.0	28	0.26
April 1993	−1.3	25	0.30
November 1993	−1.2	27	0.36

[a] Entries for economic expectations are the percentage of respondents choosing options 1 and 2 in response to the following question: 'Over the next 12 months, do you expect that the financial situation of your household will (1) get much better; (2) get a little better; (3) stay the same; (4) get a little worse; (5) get much worse?' Entries for satisfaction with democracy are the percentage answering 'very' or 'fairly satisfied' to the question: 'On the whole, are you very satisfied, fairly satisfied, not very satisfied, or not at all satisfied with the way democracy is developing in [our country]?'

[b] Entries for economic evaluations are the mean values of a composite index which sums responses to two items: 'To what extent do you agree that . . . (E) The present economic situation is very favourable to me and my family: . . . (K) The way things are in our country people like me and my family have a good chance of getting ahead in life'. Both items used a four-point agree–disagree scale. Negative values of the index indicate that more people agreed with the first than with the second item. Entries for satisfaction with democracy are the percentage answering 'very' or 'fairly satisfied' to the question: 'On the whole, are you very satisfied, fairly satisfied, not very satisfied or not at all satisfied with the way democracy is functioning in . . . [country]?

Sources: part (*a*), Central and Eastern Eurobarometers and Commission of the European Communities (1993); part (*b*), CEU (1992, 1993*a*, 1993*b*, 1994).

the remaining eleven observations the aggregate level correlation rises to 0.79 and is statistically significant.

The findings for Czechoslovakia in 1990 seem to be fairly consistent with the assumption of a strong 'system honeymoon' effect (hypothesis 4). In both the Czech and the Slovak republics, the extremely high levels of satisfaction with democracy registered in January 1990 evaporated without the economic expectations of the population becoming more pessimistic. As the initial euphoria faded, the individual level correlation between the two variables became stronger. As the 1991–3 data for the two republics witness (see Tables 12.3*a* and 12.3*b*), after the evaporation of this honeymoon effect, changes in economic evaluations became positively correlated with changes in the percentage satisfied with democracy in these countries too.

The CEU surveys examined in Table 12.3*b* covered the 1992–4 period, during which we did not expect to observe any system honeymoon effects. Indeed, in this second set of surveys the individual level correlations between the index of economic evaluations and satisfaction with democracy are always remarkably high, and the correlation between the two variables is also high at the aggregate level ($r = 0.88$, $p = 0.001$).

The data confirm that countries showing lower levels of political satisfaction also tend to be more pessimistic about economic prospects. In the Eastern Eurobarometer series, the correlation between the country means (not shown here)[6] for satisfaction with the development of democracy and the expectation of favourable economic trends is insignificant ($r = 0.36$, $p = 0.32$) but, with only four cases in the analysis, this is not strong evidence against our hypothesis. On the other hand, for the Czech and Slovak republics, when the three data-points apparently biased by the 'honeymoon' effect are excluded from the computation of the country means, the coefficient increases to 0.89 ($p = 0.055$). In the CEU time series shown in Table 12.3*b*, the correlation between the country means of satisfaction with democracy and the index of economic expectations is extremely similar again ($r = 0.94$, $p = 0.03$).

The story is about the same regarding national-level change over time. In the Eastern Eurobarometer series (Table 12.3*a*), there are ten cases which allow us to analyse how strongly changes in economic optimism and political support correlate with each other within one country between two successive time points: two each for Poland and Hungary (October 1990 compared with October 1991, and October 1991 compared with November 1992), and three each for the Czech and Slovak republics. Again, the correlation is statistically insignificant at first sight (0.36, $p = 0.16$), but after removing the conspicuous cases noted above, the correlation rises to 0.77 ($p = 0.02$). In the CEU time series (Table 12.3*b*), where ten observations indicate change over time, the resulting correlation coefficient is strikingly similar ($r = 0.72$, $p = 0.01$).

Thus, it appears that increased economic optimism tends to go along with increased political support; and decline in economic optimism tends to be simultaneous with decline in political support.[7] The decisive influence of economic evaluations on regime support may also explain the robust East–West difference in satisfaction with democracy shown in Table 12.1.[8]

Regime Support and Changes in Government

We also regressed the percentage satisfied with democracy on the aggregate data for economic optimism, excluding the three cases biased by the honeymoon effect (data not shown here). The results from the Eastern Eurobarometer data suggest that a one unit change in the percentage expecting favourable economic trends between two successive data-points in the same country yields a 0.9 percentage point change in satisfaction with democracy (cf. Table 12.3a). In the CEU data, a 0.1 point increase in the index of economic evaluations yields a 1.2 percentage point increase in satisfaction with democracy (cf. Table 12.3b). We can easily test hypothesis 5 about the effect of government alternation by looking at the deviations from these projections.

We argued that changes in the partisan composition of the government affect satisfaction with democracy only if the change alters the ratio of government and opposition supporters. We expected the January 1992 change in Hungary and the spring 1992 change in Slovakia to have depressed regime support, since they reduced the partisan basis of the governments. And, indeed, there was a bigger decline in satisfaction with democracy in both Hungary and Slovakia between October 1991 and November 1992 than might be expected on account of changes in economic evaluations: a decline of 11 percentage points and 9 points respectively in satisfaction with democracy as against a decline of 8 percentage points and an increase of 7 points in evaluations of favourable economic trends (see Table 12.3a).

We also argued that the June 1992 change in the Czech government, and the December 1990, December 1991, and July 1992 changes in the Polish government were unlikely to bring about changes in the ratio of government vs. opposition supporters. Indeed, the two changes in Poland were accompanied by slightly bigger than projected declines in satisfaction with democracy. Although one can see a 5 percentage point increase in satisfaction with democracy against the anticipated change of rather less than one percentage point (0.9) in the Czech Republic between October 1991 and November 1992, we doubt that this would reflect an alternation of government effect. As a matter of fact, all data-points for the Czech Republic after October 1991 show bigger increases in satisfaction with democracy than projected by the regression analysis.

We cannot solve this Czech puzzle here. More significant is whether the July 1992 change in the Slovak government and the September 1993 change in the Polish government brought about the expected increase in regime support. In the Polish case, there is no significant deviation from our projection: a 0.3 point increase on the index of economic evaluations leads us to expect 3.6 point increase in satisfaction with democracy; in the event the increase was 4 percentage points (see August and October 1993 Polish data in Table 12.3b). In the Slovak case, however, the hypothesis is confirmed: on account of the increase of 3 percentage points in economic optimism between October 1991 and November 1992, we anticipated a 2.7 point increase in satisfaction with democracy; in fact, satisfaction with democracy increased by 7 points (see Table 12.3a).

All in all, our data suggest that hypothesis 5 should be rejected: changes in the partisan composition of government do not automatically boost regime support. We found rather more support for the expectation that the magnitude and direction of the alternation of government effect on regime support would reflect changes in the ratio of government vs. opposition supporters. Ironically, however, support for this hypothesis is provided mostly by those changes in governments which reduced, rather than expanded, the electoral base of government parties. These political changes seem to have been accompanied by larger declines in regime support than expected on account of changes in economic expectations.

The Structure of Political Support

The pervasive effects of economic factors on regime support trigger speculation about the structure of political support in new democracies. In Table 12.4 we show the effect of economic evaluations on different types of political support. Measures of voting support for government parties, satisfaction with government, and satisfaction with democracy were regressed on economic evaluations in the thirteen CEU surveys. Identical measures were used for each variable. Support for the incumbents is measured by party preferences and satisfaction with govern-

TABLE 12.4. *Dependence of different forms of political support on economic evaluations*

Survey dates	Czech Republic	Hungary	Poland	Slovakia
Voting support for government parties				
September–October 1992	15	5	3	1
January–April 1993	22	6	1	3
August–December 1993	21	4	6	7
April 1994	—	6	—	—
Satisfaction with government				
September–October 1992	18	12	4	2
January–April 1993	22	13	5	9
August–December 1993	30	14	13	14
April 1994	—	10	—	—
Satisfaction with democracy				
September–October 1992	13	10	13	7
January–April 1993	20	11	7	9
August–December 1993	23	10	13	13
April 1994	—	13	—	—

Notes: Entries are adjusted R^2 (multiplied by 100) resulting from regressing four different measures of political support on two items: 'To what extent do you agree that . . . (E) The present economic situation is very unfavourable to me and my family; . . . (K) The way things are in our country people like me and my family have a good chance of getting ahead in life.' Both items used a four point agree–disagree scale. Voting support was measured by responses to the question: 'If there were to be a general election next weekend, which party would you vote for?' Supporters of governing parties are coded 1, opposition supporters 0. All others (including respondents naming some extremely small extra-parliamentary parties, plus Polish respondents naming NSZZ 'Solidarnosc', Slovak respondents naming SDL or SKDH, and Hungarian respondents naming FKGP) are excluded from the analysis. Satisfaction with government is measured on a four-point scale recording responses to the question 'In your opinion, has the present government showed a (1) very good; (2) good; (3) weak; or (4) very weak performance since it came into office?' The item measuring satisfaction with democracy is: 'On the whole, are you (4) very satisfied; (3) fairly satisfied; (2) not very satisfied, or (1) not at all satisfied with the way democracy works in . . . [country]?'

Sources: See Table 12.3b.

ment performance. Regime support is measured by satisfaction with the functioning of democracy.

With the possible exception of the Czech Republic, the results overwhelmingly show that all of these different types of political support are strongly influenced by economic evaluations, including regime support (satisfaction with democracy). In the Czech Republic, satisfaction with government is the most influenced by economic evaluations, but the other two measures of political support are only rather less influenced.

In the other three countries, voting preferences are the least affected by economic evaluations. With a few insignificant exceptions, satisfaction with democracy and political efficacy are at least as much influenced by economic evaluations as satisfaction with government.

In Poland and Slovakia, support for the incumbents is, in fact, much less affected by economic evaluations in late 1992 and early 1993 than the two measures of regime support. The data provide a clear and plausible explanation for this. There were substantial changes in the composition of the Slovak and Polish governments in July 1992, and at the beginning of their tenure the new governments were apparently not held strongly responsible for the state of the economy. However, about a year after the installation of these governments, economic effects on satisfaction with government and party preferences were as strong in Poland and Slovakia as in Hungary. In the Czech Republic, the Klaus government—inaugurated after the June 1992 election—was apparently not given such a honeymoon. This is understandable, however, as the Klaus government was dominated by precisely those parties which held the economic portfolios between 1990 and 1992.

Thus, the short tenure of governments in some countries can explain why economic effects are sometimes stronger on regime support than on support for the incumbent authorities. But government instability cannot explain the Hungarian results. In Hungary, essentially the same government was in office from May 1990 to May 1994, except for routine reshuffles and the January 1992 change noted earlier. Yet, throughout the 1992–4 period, economic effects on regime support are about as strong as on satisfaction with government. One possible explanation would be that hypothesis 4 is correct: that this is the natural state of affairs in new democracies, because diffuse support is largely absent.

In the Czech Republic, economic evaluations appear to have a rather stronger effect on satisfaction with government, and probably also on voting preferences, than on regime support. However, regime support is even more dependent on economic evaluations in the Czech Republic than in Hungary. The following rule may provide the answer to this puzzle: the stronger the effect of policy evaluations on support for the incumbents, the stronger these effects on regime support will be. Beyond a certain level, however, the effects of policy evaluations on regime support will be smaller than their effects on support for the incumbents. The theoretical rationale for this rule is provided by the notion of regime commitments. If the government and opposition parties are not believed to pursue widely different policies, then, first, support for the incumbents cannot really be based on policy evaluations, and, secondly, government policies will be perceived as regime commitments. Consequently, regime support will be more strongly affected by policy evaluations than support for the incumbents. Note that the rule is consistent with Weil's proposition that regime support is related not to policy evaluations, but to the capacity of the party system to 'present voters with clear alternatives, each capable of rotating into office, and none likely to destroy democracy. And governing coalitions should be stable and reflect voters' choices as directly as possible' (Weil 1989: 684).

We can come to a better judgement of our results by comparing them with similar data for an old democracy. We have chosen Britain for this purpose. The data sources are the 1987 British General Election Study and the CEU (1992) survey. Britain is an old democracy, with a relatively unfragmented party system, and a 'responsible' system of party government. Thus, whatever unambiguous systematic differences may exist between Western and Eastern democracies must be evident in this comparison, irrespective of the technical problems of comparability.

Even so, the conclusions from this comparison must be regarded as tentative. Whereas the variables used in this analysis were measured identically in the East–Central European countries, they were measured rather differently in Britain. Therefore, any differences between Britain, on the one hand, and Poland, Hungary, and the Czech and Slovak republics, on the other, may be due to measurement differences rather than to real differences. But we are on safer ground with the similarities: it is intuitively improbable that robust differences can be obscured by slightly different measures.[9] Furthermore, because of the limitations of the data, the comparison is restricted to two effects: that satisfaction with democratic political systems is boosted simply by the fact that many citizens feel represented by one of the major political actors (hypothesis 6); the extent to which the different forms of political support vary together with perceived or anticipated policy outputs and economic conditions.

Support for the government is measured by whether or not respondents named a government party as their preference when voting. Satisfaction with the working of the political system is measured by a different item in the two surveys. However, the survey by Dohnalik *et al.* (1991) used close equivalents for both items; analysis of these items (data not shown) shows that, although they were not only intended to measure the same phenomenon, they appear to be functionally equivalent in all four East–Central European countries.

Evaluations of perceived (and anticipated) policy outputs and economic conditions are measured by two variables in each country. We assume that the greater the probability that respondents would vote for a government party (based on issue attitudes), the closer they are to the government's ideological profile. We take closeness to the government's ideological profile as the best indicator of the respondent's generally positive evaluation of the governments' past and anticipated future actions. Respondents' scores on this variable were obtained from a discriminant analysis which predicted voting preference from whatever items on issue attitudes were available in the surveys. Unfortunately, entirely different measures of the evaluation of economic conditions had to be used in Britain and in the four East European countries. In Britain, we use a composite index about retrospective evaluations of developments in the national economy between the 1983 and 1987 general elections. In the Eastern countries, we use a composite index about the evaluations of the impact of current economic developments on the respondents' personal situation.

For each of the significant political parties,[10] one binary variable was created, according to whether the respondents felt the party in question represented them. There was a technical difference in the measurement of this item which meant that British respondents were allowed to name only one party, while in the Eastern countries they could rate several parties equally favourably. Since several pairs of the East–Central European parties are ideologically very close to each other, it seemed reasonable, for both substantive and technical reasons (for example, to avoid disturbing multicollinearities between the resulting variables), to treat these pairs as one party rather than two.

The explanatory power of different models of political support is shown in Table 12.5. In Model 1, we have two predictor variables: evaluation of economic conditions, and ideological distance from the governing parties. In Model 2, we also add the party related variables.[11] The standardized parameter estimates obtained with Model 2 are shown in Table 12.6. Several alternative models, including socio-cultural background variables and satisfaction with government performance among the predictors, were used to test the robustness of the reported findings. Since these parameter estimates did not show any theoretically interesting change across these alternative specifications, the details of these tests are not discussed here.

TABLE 12.5. *Determinants of political support in Britain and East–Central Europe*

	Czech Republic	Hungary	Poland	Slovakia	Britain
Voting support for government parties					
Model 1	38	11	8	27	46
Model 2	44	22	15	42	54
N	805	1,118	1,081	707	3,033
Political efficacy					
Model 1	21	14	10	12	10
Model 2	21	14	10	12	13
N	797	1,053	1,042	701	2,995
Satisfaction with the political system					
Model 1	19	7	14	10	20
Model 2	19	9	14	12	21
N	805	1,057	1,059	705	3,006

Notes: Entries are adjusted R^2 (multiplied by 100) resulting from regressing the three measures of political support on two sets of independent variables. The number of cases is shown in parentheses. The independent variables in Model 1 are economic evaluations and ideological closeness to government parties; in Model 2, as in Model 1, plus party representation variables. For further details, see n. 11.

Sources: British Election Study (1987) and CEU (1992).

Consider first the effect of economic evaluations and ideological closeness on political support. Advocates of structural differences in the origins of political support between new and old democracies may take some comfort from the results for Poland and Hungary. In these two cases, policy evaluations explain at least as much of the variance in efficacy and satisfaction with the political system as in voting support.

Ideological closeness to the governing party, however, has a much stronger effect on both efficacy and satisfaction with the political system in Britain than in East–Central Europe. The size of these effects appears to be proportionate to the size of issue and attitude effects on voting support for government and opposition parties (cf. Table 12.6). They all tend to be stronger in Britain than in the Czech Republic, stronger in the Czech than in the Slovak Republic, and, again, stronger in Slovakia than in Poland or Hungary. It is hardly surprising that issue attitudes are more closely related to vote in Britain's fairly old party system than in East–Central Europe, where the complicated patterns of

TABLE 12.6. *Determinants of political support in Britain and East–Central Europe, by country*

	Dependent variable	
	Voting support	Satisfaction with political system
CZECH REPUBLIC		
Economic evaluations	0.05	0.20**
Ideological closeness	0.44**	0.25**
Represented by		
CSSD or LSU	−0.11**	−0.01
HSD-SMS	−0.04*	−0.00
KDU-CSL	0.07**	0.03
KSCM	−0.02	−0.03
ODS or ODA	0.21**	0.06
SPR-RSC	−0.09	−0.04
HUNGARY		
Economic evaluations	0.03	0.24**
Ideological closeness	0.25**	0.07**
Represented by		
FKGP	0.03	−0.02
MDF or KDNP	0.20**	0.03
MSZP	0.09**	−0.11**
SZDSZ or FIDESZ	−0.27**	−0.07**
POLAND		
Economic evaluations	0.06**	0.30**
Ideological closeness	0.22**	0.14**
Represented by		
KPN	−0.10**	−0.00
PSL	−0.14**	0.03
PC	−0.07**	0.03
SdRP	−0.09**	−0.07**
UD or KLD	0.19**	0.02
ZChN	0.06**	0.03
SLOVAKIA		
Economic evaluations	0.00	0.24**
Ideological closeness	0.37**	0.20**
Represented by		
DS or ODU	−0.12**	−0.04
HZDS or SNS	0.33**	0.06
KDH	−0.14**	0.07*
MKM-EWS-MLS	−0.08*	0.00
SDL	−0.11**	−0.14**

TABLE 12.6. *Cont.*

	Dependent variable	
	Voting support	Satisfaction with political system
BRITAIN		
Economic evaluations	0.02*	0.05**
Ideological closeness	0.48**	0.40**
Represented by		
Alliance	−0.17**	0.02
Conservatives	0.22**	0.10**
Labour	−0.11**	0.06**

$*p < 0.10$ $**p < 0.05$

Notes: Entries are the standardized regression coefficients in Model 2 of voting support for governing parties, and satisfaction with the political system. On the variables, see notes to Table 12.5. For details of the variables, see n. 10. For details of the parties, see n. 9. The British and East–Central European results are not strictly comparable owing to some measurement differences.

Sources: British Election Study (1987) and CEU (1992).

coalition politics sometimes divide both the government and the opposition. But this seems to result in regime support, too, being more sensitive to issue effects in Britain than in the new democracies. In so far as ideological closeness to the governing parties is a good indicator of policy evaluations, the results obtained with Model 1 do not support the notion that generalized forms of political support are less sensitive to perceived policy outputs in consolidated democracies than in the new democracies.

With respect to policy evaluations, then, the dividing line is not between the new democracies and Britain, but between Poland and Hungary on one side, and the rest on the other. Moreover, the really striking difference between Poland and Hungary, on the one hand, and Britain, on the other, appears to be in the structure of voting support rather than regime support. Although the determinants of voting support are similar in the two contexts, their explanatory power is spectacularly larger in Britain, the Czech and Slovak republics than in Hungary or Poland (see Table 12.5). These differences far exceed what we would expect from differences in the measures used.

In our view, these differences are due to real differences in the popularly perceived ideological distinctiveness of the governing parties. In other words, the data suggest that it is probably not the supply of diffuse support which explains differences in the structure of political support but, rather, the rule we specified earlier. Where the policy preferences of government and opposition are not very clearly differentiated, policy evaluations have equally weak effects on both support for particular incumbents and on regime support. Where ideological differences are more clear-cut, policy evaluations have a greater effect on both kinds of support, but the effects on voting support are stronger than the effects on regime support.

The effects of the party-related variables on voting support are robust and their signs vary with the opposition or governing status of the parties in question. The picture is entirely different in the case of more generalized forms of political support. In Britain, all three party-related variables have an invariably positive direct effect on both efficacy and satisfaction with the political system, and (with one minor exception) these effects are statistically significant. In East–Central Europe, almost none of the party variables has a statistically significant positive effect on generalized support; most effects are insignificant and quite a few are, in fact, negative. Clearly, one peculiarity of the East European party systems immediately makes its mark on the structure (and possibly on the level) of generalized support: feelings about being represented by the former communist parties[12] have an invariably negative effect on satisfaction with the political system, and three of these effects are statistically significant. Although individual-level data alone cannot provide decisive evidence on this score, the British system of party representation appears to generate support for the political system, but the East–Central European parties probably do not.

Conclusions

We have presented empirical evidence that, in terms of satisfaction with the functioning of democracy, popular support for the political regime is substantially lower in East–Central than in Western Europe. We have also shown that this difference can be related to popular evaluations of economic conditions. In the new democracies, we found a substantial correlation between regime support and popular evaluations of economic conditions, at both the individual and at the aggregate level. Individual-level data for East–Central Europe demonstrate that, at least in some countries, economic evaluations may have as strong an effect on satisfaction with the political system as on support for particular incumbents. Evaluations of economic conditions, in particular, may have an even stronger effect on regime support than on support for the incumbents, provided that the government is relatively new—which has been almost always true in Poland and Slovakia since 1989.

Support for particular incumbents is unusually weakly related to policy evaluations in the new democracies, where an overarching consensus between the significant political actors or some other factor prevents the emergence of a close link between issue attitudes and party preferences. It is probably this factor, rather than the absence of a reservoir of diffuse support, which may account for the differences in the structure of political support between some of the new democracies and the consolidated democracies. We have also shown that some of the satisfaction-generating mechanisms of democracies—the alternation of government or the feeling of being represented—are not fully effective in the four new East–Central European democracies.

The lack of comparable data for 1989 and early 1990 means that we cannot tell whether the evaporation of a short-term 'system honeymoon' ever occurred in Poland and Hungary. In the case of Czechoslovakia in 1990, however, it seems very difficult to find any other factor which would explain either the spectacular decline of satisfaction with democracy, or the increase in the individual-level correlation between regime support and economic expectations during that period. Our findings do not imply that there are no enduring effects from a 'system honeymoon' or from an adjustment of economic expectations at work in Eastern Europe. But even if they do exist, they do not cancel out entirely the effect of other—mainly economic—factors in depressing regime support.

There is, however, no indication of a more or less permanent decline in regime support in East–Central Europe. This, we argued, should speak against government overload theory. Somewhat ironically, the thesis about the economic determinants of regime support can explain this finding. Tables 12.3a and 12.3b presented evidence of a decline, rather than an increase, in economic pessimism in East–Central Europe since 1990. And these changes in the perception of personal economic prospects were quickly converted into increasing satisfaction with democracy.

Finally, what grounds are there for supposing that democratic stability may yet prove fragile in Eastern Europe? After all, the threat of a military coup in these countries is generally thought to be absent (cf. di

Cortona 1991: 326–7): even the most sceptical observers find it difficult to identify any non-democratic alternative which would appear as credible and attractive for any significant minority of the citizenry. Even the minority of East Europeans who rate the previous authoritarian regime more favourably than the new political system tend to be fairly negative, in absolute terms, in their evaluation of the authoritarian regime. They are better described as sceptics rather than as die-hard opponents of the new regimes (Rose and Mishler 1993). Of course, we might argue that a high level of popular dissatisfaction would lead governments to sacrifice some degree of consistency and efficiency in their economic policies in an attempt to accommodate dissatisfaction among the mass public. But this is to reiterate the government overload argument, instead of proving that it correctly predicts an emerging crisis. Moreover, although the economic reforms in East European countries became associated with declining real incomes, the only known case (up to 1993) of an economic reform programme being effectively undermined gained its impetus from factors other than widespread mass protest against deteriorating living standards (see Russia Survey 1992). Arguably, then, the process of democratic consolidation is even less likely than the economic reforms to be slowed down or endangered by economic dissatisfaction on its own.

None the less, several recent East–Central European examples[13] suggest that there might be an indirect causal link between the mass attitudes analysed in this chapter and potential threats to democratic consolidation. First, the readiness of citizens to express dissatisfaction with the functioning of the political system suggests that professional political actors may expect to gain increased support from campaigns aimed at revising the rules of the game. Secondly, it seems reasonable to assume that, under otherwise identical conditions, politicians are more ready to revise elements of a relatively new institutional framework than in the case of a relatively old one. If both conjectures hold true, and popular support for the political regime remains relatively low in East–Central Europe, we can expect a much higher incidence of campaigns to refashion political institutions in the Eastern democracies than in the West. Some of these campaigns may eventually strengthen the legitimacy of the political system; probably many people expected such benefits from the 1993 Italian referendum on electoral reform, and many in Britain, too, expect political benefits from institutional reform. The third conjecture is that, beyond a certain frequency, such campaigns are more likely to increase mutual distrust between politicians and their scepticism about the benefits of complying with the rules of the game than to increase popular satisfaction with the functioning of the political system. The disruption of the political order may, of course, require a little more than that, but these outcomes alone may slow down the consolidation of new institutional arrangements. Thus a causal link between popular attitudes towards the functioning of the political system and potential threats to democratic stability looks more likely in the new democracies than in the older democracies. These three suppositions, and the links between them, seem more tenable than those upon which the supposed link between government overload, 'new politics', and a coming crisis of Western democracies were founded.

NOTES

1. For example, the former communist parties, the Polish KPN, the Czech Republican (SPR-RSC), and the Hungarian Small Holders (FKGP).
2. That there was any real short-term trend is contradicted by Bruszt and Simon (1992) and Simon (1992), who recorded the same level of 'satisfaction with the way democracy functions in our country' in November 1990 and December 1991. The October 1990 Central and Eastern Eurobarometer presumably measured a low point of political satisfaction in Hungary during 1990–2. In October 1990, Hungary went through a small political crisis; its peaceful ending might have been echoed by Simon and Bruszt's November 1990 data. The difference between their data and ours may be due to monthly fluctuations.
3. This finding is also supported by the October 1991 comparative survey of Dohnalik *et al.* (1991). In that study too, Poles and Hungarians were less satisfied 'with the functioning of democracy' than Czechs and more satisfied than Slovaks. Poles were slightly, but significantly, more satisfied than Hungarians.
4. This conclusion is somewhat contradicted by a comparison of the 1991 and 1992 Eurobarometer results (see Table 12.3*a*). These data suggest a decline of political support in Hungary but a small increase in Poland between October 1991 and November 1992.
5. The field work was conducted by local polling agencies: Centre for Empirical Social Research (STEM) in Slovakia and the Czech Republic; Median Public Opinion and Market Research Institute in Hungary; Centre for Public Opinion Research in Poland.
6. The unweighted national average of the percentage reported in Table 12.3*a* was used as the 'country mean'.
7. The same analysis of correlations in the Eastern Eurobarometer data between satisfaction with the development of democracy and economic expectations was repeated by substituting the data about personal economic expectations with responses to the question 'Over the next 12 months, do you think the general

economic situation in [our country] will (1) get much better; (2) get a little better; (3) stay the same; (4) get a little worse; (5) get much worse' (data not shown). The theoretical difference between these two sorts of expectations notwithstanding, the results obtained were similar, except that for the national economy, no 'system honeymoon' effect was detectable. We argued above that it could have been present in the 1990 Czechoslovak data. This minor difference and the slightly stronger correlation coefficients encountered in this second analysis may have been due to the presence of the same acquiescence bias both in responses about the national economy and satisfaction with the development of democracy, but not (or less so) in responses about personal economic expectations.

8. In May 1991 the *Washington Times–Mirror* (1991) survey found around 50 per cent of Spaniards and French, around 60 per cent of Italians and Britons, and 70 per cent of West Germans agree with the statement that 'I am pretty well satisfied with the way things are going for me financially.' These percentages were only 34, 25, and 21 in Czechoslovakia, Poland, and Hungary, respectively. With the exception of Italy, the percentage differences between the individual countries seem parallel to 1991 Eurobarometer and Eastern Eurobarometer findings about differences in the rates of satisfaction with democracy.

9. For this to happen, the measurement differences would have had similarly large, but exactly opposite, effects on the results of the analysis as the differences between the countries.

10. The parties are: CSSD, Czechoslovak Social Democratic Party; LSU, Liberal Social Union; HSD-SMS, Movement for Self-Governing Democracy—Rally for Moravia and Silesia; KDU-CSL Christian Democratic Union—Czech People's Party; KSCM, Communist Party of the Czech and Moravian Lands; ODS, Civic Democratic Party; ODA, Civic Democratic Alliance; SPR-RSC, Republican Party; FKGP, Independent Small Holders Party; MDF, Hungarian Democractic Forum; KDNP, Christian Democratic People's Party; MSZP, Hungarian Socialist Party; SZDSZ, Alliance of Free Democrats; FIDESZ, Federation of Young Democrats; KPN, Confederation for an Independent Poland; PSL, Polish People's Party; PC, Centre Alliance; SdRP, Social Democratic Party of Poland; UD, Democratic Union; KLD, Liberal-Democratic Congress; ZChN, Christian National Unity; DS, Democratic Party; ODU, Civic Democratic Union; HZDS, Movement for Democratic Slovakia; SNS, Slovak Nationalist Party; KDH, Christian Democratic Movement; MKM-EWS-MLS, Hungarian Christian Democratic Movement—Coexistence—Hungarian People's Party; SDL, Party of the Democratic Left.

11. The 'ideological closeness to government parties' variable was created by discriminant analysis, with voting intention (see coding below) as the dependent variable. Respondents who were coded 0.5 were excluded. The resulting discriminant function scores were then used as the ideological closeness variable; where necessary, the original scores were multiplied by −1, to make the highest scores mean closeness to government party. The independent variables in the discriminant analysis included V26A, V26B, V27, V30B, V33A-V33F, V37A, V37B, V38A-V38D, V42A, V43A-V43O, V110-V112, V121A-V121Q of the British Election Study, and Q16C, Q16D, Q16F-Q16I, Q16M-Q16R, Q18A-Q18T of the CEU (1992) survey. Before running the discriminant analyses,

missing values were substituted by the variable means. For further details, see the original codebooks.

The economic evaluations index for East–Central Europe summed responses to two items: 'The present economic situation is very unfavourable to me and my family'; and 'The way things are in . . . [country] people like me and my family have a good chance of getting ahead in life.' Both items used a four-point agree–disagree scale. High scores on the index stand for high satisfaction with economic conditions. For Britain, the index summed responses to three elements of an item series: 'Since the last general election in June 1983, would you say that (a) prices, (b) unemployment, (c) taxes have increased or fallen?' The items used a five-point scale running from 1 (increased a lot) to 5 (fallen a lot).

For 'feelings about being represented by parties', the British data are based on the question ' . . . do you feel that any of the political parties in Britain properly represent the views of people like you? If yes: Which one?' Three variables were created: one each for the Conservative Party, Labour, and the former Alliance parties. Respondents are coded 1 if the respondent felt 'properly represented' by the party named, 0 otherwise. In East–Central Europe, an item series asked respondents to rate the six to eight most important parties in the country on a seven-point scale, according to the extent 'these organizations express or opposes your views and interests'. On the party-related variables used in the analysis, responses are coded 1 if respondents said that the party in question expressed their 'views and interests very well', 0 otherwise. As some pairs of the original variables had very strong (0.40 or higher) correlations with each other, these pairs of parties are treated as one party, and respondents are coded 1 on the resulting variable if they gave the maximum rating to any of these two parties. These pairs included two liberal governing parties in Poland; two conservative–liberal opposition and the two nationalist governing parties in Slovakia; two centre-left opposition parties in the Czech Republic; and two liberal opposition parties and two Christian–nationalist governing parties in Hungary.

For East–Central Europe, the dependent variable voting support is based on the question, 'If there were to be a general election next weekend, which party would you vote for?' In Britain, party preference was measured by 1987 vote as recalled in the post-election survey. Supporters of governing parties are coded 1, opposition supporters 0, and everybody else 0.5 (including respondents naming some extremely small extra-parliamentary parties, plus Polish respondents naming NSZZ 'Solidarnosc', Slovak respondents naming SDL or SKDH, and Hungarian respondents naming FKGP).

The efficacy index was created by summing responses to two items: 'People like me have no say in what government does' and 'Parties are only interested in people's votes, but not in their opinion.' The CEU survey used a four-point agree–disagree scale; the BES survey used a five-point scale. High scores on the index stand for disagreement with both statements.

For East–Central Europe, satisfaction with the political system was based on the question 'On the whole, are you very satisfied, fairly satisfied, not very satisfied, or not at all satisfied with the way democracy works in . . . [country]?' Responses are coded on a four-point scale, with 4 meaning 'very satisfied'. In Britain, the item is 'All in all, how well do you think the system of democracy in Britain works these days?' The codes are 4, 'It works well and needs no changes'; 3, 'It works well and needs some changes'; 2, 'It does not work well and needs a lot of changes'; 1, 'It does not work well and needs to be completely changed'.

12. These are KSCM (Communist Party of the Czech and Moravian Lands); MSZP (Hungarian Socialist Party); SdRP (Social Democratic Party of Poland); and SDL (Party of the Democratic Left).

13. Somewhat *ad hoc* examples are: the Slovak separatist movement; the questioning by Samoobrona, an agricultural organization, of the right of the Polish legislature and government to outlaw violent political protest over economic conditions; the efforts of the Society of People with Incomes Below Subsistence Level to initiate a referendum on dissolving the Hungarian parliament and calling new elections long before the end of its term. These campaigns varied widely in their popular approval and success. But all three questioned the legitimacy of existing institutional arrangements and called for their revision in the name of greater democracy or greater liberalism. Whatever public support they enjoyed was much more likely to have been fed by dissatisfaction with the economic conditions and the existing political system than by anti-democratic sentiments.

13

Support for Democratic Values

JACQUES THOMASSEN

Developments in support for the democratic system in Western Europe were analysed in Chapter 11, using the level of satisfaction with democracy as an indicator of support. In order to assess support for democratic values, however, this analysis needs further refinement. The purpose of this chapter is, first, to develop a more refined operationalization of democratic values and, secondly, to assess the development of support for democratic values in Western Europe.

The indicator 'satisfaction with democracy' measures a felt discrepancy between democratic norms and the actual democratic process. It does not, therefore, measure support for basic democratic norms and values. Dissatisfaction with democracy does not necessarily mean that people do not support democratic principles. It might just as well mean the opposite; it is not unlikely that people may be dissatisfied with democracy because the actual political process does not meet their high democratic standards. Therefore, as argued in Chapter 11, it is only natural that the level of satisfaction with the functioning of democracy will be lower than support for democracy as a form of government or for democratic values. This turned out to be the case. Whereas in general support for democracy as a form of government was significantly higher than satisfaction with the functioning of democracy, support for the idea of democracy was astonishingly high. In all EC

The research assistance of Ilse Hento, Raymond Horstman, and Roland Pierik is gratefully acknowledged. I am also very grateful to Professor Ruud de Moor and Dr Loek Halman of the Catholic University of Brabant for giving me early access to the data from the 1990 World Values Survey.

countries at the end of the 1980s, more than 90 per cent of citizens supported the idea of democracy (see Table 11.1).

As far as support for the idea of democracy can be considered a valid indicator of support for democratic values, we might conclude that support for democratic values is high. However, using a single indicator to measure support for democratic values might suggest that democracy is an unequivocal and unidimensional concept. In the next section we argue that it is not.

Two Conceptions of Democracy

In order to understand what people mean when they say they support the idea of democracy we should know more about what they understand by 'democracy'. A simple way to find out is to ask them. Unfortunately, an open-ended question about what democracy means to people has, to our knowledge, never been asked in comparative research. But the one occasion when such a question was put to a sample of the mass public is sufficient to support the argument that democracy is a multi-dimensional concept.

In a Dutch mass survey in the early 1970s people were asked what they thought of when they heard the word 'democracy'. An overview of the more frequent responses is presented in Table 13.1. Obviously democracy means different things to different people. The most remarkable finding is that most answers do not refer, directly or indirectly, to the literal meaning of democracy—government by the people or popular sovereignty. According to these data, most people associate democracy with liberty. Similar results were obtained by a different method in West Germany in 1978 when people were asked to choose the most important characteristics of democracy from a list of possible characteristics. The characteristic chosen by most people (85 per cent) was freedom of the press and opinion. The possibility of choosing between different political parties was mentioned by 79 per cent. But for a characteristic such as citizens participating in the decision-making of the state, the score was no higher than 51 per cent (Noelle-Neumann and Piel 1983: 218; Conradt 1981; see also Table 11.1).

These results may be counter-intuitive, but they are not inconsistent with the development of Western liberal democracy. Liberal democracy can be considered as an historical compromise between two different principles. The first is the principle of popular sovereignty:

TABLE 13.1. *Conceptions of democracy*

Answer	%
Freedom of expression, freedom of press	18.3
Freedom, being free, free country	15.2
Equality	4.9
Equal rights and duties	3.6
Having a say in political decisions	7.7
Popular sovereignty	3.5
Don't know/No answer	14.1
N	1,036

Notes: Entries are proportion of respondents who give this type of answer to the question: 'What do you think of when you hear the word democracy?' Only answers given by more than twenty respondents are presented here, therefore the percentages do not add up to 100 per cent

Source: Bertrand (1981: 5).

the sovereign power is exercised by, or in the name of, the people. The second principle, and at least as important, is that the liberty of individual citizens must be protected against the power of the state, whether or not this is legitimized by the (majority of the) people.

It is essential for the further argument in this chapter that there is no fixed balance between these two principles which, together, constitute the normative basis of Western liberal democracies. The relative weight of the two principles can be different in different states, or within one state at different times, and different people can give them different weights. It is argued in this chapter that the relative weight of these two principles in the value orientations of the mass publics in West European democracies has changed in favour of the second principle. However, in order to underpin this argument, we need a more detailed description of the two basic principles.

It is generally recognized that two different strands of thought can be distinguished in normative democratic theory. Although various labels are used to indicate essentially the same distinction, they can be identified as the *individualist* versus the *collectivist* theory (Pennock 1979), or the Anglo-American or liberal theory versus the French or Continental theory (Sabine 1952). More or less the same distinction can be found in several well-known works on democratic theory. To mention only two, both Dahl's (1956) distinction between populist and Madisonian democracy and Lijphart's (1984) distinction between

majoritarian and consensus government are based on the same philosophical roots. The difference between the two theories can also be
indicated by the distinction between the theory of the rule of law or the
Rechtsstaat and the theory of democracy in the sense of 'popular
sovereignty'. The differences between the two theories largely reflect
those between Locke and the English Revolution on the one hand, and
Rousseau and the French Revolution on the other (Sabine 1952).

Before going on to indicate a number of ways in which the two
theories differ, we make some preliminary remarks about the status
of the distinction between these two theories and its analytic use. It
might be clear that the distinction between the two theories of democracy is an analytic one and hardly one of political practice. Democracy
and *Rechtsstaat* have different intellectual roots but have been integrated in Western democratic institutions. Nevertheless, the two theories clearly exist as different views on democratic values and
institutions. But it might be better to consider them as ideal types in
the Weberian sense; in reality, we will seldom find these ideal types but,
rather, mixed types.

However, if these theories have any substantive meaning, one might
expect a certain correlation between their different aspects, both in
democratic thought and political institutions. Lijphart (1984), for
instance, found that at the institutional level different aspects of the
two theories tend to cluster together. Therefore, he was able to distinguish between majoritarian and consensus types of government on
empirical grounds. One of our objectives is to test to what extent
attitudes with respect to different aspects of democracy are also constrained by the same dimensional structure. But first we need a more
specific distinction between the two theories of democracy.

The difference between them can be clarified by a number of pairs of
concepts: liberty versus equality, small versus big government, pluralism versus the common good, and an instrumental versus a developmental view of participation. Clearly, not all these pairs of concepts are
at the same level of abstraction. Liberty, equality, and the common
good refer to basic democratic values. The size of government and
views on political participation reflect political norms of a lower
level, because they can logically be deduced from the basic values of
liberty and equality.

Aspects of Democracy

The first distinction between the two theories refers to the basic democratic values of *liberty* and *equality*. However, it would be too simple to say that the difference between the two theories reflects the classic tension between liberty and equality. Liberty plays a prominent role in both theories, but the conceptualization of liberty associated with these two theories is totally different. In both theories, liberty refers to the relationship between the citizen and the state, but in a different way.

According to the collectivist theory, a free citizen is a citizen who takes part in the process of decision-making—who actively participates in politics. In its most extreme form, this idea of democracy has been expressed by Rousseau. In his view, freedom and participation in the legislative process are the same thing. Participation in law-making means that the citizen still has to obey the laws but, because these laws are of his own making, he remains his own master. According to this 'positive' concept of liberty (Berlin 1969), there is a logical relationship between liberty and self-government, participation, and democracy (Charmant and Lehning 1989: 25). It is anything but inconsistent with political equality.

The individualist view on liberty is totally different, and is usually referred to as the 'negative' or protective concept of freedom. Freedom is interpreted as freedom from constraints by other human beings, in particular by the state or the government. This view supports the desirability of civil liberties such as freedom of speech and press, of association, assembly and religion, the rights of privacy and lifestyle, the right of due process (McClosky and Brill 1983), the protection and tolerance of minorities, and cultural and political diversity. The participation of citizens in the political process is an instrument which can be helpful in protecting this freedom but is certainly not identical with it (Kleimansegg 1988: 81). It is not the right to participate in the power of the state that is essential but the right to be left alone by the state, whether or not its power is legitimated by the will of the people. This negative concept of liberty has a less comfortable relationship with equality, but the extent to which this is the case depends also on the interpretation of equality.

The principle of equality can be interpreted either as political equality or social equality. Political equality in a formal sense is hardly an issue. It is an accepted principle in both theories. Moreover, there is no

inherent tension between political equality and liberty. Quite the contrary: the individualist interpretation of democracy demands that, once
it is recognized that the people should make political decisions, then all
the constituent individuals should have an equal say (Holden 1988: 15).

There is a tension between liberty and social equality, however. The
individualist theory of democracy emphasizes that a policy to enforce
social equality is a threat to liberty. But the extent to which this is the
case depends on the form of equality referred to. One form refers to
equality of opportunity. In its most basic form, this means no more than
that individuals should have equal chances. This can hardly be seen as a
threat to liberty. However, the matter becomes more complicated when
it is maintained that opportunities for certain groups are, in fact, not
equal because they do not have an equal start. From this perspective, it
can be argued that government policy should improve the opportunities
of disadvantaged groups, for instance by affirmative government action
to compensate women, blacks, and other minorities. Such policies can
be enforced only by limiting the freedom of people to a certain extent.

The welfare state can be seen as the embodiment of this broader
concept of democracy, in which not only civil rights and political
equality but also social rights and social equality are considered
fundamental rights. In this context, the ideal of social equality tends
to imply not only equality of opportunity but also equality of condition.
If social equality is literally supposed to mean that all people have
available the same resources, this is obviously inconsistent with the
principle of liberty. It could only be attained and maintained by
suppression.

Thus, no society which adheres to both liberty and equality can define
equality as equality of condition (Pennock 1979: 36), at least not in an
absolute sense. At the same time, for reasons of legitimacy, no political
system can afford to be insensitive to the fact that unlimited liberty will
lead to an inequality of condition which will not be acceptable to its
citizens. The most obvious case is the responsibility of the government
to reduce the gap between rich and poor (Verba *et al.* 1987: 99).
Therefore, all democratic societies will find a compromise somewhere
between the two extremes of unlimited liberty at the risk of extreme
differences in the social condition of its people, and complete social
equality which can only be achieved—and even then in theory only—by
an oppressive political system. But even in a mild form, the reduction of
social inequality will not come into being spontaneously. It will have to
be enforced by government intervention. For this reason, as we will see

below, people's opinion on social equality will be affected by their attitude to the role of government.

The *role of government* is another respect in which the two theories differ. In a radical democratic view the state is the embodiment of popular sovereignty—the expression of the will of the people. This will is supreme: there is nothing the people are not allowed to do (Holden 1988: 70). Therefore, there is no reason to limit the power of the government in directing societal development and taking care of the people's welfare. Government intervention and regulation are not inimical to democracy but are democratic instruments steering society in accordance with the view of the elected government.

According to the individualist view, government intervention should be limited to a minimum. The identification of the power of the state with the will of the people, and hence the argument that the power of the state needs no constraints, is considered as the very definition of a totalitarian state. This view makes no distinction between the will of the people as a whole and the right of individual citizens to be protected against that will. Even though this extreme version of the collectivist view has few adherents in Western democracies, from the individualist perspective increasing government intervention and regulation are seen as a fundamental threat to the essential value of democracy—individual freedom.

The development of the welfare state seems to leave no doubt about which view has won the argument. It is widely recognized—even in the Constitution in some countries—that the government is responsible for public welfare; for example, for minimum wages, public health, public transport, education, full employment, public housing, incomes and prices, in addition to individual rights to liberty. However, in most countries, increasing state intervention and regulation has become a political issue. For several reasons, the idea that the government should direct and regulate societal developments has become less popular.

A third aspect in which these theories differ is in the notion of the *general will* as against *pluralism*. A radical interpretation of popular sovereignty is incompatible with the existence of intermediary institutions between the individual and the state. Interest groups can only lead to factionalism and are inimical to the general interest. The debate on the positive and negative aspects of 'factions' has a long history and has its modern variant in the debate on pluralism. On the one hand, pluralism has been praised as the ultimate form of democratic government, reconciling the tension between majority rule and respect for minorities (Dahl 1956). On the other hand, from a different perspective, it is condemned as 'interest-group-liberalism' (Lowi 1969; McConnell 1966). Whereas the positive interpretation of pluralism envisages a self-correcting system in which the invisible hand of political bargaining inevitably restrains the concentration of power, both Lowi and McConnell foresee the fragmentation of the polity into a series of small, autonomous, fiefdoms which are all independent of each other.

Again this is a matter of perspective. Where a liberal democrat welcomes a contribution to the intricate web of checks and balances, the radical democrat sees an intrusion on the general interest and the general will of the people as expressed by the power of the state. Whereas the latter view implies government as a power above partial interests, a pluralist vision implies a more horizontal view, in which the government is, to a large extent, part of a complicated network of groups and agencies which are more or less permanently involved in negotiations with each other.

Both the individualist and the collectivist theory of democracy value *political participation* positively. However, the interpretation of the value of political participation is different. A fundamental characteristic of the collectivist theory is that it hardly recognizes representative democracy as a type of democracy *sui generis* but, rather, as a surrogate of true democracy—which is direct democracy. Hence, the importance of the idea of a 'participatory democracy' which, according to this view, 'fosters human development, enhances a sense of political efficacy, reduces a sense of estrangement from power centres, nurtures a concern for collective problems and contributes to the formation of an active and knowledgeable citizenry capable of taking a more acute interest in governmental affairs' (Held 1987: 259–60). In a romantic version of this view, decision-making should be decentralized to smaller communities or groups in which forms of direct democracy might be feasible. Opportunities for participation should not be limited to state affairs; people should also be involved in decision-making processes outside the sphere of government, such as economic enterprises and other central institutions of society (Held 1987: 259).

According to the individualist theory of democracy, representative democracy should not be confused with direct democracy. In general, politics should be left to politicians. In normal circumstances, most citizens take this division of labour for granted—probably because they have more important things to do than spend their time on politics. But they will spring to arms when their personal interests are at stake. Therefore, in this so called instrumental theory of participation, political participation is considered as nothing more than an instrument to protect one's personal interests (Pateman 1970: ch. 2). This perspective on political participation is typical of a utilitarian theory of democracy which accepts that individual citizens primarily act to satisfy their individual wants, not the common good. It is the function of political parties and government to reconcile those different wants (Lively 1975: 122).

The Dimensional Structure

The first objective of this study is to test the hypothesis that attitudes towards different aspects of democracy cluster according to the distinction between the individualist and the collectivist theory. So, ideally, we need data from a survey tapping opinions on the different aspects of democracy identified above. To our knowledge, such a survey does not exist. However, the 1985 ISSP study asked a number of questions about liberty and equality in relation to the role of government. These cover some of the main aspects of the two different theories.

Theoretically, one would expect these items to be based on one single dimension with the items on liberty at one pole, and the items on equality and the role of government at the other. However, factor analysis of these items yields a two-factor solution. This result, shown in Table 13.2, corroborates nicely our distinction between the two dimensions of democracy.

The first factor stands for the collectivist theory. All the items with a substantial loading on this factor refer either to the role of government in reducing income differences or to the responsibility of government for the welfare of different groups of people. Thus an interpretation of this factor in terms of social equality seems warranted. The items with the highest loadings refer either directly to a reduction of income differences, or to the transfer of tax money to disadvantaged groups, such as the elderly and the unemployed. Items referring to government spending in policy sectors less directly relevant for the distribution of income, like health and education, have lower loadings.

The second factor can be interpreted as an individualist dimension. The items with high loadings on this factor refer to basic liberties, such as freedom of speech and assembly. The items with the highest loadings measure acceptance of the civil rights of politically deviant groups such

TABLE 13.2. *Factor analysis of democratic values, 1985*

	Factor 1	Factor 2
Organizing protest meetings allowed	−0.003	0.505
Publishing protest pamphlets allowed	0.009	0.525
Protest demonstrations allowed	0.118	0.491
Occupying government offices allowed	0.281	0.307
Organizing nation-wide strikes against government allowed	0.386	0.399
Revolutionaries should be allowed to hold public meetings	0.029	0.700
Revolutionaries should be allowed to publish books	−0.014	0.774
Racists should be allowed to hold public meetings	−0.173	0.650
Racists should be allowed to publish books	−0.183	0.696
Support for progressive income tax	0.451	0.018
Government should reduce income differences	0.631	−0.046
More government spending on health	0.449	−0.024
More government spending on education	0.306	0.094
More government spending on old age pensions	0.498	−0.086
More government spending on unemployment benefits	0.613	0.051
Government should provide jobs for everybody who wants one	0.662	−0.026
Government responsible for health care	0.563	−0.035
Government responsible for the old	0.554	−0.067
Government responsible for the unemployed	0.682	0.044
Government should reduce income differences	0.745	−0.035

Notes: R^2 = 34.8 per cent. Quartimax rotation; maximum likelihood extraction.
Source: ISSP (1985).

as revolutionaries and racists. Lower, but still significant, loadings are found for items which—according to Political Action (Barnes, Kaase, *et al*. 1979)—refer to protest approval. Items indicating approval of the publication of protest pamphlets, protest meetings, and protest demonstrations have loadings of about 0.50. Items standing for approval of more vigorous action, such as occupying government offices and the organization of nationwide strikes against the government, have lower loadings of 0.31 and 0.40 respectively. Interpreting the approval of, at least, the milder forms of unconventional behaviour in terms of basic civil rights is significant for our later discussion of political participation. There we shall argue that increasing approval of these forms of political participation should not be seen as growing support for participatory democracy but, rather, as support for an expansion of civil rights.

However, we should not exaggerate the extent to which the opinions of the mass public on these different aspects of democracy are constrained according to our theoretical scheme. The results of the factor analysis are not very impressive. The two-factor solution, which seems optimal, explains no more than 34.8 per cent of the variance. This is not surprising. Even on issues of everyday politics, the attitudes of most people are only partly constrained by ideological conceptions (Converse 1964). Therefore, it would be naïve to expect people's attitudes towards the more complicated aspects of a democratic system to fit neatly with our theoretical framework. But the extent to which they do suggests that our theoretical scheme, with its distinction between two different conceptions of democracy, is a useful instrument for examining developments in support for democratic values. In the next section, we argue that there are good reasons for anticipating that support for the two conceptions of democracy has developed differently.

Support for Democratic Values

The literature anticipating declining support for representative democracy was reviewed at the outset of this volume (see Chapter 1). But such an expectation has not always been the general wisdom. In their classic study *The Civic Culture* (1989), Almond and Verba predicted gradually increasing support for democratic values in Western societies. Their prediction was based on the presumption that a number of forces, such as education, the democratization of authority systems in the family, the school, and the workplace would lead to the development of democratic values. However, in the last chapter of *The Civic Culture Revisited*, Almond concludes that 'the implicit prediction in *The Civic Culture* of a tendency toward more widely held "civic" attitudes has not been borne out' (Almond and Verba 1989: 399). In our view, both the original prediction and the latter-day conclusion are too broad and too general. Instead, we expect to find a more differentiated pattern of development.

The hypothesis that support for the individualist aspects of democracy has increased while support for the collectivist aspects has declined was presented in Chapter 1. The hypothesis was deduced from more general theories of modernization. In most of these theories, economic and technological developments are considered to be the principal impetus to social change. The process of industrialization led to urbanization, a further division of labour, secularization, and rising levels of education—all of which have influenced the values and attitudes of people in modern societies. There seems to be a general understanding as to the direction of these changes, in which the key-words are independence, self-fulfilment, and emancipation.

More generally, these developments can be characterized as the process of individualization. Positive interpretations of this process emphasize that individuals have become more prepared to challenge traditional sources of authority and to decide life-styles for themselves. On the shadow side, we might observe increasing anomie, loneliness, and selfishness (Flanagan 1982*a*, 1982*b*; Van Deth 1984: 16–26). But both interpretations point to an increasing emphasis on the individual rather than society as a whole. However, this development might be more linear than is often suggested. In many interpretations of social developments during the last decades in advanced industrial democracies, it is argued that, after a sharp turn to the left in the 1960s and early 1970s, the tide has turned again and politics has returned to conservatism. However, our distinction between two dimensions of democracy allows us to take a more differentiated view.

The hypothesis of declining support for the collectivist dimension of democracy and increasing support for the individualist dimension predicts declining support for leftist issues like the redistribution of income and a further expansion of the welfare state. It also predicts declining enthusiasm for participatory democracy. But at the same time, it predicts a continuous growth of support for other values associated with leftist politics, such as civil liberties and the tolerance of minorities and deviant groups. However, once one accepts the distinction between the two theories of democracy, these trends are not at all contradictory. Support for individualist values in the economic domain is usually considered conservative, whereas individualism in the socio-cultural domain is associated with anti-traditionalism, and is thus considered progressive or leftist. Therefore, the hypothesis of declining support for collectivist values and increasing support for individualist values predicts precisely this seemingly inconsistent development.

Support for our hypothesis can be found in a longitudinal study conducted by Middendorp in the Netherlands (1991). He distinguishes between two ideological dimensions which strongly resemble ours: 'socio-economic left–right' and 'politico-cultural libertarianism–authoritarianism'. The trends on these two dimensions during the period 1970–85 are presented in Figure 13.1.

This figure is consistent with our hypothesis. First, there is an impressive turn to the right on the socio-economic dimension. This trend is based on a large number of indicators and stands for increasing

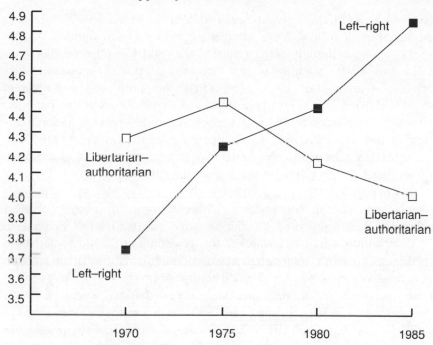

FIGURE 13.1. *Ideological dimensions among the Dutch electorate, 1970–85*

Note: Entries are the mean scores on the left–right and libertarian–authoritarian dimensions measured on a ten-point scale.

Source: Middendorp (1991: 148).

'opposition to egalitarian government policies in socio-economic terms; a tendency away from welfare state policies, away from government interference and government spending generally' (Middendorp 1991: 149). The second trend, also based on several indicators, stands for 'an increase in libertarianism, i.e. tolerance, less respect for traditional ways of life (freedom to express individual life-styles)' (Middendorp 1991: 149–50). Although the trend on this second dimension is not monotonic, there can be no misunderstanding about its direction—as predicted by our hypothesis.

There are few time-series data for other countries which would allow us to compare trends on these two dimensions. Heath *et al.* (1991), in their study of political change in Britain, distinguish the same two dimensions and present longitudinal data on individual items representing these dimensions. However, the wording on individual items is not exactly the same in every year, and these inconsistencies preclude them using scales rather than individual questions (Heath *et al.* 1991: 184).

Even so, their findings give us some idea of the extent to which British public opinion followed the same direction as Dutch opinion. In the socio-economic domain, a sharp turn to the right was observed between 1974 and 1979, 'running in the direction of privatization and self-reliance' (Heath *et al.* 1991: 175). Thereafter, public opinion appears to have turned left again, at least on an issue like welfare benefits, although there were no major changes in attitudes towards nationalization or the redistribution of income and wealth. On the libertarian–authoritarian dimension, too, there was no clear pattern of change. As far as there was, it points in the libertarian direction.

However, as Heath *et al.* recognize, the data they present are difficult to interpret. Respondents to the British election studies have not been asked for their opinion on income equality, nationalization, or welfare in an absolute sense, but whether the government should redistribute income and wealth, nationalize more companies, and whether welfare benefits have gone too far. The difficulty with interpreting answers to these questions is—as the authors observe—that the world has been changing around the electorate. In 1987 there were fewer nationalized industries than in 1974, the eligibility rules for welfare benefits were changed, and income inequality increased. Therefore, changed responses may simply reflect the changing situation people face. Against this background 'it could be argued . . . that there has been public acceptance of the increase in inequality just as there has been for the programme of privatization' (Heath *et al.* 1991: 176).

In all, the British data support our hypothesis less convincingly than the Dutch data but at least they are not inconsistent with it. Data for other countries are even more limited than for Britain. Therefore, we have to rely on whatever data we can find which are relevant to the several aspects of the two dimensions of democracy. In what follows, the general hypothesis will be argued, specified, and tested for each aspect of the two conceptions of democracy discussed earlier.

Liberty and Equality

With respect to the values of liberty and equality, our hypothesis predicts a gradual increase in support for civil liberty and declining support for equality. The main argument for predicting increasing support for liberty is that a certain degree of political sophistication is essential to grasp the meaning of civil liberties. The point is well made by McClosky and Brill (1983: 415–16):

The inclination to tolerate beliefs or conduct that one considers offensive or dangerous is not an inborn trait, but is learned behaviour . . . Those who become defenders rather than foes of civil liberties need to acquire a greater measure of information and intellectual sophistication about libertarian norms, a sense of relevant principles such as reciprocity, and an ability to understand the rules of the democratic game. Learning the arguments for freedom and tolerance . . . is no simple task. Many of those arguments are subtle, esoteric, and difficult to grasp. Intelligence, awareness, and education are required to appreciate them fully.

The increasing levels of education and political sophistication of the mass public in Western societies are often referred to as a process of 'cognitive mobilization' (Inglehart 1990: 337). But in addition, McClosky and Brill (1983: 434–5) observed that younger generations are significantly more tolerant than older generations even after accounting for differences in education. In their view, the stronger libertarianism of the younger generations, apart from reflecting differences in education, is a sign of greater freedom in the home and in schools, greater geographic and social mobility, growing urbanization, increasing secularism, and increasing social exchange and communication. According to McClosky and Brill (1983. 435). 'The higher levels of tolerance exhibited by the incoming generations, in turn, provide reason to believe that, as each new generation matures into adulthood, the general level of freedom and tolerance in the society as a whole will rise.'

Scattered data from studies in several countries seem to support the hypothesis of a gradual increase in the level of tolerance and support for civil liberties. In the United States, a substantial increase in the level of tolerance has been found since the first study on tolerance by Stouffer in 1954 (Davis 1975; Nunn, Crockett, and Williams 1978). However, Piereson, Sullivan, and Marcus (1980: 166) argue that these results can be biased because the level of tolerance is measured by referring to generally unpopular groups, such as communists, socialists, and atheists. According to Piereson, a reliable measure of tolerance should refer to groups in society to which respondents themselves are hostile. The same caution is probably warranted with respect to similar studies in other countries.

A gradual increase in support for civil liberties has been found in

TABLE 13.3. *Tolerance of various groups of people as neighbours*

	Denmark	Iceland	Norway	Sweden	Belgium	Britain	West Germany	Ireland	Netherlands	France	Italy	Spain
People with criminal records												
1981	17	13	35	27	22	39	28	44	17	11	39	35
1990	28	24	37	35	28	41	28	52	29	20	48	38
People of different race												
1981	4	4	9	6	12	10	11	7	10	5	7	9
1990	7	8	12	7	17	9	10	6	8	9	13	9
Left–wing extremists												
1981	7	22	19	21	21	27	51	21	39	10	37	25
1990	6	30	19	24	34	34	51	29	48	24	30	25
Right–wing extremists												
1981	3	20	18	17	17	22	45	17	35	14	40	24
1990	7	29	22	29	38	28	62	21	53	33	34	28
Heavy drinkers												
1981	29	52	33	44	39	48	67	33	51	47	44	38
1990	34	61	32	45	50	48	64	34	59	50	51	41

Immigrant-foreign workers												
1981	9	2	10	4	15	13	21	6	17	6	4	2
1990	12	8	16	9	21	12	16	5	10	13	15	8
Minority religious groups												
1981	15	13	6	9	12	22	31	13	20	13	16	14
Jews												
1990	3	7	9	6	13	7	7	6	4	7	13	8
Hindus												
1990	6	8	14	9	16	12	13	10	8	8	13	8
Muslims												
1990	15	12	21	17	26	17	20	13	15	18	15	11
Homosexuals												
1990	12	20	20	18	24	31	34	33	12	24	39	32

Notes: Entries are percentages of people who do not want to have a specific group as neighbours. The first data for Iceland were collected in 1984, for Norway in 1982. The sample size for 1981 varies between 927 (Iceland) and 2,303 (Spain); for 1990 the sample size varies between 702 (Iceland) and 2,792 (Belgium).

Sources: European Values Survey (1981); World Values Survey (1990).

Germany and the Netherlands. In Germany, the number of people who believed that one could talk freely about politics increased from 55 per cent in 1953 to 84 per cent in 1971 (Conradt 1974: 226–7). Also, support for the right to take one's political beliefs into the streets, and for the right to strike and to demonstrate, even when doing so could lead to public order disturbances, increased slightly between 1968 and 1982 (Gabriel 1987: 41).

A longitudinal study in the Netherlands by the Social and Cultural Planning Bureau offers a richness of data on tolerance and support for civil liberties. Support for civil liberties has gradually increased since the early 1970s (SCP 1992: 452; see also Figure 13.4 below). Tolerance of minorities, however, does not follow the same pattern. The acceptance of neighbours of a different race is one of the few items on which information from the mid-1960s onwards is available. As measured by these items, tolerance of minorities is stable in the 1980s, but there is a clear indication that tolerance was much higher in the 1960s. Perhaps the development towards a multi-racial society has had a negative effect on levels of tolerance; the likelihood of having a neighbour of a different race has become much less theoretical in the 1980s than it was in the 1960s (SCP 1992: 469).

Data from the 1981 European Values Survey and the 1990 World Values Survey allow us to go some way in describing developments in tolerance levels across a number of countries in a systematic way. In these studies, respondents were shown a list of various groups of people and asked to pick out the groups they would not like to have as neighbours. The results are presented in Table 13.3. Unfortunately, the list of groups was not exactly the same in 1981 and 1990. Therefore, the hypothesis that tolerance has increased can be tested with data for only six groups in twelve different countries. This yields seventy-two comparisons. No more than thirteen of these are consistent with the hypothesis. In general, tolerance has not increased but declined between 1981 and 1990. However, it would be only part of the truth to interpret these data exclusively as a sign of increasing racial discrimination in Western Europe.

First, compared to other categories—such as people with a criminal record, heavy drinkers, or homosexuals—the willingness to accept people of a different race, a minority religious group, or Jews, Hindus, or Muslims is still relatively high. In most countries the percentage of people who admit that they do not want people of a different race or Jews as their neighbours is still below 10 per cent. In the case of foreign workers, the average percentage is somewhat higher, but still far below the general mean in the table. Secondly, as far as there is an increase of intolerance towards racial minorities, it is certainly not stronger than the general trend of increasing intolerance towards all groups which for one reason or the other might cause social problems, such as people with a criminal record and heavy drinkers.

Of course, one might argue that the items in Table 13.3 refer to social tolerance rather than political tolerance. It is the latter which counts in a democracy. People can refuse to socialize with particular groups of people without denying them their political rights. It was demonstrated before that this, indeed, is often the case. Sullivan, Piereson, and Marcus found that in the United States the percentage of people who would be unwilling to invite a member of a minority they disliked to dinner, would be upset if a member of that group moved in next door, or would feel negatively about their son or daughter dating a member of that group, was much higher than the percentage who were generally intolerant of political activities by members of these same groups (Sullivan, Piereson, and Marcus 1982: 237).

However, this is not to say that the decline of social tolerance is irrelevant for the fate of liberal democracy. Sullivan, Piereson, and Marcus (p. 238) also found that the largest explanatory factor by far, for both social and political intolerance, is the perception of certain groups as threatening. It is the same perceived threat, expressed in xenophobic feelings towards minority groups—foreign workers, Jews, Hindus, Muslims, and people of a different race—which forms the breeding ground of right-wing political movements. With respect to all these groups, at least in 1990, Belgium had the highest proportion of people who do not want to accept members of these minorities as neighbours. Perhaps it is a bit far-fetched to see here the explanation for the success of the Flemish Bloc—a party which is not ashamed of a *Blut und Boden* ideology—in the parliamentary elections of 1991. But at least the data do not contradict it.

People were also confronted with the choice between liberty and equality in both the 1981 European Values Survey and the 1990 World Values Survey. The question was phrased as follows:

Which of these two statements comes closest to your own opinion?

A: I find that both freedom and equality are important. But if I were to choose to make up my mind for one or the other, I would consider personal freedom more important, that is, everyone can live in freedom and develop without hindrance

B: Certainly both freedom and equality are important. But if I were to choose to make up my mind for one or the other, I would consider equality more important, that nobody is underprivileged and that social class differences are not so strong.

If both of our predictions—of an increase in support for liberty and a decline in support for equality—are correct, we should expect an increase in the number of people who prefer freedom to equality. However, as we can see in Table 13.4, this is the case in only six of the twelve countries. In the other six the percentage of people who prefer freedom above equality has declined.

It is hard to think of an explanation for these different patterns. One might speculate that they are caused by a sort of 'ceiling and floor' effect: in countries where the percentage of people who prefer freedom above equality has increased, this percentage will tend to decrease; where the percentage has declined, it will tend to increase. There may be something to this. Of the five countries with the highest proportion of people who prefer freedom above equality in 1981, four show a decline in 1990, whereas the three countries with the lowest percentage in 1981 show an increase in 1990. But this kind of speculation cannot save the hypothesis of a uniform change in the direction of a

TABLE 13.4. *Preference for freedom over equality*

	1981	1990	Difference	Average N
Denmark	62	66	+4	1,106
Iceland	52	47	−5	815
Norway	66	68	+2	1,145
Sweden	62	70	+8	1,001
Belgium	64	58	−6	1,969
Britain	75	67	−8	1,326
West Germany	49	73	+24	1,703
Ireland	55	46	−9	1,109
Netherlands	63	59	−4	1,730
France	63	53	−10	1,101
Italy	48	49	+1	1,683
Spain	48	53	+5	2,470

Notes: Entries are percentages preferring freedom (option A) over equality (option B). See also notes to Table 13.3

Source: See Table 13.3.

greater preference for liberty. However, we should note the remarkable increase in the preference for freedom observed in Germany. We might surmise that this dramatic change was due to the fall of the communist regime in East Germany which—at least temporarily—boosted the spirit of liberty in West Germany.

Expectations with respect to equality are mixed. Political equality is as much an individualist value as a collectivist value. Of course, universal suffrage had to be fought for, but the indisputable argument to enfranchise all adults was the equal rights argument, one of the basic elements of liberal democracy. And there is no reason to expect a decline in support for basic political rights. The same argument applies to support for equality of opportunity; in this case, too, there is no reason to expect a decline. Only with respect to support for equality of condition is the prediction unequivocal. Here we anticipate a decline or, at least, a flattening curve.

The 1981 and 1990 Values Studies included an interesting question which presented people with a context in which they were asked to choose between two options, one representing equality of opportunity and one representing equality of condition. The question reads as follows:

I'd like to relate an incident to you and ask your opinion of it. There are two secretaries, of the same age, doing practically the same job. One of the secretaries finds out that the other one earns £10 a week more than she does. She complains to her boss. He says, quite rightly, that the other secretary is quicker, more efficient and more reliable at her job. In your opinion, is it fair or not fair that one secretary is paid more than the other?

The answer that this situation is fair can be interpreted as support for equality of opportunity rather than equality of outcome or of condition. If one thinks of this situation as unfair one would probably also support equality of condition. The answers to this question in the same twelve countries as before are summarized in Table 13.5.

The difference between 1981 and 1990 is fascinating. In all countries but one, the proportion of people who agree with the statement that it is fair to pay the quicker secretary more has increased. In most countries this increase is sizeable. In Italy it is as much as 30 percentage points. These data show in a dramatic way the cultural changes which have occurred in Western Europe in the 1980s. The egalitarian values so prominent in the 1960s and 1970s have given way to a mentality which more easily accepts reward according to achievement.

TABLE 13.5. *Agreement with statement that a faster secretary should be paid more*

	1981	1990	Difference
Denmark	60	76	+16
Iceland	66	75	+9
Norway	54	54	0
Sweden	59	62	+3
Belgium	63	73	+10
Britain	68	79	+11
West Germany	71	85	+14
Ireland	60	73	+13
Netherlands	61	72	+11
France	63	79	+16
Italy	49	79	+30
Spain	70	74	+4

Notes: Entries are percentages. For sample size, see Table 13.4.

Sources: See Table 13.3.

The Role of Government

Opinions on equality of condition can hardly be separated from opinions on the role of the government to enforce this equality. Above it was argued that, in the welfare state, government is held responsible for public welfare. The allocation of state benefits is strongly related to the issue of equality, in particular equality of income. Income redistribution is not necessarily an explicit purpose of welfare policy. It might just as well be a side effect of welfare programmes. Even the most minimal welfare state affects the distribution of income by transferring resources from the rich to the poor. And as the welfare state expands its services, government programmes have more impact on the distribution of income (Verba *et al.* 1987: 2–4). Therefore, the argument predicting declining support for this form of equality applies at least as much to the role of the government as to the outcome of its policies to reduce inequality.

The development of opinions about the scope of government is discussed at greater length elsewhere (see Volume iii). But we consider what might be an interesting paradox about the welfare state. The hypothesis to be tested here is that support for the welfare state among the mass public has gradually declined. However, this is not due to a failure of the welfare state but, rather, to its success. In the first place, mainly due to the welfare state, education levels have dramatically increased in all advanced industrial societies. In addition, at least in the more developed welfare states, people have become financially more independent. The elderly no longer depend on their children, adolescents increasingly enjoy a life separate from their parents. Thus, it might be argued, the welfare state has furthered the development of individualism in society. One of the characteristics of individualism is that people are not inclined to accept interference with their personal life. And the paradox of the welfare state might very well be that people are increasingly inclined to resist the only remaining meddler—state bureaucracy, the inevitable companion of the welfare state.

In the second place, the development of attitudes to the welfare state may reflect diminishing marginal utility. The very success of the welfare state might lead people to take for granted the provisions of the welfare state, but they are no longer willing to accept the high tax burden which inevitably goes with it. This thesis has been tested by Inglehart. He argues that as a society approaches perfect equality, it necessarily reaches a point of diminishing returns. Thus, as a society moves closer to an equal distribution of income, political support for further redistribution declines. And, indeed, evidence from the Eurobarometer surveys suggests that at high levels of economic development, public support for the classic economic policies of the left tends to diminish.

In Eurobarometer surveys carried out in 1979, 1981, and 1983 in the ten member nations of the European Community,[1] the following questions were asked:

We would like to hear your views on some important political issues. Could you tell me whether you agree or disagree with each of the following proposals? How strongly do you feel?

1. Greater effort should be made to reduce income inequality.
2. Government should play a greater role in the management of the economy.[2]
3. Public ownership of industry should be expanded.

According to Inglehart the answers to these questions were counter-intuitive. It was not the developed welfare states like Denmark, with their advanced social legislation, progressive taxation, a high level of income equality, and a large proportion of the GNP going to the public sector, which showed the highest level of support for a further extension of welfare provision. Instead, Greece—by far the poorest of the ten countries—had the highest proportion supporting a further reduction of income inequality, more government management of the economy, and more nationalization of industry. The ten societies show an almost perfect fit between level of economic development and support for these elements of welfare policy.[3] This is not to say that support for the welfare state and an egalitarian society has diminished in the advanced welfare states of Western Europe, but it does indicate that the principle of diminishing marginal utility applies to the attitudes of citizens in these nations.

If both the arguments of further individualization and of diminishing marginal utility are valid, one might also expect a gradual decline in support for an extension of egalitarian welfare policies. In Table 13.6 we present data about support for a further reduction of income inequality in the EC member states. The data are from the same surveys used by Inglehart. In all countries except Denmark, support for a further reduction of income inequality declined steadily over the four years 1979–83, which is consistent with the general hypothesis.

Of course, these Eurobarometer data refer to a very limited timespan. The Netherlands is the only country for which there is a much longer time series: data on opinions about which activities should be financed by the government were collected by the Dutch Social and Cultural

TABLE 13.6. *Support for a further reduction of income inequality*

	1979	1981	1983	Average N
Denmark	35	24	31	1,014
Belgium	62	56	50	1,006
Germany	33	32	30	1,006
Ireland	37	37	32	994
Luxembourg	67	58	54	364
Netherlands	51	47	47	985
Britain	28	24	24	1,365
France	70	65	62	1,018
Italy	62	51	48	1,044
Greece	—	85	82	1,000

Note: Entries are percentages agreeing strongly.

Sources: Eurobarometer, Nos. 11, 16, and 19.

Planning Agency (SCP) from 1970 onwards. People were asked to indicate their degree of approval for government spending on public nurseries, cultural grants, compulsory education, fighting pollution, free education, housing, scholarships, and learning facilities. In Figure 13.2, we set out the trend in support levels for government spending in these policy areas over the last twenty years.

It is quite clear that support for expenditures on these items has

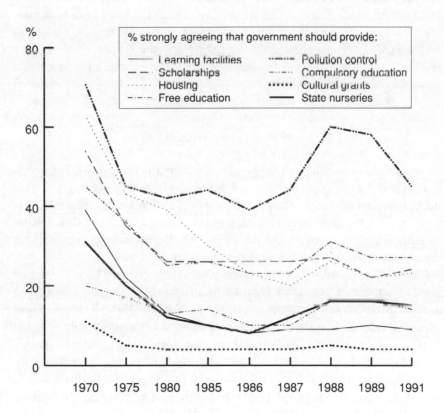

FIGURE 13.2. *Trends in support of government spending on services in the Netherlands, 1970–91*

Source: SCP (1992: 447–8).

declined dramatically, particularly during the 1970s. This is consistent
with our hypothesis. However, the latest developments seem to indicate
a stabilization, if not a reversal, of opinion. Probably the same law of
diminishing returns that made people oppose the ever-increasing tax
burden of the welfare state in the 1970s is causing a reversal of the
trend. After a time, people begin to feel the effects of budget cuts and
withdraw their support for a further reduction of welfare expenditure.
This kind of development can be seen in Britain, where the proportion
of people supporting a reduction of government spending on health and
education declined steadily from an already low 14 per cent in 1983 to 7
per cent in 1989 (Taylor-Gooby 1993). Years of Thatcherism apparently exhausted support for a further reduction of expenditure on health
and education. Thus, what both the Dutch and the British data indicate
is that declining support for the welfare state is not an irreversible
process.

General Interest versus Pluralism

It is difficult to think of a good operationalization of the tension
between the notion of the general interest or the common good, and
the realization that there are positive aspects to conflicting interests. It is
even more difficult to find a successful operationalization of this tension
in earlier empirical research. As far as we are aware, no comparative
data on support for the associated values are available.

The only relevant data we found are for Germany. In 1968, 1979, and
1982, a sample of people in West Germany were asked their opinion on
a few items which can be interpreted as indicators of support for
pluralist values. The item 'A viable democracy is unthinkable without
a political opposition' still refers to the formal rules of the game.
Therefore, it is no wonder that the proportion of people agreeing with
this principle was as high as about 90 per cent in all three years.
Rejecting the statement 'It is not the task of the political opposition
to criticize the government, but to support it in its work' can be
interpreted as support for pluralist values. The proportion of people
doing so was rather low, but increased from 28 per cent in 1968 to 34
per cent in 1982. About the same low proportion disagreed with the
statement that conflicts between interest groups and their demands on
the government are damaging democracy. That the interests of the
people as a whole should always take precedence over the specific

interests of individuals was rejected by less than 10 per cent in all three years. The obvious conclusion is that it is very difficult for the mass public to discern the positive functions for democracy of the political opposition, and even more so of the permanent conflicts of interests between different groups. The changes over time were small, but they are in the direction of increasing support for pluralism (Gabriel 1987: 40–1).

Political Participation

We have argued that both the individualist and the collectivist theories of democracy value political participation. However, the view on political participation derived from the two theories is different. As we noted earlier, a central element of the collectivist theory is the idea of participatory democracy, whereas 'instrumental participation' is derived from the individualist theory. According to our general hypothesis, we anticipate declining support for the idea of participatory democracy and increasing support for the instrumental view.

This prediction might sound counter intuitive. Is participatory democracy, at least as an ideal, not the main heritage of the 1960s? True enough, the idea of participatory democracy seemed to play an important role in the turbulences of the 1960s. However, even though this view—expressed in such demands as 'one man one vote' in universities and the founding of communes—was one of the most visible characteristics of the direct action movements, it hardly had a lasting impact. The idea of direct democracy, apart from being unrealistic, rejoiced in popularity for only a short time.[4] However, this is not to say that a positive attitude to political participation did not exist or exists no longer. But in our view, this attitude has little to do with the collectivist view on political participation or a participatory democracy. It is more likely that in modern society people nurse an instrumental attitude to political participation. Better educated people with more political skills than their parents are prepared to use all available means to influence political decision-making in their favour. Therefore, we expect increasing support for forms of participation which enable people to pursue their individual and group interests, but declining or stable support for forms of political participation which are tinged with direct, participatory democracy.

We could find no extensive comparative data on the development of support for forms of political participation that can be associated with the idea of participatory democracy. Only for the Netherlands are there longitudinal data on a whole battery of items. Figure 13.3 shows the development of support for different forms of participation. It presents the percentage of people who support a greater 'say' for workers in management, citizens in local and provincial decisions, students in the administration of universities, and pupils and parents in the administration of high schools.

The pattern of development is quite clear. Support for a further increase of all these forms of participation declined strongly between 1970 and 1975. Thereafter, the level of support is rather stable. Of course, we should be very cautious in interpreting this kind of data.

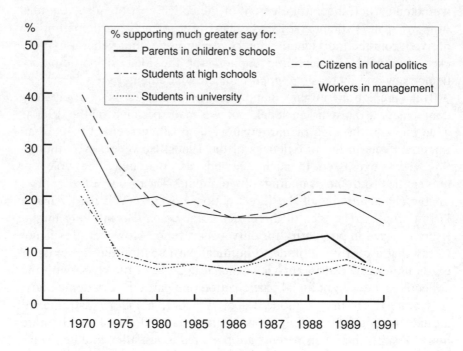

FIGURE 13.3. *Trends in support of different forms of participation in the Netherlands, 1970–91*

Source: SCP (1992: 453).

Declining support for a further increase of political participation does not necessarily mean that support for a certain level of political participation is declining. The negative trends in Figure 13.3 could go together with increasing support for a certain level of political participation. This will be the case when the actual opportunities to participate grow faster than the desire for more participation. Also, strictly speaking, not all these forms of participation refer to political participation. But at least one can say that, gradually, fewer people want a further expansion in certain forms of political participation. On the other hand, we should note that the proportion of people in Britain agreeing with the statement 'government should give workers more say in running the places where they work' increased from 58 per cent in 1974 to 76 per cent in 1987 (Heath *et al.* 1991). This finding, of course, contradicts our hypothesis.

Seemingly in contradiction to declining support for these forms of participation in the Netherlands, is the fact that support for all manner of unconventional behaviour, or protest approval, has increased in the same period. However, as we have argued elsewhere (Thomassen and Van Deth 1989: 72–3), this development has hardly anything to do with the idea of a participatory democracy. Protest approval can be interpreted as support for a growing repertoire of civil rights. As shown in Figure 13.4, approval of different kinds of protest behaviour tends to increase when it involves classic civil rights like freedom of speech.

The trends here would seem to contradict the trends in Figure 13.3. However, the factor analysis of democratic values (Table 13.2) yields a cluster consisting of both classic civil rights and forms of protest behaviour. If this interpretation is correct, there is no contradiction between the declining curves in Figure 13.3 and the rising curves in Figure 13.4. Quite the contrary: in this interpretation it corroborates the general hypothesis of declining support for participatory democracy, as part of the collectivist dimension of democracy, and increasing support for an expanding repertoire of civil rights as part of the individualist dimension.

Conclusion

At the beginning of this chapter we distinguished between two theories of democracy, the individualist and the collectivist theory. From general theories of modernization, we deduced the hypothesis that

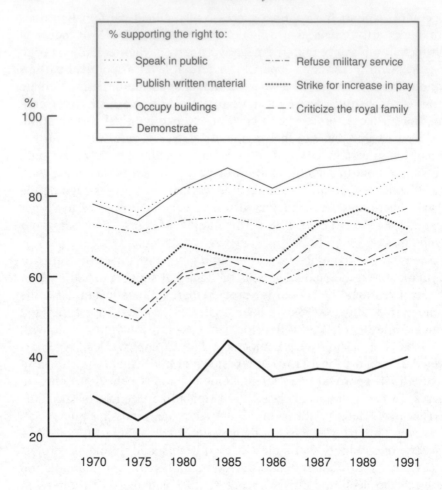

FIGURE 13.4. *Trends in levels of support for civil liberties in the Netherlands,*
1970–91

Source: SCP (1992: 452).

support for the individualist aspects of democracy has increased while
support for the collectivist aspects has declined. The empirical evidence
with respect to this hypothesis is mixed. The most convincing evidence
in support of the hypothesis is Middendorp's finding that, at least in the
Netherlands, there is a clear increase in libertarianism, which is strongly
related to the individualist dimension of democracy, accompanied by a

turn to the right on the socio-economic dimension, which is at least part of the collectivist dimension of democracy.

The further evidence in this chapter refers to the more specific aspects of the two dimensions. The hypothesis predicts increasing support for liberty and declining support for equality. Not all the available empirical evidence is consistent with this prediction. Although there seems to be a general increase in support for civil liberties, there is also strong evidence that people have become less, rather than more, tolerant towards minorities. The evidence with respect to social equality and the role of government is unequivocal. Support for equality of outcome and 'big' government has definitely declined. At the same time, there is some indication that this decline had reached bottom by the end of the 1980s.

The evidence with respect to political participation seems at first sight to be contradictory. The limited data available suggest that support for unconventional political participation has increased whereas support for conventional participation has not. However, we have interpreted the former as an indication of support for a further expansion of the civil rights repertoire, and therefore of an expansion of individual civil rights. The latter we have interpreted as lack of support, or at least less support, for a further development in the direction of participatory democracy. In general, we might conclude that the main hypothesis has been borne out, although in several aspects the evidence is certainly not conclusive.

What does this tell us about the future development of democracy in Western Europe? What can we say about a democracy in which individual liberty prevails to the extent that the role of the government and institutionalized politics is increasingly questioned, where a pluralist process of decision-making leaves little room for an impartial interpretation of the general interest, where political participation seems to be directed to individual and private ends at the expense of the recognition and pursuit of the public good (cf. Putnam 1993: 88). Should it not remind us of Huntington's prediction that 'postindustrial politics is likely to be the darker side of postindustrial society'? (Huntington 1974: 190). Does this development not deprive the political culture of the 'plus something else' which, according to Almond and Verba (1989: 29), distinguishes the civic culture from the 'rationality-activist' model of political culture?

This kind of speculation underestimates the self-correcting capacities of democratic regimes. Political changes, certainly when they are initiated by a sudden outburst, tend at first to move from one extreme to the other before they reach a new equilibrium. A single example to illustrate this point comes from the development of attitudes towards different forms of unconventional behaviour in the Netherlands. Before the 1960s the Netherlands could be characterized as a conservative country with a very low rate of political participation. According to *Political Action* (Barnes, Kaase, *et al*. 1979), this situation had changed dramatically by the early 1970s. Not that the Dutch all of a sudden had become extremely active in politics: on the contrary, certainly in the domain of unconventional political participation, they were still relatively inactive. But in terms of attitudes towards unconventional political participation, they had become by far the most tolerant nation examined in the study. The level of protest approval was higher than in any other country. The most impressive difference between the Netherlands and the other nations concerned the development in repression potential. Compared to the other countries, approval of repressive government action against those engaging in protest behaviour rose quite dramatically: 'Whereas in the other four countries between 12 per cent and 19 per cent will sanction no counteraction against unruly demonstrators, in the Netherlands this figure is 47 per cent' (Marsh and Kaase 1979: 90).

The level of repression potential was measured again in the second wave of the Political Action study, conducted in 1979–80 in the Netherlands, the United States, and West Germany (Jennings, Van Deth, *et al*. 1989) and also in Eurobarometer, No. 31 (1989). Thus we can compare the level of repression potential in the Netherlands and West Germany in 1974, 1979, and 1989, and in Britain in 1974 and 1989. The relevant figures are presented in Table 13.7.

Clearly, both the absolute and the relative position of the Netherlands completely changed after 1974. Whereas repression potential on almost all items gradually declined in West Germany and Britain, the development in the Netherlands was exactly the opposite. Only with respect to such an unlikely event as using troops to break strikes has repression potential not increased. As a result, repression potential in the Netherlands was, in 1989, the highest of all EC countries after Denmark (Kaase and Neidhardt 1990: 61).

The most plausible explanation for this development is that in the early 1970s, in reaction to the relatively passive and dull politics of the past, indiscriminate approval of all manner of political behaviour and protest became common in the Netherlands. Then, as a reaction to the

TABLE 13.7. *Repression potential in three West European countries, 1974–89*

	Germany			Netherlands			Britain	
	1974	1979	1989	1974	1979	1989	1974	1989
Police using force against demonstrators	49 (2,247)	42 (1,989)	23 (983)	36 (1,142)	41 (775)	63 (1,008)	73 (1,389)	36 (1,198)
Courts giving severe sentences to protestors who disregard police	77 (2,257)	67 (2,000)	63 (977)	39 (1,153)	49 (769)	71 (995)	82 (1,399)	54 (1,178)
Government passing law to forbid all public protest demonstrations	53 (2,245)	52 (1,900)	39 (970)	13 (1,169)	12 (775)	23 (989)	25 (1,380)	35 (1,203)
Government using troops to break strikes	38 (2,210)	43 (1,976)	30 (967)	21 (1,134)	28 (765)	22 (994)	47 (1,337)	30 (1,188)

Notes: Entries are percentages who strongly approve of proposed repression methods. The percentage base is shown in parentheses.

Source: Political Action (1974, 1979); Eurobarometer, No. 31.

negative consequences of this relaxed attitude, the Dutch apparently made another radical turn. There may be several more oscillations before attitudes towards new forms of political participation reach a new equilibrium. That equilibrium will, in all likelihood, be at a higher level of acceptance than in the 1960s, but it will no longer reach the level of the 1970s.

Perhaps the lesson to be learned from this single example is that social and political changes tend to follow the pattern of a pendulum rather than a linear trend: the stronger the initial swing, the stronger also the reaction will be. Each oscillation will be followed by a smaller one, until the pendulum reaches its original equilibrium again. Here the analogy ends: in the case of social and political change the new equilibrium might be different from the original one. But it may be far less different than observers at the time will be inclined to think.

NOTES

1. Greece, not then being an EC member state, was not included in the 1979 survey.
2. In 1983, this item was reversed to refer to 'a small role'.
3. It might be argued in the case of the first item, the reduction of income inequality, that income distribution rather than the level of economic development is relevant. Using the same data, Edeltraud Roller finds a stronger relationship between support for income distribution using the Gini index than for GDP per capita. However, using the 1987 ISSP study, she found a significant relationship between support for income redistribution and GDP per capita but not the Gini index. See Vol. iii of this series, Ch. 3.
4. One might even question its popularity among the mass public at the time. Perhaps many social scientists working in universities in the late 1960s and the early 1970s have mistaken student activism for the mood of the society at large.

PART IV

Citizens and the State

14

Citizens and the State: A Relationship Transformed

DIETER FUCHS AND HANS-DIETER KLINGEMANN

This concluding chapter begins with a brief account of the issues addressed in Chapter 1. We then summarize the most important findings from the empirical analyses in the volume and, on this basis, attempt to answer the question about the challenge to representative democracy. This is followed by an evaluation of the change in the relationship between citizens and the state. However, since most of the trend data analysed in this volume do not go beyond the end of the 1980s, our answer can be addressed only to the historical phase which ended with the collapse of the state socialist systems in Central and Eastern Europe. We conclude, therefore, with a discussion of the consequences which the ensuing change in the global constellation might have for the representative democracies of Western Europe.

The Issues

The development of West European societies over the past decades has been characterized by manifold and profound processes of social change. These can be integrated within a theory of modernity and concentrated in such a way as to lend them a uniform direction of development. Bell's (1973, 1976) concept, postulating a transformation of industrial into post-industrial society, has gained wide recognition in characterizing this transformation. This development has been investigated in numerous studies, especially studies of economic and cultural systems. Economic transformation into post-industrial society can be characterized primarily by the expansion of the service sector. Cultural transformation can be described in terms of a change in values in favour of postmaterialist value priorities.

The political system is apparently more problematic. In principle, general societal transformation does not bypass the political sphere. This is all the more true because the political system is the only societal subsystem capable of making binding decisions for society as a whole. Thus, if there is still such a thing as a control centre in modern societies, it is the political system. Many problems consequent on social change are, therefore, likely to be manifest as political problems. Or, at least, this is likely to be the case with problems demanding solutions which are binding for society as a whole. This raises the question of the capacity of representative democracy to absorb and process the problems produced by transformation into post-industrial societies. This is still very much an open question which can be answered in a variety of ways.

The point of departure for the empirical analyses in our volume is a series of critical diagnoses of the condition of Western democracies, which postulate a particular answer. With varying degrees of explicitness, the common theme of these diagnoses is that the problem-solving capacity of current representative democracy is no longer adequate. Thus, these diagnoses claim, a *challenge* to representative democracies has arisen which can be met only by decisive structural reform of some kind. The proposed direction of this structural reform generally amounts to implementing forms of direct democracy within the institutional context of representative democracy. However, the authors of the present volume did not choose this point of departure because they agree with it. Rather, in the first place, these critical diagnoses serve a heuristic purpose in specifying meaningful and testable hypotheses. Secondly, the rhetoric of crisis has found a considerable echo in both academic and public discussion at least since the mid-1970s. And, finally, if the hypothesis that there is a challenge to representative democracies is empirically tenable, its political significance would make it an extremely important finding. Alternatively, if the hypothesis proves unfounded, this volume will have contributed towards directing attention to more specific issues *within* representative democracy.

Whatever the challenge to representative democracy, it cannot be understood as something which either exists or not at any given point in time. Rather, it is a process which extends over a long period, at the end of which there may be structural transformation. But that is likely only if there is a convincing alternative. The most credible alternative is the institutionalization of some form of direct democracy—at least, other alternatives are scarcely discussed and would probably have little chance of attracting support from citizens. But hitherto there has been little sign of institutional change in West European democracies—certainly, none in the direction of this most likely alternative. Thus, if representative democracy is being challenged, the process must be at an early stage.

A process of challenging the institutional structure of a democracy can start only if the citizenry becomes dissatisfied with its specific institutions, mechanisms, and major collective actors. The relationship between citizens and the state would then have to change fundamentally. In a representative democracy, this change would affect the way in which the demands of the citizens and the decisions of the state are accommodated. This would occur primarily via the competitive party system, by which citizens select certain parties or political leaders to occupy decision-making positions. Proceeding on the premiss that there is a challenge to representative democracy, any change on the part of citizens would necessarily relate to this core institution of representative democracy.

Accordingly, in Chapter 1, several hypotheses are formulated which are tested in the subsequent empirical analyses. Figure 1.2 presents a synopsis of these hypotheses and Figure 1.1 shows the connections between them in schematic form. The thrust of the arguments underlying the hypotheses are reiterated in this chapter.

The most direct empirical evidence in favour of the challenge hypothesis would be a demonstration that citizen dissatisfaction has been *generalized* to affect the systemic level. This would take the form of a decline in support for specific government institutions or for the democratic system as a whole. Support for a systemic change can be plausibly assumed only where support for a given political system has declined. Whether or not this leads to a change in the system depends—apart from the extent of the erosion in support—on the attractiveness of the alternative.

Our answer to the question of the challenge to representative democracy is set against the background of the findings emerging from the empirical analyses. In the following sections, these findings are presented in summary form, following the sequence in which the hypotheses are presented in Figure 1.2.

Political Involvement

Was there a decline in institutional political participation (hypothesis 1)? This question is addressed by Topf in Chapter 2. He analyses electoral participation over the period from 1945 to 1989 in eighteen West European countries. Overall, across Western Europe as a whole, the mean turnout level was 83 per cent. Comparing turnout during five-year periods against this overall mean, the level for the last period (1985–9) was 80 per cent—the lowest for any five-year period. The highest level was 85 per cent in 1960–5. But the European-wide figures conceal considerable variation. Grouping countries by the direction of trends for the last decade reveals eight countries where the curves fell, and ten where they were stable or rising. Thus, the evidence indicates that over recent years there was no general trend towards a decline in institutionalized political participation. At the European level, the picture for the 1945–89 period was of remarkable stability. This contradicts hypothesis 1.

Was there an increase in non-institutionalized political participation (hypothesis 2)? The answer to this question is a resounding 'yes', as demonstrated by the analyses reported by Topf in Chapter 3. Non-institutionalized participation is measured by a cumulative index based on items first used in the Political Action surveys (Barnes, Kaase, *et al.* 1979). The index distinguishes between groups of respondents who had engaged in (1) none of the forms of political participation in the battery of items, (2) some of the forms (that is one or two), and (3) several of the forms (that is, three or more). Data for four time points (1959, 1974, 1980, and 1989/90) can be compared. At the European level, the results show that 85 per cent of respondents had not engaged in non-institutionalized political activities in 1959. By 1990 this percentage had almost halved to 44 per cent. This increase in political participation is truly remarkable. Note, however, that the data for 1959 are based on only three countries and those for 1974 on five countries; only for 1980 and 1990 are data available for twelve countries. Notwithstanding the insurmountable difficulty of the lack of data, the trend towards an extended action repertory among citizens is consistent across all countries for which data are available. Thus, hypothesis 2 is clearly confirmed.

Was there an increase in political apathy (hypothesis 3)? An answer to this question is presented in Chapter 3. Following the early work of Barnes, Kaase, and their colleagues (1979), Topf identifies four modes of political involvement: (1) political apathy (no political interest and no political action); (2) political detachment (political interest and no political action); (3) expressive activism (no political interest and political action); and (4) instrumental activism (political interest and political action). At a general, European-wide level, the findings reveal an increase in political apathy between 1974 and 1980 (from 28 to 37 per cent) and a subsequent decline of similar magnitude (from 37 per cent in 1980 to 29 per cent in 1990). The picture is even clearer when we look at individual countries. In ten out of twelve countries, political apathy declined between 1980 and 1990. The proportion of the politically apathetic increased only in France; in Spain, the proportion was almost stable (52 per cent in 1980, 54 per cent in 1990). Of the five countries where data for three time points are available, three (Finland, Britain, Italy) showed a continuous decline in political apathy, whereas for two countries apathy increased from 1974 to 1980 and then fell again from 1980 to 1990.

Indeed, contrary to hypothesis 3, instrumental political action remained the dominant mode in all the countries for which we have data. There is little evidence that the large increase in non-institutionalized political participation was primarily due to an increase in expressive modes of action. At the European level, expressive action increased by about 6 percentage points compared to instrumental action between 1974 and 1990. However, given the much greater overall expansion in non-institutionalized political participation, this small increase in expressive activism seems quite plausible. Of course, we have to bear in mind the limitations of our data: for 1974, we have data for only five countries; for 1980, there are data for thirteen countries; for 1990, for twelve countries. Even so, the available evidence does not support hypothesis 3.

On a Europe-wide basis, then, the results presented in Part I of this volume can be readily summarized. First, institutional political participation was stable. Secondly, non-institutionalized political participation increased dramatically. And, thirdly, political apathy declined.

Political Linkage

Was there a decline in attachment to interest organizations (hypothesis 4)? Aarts addresses this problem in Chapter 8. He singles out three groups of respondents: (1) those who had never been a member of social and political organizations during the period 1959–90 (nine countries); (2) those who had been members of trade unions, covering the period 1950–85 for trade-union density (eight countries), and 1955–90 for trade-union membership (nine countries); and (3) those who had supported new social movements during the 1982–9 period (five countries). For all three groups, large variations are evident—both cross-nationally and over time. In summarizing these results, we concentrate first on union membership. Attachment to new political actors is discussed at a later point.

Overall, at the European level, union density was at about the 50 per cent level. It was high in Denmark, Norway, and Sweden (on average 70 per cent during 1950–85); at a medium level in Germany, Britain, Italy, and the Netherlands (42 per cent); and low in Portugal, Spain, and Greece. It was lowest of all in France (19 per cent). However, comparisons over time indicate that we cannot speak of a general decline in union density or union membership. Comparing the earliest and latest time points, union density declined in just two of the eight countries during the period under consideration. In a slightly different set of countries, union membership grew in four countries, declined in four, and stayed about the same in one. Overall, except in Belgium, Denmark, and Britain, there was a positive relationship between union membership and party preference. It is still true that supporters of left-wing parties were more numerous among union members. However, there is little evidence of clear trends over time. Cross-cultural variations and trendless fluctuation accounted for most of the differences. Hypothesis 4 is, thus, not confirmed.

Was there a decline in attachment to political parties (hypothesis 5)? Three chapters take up this question, discussing the development of party attachments, party membership, and party de-alignment. In Chapter 4, Schmitt and Holmberg report the empirical evidence for fourteen West European countries and the United States, using data from national election studies (Denmark, Germany, Britain, Norway, Sweden, and the United States) and the Eurobarometer surveys (twelve countries). The time span covered by the national election studies ranges from 1956 to 1991 for Sweden and from 1971 to 1989 for Denmark and the Netherlands. The time span for the Eurobarometer data also differs across countries, covering 1975–92 for France, Luxembourg, Germany, the Netherlands, and Belgium; 1976–92 for Denmark; 1978–92 for Ireland, Italy, and Britain; 1981–92 for Greece; and 1985–92 for Portugal and Spain.

In 1978, based on the EC-9 countries, party identifiers, on average, comprised 71 per cent of the adult population, of which about half were strong identifiers (36 per cent). Both groups have declined over time; identifiers by 0.9 per cent, strong identifiers by 0.5 per cent per year. Again, however, there is much variation across countries. Setting aside the United States, and taking as our criterion a significance level of 0.05 for the regression slope, the results show that both the proportion of identifiers and strong identifiers has declined in Britain, France, Ireland, Italy, Luxembourg, and Sweden. Furthermore, the proportion of strong identifiers—but not identifiers—has declined in Denmark and the Netherlands, but has increased in Spain. However, no decline in party identification can be observed by this method in Belgium, Germany, Norway, Portugal, and Greece. The slopes are negative in some of these latter cases but they do not reach the 5 per cent criterion. Thus, in eight of the fourteen West European countries covered by the analysis there was some measure of decline in party identification.

This general picture is reflected in Widfeldt's account of party members in Chapter 5. Examining data from both party records (ten countries) and surveys (fifteen countries) for at least three time points, he reveals a downward trend in party membership for the Scandinavian countries (Finland, Norway, Sweden, and, although somewhat weaker, in Denmark), Britain, the Netherlands, and Italy. In the eight remaining countries, the proportions of party members had not changed much; in some cases the proportions even increased (Belgium, Ireland, Germany, and Greece).

In Chapter 7, Biorcio and Mannheimer add another perspective. They analyse data for five countries in 1989. They construct a typology distinguishing between the 'de-aligned', the 'pragmatic', the 'identifying', and the 'integrated' voter. They find a high degree of de-alignment in Spain, France, and Italy, but a lesser degree in Britain and Germany. De-alignment was at its highest among the young and lowest among the elderly. From this evidence, they conclude that the relationship between citizens and parties was changing in the direction of de-alignment. Although the evidence varies, it is fair to say that the overall impression is of declining attachment to political parties. This finding is in line with hypothesis 5.

That we have to be cautious about the conclusions we draw from these results is shown by Klingemann's analysis in Chapter 6, in which he compares party positions and voter orientations. Data from party manifestos are used to measure party policy positions, and data from the

Eurobarometer surveys as well as national election surveys are used to measure voter orientations on a left–right self-placement scale. The analysis covers twelve countries and a period of twenty years (1970–89). His results show that the policy positions of political parties matched the orientations of their supporters rather well. To the extent that there was change, it is in the direction of a more faithful representation of popular wishes by the political parties. These findings run counter to the notion that parties no longer performed their traditional linkage function.

Was there an increase in attachment to new collective actors (hypothesis 6)? The empirical evidence presented in Chapter 8 by Aarts relates to five countries (France, Germany, Britain, Italy, the Netherlands) and four time points (1982, 1984, 1986, and 1989). There was no general trend from the beginning of the 1980s to the end of the decade. Comparing 1982 and 1989, support for new social movements increased in Germany and the Netherlands, and declined in Britain, France, and Italy. Thus, there was no general increase in attachment to new collective actors in the countries and in the period we were able to observe. These findings do not support hypothesis 6.

In sum, with regard to the hypotheses on political linkage, we have clear answers. On the one hand, there was no general decline in attachment to interest organizations (hypothesis 4), and there was no general increase in attachment to new collective actors (hypothesis 6). These findings contradict the initial hypotheses. On the other hand, there is evidence pointing towards a decline in attachment to political parties, which, after all, are some of the most important intermediary collective actors. This latter result supports hypothesis 5. Thus, the overall picture for political linkage is rather mixed.

The Political System

Was there a decline in support for politicians (hypothesis 7)? In Chapter 9, Listhaug examines trends in support for politicians by analysing what people think of politicians in general. Generalized trust in politicians is measured by a set of political support items, such as 'Do you think that most of our politicians can be trusted?'. Factor analysis of several trust items confirmed that trust in politicians constitutes one dimension. Data were available from national election studies for four countries: Norway (six time points, 1969–89); Sweden (seven time points, 1968–88);

Denmark (seven time points, 1971–84); and the Netherlands (seven time points, 1971–89). As similar items are not always available, it is difficult to compare the findings across the four countries. Even so, it is safe to conclude that there was no general downward trend for the countries and periods under study. At the beginning of the period, Swedish people seemed to be more trusting than the Norwegians, the Dutch, and the Danes. At the end of the period, the Dutch were most trusting, followed by the Norwegians, the Swedes, and the Danes. If anything, we can observe a downward trend in Sweden and Norway and a slight upwards move in the Netherlands and Denmark. These results do not generally confirm hypothesis 7.

Was there a decline in support for government institutions (hypothesis 8)? In Chapter 10, Listhaug and Wiberg compare trust measures for ten political and private institutions in twelve countries in 1981 and 1990. The results show there was no widespread and severe decline in public confidence in institutions across Western Europe. There was a slight downward trend in trust levels for 'order' institutions such as the church, the armed forces, and the legal system. But support for the civil service and parliament was stable, while support for other institutions, such as the education system, has increased. The most consistent improvement was in confidence in 'major companies', which was evident in all countries except Britain. Although it narrowed, there was still a confidence gap in favour of government institutions. Looking at individual countries, however, support for government institutions declined, on average, in six of the eleven countries. This finding tends to favour hypothesis 8. At best, however, the evidence is mixed.

Was there a decline in support for the democratic system (hypothesis 9)? This question is tackled by Fuchs, Guidorossi, and Svensson in Chapter 11. The answer to this question is particularly important because dissatisfaction of this kind relates not just to a specific government but to the democratic system in general. System support was measured at a relatively low level of generalization, using the Eurobarometer question: 'On the whole, are you very satisfied, fairly satisfied, not very satisfied or not at all satisfied with the way democracy works (in your country)?' Data are available for thirteen countries over a fifteen-year period (1976–91). On average, European-wide, the proportion of citizens satisfied with the way democracy works in their country was 57 per cent—ranging from a minimum of 49 per cent (autumn 1980) to a maximum of 59 per cent (autumn 1989). According to this measure, with the exception only of Italy, a majority of citizens in member countries of the European Community was satisfied with democracy over the entire period. This finding is confirmed by linear regression analysis. However, most of the longitudinal analyses at the country level yield a more varied picture. Trend lines were positive in five out of fourteen countries; in eight countries, there was no trend; in only one country was the trend line negative, as suggested by hypothesis 9. These results do not confirm the hypothesis.

In Chapter 12, Tóka presents four similar findings for four Central and East European countries. Although the levels of support for democracy were lower than in Western Europe (with the exception of Italy), the trend is by no means uniformly declining. Rather, what Tóka demonstrates is that generalized support for democracy is closely linked to perceptions of the economic situation. Thus, output performance seems to be of overriding importance for the consolidation of democratic regimes in Central and Eastern Europe. Below we shall argue that this pattern may become typical for future developments in Western Europe as well.

Was there an increase in support for individualist democratic values (hypothesis 10)? Thomassen discusses this question in Chapter 13. Using the 1985 ISPP surveys (four countries), he demonstrates that the concept of individualist democratic values (civil rights and liberties) as opposed to the concept of collectivist democratic values (social equality) is reflected in these data. The loading of items approving milder forms of unconventional political participation on the individualist dimension is interpreted as support for an expansion of civil rights. Changing levels of support for different aspects of individualist democracy are reported, using data on (social) tolerance from the 1981 European Values Survey and the 1990 World Values Survey (twelve countries). Thomassen's findings show that tolerance levels have declined in ten out of twelve countries, with Germany and Britain the exceptions. This finding is not consistent with the original hypothesis.

In another question from the two Values Surveys, respondents were confronted with a direct choice between liberty and equality. An increase in the proportion of citizens valuing liberty more highly than equality was observed in only six countries, whereas in the other six countries the proportion declined. With respect to the general hypothesis, this is an ambivalent finding. A third measure from the Values Surveys, relating to attitudes towards egalitarian values (collectivist democracy), showed that in all countries except Norway egalitarian values were declining. This finding is interpreted as supporting the hypothesis. In addition, Eurobarometer data for 1979, 1981, and 1983 (ten countries) showed that in all countries except Denmark support for a further reduction of income inequality had declined. This finding also supports the hypothesis. Thus, overall, it seems justified to conclude that there was increasing support for individualist democratic values. This conclusion is in line with hypothesis 10.

With respect to attitudes towards the political system, then, the overall picture is mixed. The evidence on generalized trust in politicians (hypothesis 7) is inconclusive; there was a slight decline in support for government institutions (hypothesis 8); and there was an increase in support for both individualist democratic values (hypothesis 10) and the democratic system (hypothesis 9).

Before we go into what these findings mean for the general question of the challenge to representative democracy, we summarize the empirical results presented in this volume. Table 14.1 shows, for each hypothesis, whether it was confirmed in the majority of countries under consideration. In assessing and comparing the findings, however, bear in mind that they relate to a varying number of countries and varying time periods.

It is evident that three of the ten original hypotheses are confirmed. In the majority of countries for which data are available, there is a clear increase in non institutionalized participation and a clear decline in attachment to political parties. Increasing support for individualist democratic values is also observed. As far as the other six hypotheses are concerned, the empirical findings either present a mixed picture or refute the hypothesis.

The Challenge to Representative Democracy

The hypotheses we tested are based on the premiss that a fundamental change had taken place in the relationship between citizens and the state, provoking a challenge to representative democracy. The data failed to confirm most of the hypotheses. This means, for one thing, that the postulated fundamental change in the citizens' relationship with the state largely did *not* occur. And since such a change is a prerequisite for any challenge to representative democracy, this finding does not support the general challenge hypothesis. However, two hypotheses, relating to essential aspects of the relationship between citizens and the state, are confirmed. They concern non-institutionalized participation

TABLE 14.1. *Summary of major empirical findings*

Hypotheses	Confirmed	Not confirmed	Number of countries	Time period
Part I: Political Involvement				
H1 Decline in institutional political participation[a]	8	10	18	1945–89[v]
H2 Increase in non-institutional policital participation[b]	3	—	3	1959–90
	5	—	5	1974–90
	12	1	13	1980–90
H3 Increase in political apathy[c]	—	4	4	1974–90
	2	10	12	1980–90
	2	3	5	1974–80
Part II: Political Linkage				
H4 Decline in attachment to interest organizations[d]	2	6	8	1950–85[v]
	4	5	9	1955–90[v]
H5 Decline in attachment to political parties[e]	8	6	14	1956–92[v]
	7	8	15	1960–89[v]
H6 Increase in attachment to new collective actors[f]	2	3	5	1982–89
Part III: Political System				
H7 Decline in support (trust) for politicians[g]	2	2	4	1968–89[v]
H8 Decline in support (trust) for governmental institutions[h]	6	5	11	1981–90
H9 Decline in support for the democratic system[i]	1	13	14	1976–91
H10 Increase in support for individualist values[j]	11	1	12	1981–90
	9	1	10	1979–83

Notes: Where more than one row of figures are presented for a hypothesis, they refer to either different time periods or different specific indicators for the same general concept. Time periods marked 'v' vary between countries; the table shows the earliest and latest year mentioned.

Sources: [a] Figures 2.5 *a–c*   [b] Table 3.3   [c] Table 3.6   [d] Table 8.5, 8.6
[e] Table 4.1, 5.1 *a–b*   [f] Table 8.9   [g] Figures 9.1 *a–d*   [h] Table 10.1
[i] Table 11.7   [j] Table 12.3, 12.5

and identification with the political parties. We should not, therefore, put aside the challenge hypothesis too hastily.

The observed increase in non-institutionalized participation in practically all countries is the most unambiguous finding in this volume. This change in citizens' political involvement could have a considerable impact on the political process, because it alters essential aspects of communication between rulers and the ruled. Non-institutionalized forms of participation differ from voting as the dominant type of participation in representative democracies in two regards. First, they are generally used in pursuit of specific goals, and secondly, they result in political decision-makers being addressed directly by citizens. The fundamental characteristic of representative democracy, however, is that there is mediation between the demands made by citizens and the decisions made by the state. This mediation is undertaken by the political parties. Through competitive elections, citizens select certain parties for decision-making positions, which then act as the representatives of the citizens in these decision-making positions. However, a vote for a certain party grants only a general mandate to implement, during the coming legislative period, the government platform presented to the electorate during the election campaign. Thus, the primary sense of the communication between rulers and the ruled, mediated via elections and parties, is to give rulers relative autonomy in their actions *vis-à-vis* the varying and fluctuating demands of citizens. This relative autonomy is, at least in principle, the precondition for the effective implementation of programmatic goals in face of a multitude of constraints.

Non-institutionalized forms of participation, by contrast, are characterized precisely by the bypassing of elections and parties. The increase in this type of participation can, therefore, be interpreted as a symptom of the erosion in the legitimacy of the competitive party system as the central institutional mechanism of representative democracy. This interpretation appears to be supported by the decline in the identification of citizens with political parties. The political parties are, after all, the mediators between citizens and the state. However, we need a supplementary argument before we can conclude that the legitimacy of the central institutional mechanism of representative democracy suffered erosion. The two trends we have identified—increasing non-institutional participation and declining identification with parties—have been interpreted as the expression of profound dissatisfaction among citizens. And it is precisely this argument which appears to be unjustified. In the first place, these two phenomena can be interpreted in other ways and, in the second place, further empirical evidence tends to counter this supplementary assumption.

An alternative interpretation of the two trends arises from the same theory of modernity used as our framework in Chapter 1. The individual modernization in Western societies described there means, among other things, a considerable increase in the skills of citizens. These concern both the capacity to appropriate the environment cognitively and to attain goals through one's own action in this environment. From this perspective, it is perfectly rational to take up additional options for action with the purpose of pursuing one's interests in politics. This is especially true if one's investment is not very high. And this is more or less the case with non-institutionalized forms of action. Most citizens participate in petitions, demonstrations, traffic blockades, and the like, which are organized by others. Participation takes place intermittently and seldom involves investing a great deal of time.

The increase in non-institutional forms of participation can, accordingly, be understood as an extension of the citizens' repertory of action beyond merely participating in elections. The two types of participation have different advantages and disadvantages for individual actors, and can therefore be considered complementary. This assumption was confirmed, empirically, by the Political Action study (Kaase and Marsh 1979; Kaase 1989). Citizens use non-institutionalized forms of action because these forms offer their own possibilities for attaining political goals—not because citizens are dissatisfied with conventional forms of action. This is also apparent from the evidence that electoral participation in West European countries has apparently suffered only slight decline, or none at all. This latter finding is remarkable, if for no other reason than that in a cost–benefit analysis of action alternatives in asserting interests, electoral participation is unlikely to show an overly favourable balance.

A further consequence of increasing cognitive competence among citizens is their greater capacity for criticism and a greater willingness to do so. It is highly unlikely that parties and governments will be spared. Competition between government and opposition in the election campaign, and the confrontation between government and opposition in parliament, constitute a built-in mechanism in representative democracies which further increases the potential for criticism among citizens. From this perspective, it is only to be expected that citizens will take a more sceptical view of political actors as a whole, and thus of political parties. This critical potential would become a problem for representative democracies only if it knows no bounds and completely exhausts loyalty to the political parties.

The data presented in this volume hints in the direction of this argument. In five of the fourteen countries investigated, no significant decline whatsoever in identification with parties was uncovered; in one country identification increased; and in most of the remaining countries the decline was not particularly dramatic.[1] Thus, there is something to be said in favour of Sniderman's (1981) thesis that, although citizens in Western democracies have become more critical, they have also become more realistic. They recognize the errors and weaknesses of political actors and criticize them, too, but they do not 'throw out the baby with the bathwater', for 'nobody is perfect'.

The hypotheses of an increase in non-institutionalized participation by citizens and a decline in identification with parties were confirmed. However, the empirical findings hardly lend themselves to construing a challenge to representative democracy. Certainly, in view of the generalized support for democracy evident in West European countries, it is difficult to contest this view. Contrary to theoretical expectations, we found no decline in generalized support for democracy among the citizens of Western Europe. Rather, there was a slight but significant increase. Notwithstanding how one judges citizens' dissatisfaction with the possibilities for political participation, with the outcomes of political decision-making processes, and with the activities of political actors, no generalization of this dissatisfaction to the system level was observed. It should be remembered that the indicator measuring generalized support for democracy refers to the functioning of democracy in the respondent's own country, and is thus related to the reality of people's experience of a democratic system. If dissatisfaction had been generalized to the system level, it should have been recorded by this indicator.

Let us once again consider the empirical findings in relation to the critical analyses of the state of Western democracies which are reviewed in Chapter 1. This allows us to draw some final conclusions. The common core of these analyses is, first, the thesis that transformation into post-industrial societies has generated new demands among citizens, both in relation to new issues and new forms of participation. The second thesis is that these new demands have led to a disturbance in the balance between citizens and the state,[2] involving serious problems of adaptation for the state. If it is then claimed that these adjustment problems cannot be resolved within the existing institutional context, one is justified in speaking of a challenge to representative democracy. The point is well made by Dalton (1988: 73; emphasis added):

It is clear that contemporary democracies face new challenges, and their future depends on the nature of the response . . . *Democracies must adapt to survive* . . . Democracy is threatened when we fail to take the democratic creed literally and reject these challenges.

However, a disturbance in the balance between citizens and the state, provoking the 'new challenges' and problems of adaptation, will occur only if citizens withdraw their support from the state as a whole, or, at least, from core structural elements. The data presented in this volume reveal that this was not the case, and that there was no sign of such a development. This invites the following conclusion: up to the end of the 1980s there was no challenge to the representative democracies of Western societies.

In the light of this conclusion, what are the reasons for the false assessments suggesting a challenge to democracy? Clearly, in the period under observation, there was societal change in Western Europe, in the sense of societal and individual modernization, which provoked new citizen demands. This is borne out by several empirical studies (cf. Dalton 1988; Jennings, Van Deth, *et al.* 1989; Inglehart 1990). In our view, there are principally two aspects to this question. The first concerns the sources of generalized support for Western democracies. Most of the crisis theories of the 1970s and the challenge theories of the 1980s implicitly assume that support for these democracies depends on a 'balance between citizen demands and state capacity to satisfy the demands' (Weil 1989: 683). According to these theories, then, the source of generalized support is primarily the performance of the state. Another source is the legitimacy of democracy, and legitimacy means that, in the perception of the citizens, the institutional structure of democracy corresponds to the values and norms they hold. It is especially this type of generalized support which contributes to the stability and persistence of political systems. This has been theoretically elaborated and empirically demonstrated in numerous studies. In contrast to the state socialist systems, Western democracies appeared to be without alternatives, and the values and norms underlying them were, so to speak, permanently stabilized by the contrast. In the last section we discuss what the end of this east–west conflict could mean for the legitimation of Western democracies.

The other aspect of the erroneous assessments, in our opinion, is the underestimation of the adaptive capacity of representative democracy. Transformation into post-industrial societies not only generated new political problems but also provided solutions to these problems. And this occurred within the institutional framework of representative democracy. In the next section we consider this assertion at greater length.

The Transformation of Representative Democracy

The citizens of West European countries have not withdrawn support from their democracies in recent decades. This holds true for both democracy as a form of constitutionally defined government and for the reality of democracy. For this reason alone, there can have been no challenge to the representative democracy of Western societies. The discourse of challenge during the 1970s and 1980s was thus presumably an élite discourse without any real mass basis. However, rejecting the challenge hypothesis does not mean that there was no change in the relationship between citizens and the state. A change quite obviously did take place, and this also alters the reality of representative democracy in Western Europe. With reference to Dahl (1989), we call this process *democratic transformation*.

Any such transformation can be determined only on the basis of an initial state which, in changing, results in a new state. Defining this initial state is not unproblematic since the institutional framework of representative democracy is compatible with a broad range of realities. It has become customary to contrast the changes affecting Western democracies since about the mid-1960s with the 'quiet' 1950s. In the 1950s there was a remarkable consonance between the democratic practice of citizens and theories of democracy which, to a certain extent, brought the essence of the idea of representation to the fore, vesting it with a claim to normative status.[3] In this understanding of the concept, representative democracy was largely restricted to the selection, by the electorate, of political élites for decision-making positions. Representative democracy thus meant relatively seldom and limited political participation by citizens. A very strong role for political parties in the political process complemented this rather weak form of citizen participation (Hirst 1990). It was essentially the political parties which articulated citizens' interests on their behalf, and it was the parties which introduced citizen interests into the decision-making processes.

The extension of the citizens' action repertory and the use made of this repertory, however, has breached the restrictive practice of democracy. Citizens have become more demanding and more critical towards politicians and parties. Above all, citizens have developed the capacity, and the readiness, to back up their demand by using the entire range of their potential for action.

The action repertory of citizens has been extended mainly in the field of non-institutionalized forms of action. But, as we have already discussed, it is precisely these forms of participation which circumvent the mediation of citizens' interests by the political parties. However, from this point of view, we might suppose that representative democracy has, in fact, been undermined by the way citizens use this extended action repertory. But there are several reasons why this is not so. First, the vote is still the only form of action through which citizens decide who governs. Thus, the impact of non-institutionalized action on decision-makers depends less on the actions themselves than on their possible consequences for citizens' party preferences. In other words, those collective actions which use non-institutionalized forms of action attempt, primarily, to mobilize public opinion. This may, or may not, influence people's party preferences. Secondly, the evidence we have uncovered relates, principally, to extending the repertory for action. However, the repertory is relatively seldom put to use. In short, there is a considerable gap between the potential for mobilizing citizens for collective action and actual mobilization (cf. Fuchs and Rucht 1994). Thirdly, if we disregard the relatively non-committal signing of petitions, participation in elections is still by far the most frequent political activity undertaken by citizens in Western democracies. Thus, political participation by citizens still focuses on taking part in elections. Voting is complemented—but not replaced—by non-institutionalized political action.

Nevertheless, the informal rules of interaction between citizens and politicians did change. On the one hand, citizens could intervene politically when necessary through their own activities, and they did so more or less frequently. Politicians, on the other hand, constantly had to take account of this possibility, even when there was no mobilization of citizens worth mentioning. The actions and decisions of politicians were consequently far more subject to influence and scrutiny by the citizens than in the quiet 1950s. The role played by the mass media also changed the rules of the game in politics. The individual and collective actors of the polity were permanently exposed to critical observation through mass communication. Public opinion generated by mass communication had a feedback effect on the opinions and preferences of voters. In the main, this feedback effect led the major political actors to consider, continuously and systematically, the opinions and preferences of voters.

These changes in the nature of the interaction between the actors of the polity and the public we call a process of *democratic transformation*. The process produced greater responsiveness on the part of the major political actors towards the demands of the citizens. And citizens became more active as well as more effective in the political process.

The substance of this democratic transformation was characterized by the exhaustion of the possibilities contained in the rights of citizens in representative democracies. This openness was decisive for democratic transformation *within* the institutional framework of representative democracies. The process of transformation merely altered the reality of representative democracies. It is probably this change which accounted for the relatively high levels of satisfaction with the functioning of democracy in their own countries which we found among West European citizens. In view of our evidence, it cannot be said that engaging in non-institutionalized forms of action, or the formation of new collective actors outside the party system, was a consequence of fundamental dissatisfaction among citizens. It is far more likely that the relatively high degree of citizen satisfaction with their democracy persisted because the transformation had taken place.[4]

From this perspective, we do not see the increase in non-institutionalized participation and the coming into being of new political actors, such as citizen initiative groups and new social movements, as an expression of a participation problem which can and must be solved through institutional reform. Rather, these developments appear to be the solution to the new participation demands of citizens. Moreover, through this solution, a chronic problem about the allocation of time— largely due to incompatible goals—can also be reduced. On the one hand, citizens wished to have greater influence on political actors and to supervise their actions more closely. On the other hand, they wished to take up some of the many activities available outside the political sphere in modern societies. Occasional and brief participation in collective action organized by citizen initiative groups and social movements is a useful compromise between these conflicting goals.

And this compromise was made possible by, among other things, the fact that such participation was not institutionalized.

The process of democratic transformation primarily concerns the forms of interaction between citizens and the state. It can be seen as a successful adaptation of representative democracy to the new participation demands of their citizens. This is one aspect of the new demands which arose in the context of the transition to post-industrial society. Demands relating to new issues are the other aspect. We can also identify forms of adaptation to these demands. They consist, first, in the emergence of new collective actors who articulated such new issue demands in their collective actions. But they are also apparent in changes to the party systems, whether in the form of adjustments to party programmes or the emergence of new parties. On the whole, as evidenced in Chapter 6, these adjustments appear to have led to a *rapprochement* between party programmes and voter orientations.

The capacity of the representative democracy of Western societies to absorb and process the problems arising from the transition to post-industrial society has apparently been adequate. The ability to adapt to the resulting problems is grounded in the alterations which took place in the informal rules for interaction between citizens and state actors, and in the adaptation of parties to the new demands. These adaptive mechanisms led to a change in the reality of democracy which we refer to as 'democratic transformation'. This democratic transformation, which occurred at a level below the formal structure of representative democracy, can be regarded as the political dimension of the transformation to post-industrial society.

All this said, however, we envisage that the changes in the global constellation which took place in the late 1980s preclude a mere continuation of this period of political development. So we conclude with a discussion of the prospects for representative democracy in Western Europe which arise from the different world emerging in the 1990s.

A New Global Constellation

The end of the 1980s represents something of a historical *caesura* for West European societies. With the collapse of the state socialist systems in Central and Eastern Europe, East–West global conflict largely came to an end. In addition, at about much the same time, citizens in Western

Europe have been increasingly confronted by the problems resulting from global economic competition. Moreover, the effects of this structural change in economic development were exacerbated by the recession which started in Western Europe around 1988–9. These two changes in the global constellation are unlikely to leave unscathed the legitimating conditions for West European democracies.

One of the effects of these altered conditions is likely to be a change in the agenda of problems for Western societies. Economic and security concerns can be expected to regain the edge over postmaterialist concerns. There are already signs of such a development in terms of value priorities among West European citizens. Since the late 1980s, the proportion of postmaterialists relative to materialists has either ceased to increase or has even declined in several West European countries (Inglehart and Abramson 1994: 338). This is most marked in West Germany, where, since 1988, there has been a striking decline in the proportion of postmaterialists. This is not surprising: German unification and Germany's geographical position render these developments particularly palpable to the people of former West Germany.

We surmise, then, that the postmaterialist age has, for the moment at least, come to a halt. We leave open the question of whether this is only a pause or a lasting change. But for the foreseeable future, the altered problem agenda means that the attention of citizens will be directed more strongly than before to the performance of the state in the fields of economy and security. For this reason, the legitimation of Western democracies will depend more heavily on the performance of governments. In this case, it is a matter of output-related performance.

The end of the East–West contrast in political systems touches on the legitimation conditions for Western democracies in another regard as well. We noted earlier that this opposition put Western democracies in a relatively comfortable position. The contrast with the dictatorships in Central and East European countries highlighted the relevance of basic Western democratic values. Reference to these basic values made it considerably easier to legitimate the institutional structure of democratic systems in Western Europe. In other words, East–West confrontation was an important factor in legitimating the representative democracies of the West. With the disappearance of this confrontation, the attention of citizens is likely to concentrate more on the functioning of democracy in their own country rather than the general principles of democracy. Citizens are likely to judge the reality of democracy as they experience it against general democratic values and norms, and through comparison with other Western democracies. From this perspective, too, the degree to which the legitimation of Western democracy depends on performance is likely to increase. However, in this case it is not a matter of output-related performance but of democratic performance.

We have postulated that, due to the new global constellation, Western democracies will become increasingly dependent on performance for securing their legitimacy. This claim relates to both the capacity of democratic systems to solve certain societal problems and to attain certain democratic standards. Thus, the legitimation of democracy by its citizens becomes conditional in two ways. The source of support for a democratic system is therefore likely to shift away from 'ideal normative agreement' towards 'instrumental acceptance' (Held 1987: 238). If, over and beyond this conditional support, the critical competence of citizens is taken into account, then we can expect a more sceptical attitude on the part of citizens towards the reality of

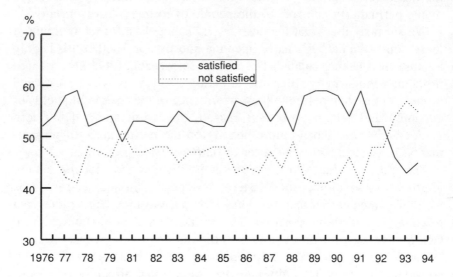

FIGURE 14.1 *Trends in satisfaction with democracy in Western Europe, 1976–94*

Notes: Proportions are based on total population. The data are pooled and weighted by proportion size. EC-12 consists of Belgium, Britain, Denmark, France, Germany, Greece, Ireland, Italy, Luxembourg, Netherlands, Portugal, and Spain. Northern Ireland and East Germany are entered as separate cases.

Sources: Eurobarometer, Nos. 6–41.

democracy. We test this supposition with the help of the Eurobarometer indicator recording citizens' satisfaction with the functioning of democracy in their own country. Figure 14.1 shows the trend in satisfaction with democracy from late 1976 to early 1994.

According to this time series, satisfaction with democracy among citizens in Western Europe reached its highest level for the entire period under observation in autumn 1989. Since then, an almost continuous decline has been recorded. This was interrupted only by the intermediate peak in spring 1991. In autumn 1992 the proportion of the dissatisfied was, for the first time, markedly higher than the proportion of those expressing satisfaction. Moreover, comparing the trend in satisfaction with democracy with the most important economic trends, we find a distinct parallel between the decline in satisfaction with democracy and the fall in economic growth rates and the rise in unemployment rates in Western Europe (data not shown here). In the earlier period, this parallel between developments in satisfaction with democracy and developments in the economy either did not exist or were considerably less pronounced.

On the one hand, this evidence of the linkage between the two trends since 1989 supports our argument that citizen support for democracy is becoming increasingly dependent on performance. On the other hand, the extent of the erosion of satisfaction suggests that 'the crisis of democracy', rather than being a matter of rhetoric, is actually materializing. If so, that would run against our general argument. However, for a number of different reasons, we do not believe that to be the case.

That citizens' satisfaction with the reality of democracy in their own country depends on performance can have either negative or positive effects. In spring 1994, the economic macro-data indicated an improvement in the economic situation in Western Europe for the first time since 1988–9. There was a corresponding marked rise in satisfaction with democracy among citizens at the same time. It can, therefore, be assumed that this rise will continue with the consolidation of economic development.

The links we found between economic development and satisfaction with democracy have been recorded at a highly aggregated level, taking Western Europe as a whole. This conceals highly divergent circumstances and developments in individual countries. The linkage between economic development and satisfaction with democracy did not exist at all in Luxembourg, Denmark, Ireland, Northern Ireland, Britain, and Greece. Moreover, trends in satisfaction with democracy differed widely from country to country (data not shown here). Thus, there must be other, especially country-specific factors, also influencing citizen satisfaction with democracy. In fact, the relatively strong linkage with economic developments uncovered for Western Europe as a whole is largely attributable to the particularly pronounced relationship in France, Italy, and Germany. However, when the data for each country are given equal weighting—rather than weighted by population size—the proportion of respondents who are dissatisfied with the functioning of democracy in their country at no time exceeds the proportion of those who are satisfied. Thus, whatever the effect of the new global constellation, it does not have a uniform effect on the development of West European democracies. In short, how the problems created by the new constellation are to be solved depends on the policies and politics—on the functioning of political institutions—in the individual countries.

The new global constellation has certainly made the legitimation of Western democracies more difficult. East–West confrontation had a stabilizing effect on legitimizing democratic regimes. With the end of East–West conflict this frame of reference has vanished and the dependence of legitimation on performance is likely to grow. However, on the experiences of the last decades, there is no reason to doubt that representative democracy has the flexibility to solve these new problems. In addition, now more than ever, there is no alternative to representative democracy—at least as far as its basic institutional structure is concerned.

How well legitimization is achieved in future is determined not at the general level but, finally, in individual countries. For this reason alone, a comprehensive crisis of democracy in Western Europe during the 1990s is unlikely. It is another matter, however, whether a crisis occurs in a particular country, as has been the case in Italy. But even then, the point of reference for overcoming the crisis is not an alternative to representative democracy but an alternative within representative democracy. If we are correct in concluding that the new global constellation has made the legitimation of Western democracies more dependent on performance, then the direction in which an alternative is sought also has to change. The centre stage is then likely to be occupied by structural variants of representative democracy which enhance the effectiveness of problem-solving rather than democratic responsiveness to the demands of citizens.

NOTES

1. Moreover, it is a moot point whether a party system presupposes identification with the parties by citizens. The development of a preference is presumably sufficient. This can occur on the basis of rational calculation and can change. All that is important is that as many citizens as possible develop such a preference.
2. In our context, the general concept of the state refers exclusively to the specific state form associated with representative democracy.
3. For a discussion of these theories of democracy, see Held (1987: chs. 5, 6).
4. This interpretation can explain why it is that precisely those West European citizens with an above-average desire to participate in politics—the postmaterialists—have shown an above-average increase in satisfaction with democracy since the mid-1970s. See Ch. 11.

REFERENCES

Aberbach, J. D., Putnam, R. D., and Rockman, B. A. (1981). *Bureaucrats and Politicians in Western Democracies*. Cambridge, Mass.: Harvard University Press.

Abramson, P. (1977). *The Political Socialization of Black Americans*. New York: Free Press.

—— (1983). *Political Attitudes in America: Formation and Change*. San Francisco: W. H. Freeman.

—— and Ostrom, C. W., Jr (1991). 'Macropartisanship: An Empirical Reassessment'. *American Political Science Review* 85: 181–203.

Adorno, T. W., Frenkel-Brunswick, E., Levinson, D., and Sanford, R. (1950). *The Authoritarian Personality*. New York: Harper.

Allsop, D., and Weisberg, H. F. (1988). 'Measuring Change in Party Identification in an Election Campaign'. *American Journal of Political Science* 32: 996–1017.

Allum, P. A. (1979). 'Italy'. In *Political Parties in the European Community*, ed. S. Henig. London: George Allen and Unwin.

Almond, G. A. (1960). 'Introduction: A Functional Approach to Comparative Politics'. In *The Politics of the Developing Areas*, ed. G. A. Almond and J. S. Coleman. Princeton, NJ: Princeton University Press.

—— (1980) (1989, 2nd edn.). 'On Revisiting the Civic Culture: A Personal Postscript'. In *The Civic Culture Revisited*, ed. G. A. Almond and S. Verba. London: Sage.

—— and Verba, S. (1963) (1989, 2nd edn.). *The Civic Culture: Political Attitudes and Democracy in Five Nations*. Princeton, NJ: Princeton University Press (Newbury Park, Sage).

—— Powell, G. B., Jr, *et al.* (1978, 2nd edn.) (1960, 1st edn.). *Comparative Politics: System, Process, and Policy*. Boston, Mass.: Little, Brown.

Alt, J. (1984). 'Dealignment and the Dynamics of Partisanship in Britain'. In *Electoral Change in Advanced Industrial Democracies*, ed. R. J. Dalton, S. C. Flanagan, and P. A. Beck. Princeton, NJ: Princeton University Press.

Asp, K. (1986). *Mäktiga massmedier*. Stockholm: Akademilitteratur.

Baker, K. L., Dalton, R. J., and Hildebrandt, K. (1981). *Germany Transformed: Political Culture and New Politics*. Cambridge, Mass: Harvard University Press.

Barber, B. R. (1984). *Strong Democracy: Participatory Politics for a New Age*. Berkeley, Calif.: University of California Press.

Barnes, S. H. (1977). *Representation in Italy*. Chicago: University of Chicago Press.

—— (1984). 'Political Mobilization and the New Citizen'. Paper prepared for the Beliefs in Government conference, European University Institute, Florence.

—— (1989). 'Partisanship and Electoral Behavior'. In M. K. Jennings, J. W. Van Deth, *et al.*, *Continuities in Political Action*. Berlin: de Gruyter.

—— Kaase, M., *et al.* (1979). *Political Action: Mass Participation in Five Western Democracies*. Beverly Hills, Calif.: Sage.

—— McDonough, P., and Lopéz Pina, A. (1985). 'The Development of Partisanship in New Democracies: The Case of Spain'. *American Journal of Political Science* 29: 695–720.

—— Jennings, M. K., Inglehart, R., and Farah, B. (1988). 'Party Identification and Party Closeness in Comparative Perspective'. *Political Behaviour* 10: 215–31.

Bartolini, S., and Mair, P. (1990). *Identity, Competition and Electoral Availability: The Stabilization of European Electorates 1885–1985*. Cambridge: Cambridge University Press.

Beck, U. (1986). *Risikogesellschaft: Auf dem Weg in eine andere Moderne*. Frankfurt: Suhrkamp. English trans.: *Risk Society: Towards a New Modernity*. London: Sage, 1992.

Beer, S. H. (1982). *Britain against Itself*. London: Faber and Faber.

Bell, D. (1973). *The Coming of Post-Industrial Society: A Venture in Social Forecasting*. New York: Basic Books.

—— (1976). *The Cultural Contradictions of Capitalism*. London: Heinemann.

—— (1988) (1960, 1st edn.). *The End of Ideology: On the Exhaustion of Political Ideas in the Fifties*. New York: Free Press.

Berger, M. (1977). 'Stabilität und Intensität von Parteineigungen'. In *Wahlsoziologie heute*, ed. M. Kaase. Opladen: Westdeutscher verlag.

Berlin, I. (1969). *Four Essays on Liberty*. Oxford: Oxford University Press.

Bertrand, A. (1981). *Politieke demokratie en welzijn*. Alphen aanden Rijn: Samsom.

Biorcio, R., and Mannheimer, R. (1985). *Misurare la politica: Ricerche empiriche sulla cultura politica, le scelte di voto e il comportamento elettorale degli italiani negli anni '70 e '80*. Milan: Unicopli.

Birch, A. H. (1984). 'Overload, Ungovernability and Delegitimation: The Theories and the British Case'. *British Journal of Political Science* 14: 135–60.

Borre, O., and Katz, D. (1973). 'Party Identification and its Motivational Base in a Multiparty System: A Study of the Danish General Election of 1971'. *Scandinavian Political Studies* 8: 69–111.

Bowler, S., and Farrell, D. M. (1991). 'Party Loyalties in Complex Settings: STV and Party Identification'. *Political Studies* 29: 350–62.

Boynton, G. R., and Loewenberg, G. (1973). 'Der Bundestag im Bewußtsein der Öffentlichkeit 1951–1959'. *Politische Vierteljahresschrift* 14: 3–25.

Brittan, S. (1975). 'The Economic Contradictions of Democracy'. *British Journal of Political Science* 5: 129–59.

Brody, R. A., and Rothenberg, L. S. (1988). 'The Instability of Partisanship: An Analysis of the 1980 Presidential Election Campaign'. *British Journal of Political Science* 18: 445–65.

Bruszt, L., and Simon, J. (1992). *Political and Economic Orientations during the Transition to Democracy*. Codebook. Budapest: TTI.

Buchanan, J. M. (1991). *The Economics and the Ethics of Constitutional Order*. Ann Arbor: University of Michigan Press.

Budge, I., Crewe, I., and Farlie, D. (eds.) (1976). *Party Identification and Beyond: Representations of Voting and Party Competition*. London: John Wiley.

—————— Robertson, D., and Hearl, D. (eds.) (1987). *Ideology, Strategy, and Party Change: Spatial Analysis of Post-War Election Programmes in Nineteen Democracies*. Cambridge: Cambridge University Press.

Butler, D., and Stokes, D. (1969) (1972, rev. edn.; 1974, 2nd edn.). *Political Change in Britain: The Evolution of Electoral Choice*. London: Macmillan.

Caldeira, G. A. (1986). 'Neither the Purse nor the Sword: Dynamics of Public Confidence in the Supreme Court'. *American Political Science Review* 80: 1209–26.

Campbell, A., and Valen, H. (1966). 'Party Identification in Norway and the United States'. In *Elections and the Political Order*, ed. A. Campbell, P. E. Converse, W. E. Miller, and D. Stokes. New York: John Wiley.

—————— Converse, P. E., Miller, W. E., and Stokes, D. (1960). *The American Voter*. New York: John Wiley.

Castles, F. G. (ed.) (1982). *The Impact of Parties: Politics and Policies in Democratic Capitalist States*. London: Sage.

—————— and Mair, P. (1984). 'Left–Right Political Scales: Some "Expert" Judgments'. *European Journal of Political Research* 12: 73–88.

CEU (Central European University) (1992). 'The Development of Party Systems and Electoral Alignments in East Central Europe: The Fall 1992 Survey'. Machine-readable data file. Budapest: Department of Political Science, Central European University.

—————— (1993*a*). 'The Development of Party Systems and Electoral Alignments in East Central Europe: The January 1993 Survey in Poland and Hungary and the April 1993 Survey in the Czech Republic and Slovakia'. Machine-readable data file. Budapest: Department of Political Science, Central European University.

—————— (1993*b*). 'The Development of Party Systems and Electoral Alignments in East Central Europe: The August–October 1993 Election Panel Study in Poland and the November–December 1993 Survey in the Czech

Republic, Hungary and Slovakia'. Machine-readable data file. Budapest: Department of Political Science, Central European University.

—— (1994). 'The Development of Party Systems and Electoral Alignments in East Central Europe: The April–May 1994 Election Panel Study in Hungary'. Machine-readable data file. Budapest: Department of Political Science, Central European University.

Chapman, J. (1990). 'Politics and Personal Rewards'. Paper presented to the ESF/ESRC Conference on Political Participation in Europe, University of Manchester.

Charlot, J. (1986). 'La Transformation de l'image des partis politiques français'. *Revue Française de Sciences Politiques* 36: 5–13.

Charmant, H., and Lehning, P. B. (1989). *Afscheid van de verlichting*. Rotterdam: Donner.

Chisholm, L. (1992). 'A Crazy Quilt: Education, Training and Social Change in Europe'. In *Social Europe*, ed. J. Bailey. London: Longman.

Citrin, J. (1974). 'Comment: The Political Relevance of Trust in Government'. *American Political Science Review* 68: 973–88.

Clarke, H. D., and Stewart, M. C. (1984). 'Dealignment of Degree: Partisan Change in Britain, 1974–83'. *British Journal of Political Science* 46: 689–718.

Cohen, C. (1971). *Democracy*. New York: Free Press.

Cohen, J. L. (1985). 'Strategy or Identity: New Theoretical Paradigms and Contemporary Social Movements'. *Social Research* 52: 663–716.

Commission of the European Communities (1993). *Central and Eastern Eurobarometer: Eighteen Countries Survey, Autumn 1992*. Research Report. Brussels: Commission of the European Communities.

—— (1994). *Eurobarometer Trends 1974–1994*. Brussels: Commission of the European Communities.

Conradt, D. P. (1974). 'West Germany: A Remade Political Culture? Some Evidence from Survey Archives'. *Comparative Political Studies* 7: 222–38.

—— (1980). 'Changing German Political Culture'. In *The Civic Culture Revisited: An Analytic Study*, ed. G. A. Almond and S. Verba. Boston: Little, Brown.

—— (1981). 'Political Culture, Legitimacy and Participation'. *West European Politics* 4: 18–34.

Converse, P. E. (1964). 'The Nature of Belief Systems in Mass Publics'. In *Ideology and Discontent*, ed. D. Apter. New York: Free Press.

—— 1969. 'Of Time and Partisan Stability'. *Comparative Political Studies* 2: 139–71.

—— (1975). 'Public Opinion and Voting Behavior'. In *Handbook of Political Science*, iv. *Nongovernmental Politics*, ed. F. I. Greenstein and N. W. Polsby. Reading, Mass.: Addison-Wesley.

—— and Pierce, R. 1986. *Political Representation in France*. Cambridge, Mass.: Belknap Press.

Crepaz, M. M. L. (1990). 'The Impact of Party Polarization and Postmaterialism on Voter Turnout'. *European Journal of Political Research* 18: 183–205.

Crewe, I. (1981). 'Electoral Participation'. In *Democracy at the Polls*, ed. D. Butler, H. R. Penniman, and A. Ranney. Washington, DC: American Enterprise Institution.

—— and Denver, D. (1985). *Electoral Change in Western Democracies*. London: Croom Helm.

—— Fox, T., and Alt, J. (1977). 'Non-Voting in British General Elections 1966–October 1974'. In *British Political Sociology Yearbook,* iii, ed. C. Crouch. London: Croom Helm.

—— Day, N., and Fox, A. (1991). *The British Electorate 1963–1987: A Compendium of Data from the British Election Studies*. Cambridge: Cambridge University Press.

Crook, S., Pakulski, J., and Waters, M. (1992). *Postmodernization: Change in Advanced Society*. London: Sage.

Crozier, M., Huntington, S. P., and Watanuki, J. (1975). *The Crisis of Democracy: Report on the Governability of Democracies to the Trilateral Commission*. New York: New York University Press.

Dahl, R. A. (1956). *A Preface to Democratic Theory*. Chicago: University of Chicago Press.

—— (1982). *Dilemmas of Pluralist Democracy: Autonomy versus Control*. New Haven, Conn.: Yale University Press.

—— (1989). *Democracy and its Critics*. New Haven, Conn.: Yale University Press.

Dalton, R. J. (1984). 'Cognitive Mobilization and Partisan Dealignment in Advanced Industrial Democracies'. *Journal of Politics* 46: 264–84.

—— (1988). *Citizen Politics in Western Democracies: Public Opinion and Political Parties in the United States, Britain, West Germany and France*. Chatham, NJ: Chatham House.

—— and Küchler, M. (eds.) (1990). *Challenging the Political Order: New Social and Political Movements in Western Democracies*. Cambridge: Polity Press.

—— and Rohrschneider, R. (1990). 'Wählerwandel und die Abschwächung der Parteineigung von 1972 bis 1987'. In *Wahlen und Wähler: Analysen aus Anlaß der Bundestagswahl 1987*, ed. M. Kaase and H. D. Klingemann. Opladen: Westdeutscher Verlag.

—— Flanagan, S. C., and Beck, P. A. (eds.) (1984). *Electoral Change in Advanced Industrial Democracies*. Princeton, NJ: Princeton University Press.

—— Küchler, M., and Bürklin, W. (1990). 'The Challenge of New Movements.' In *Challenging the Political Order: New Social and Political*

Movements in Western Democracies, ed. R. J. Dalton and M. Küchler. Cambridge: Polity Press.

Davis, J. A. (1975). 'Communism, Conformity, Cohorts and Categories: American Tolerance in 1954 and 1972–73'. *American Journal of Sociology* 81: 491–513.

Davis, J. C. (1962). 'Toward a Theory of Revolution'. *American Sociological Review* 27: 5–19.

Day, A. J. (ed.) (1988, 3rd edn.). *Political Parties of the World: A Keesing's Reference Publication*. Harlow: Longman.

—— and Degenhardt, H. W. (eds.) (1984, 2nd edn.). *Political Parties of the World*. Harlow: Longman.

Denver, D. (1985). 'Conclusion.' In *Electoral Change in Western Democracies*, ed. I. Crewe and D. Denver. London: Croom Helm.

di Cortona, P. G. (1991). 'From Communism to Democracy: Rethinking Regime Change in Hungary and Czechoslovakia'. *International Social Science Journal* 43: 315 30.

Dittrich, K., and Johansen, L. N. (1983). 'Voting Turnout in Europe, 1945–1978: Myths and Realities'. In *Western European Party Systems: Continuity and Change*, ed. H. Daalder and P. Mair. London: Sage.

Dohnalik, J., Hartl, J., Jasiewicz, K., Markowski, R., Mateju, P., Rezler, L., Töka, G., and Tucek, M. (1991). 'Dismantling of the Social Safety Net and its Political Consequences in East Central Europe: An International Comparative Study Initiated and Sponsored by the Institute of East–West Studies'. Machine-readable data file. Distributors: IEWS, New York and TARKI, Budapest.

Döring, H. (1990). 'Aspekte des Vertrauens in Institutionen'. *Zeitschrift für Soziologie* 19: 73–89.

—— (1992). 'Higher Education and Confidence in Institutions'. *West European Politics* 15: 126–46.

Downs, A. (1957). *An Economic Theory of Democracy*. New York: Harper and Row.

Duverger, M. (1954). *Political Parties*. New York: John Wiley.

Easton, D. (1965) (1979, 2nd edn.). *A Systems Analysis of Political Life*. New York: John Wiley.

—— (1975). 'A Re-assessment of the Concept of Political Support'. *British Journal of Political Science* 5: 435–57.

—— Dennis, J., et al. (1969). *Children in the Political System: Origins of Political Legitimacy*. New York: McGraw-Hill.

Edelman, M. (1964). *The Symbolic Uses of Politics*. Urbana, Ill.: University of Illinois Press.

Epstein, L. D. (1967). *Political Parties in Western Democracies*. New York: Praeger.

Eulau, H., and Karps, P. (1978). 'The Puzzle of Representation: Specifying

Components of Responsiveness'. In *The Politics of Representation*, ed. H. Eulau and J. C. Wahlke. Beverly Hills, Calif.: Sage.

—— and Wahlke, J. C. (eds.) (1978). *The Politics of Representation*. Beverly Hills, Calif.: Sage.

Falter, J. W. (1977). 'Einmal mehr: Läßt sich das Konzept der Parteiidentifikation auf deutsche Verhältnisse übertragen?' In *Wahlsoziologie heute*, ed. M. Kaase. Opladen: Westdeutscher Verlag.

—— and Rattinger, H. (1983). 'Parteien, Kandidaten und politische Streitfragen bei der Bundestagswahl 1980: Möglichkeiten und Grenzen der Normal-Vote-Analyse'. In *Wahlen und politisches System: Analysen aus Anlaß der Bundestagswahl 1980*, ed. M. Kaase and H.-D. Klingemann. Opalden: Westdeutscher Verlag.

Farrell, D. (1992). 'Ireland'. In *The Development of Party Organizations in Western Democracies 1960–1990: A Data Handbook*, ed. R. Katz and P. Mair. London: Sage.

Featherstone, M. (1988). 'In Pursuit of the Postmodern'. *Theory, Culture & Society* 5: 195–215.

Finkel, S., and Opp, K. D. (1991). 'Party Identification and Participation in Collective Political Action'. *Journal of Politics* 53: 339–71.

Fiorina, M. P. (1981). *Retrospective Voting in American National Elections*. New Haven, Conn.: Yale University Press.

Flanagan, S. C. (1982*a*). 'Changing Values in Advanced Industrial Societies: Inglehart's Silent Revolution from the Perspective of Japanese Findings'. *Comparative Political Studies* 14: 403–44.

—— (1982*b*). 'Measuring Value Change in Advanced Industrial Societies: A Rejoinder to Inglehart'. *Comparative Political Studies* 15: 99–128.

Flickinger, R. S., and Studlar, D. T. (1992). 'The Disappearing Voters? Exploring Declining Turnout in Western European Elections'. *West European Politics* 15: 1–16.

Flora, P. (ed.) (1986*a*). *Growth to Limits: The Western European Welfare States since World War II*, i. Berlin: de Gruyter.

—— (ed.) (1986*b*). *Growth to Limits: The Western European Welfare States Since World War II*, ii. Berlin: de Gruyter.

Franklin, C. H. (1984). 'Issue Preferences, Socialization, and the Evolution of Party Identification'. *American Journal of Political Science* 28: 459–78.

—— and Jackson, J. E. (1983). 'The Dynamics of Party Identification'. *American Political Science Review* 77: 957–73.

Franklin, M., Mackie, T., Valen, H., *et al.* (1992). *Electoral Change: Responses to Evolving Social and Attitudinal Structures in Western Countries*. Cambridge: Cambridge University Press.

Fuchs, D. (1989). *Die Unterstützung des politischen Systems der Bundesrepublik Deutschland*. Opladen: Westdeutscher Verlag.

—— (1990). 'The Normalization of the Unconventional: Forms of Political

Action and New Social Movements'. Discussion Paper FS III 90–203. Berlin: Wissenschaftszentrum Berlin.

—— (1993*a*). 'Trends of Political Support in the Federal Republic of Germany'. In *Political Culture in Germany*, ed. D. Berg-Schlosser and R. Rytlewski. London: Macmillan.

—— (1993*b*). 'A Metatheory of the Democratic Process'. Discussion Paper FS III 93–203. Berlin: Wissenschaftszentrum Berlin.

—— and Klingemann, H-.D. (1989). 'The Left–Right Schema'. In *Continuities in Political Action: A Longitudinal Study of Political Orientations in Three Western Democracies*, ed. M. K. Jennings and J. W. Van Deth *et al.* Berlin: de Gruyter.

—— and Rucht, D. (1994). 'Support for New Social Movements in Five Western European Countries'. In *A New Europe? Social Change and Political Transformation*, ed. C. Rootes and H. Davis. London: UCL Press.

Gabriel, O. W. (1986). *Politische Kultur, Postmaterialismus und Materialismus In der Bundesrepublik Deutschland*. Opladen. Westdeutscher Verlag.

—— (1987). 'Demokratiezufriedenheit und demokratische Einstellungen in der Bundesrepublik Deutschland'. *Aus Politik und Zeitgeschichte* 22: 32–45.

Gamson, W. A. (1968). *Power and Discontent*. Homewood, Ill.: Dorsey Press.

Gibbins, J. R. (1989). *Contemporary Political Culture: Politics in a Postmodern Age*. London: Sage.

Gilljam, M., and Holmberg, S. (1990). *Rött Blått Grönt*. Stockholm: Bonniers.

—— (1993). *Väljarna inför 90 talet*. Stockholm: Norstedts Juridik.

Girvin, B. (ed.) (1988). *The Transformation of Contemporary Conservatism*. London: Sage.

Goul Andersen, J. (1992). 'Årsaker til mistillid'. In *Vi og våre politikere*, ed. H. J. Nielsen., N. Thomsen, and J. Westerståhl. Viborg: Spektrum.

Habermas, J. (1973). *Legitimationsprobleme im Spätkapitalismus*. Frankfurt: Suhrkamp. Eng. trans. (1975). *Legitimation Crisis*. Boston: Beacon Press.

Harmel, R., and Janda, K. (1994). 'An Integrated Theory of Party Goals and Party Change'. *Journal of Theoretical Politics* 6: 259–87.

Harvey, D. (1989). *The Condition of Postmodernity*. Oxford: Basil Blackwell.

Heath, A. F., and McDonald, S. K. (1988). 'The Demise of Party Identification Theory?' *Political Studies* 7: 95–107.

—— and Pierce, R. (1992). 'It Was Party Identification All Along: Question Order Effects on Reports of Party Identification in Britain'. *Electoral Studies* 11: 93–105.

—— and Topf, R. G. (1986). 'Educational Expansion and Political Change in Britain 1964–1983'. *European Journal of Political Research* 14: 543–67.

—— Jowell, R., and Curtice, J. (1985). *How Britain Votes*. Oxford: Pergamon Press.

—— Jowell, R., Curtice, J., Evans, G., Field, J., and Witherspoon, S.

(1991). *Understanding Political Change: The British Voter 1964–1987*. Oxford: Pergamon Press.

Held, D. (1987). *Models of Democracy*. Cambridge: Polity Press.

Hermansson, J. (1988). 'A New Face for Swedish Communism: The Left Party Communists'. In *Communist Parties in Western Europe: Decline or Adaptation?*, ed. M. Waller and M. Fennema. Oxford: Basil Blackwell.

Hill, K. (1974). 'Belgium: Political Change in a Segmented Society'. In *Electoral Behaviour: A Comparative Handbook*, ed. R. Rose. New York: Free Press.

Hirschman, A. O. (1982). *Shifting Involvements: Private Interest and Public Action*. Princeton, NJ: Princeton University Press.

Hirst, P. (1990). *Representative Democracy and its Limits*. Cambridge: Polity Press.

Hobday, C. (1986). *Communist and Marxist Parties of the World: A Keesing's Reference Publication*. Harlow: Longman.

Hofferbert, R. I., and Budge, I. (1992). 'The Party Mandate and the Westminster Model: Election Programmes and Government Spending in Britain, 1948–85'. In *British Journal of Political Science* 22: 151–82.

—— and Klingemann, H.-D. (1990). 'The Policy Impact of Party Programmes and Government Declarations in the Federal Republic of Germany'. *European Journal of Political Research* 18: 277–304.

Hoffmann-Lange, U. (1987). 'Eliten als Hüter der Demokratie?' In *Politische Kultur in Deutschland*, ed. D. Berg-Schlosser and J. Schissler. Opladen: Westdeutscher Verlag.

Hofrichter, J., and Schmitt, H. (1991). 'Eher mit als gegeneinander! Zum Verhältnis von neuen sozialen Bewegungen und politischen Parteien in den achtziger Jahren'. In *Neue soziale Bewegungen in der Bundesrepublik Deutschland*. Bonn: Bundeszentrale für politische Bildung.

Holden, B. (1988). *Understanding Liberal Democracy*. Deddington, Oxon.: Philip Allan.

Holmberg, S. (1974). *Riksdagen representerar svenska folket*. Lund: Studentlitteratur.

—— (1981). *Svenska Väljare*. Stockholm: Liber.

—— (1984). *Väljare i förandring*. Stockholm: Liber.

—— (1991). 'Political Representation in Sweden'. In *Politische Klasse und politische Institutionen*, ed. H.-D. Klingemann, R. Stöss, and B. Wessels. Opladen: Westdeutscher Verlag.

—— (1992). 'The Undermining of a Stable Party System'. In *From Voters to Participants: Essays in Honour of Ole Borre*, ed. P. Gundelach and K. Siune. Aarhus: Politica.

—— and Esaiasson, P. (1988). *De folkvalda*. Stockholm: Bonniers.

—— (1993). 'The Parliamentarians'. Unpublished paper, Department of Political Science, Göteborg.

———— Gilljam, M. (1987). *Väljare och Val i Sverige*. Stocholm: Bonniers.

———— Gilljam, M., and Oskarson, M. (1988). *Valundersökning 1985: Teknisk Rapport*. Stockholm and Göteborg: Statistiska Centralbyrån and Department of Political Science.

House, J. S., and Mason, W. M. (1975). 'Political Alienation in America'. *American Sociological Review* 40: 123–47.

Howell, S. E., and Fagan, D. (1988). 'Race and Trust in Government'. *Public Opinion Quarterly* 52: 343–50.

Huber, J., and Inglehart, R. (1994). 'Expert Interpretations of Party Space and Party Placement in 42 Societies'. In *Party Politics*, i *(forthcoming)*.

Huntington, S. P. (1974). 'Postindustrial Politics: How Benign Will It Be?' *Comparative Politics* 6: 163–91.

Inglehart, R. (1977). *The Silent Revolution: Changing Values and Political Styles among Western Publics*. Princeton, NJ: Princeton University Press.

———— (1984). 'The Changing Structure of Political Cleavages in Western Society'. In *Electoral Change in Advanced Industrial Democracies: Realignment or Dealignment?* ed. R. J. Dalton, S. C. Flanagan, and P. A. Beck. Princeton, NJ: Princeton University Press.

———— (1990*a*). *Culture Shift in Advanced Industrial Society*. Princeton, NJ: Princeton University Press.

———— (1990*b*). 'Values, Ideology and Cognitive Mobilization in New Social Movements.' In *Challenging the Political Order: New Social and Political Movements in Western Democracies*, ed. R. J. Dalton and M. Kuechler, Cambridge: Polity Press.

———— and Abramson, P. R. (1994). 'Economic Security and Value Change'. *American Political Science Review* 88: 336–54.

———— and Hochstein, A. (1972). 'Alignment and Dealignment of the Electorate in France and the United States'. *Comparative Political Studies* 5: 343–72.

Inkeles, A. (1983). *Exploring Individual Modernity*. New York: Columbia University Press.

———— and Smith, D. H. (1974). *Becoming Modern: Individual Change in Six Developing Countries*. Cambridge, Mass.: Harvard University Press.

Irving, R. E. M. (ed.) (1979) *The Christian Democratic Parties of Western Europe*. London: Allen and Unwin.

Iyengar, S., and Kinder, D. R. (1987). *News that Matters*. Chicago: University of Chicago Press.

Jackman, R. W. (1987). 'Political Institutions and Voter Turnout in the Industrial Democracies'. *American Political Science Review* 81: 405–23.

Jennings, M. K., Van Deth, J. W., *et al.* (1989). *Continuities in Political Action: A Longitudinal Study of Political Orientations in Three Western Democracies*. Berlin: de Gruyter.

Johnston, R. (1992). 'Party Identification Measures in the Anglo-American

Democracies: A National Survey Experiment'. *American Journal of Political Science* 36: 542–59.

Kaase, M. (1976). 'Party Identification and Voting Behaviour in the West German Election of 1969'. In *Party Identification and Beyond*, ed. I. Budge *et al*. London: John Wiley.

—— (ed.) (1977). *Wahlsoziologie heute*. Opladen: Westdeutscher Verlag.

—— (1984). 'The Challenge of the "Participatory Revolution" in Pluralist Democracies'. *International Political Science Review* 5: 299–317.

—— (1985). 'Systemakzeptanz in den westlichen Demokratien'. In *Aktuelle Herausforderungen der repräsentativen Demokratie: Sonderheft der Zeitschrift für Politik*, ed. U. Matz. Cologne: Heymanns Verlag.

—— (1988). 'Political Alienation and Protest'. In *Comparing Pluralist Democracies: Strains on Legitimacy*, ed. M. Dogan. Boulder, Colo.: Westview.

—— (1989). 'Mass Participation.' In M. K. Jennings, J. W. Van Deth, *et al.*, *Continuities in Political Action: A Longitudinal Study of Political Orientations in Three Western Democracies*. Berlin: de Gruyter.

—— (1990). 'Social Movements and Political Innovation'. In *Challenging the Political Order: New Social and Political Movements in Western Democracies*, ed. R. J. Dalton and M. Küchler. Cambridge: Polity Press.

—— (1992*a*). 'Direct Political Participation in the Late Eighties in the EC Countries'. Unpublished manuscript.

—— (1992*b*). 'Legitimitätsüberzeugungen'. In *Lexikon der Politik*, iii. *Die westlichen Länder*, ed. M. G. Schmidt. Munich: Beck.

—— and Barnes, S. H. (1979). 'Conclusion: The Future of Political Protest in Western Democracies'. In S. H. Barnes, M. Kaase, *et al.*, *Political Action: Mass Participation in Five Western Democracies*. Beverly Hills, Calif.: Sage.

—— and Marsh, A. (1979). 'Political Action Repertory: Changes over Time and a New Typology'. In S. H. Barnes, M. Kaase, *et al.*, *Political Action: Mass Participation in Five Western Democracies*. London: Sage.

—— and Neidhardt, F. (1990). *Politische Gewalt und Repression: Ergebnisse von Bevölkerungsumfragen*. Berlin: Duncker and Humblot.

Katz, R. (1985). 'Measuring Party Identification with Eurobarometer Data: A Warning Note'. *West European Politics* 8: 104–8.

—— and Mair, P. (1992*a*). 'Changing Models of Party Organization: The Emergence of the Cartel Party'. Paper presented at ECPR joint sessions, University of Limerick.

—— (eds.) (1992*b*). *The Development of Party Organizations in Western Democracies 1960–1990: A Data Handbook*. London: Sage.

—— *et al.* 1992 'The Membership of Political Parties in European Democracies 1960–1990.' *European Journal of Political Research* 22: 329–45.

Kavanagh, D. (1980). 'Political Culture in Great Britain: The Decline of the

Civic Culture'. In *The Civic Culture Revisited*, ed. G. A. Almond and S. Verba. Boston, Mass.: Little, Brown.

Keane, John (1988). *Democracy and Civil Society*. London: Verso.

Kelley, S., Jr., Ayres, R., and Bowen, W. G. (1967). 'Registration and Voting: Putting First Things First'. *American Political Science Review* 61: 359–79.

Kielmansegg, P. G. (1988). *Das Experiment der Freiheit. Zur gegenwärtigen Lage des demokratischen Verfassungsstaat*. Stuttgart: Klett-Cotta.

Kinder, D. R., and Kiewiet, D. R. (1979). 'Economic Discontent and Political Behavior'. *American Journal of Political Science* 23: 21–44.

King, A. (1975). 'Overload: Problems of Governing in the 1970s'. *Political Studies* 23: 284–96.

Kirchheimer, O. (1966). 'The Transformation of the Western European Party Systems'. In *Political Parties and Political Development*, ed. J. LaPalombara and M. Weiner. Princeton, NJ.: Princeton University Press.

Kirchner, E. J. (ed). (1988). *Liberal Parties in Western Europe*. Cambridge: Cambridge University Press.

Kirkpatrick, J. J. (1979). 'Changing Patterns of Electoral Competition'. In *The New American Political System*, ed. A. King. Washington, DC: American Enterprise Institute.

Klandermans, B., Kriesi, H., and Tarrow, S. (eds.) (1988). *International Social Movement Research*, i. *From Structure to Action: Comparing Movement Participation Research Across Cultures*. Greenwich, Conn.: JAI Press.

Klingemann, H.-D., and Taylor, C. L. (1977). 'Affektive Parteiorientierung, Kanzlerkandidaten und Issues'. In *Wahlsoziologie heute*, ed. M. Kaase. Opladen: Westdeutscher Verlag.

——— Hofferbert, R. I., and Budge, I. (1994). *Parties, Policies, and Democracy*. Boulder, Colo.: Westview.

Kornhauser, W. (1959). *The Politics of Mass Society*. London: Routledge.

Krampen, G. (1988). 'Toward an Action-Theoretical Model of Personality'. *European Journal of Personality* 2: 39–55.

Kriesi, H. (1988). 'Local Mobilization for the People's Petition of the Dutch Peace Movement'. In *From Structure to Action: Comparing Social Movement Reseach across Cultures*, ed. B. Klandermans *et al.* Greenwich, Conn.: JAI Press.

Küchler, M. (1991). 'Issue Voting in the European Elections 1989'. *European Journal of Political Research* 19: 81–103.

Lane, J.-E., and Ersson, S. (1987) (1991, 2nd edn.). *Politics and Society in Western Europe*. London: Sage.

——— (1990). 'Macro and Micro Understanding in Political Science: What Explains Electoral Participation?' *European Journal of Political Research* 18: 457–65.

——— McKay, D., and Newton, K. (1991). *Political Data Handbook: OECD Countries*. Oxford: Oxford University Press.

LaPalombara, J. (1987). *Democracy Italian Style*. New Haven, Conn.: Yale University Press.

Lash, S., and Friedman, J. (1992). *Modernity and Identity*. Oxford: Basil Blackwell.

Lau, R. R. (1982). 'Negativity in Political Perception'. *Political Behavior* 4: 353–78.

―――― (1985). 'Two Explanations for Negativity Effects in Political Behavior'. *American Journal of Political Science* 29: 119–38.

Laver, M., and Budge, I. (eds.) (1993). *Party Policy and Coalition Government in Western Europe*. London: Macmillan.

―――― and Schofield, N. (1991). *Multiparty Government: The Politics of Coalition in Europe*. Oxford: Oxford University Press.

Lawson, K. (1988). 'When Linkage Fails'. In *When Parties Fail: Emerging Alternative Organizations*, ed. K. Lawson and P. Merkl. Princeton, NJ: Princeton University Press.

―――― and Merkl, P. H. (eds.) (1988). *When Parties Fail: Emerging Alternative Organizations*. Princeton, NJ: Princeton University Press.

Lazarsfeld, P. F., Berelson, B., and Gaudet, H. (1968, 3rd edn.). *The People's Choice: How the Voter Makes Up his Mind in a Presidential Campaign*. New York: Columbia University Press.

Lebart, L., Morineau, A., and Warwick, K. M. (1984). *Multivariate Descriptive Statistical Analysis*. New York: John Wiley.

LeDuc, L. (1985). 'Partisan Change and Dealignment in Canada, Great Britain, and the United States'. *Comparative Politics* 17: 379–98.

Lewis-Beck, M. S. (1984). 'France: The Stalled Electorate'. In *Electoral Change in Advanced Industrial Democracies*, ed. R. J. Dalton *et al.* Princeton, NJ: Princeton University Press.

Lijphart, A. (1984). *Democracies: Patterns of Majoritarian and Consensus Government in Twenty-One Countries*. New Haven, Conn.: Yale University Press.

Linz, J. (1988). 'Legitimacy of Democracy and the Socioeconomic System'. In *Comparing Pluralist Democracies*, ed. M. Dogan. Boulder, Colo.: Westview.

Lipset, S. M. (1959). *Political Man*. London: Heinemann.

―――― and Schneider, W. (1983). *The Confidence Gap*. New York: Free Press.

Listhaug, O. (1984). 'Confidence in Institutions'. *Acta Sociologica* 27: 111–22.

―――― (1989). *Citizens, Parties and Norwegian Electoral Politics 1957–1985: An Empirical Study*. Trondheim: Tapir.

Lively, J. (1975). *Democracy*. Oxford: Basil Blackwell.

Lockerbie, B. (1993). 'Economic Dissatisfaction and Political Alienation in Western Europe'. *European Journal of Political Research* 23: 281–93.

Lowi, T. J. (1969). *The End of Liberalism, Ideology, Policy, and the Crisis of Public Authority*. New York: W. W. Norton.

Luskin, R. C., McIver, J. P., and Carmines, E. G. (1989). 'Issues and the Transmission of Partisanship'. *American Journal of Political Science* 33: 440–58.

Machiavelli, N. (1975). *The Prince*. Harmondsworth, Middx.: Penguin.

Mackie, T. T. (1992). 'General Elections in Western Nations during 1990'. *European Journal of Political Research* 21: 317–32.

—— and Rose, R. (1991, 3rd edn.). *The International Almanac of Electoral History*. London: Macmillan.

MacKuen, M. B., Erikson, R. S., and Stimson, J. S. (1989). 'Macropartisanship'. *American Political Science Review* 83: 1125–42.

—— (1992). 'Question Wording and Macropartisanship'. *American Political Science Review* 86: 475–86.

Macpherson, C. B. (1977). *The Life and Times of Liberal Democracy*. Oxford: Oxford University Press

Markus, G. B., and Converse, P. E. (1979). 'A Dynamic Simultaneous Equation Model of Electoral Choice'. *American Political Science Review* 73: 1055–70.

Marsh, A. (1977). *Protest and Political Consciousness*. London: Sage.

—— and Kaase, M. (1979). 'Measuring Political Action'. In S. H. Barnes, M. Kaase, *et al.*, *Political Action, Mass Participation in Five Western Democracies*. Beverly Hills, Calif.: Sage.

Martikainen, T., and Yrjönen, R. (1991). *Voting, Parties and Social Change in Finland*. Helsinki: Tilastokeskus Statisikcentralen.

Matthews, D. R. (1985). 'Legislative Recruitment and Legislative Careers'. In *Handbook of Legislative Research*, ed. G. Loewenberg, S. C. Pattersson, and M. F. Jewell. Cambridge, Mass.: Harvard University Press.

May, J. (1973). 'Opinion Structure of Political Parties: The Special Law of Curvilinear Disparity'. *Political Studies* 21: 135–51.

McClosky, H., and Brill, A. (1983). *Dimensions of Tolerance: What Americans Believe about Civil Liberties*. New York: Russell Sage Foundation.

—— and Zaller, J. (1984). *The American Ethos: Public Attitudes toward Capitalism and Democracy*. Cambridge, Mass.: Harvard University Press

—— Hoffmann, P. J., and O'Hara, R. (1960). 'Issue Conflict and Consensus Among Party Leaders and Followers'. *American Political Science Review* 54: 406–27.

McConnell, G. (1966). *Private Power and American Democracy*. New York: Vintage.

McDonough, P., Barnes, S. H., and Pina, A. L. (1986). 'The Growth of Democratic Legitimacy in Spain'. *American Political Science Review* 80: 735–60.

McGraw, K. M. (1990). 'Avoiding Blame: An Experimental Investigation of

Political Excuses and Justifications'. *British Journal of Political Science* 20: 119–42.

McKenzie, R. T. (1982). 'Power in the Labour Party: The Issue of Intra-Party Democracy'. In *The Politics of the Labour Party*, ed. D. Kavanagh. London: George Allen and Unwin.

Melucci, A. (1989). *Nomads of the Present: Social Movements and Individual Needs in Contemporary Society*. Philadelphia: Temple University Press.

Merkl, P. H. (1988). 'Comparing Legitimacy and Values among Advanced Democratic Countries'. In *Comparing Pluralist Democracies: Strains on Legitimacy*, ed. M. Dogan. Boulder, Colo.: Westview.

Middendorp, C. P. (1991). *Ideology in Dutch Politics: The Democratic System Reconsidered, 1970–1985*. Assen, Maastricht: Van Gorcum.

Miller, A. H. (1974). 'Political Issues and Trust in Government 1964–1970'. *American Political Science Review* 68: 951–72.

—— and Borelli, S. A. (1987). 'Renewed Confidence in Government: Reagan Legacy or Missed Opportunity'. Paper presented at the Annual Meeting of the International Society for the Study of Political Psychology, San Francisco.

—— and Listhaug, O. (1990). 'Political Parties and Confidence in Government: A Comparison of Norway, Sweden and the United States'. *British Journal of Political Science* 20: 357–86.

—— (1993). 'Ideology and Political Alienation'. *Scandinavian Political Studies* 16: 167–92.

Miller, W. E. (1976). 'The Cross-National Use of Party Identification as a Stimulus to Political Inquiry'. In *Party Identification and Beyond*, ed. I. Budge *et al*. London: John Wiley.

—— (1991). 'Party Identification, Realignment, and Party Voting: Back to the Basics'. *American Political Science Review* 85: 557–68.

—— Miller, A. H., and Schneider, E. J. (1980). *American National Election Studies Sourcebook*. Cambridge, Mass.: Harvard University Press.

Muller, E. N., Jukam, T. O., and Seligson, M. A. (1982). 'Diffuse Support and Anti-system Political Behaviour: A Comparative Analysis'. *American Journal of Political Science* 26: 240–63.

Neidhardt, F., and Rucht, D. (1993). 'Auf dem Weg in die "Bewegungsgesellschaft"? Über die Stabilisierbarkeit sozialer Bewegungen'. *Soziale Welt* 44: 305–326. English trans.: 'Towards a "Movement Society"?: On the Possibilities of Institutionalizing Social Movements'. Discussion Paper FS III 94–101. Berlin: Wissenschaftszentrum Berlin.

Neumann, S. (1956). *Modern Political Parties*. Chicago: University of Chicago Press.

Niemi, R. G., and Jennings, M. K. (1991). 'Issues and Inheritance in the Formation of Party Identification'. *American Journal of Political Science* 35: 970–88.

—— Mueller, J. and Smith, T. W. (1989). *Trends in Public Opinion.* New York: Greenwood.

Noelle-Neumann, E., and Köcher, R. (1993). *Allensbacher Jahrbuch der Demoskopie 1984–1992,* ix. Munich: K. G. Saur.

—— and Piel, E. (1983). *Allensbacher Jahrbuch der Demoskopie 1978– 1983,* viii. Munich: K. G. Saur.

Norpoth, H. (1978). 'Party Identification in West Germany: Tracing an Elusive Concept'. *Comparative Political Studies* 11: 36–61.

—— (1984). 'The Making of a More Partisan Electorate in West Germany'. *British Journal of Political Science* 14: 53–71.

Norris, P. (1990). 'Gender Differences in Political Participation in Britain: Traditional, Radical and Revisionist Models'. Paper presented to the ESF/ESRC Conference on Political Participation in Europe, University of Manchester.

Nunn, C. A., Crockett, H. J., Jr., and Williams, J. A., Jr. (1978). *Tolerance for Nonconformity: A National Survey of Changing Commitment to Civil Liberties.* San Francisco: Jossey-Bass.

Oberndörfer, D. (ed.) (1978). *Sozialistische und kommunistische Parteien in Westeuropa,* i. *Südländer.* Opladen: Leske.

OECD. (1992) (1993, 2nd edn.). *Education at a Glance: OECD Indicators.* Paris: OECD.

Offe, C. (1979). 'Unregierbarkeit: Zur Renaissance konservativer Krisentheorien'. In *Stichworte zur ' Geistigen Situation der Zeit'*, i, ed. J. Habermas. Frankfurt: Suhrkamp.

—— (1985). 'New Social Movements: Challenging the Boundaries of Institutional Politics'. *Social Research* 52: 817–68.

Page, B., and Jones, C. (1979). 'Reciprocal Effects of Policy Preferences, Party Loyalties and the Vote'. *American Political Science Review* 73: 1071–89.

Parry, G. (1976). 'Trust, Distrust, and Consensus'. *British Journal of Political Science* 6: 129–42.

—— Moyser, G., and Day, N. (1992). *Political Participation and Democracy in Britain.* Cambridge: Cambridge University Press.

Parsons, T. (1951). *The Social System.* London: Routledge and Kegan Paul.

—— (1959). '"Voting" and the Equilibrium of the American Political System'. In *American Voting Behavior,* ed. E. Burdick and A. Brodbeck. New York: Free Press.

Pateman, C. (1970). *Participation and Democratic Theory.* Cambridge: Cambridge University Press.

Paterson, W. E., and Thomas, A. H. (eds.) (1977). *Social Democratic Parties in Western Europe.* London: Croom Helm.

Pedersen, M. N. (1983). 'Changing Patterns of Electoral Volatility in European Party Systems 1948–1977'. In *Western European Party Systems: Continuity and Change,* ed. H. Daalder and P. Mair. London: Sage.

Pennock, J. R. (1979). *Democratic Political Theory*. Princeton, NJ.: Princeton University Press.

Phillips, A. (1991). *Engendering Democracy*. Cambridge: Polity Press.

Piereson, J., Sullivan, J. L., and Marcus, G. (1980). 'Political Tolerance: An Overview and Some New Findings'. In *The Electorate Reconsidered*, ed. J. C. Pierce and J. L. Sullivan. Berkeley, Calif.: Sage.

Pierre, J. (1986). *Partikongresser och regeringspolitik: En studie av den socialdemokratiska partikongressens beslutsfattande och inflytande 1948– 1978*. Lund: Kommunfakta förlag.

—— and Widfeldt, A. (1992). 'Sweden'. In *The Development of Party Organizations in Western Democracies 1960–1990: A Data Handbook*, ed. R. Katz and P. Mair. London: Sage.

Pitkin, H. F. (1967). *The Concept of Representation*. Berkeley, Calif.: University of California Press.

Pizzorno, A. (1966). 'Introduzione allo studio della partecipazione politica', in *Quaderni di Sociologia* 15: 235 –87.

—— (1993). *Le radici della politica assoluta*. Milan: Feltrinelli.

Pomper, G. M. (1992). 'The Expressive Party is Empassioned'. *Journal of Theoretical Politics* 4: 143–59.

Popkin, S. (1991). *The Reasoning Voter*. Chicago: University of Chicago Press.

Poulantzas, N. (1978). *State, Power, Socialism*. London: Verso.

Powell, G. B. Jr. (1980). 'Voting Turnout in Thirty Democracies: Partisan, Legal, and Socio-Economic Influences'. In *Electoral Participation: A Comparative Analysis*, ed. R. Rose. London: Sage.

—— (1986). 'American Voter Turnout in Comparative Perspective'. *American Political Science Review* 80: 17–23.

—— (1987). 'The Competitive Consequences of Polarized Pluralism'. In *The Logic of Multiparty Systems*, ed. M. J. Holler. Dordrecht: Kluwer.

—— (1989). 'Constitutional Design and Citizen Electoral Control'. *Journal of Theoretical Politics* 1: 107–30.

Przeworski, A. (1991). *Democracy and the Market*. New York: Cambridge University Press.

Putnam, R. D. (1993). *Making Democracy Work: Civic Traditions in Modern Italy*. Princeton, NJ.: Princeton University Press.

Reimer, B. (1989). 'Postmodern Structures of Feeling'. In *Contemporary Political Culture: Politics in a Postmodern Age*, ed. J. R. Gibbins. London: Sage.

Reiter, H. L. (1989). 'Party Decline in the West: A Sceptic's View'. *Journal of Theoretical Politics* 1: 325–48.

Richardson, B. M. (1991). 'European Party Loyalties Revisited'. *American Political Science Review* 85: 751–75.

Riker, W., and Ordeshook, P. (1968). 'A Theory of the Calculus of Voting'. *American Political Science Review* 64: 24–42.

Robertson, D. (1976). *A Theory of Party Competition*. London: John Wiley.

Rödel, U., Frankenberg, G., and Dubiel, H. (eds.) (1989). *Die demokratische Frage*. Frankfurt: Suhrkamp.

Rogowski, R. (1974). *Rational Legitimacy*. Princeton, NJ: Princeton University Press.

Rose, R. (1984). *Understanding Big Government*. London: Sage.

———— and Mishler, W. T. (1993). 'Reacting to Regime Change in Eastern Europe: Polarization or Leaders and Laggards?' Unpublished paper, CSPP, University of Strathclyde, Glasgow.

Rucht, D. (ed.) (1991). *Research on Social Movements: The State of the Art in Western Europe and the USA*. Boulder, Colo.: Westview.

Rühle, H., and Veen, H.-J. (eds.) (1979). *Sozialistische und kommunistische Parteien in Westeuropa*, ii. *Nordländer*. Opladen: Leske.

'Russia Survey' (1992). *The Economist*, 5 December 1992.

Sabine, G. H. (1952). 'The Two Democratic Traditions'. *Philosophical Review* 60: 451–74.

Särlvik, B., and Crewe, I. (1983). *Decade of Dealignment*. Cambridge: Cambridge University Press.

Sartori, G. (1976). *Parties and Party Systems: A Framework for Analysis*. Cambridge: Cambridge University Press.

Scarrow, S. (1991). 'Organizing for Victory: Political Party Members and Party Organizing Strategies in Great Britain and West Germany 1945–1989'. Ph.D. dissertation, Yale University.

Schattschneider, E. E. (1942). *Party Government*. New York: Holt, Rinehart and Winston.

Schlesinger, J. A. (1965). 'Political Party Organization'. In *Handbook of Organizations*, ed. J. G. March. Chicago: Rand McNally.

Schleth, U., and Weede, E. (1971). 'Causal Models of West German Voting Behaviour'. In *Sozialwissenschaftliches Jahrbuch für Politik*, ii, ed. R. Wildenmann. Munich: Olzog Verlag.

Schmidt, M. (1989). 'Learning from Catastrophes: West Germany's Public Policy'. In *The Comparative History of Public Policy*, ed. F. G. Castles. New York: Oxford University Press.

Schmitt, H. (1983). 'Party Government in Public Opinion: A European Cross-National Comparison'. *European Journal of Political Research* 11: 353–76.

———— (1984). 'Zur Links-Rechts-Polarisierung in Mittlerer Führungsschicht und Wählerschaft in 10 Westeuropäischen Parteiensystem'. In *Politische Willensbildung und Interessenvermittlung*, ed. J. Falter *et al.* Opladen: Westdeutscher Verlag.

———— (1989). 'On Party Attachment in Western Europe and the Utility of Eurobarometer Data'. *West European Politics* 12: 122–39.

—— (1990). 'Party Attachment and Party Choice in the European Elections of 1989'. *International Journal of Public Opinion Research* 2: 169–84.

Schmitt-Beck, R. (1992). 'A Myth Institutionalized: Theory and Research on New Social Movements in Germany'. *European Journal of Political Research* 21: 357–83.

Schuman, H., and Presser, S. (1981). *Questions and Answers in Attitude Surveys*. New York: Academic Press.

Seeman, M. (1959). 'On the Meaning of Alienation'. *American Sociological Review* 6: 783–91.

Seyd, P., and Whiteley, P. (1992). *Labour's Grass Roots*. Oxford: Clarendon Press.

Simon, J. (1992). 'A demokrácia másnapja Magyarországon'. In *Political Yearbook of Hungary, 1992*, ed. S. Kurtán, P. Sándor, and L. Vass. Budapest: DKMKA-Economix.

Simons, J. (1992). 'Europe's Ageing Population: Demographic Trends'. In *Social Europe*, ed. J. Bailey. London: Longman.

Skjeie, H. (1992). *Den Politiske Betydningen av Kjønn*. Report 92: 11. Oslo: Institutt for Samfunnsforskning.

Sniderman, P. M. (1981). *A Question of Loyalty*. Berkeley, Calif.: University of California Press.

—— (1993). 'The New Look in Public Opinion Research'. In *Political Science: The State of the Discipline*, ii, ed. A. Finifter. Washington, DC: American Political Science Association.

Sociaal en Cultureel Planbureau (SCP). (1990) (1992, 2nd edn.). *Sociaal en Cultureel Rapport*. Rijswijk: SCP.

Stewart, M. C. (1992). 'Campaign Context and Partisan Change in Anglo-American Electorates'. Paper presented at ECPR Joint Sessions, Limerick.

Streeck, W. (1987). 'Vielfalt und Interdependenz: Überlegungen zur Rolle von intermediären Organisationen in sich ändernden Umwelten'. *Kölner Zeitschrift für Soziologie und Sozialpsychologie* 39: 471–95.

Street, J. (1994). 'Political Culture: From Civic Culture to Mass Culture'. *British Journal of Political Science* 24: 95–114.

Strom, K. (1990a). 'A Behavioural Theory of Competitive Political Parties'. *American Journal of Political Science* 34: 565–98.

—— (1990b). *Minority Government and Majority Rule*. Cambridge: Cambridge University Press.

Sullivan, J. L., Piereson, J., and Marcus, G. E. (1982). *Political Tolerance and American Democracy*. Chicago: University of Chicago Press.

Svensson, P. (1988). 'Legitimacy and Regime Survival'. In *Rationality and Legitimacy: Essays on Political Theory*, ed. D. Anckar, H. Nurmi, and M. Wiberg. Jyväskyla: Finnish Political Science Association.

Swaddle, K., and Heath, A. F. (1989). 'Official and Reported Turnout in the

British General Election of 1987'. *British Journal of Political Science* 19: 537–51.

Tabah, L. (1990). *World Demographic Trends and their Consequences for Europe*. Population Studies, 20. Strasbourg: Council for Europe.

Taylor, M., and Herman, V. M. (1971). 'Party Systems and Government Stability'. *American Political Science Review* 65: 28–37.

Taylor-Gooby, P. (1993). 'What Citizens Want from the State'. In *International Social Attitudes: The 10th BSA Report*, ed. R. Jowell, L. Brook, and L. Dowds. Aldershot, Hants: Dartmouth.

Thomassen, J. (1976). 'Party Identification as a Cross-National Concept: Its Meaning in the Netherlands'. In *Party Identification and Beyond*, ed. I. Budge *et al.* London: John Wiley.

—— (1992). 'Changing Party Orientations in the Netherlands'. Paper presented at ECPR Joint Sessions, Limerick.

—— and Van Deth, J. W. (1989). 'How New is Dutch Politics?' *West European Politics* 12: 61–78.

Tingsten, H. (1937). *Political Behaviour: Studies in Election Statistics*. London: P. S. King & Son.

Topf, R. G. (1989*a*). 'Political Culture and Political Participation in Great Britain and the Federal Republic of Germany 1959–1988'. Paper presented at ECPR Joint Sessions, Paris.

—— (1989*b*). 'Political Change and Political Culture in Britain 1959 87'. In *Contemporary Political Culture: Politics in a Postmodern Age*, ed. J. Gibbins. London: Sage.

—— (1992). *Some Methodological Problems in the Study of Political Action*. Oxford: Joint Unit for the Study of Social Trends.

—— (1993). 'Science, Public Policy, and the Authoritativeness of the Governmental Process'. In *The Politics of Expert Advice*, ed. A. Barker and B. G. Peters. Edinburgh: Edinburgh University Press.

Tullock, G. (1967). *Towards a Mathematics of Politics*. Chicago: University of Chicago Press.

Turner, B. S. (1989). 'From Postindustrial Society to Postmodern Politics: The Political Sociology of Daniel Bell'. In *Contemporary Political Culture: Politics in a Postmodern Age*, ed. J. R. Gibbins. London: Sage.

United Nations. (1989). *Population Studies*, xi. *World Population at the Turn of the Century*. New York: United Nations.

—— (1991). *World Population Prospects*. New York: United Nations.

Van der Eijk, C., and Niemöller, B. (1983). *Electoral Change in the Netherlands*. Amsterdam: CT Press.

—— (1985). 'The Netherlands'. In *Electoral Change in Western Democracies*, ed. I. Crewe and D. Denver. London: Croom Helm.

Van der Eijk, C., and Oppenhuis, E. (1991). 'European Parties Performance in

Electoral Competition'. In *The European Elections of June 1989*, ed. H. Schmitt and R. Mannheimer. Dordrecht: Kluwer.

Van Deth, J. W. (1984). *Politieke Waarden: Een onderzoek naar politieke waarde-orientaties in Nederland in de periode 1970 tot en met 1982*. Amsterdam: CT-Press.

—— (1989). 'Interest in Politics'. In M. K. Jennings, J. W. Van Deth, *et al.*, *Continuities in Political Action*. Berlin: de Gruyter.

—— and Horstman, R. (1989). *Dutch Parliamentary Election Studies Source Book 1971–1986*. Amsterdam: Steinmetz Archive.

Verba, S., and Nie, N. H. (1972). *Participation in America*. New York: Harper and Row.

—— and Kim, J. (1978). *Participation and Political Equality*. Cambridge: Cambridge University Press.

—— *et al.* (1987). *Elites and the Idea of Equality: A Comparison of Japan, Sweden and the United States*. Cambridge, Mass.: Harvard University Press.

Visser, J. (1989). *European Trade Unions in Figures*. Boston: Kluwer.

—— (1990). 'In Search of Inclusive Unionism'. *Bulletin of Comparative Labour Relations* 18.

Volkens, A. (1995). *Sozio-ökonomische Polarisierung zwischen Parteien, Regierung und Opposition und Regierungswechsel in den OECD-Staaten 1945 bis 1990* (forthcoming).

—— Schnapp, K.-U., and Lass, J. (1991). 'Data Handbook on Election Results and Seats in the National Parliaments for the European Countries 1945–1990'. Unpublished paper, Wissenschaftszentrum Berlin.

Von Beyme, K. (1984). *Parteien in westlichen Demokratien*. Munich: K. Piper.

—— (1985). *Political Parties in Western Democracies*. Aldershot, Hants.: Gower.

Waller, M. (1991). 'Groups, Interests and Political Aggregation in East Central Europe'. *Journal of Communist Studies* 7: 128–47.

Ware, A. (1979). *The Logic of Party Democracy*. London: Macmillan.

Washington Times (1991). 'East–West Attitude Survey'. Mirror Center for The People and The Press. Machine-readable data file.

Wattenberg, M. (1990). *The Decline of American Political Parties 1952–1988*. Cambridge, Mass.: Harvard University Press.

—— (1994). *The 1992 Election: Ross Perot and the Independent Voter*. Berkeley, Calif.: University of California Press.

Weber, M. (1949). *The Methodology of the Social Sciences*. New York: Free Press.

—— (1968). *Economy and Society*. Berkeley, Calif.: University of California Press.

Weil, F. D. (1989). 'The Sources and Structure of Democratic Legitimation in Western Democracies: A Consolidated Model Tested with Time-Series Data in Six Countries Since World War II'. *American Sociological Review* 54: 682–706.

Wellhofer, E. S., and Hennessey, T. M. (1974). 'Models of Political Party Organization and Strategy: Some Analytical Approaches to Oligarchy'. In *Elites in Western Democracy*, ed. I. Crewe. London: Croom Helm.

Westle, B. (1992). 'Politische Partizipation'. In *Die EG-Staaten im Vergleich. Strukturen, Prozesse, Politikinhalte,* ed. O. Gabriel. Opladen: Westdeutscher Verlag.

Whiteley, P. F. (1988). 'The Causal Relationships between Issues, Candidate Evaluations, Party Identification, and Vote Choice—the View from "Rolling Thunder"'. *Journal of Politics* 50: 961–84.

Wiberg, M. (1986). 'Wrong Persons are Making Right Decisions Without Hearing Us: Political Trust, Responsiveness of Politicians and Satisfaction with Governmental Policies in Finland'. *Scandinavian Political Studies* 9: 141–56.

Widmaier, U. (1990). 'Political Stability in OECD Nations', *International Political Science Review* 11: 219–42.

World Bank (1992). *World Tables 1992.* Baltimore: Johns Hopkins University Press.

Wright, J. D. (1975). 'Does Acquiescence Bias the "Index of Political Efficacy"?' *Public Opinion Quarterly* 39: 219–26.

Wright, W. E. (1971). 'Comparative Party Models: Rational-Efficient and Party Democracy'. In *A Comparative Study of Party Organization,* ed. W. E. Wright. Columbus, Oh.: Merrill.

AUTHOR INDEX

SUBJECT INDEX

action:
  expressive political 21, 56, 72, 74, 76, 423
  instrumental political 21, 72, 74, 76, 423
action repertory 432, 435
actors:
  collective 14, 15, 17, 19, 21, 421, 437, 438
  intermediary 13, 17, 426
adaptation 433, 434, 438
  structural 7
apathy, political 7, 20, 21, 73, 422, 423, 430
attachment:
  to interest groups 14
  to interest organizations 11, 17, 423, 426, 430
  to new collective actors 11, 17, 19, 426, 430
  to political parties 11, 14, 17, 424, 426, 429, 430

challenge to representative democracy 1, 7–10, 13, 14, 21–3, 325, 326, 350, 354, 420, 421, 429, 433–5
change:
  cultural 20
  social 7, 8, 11, 13, 21, 419, 420, 434
  structural or institutional 4, 7–9, 343, 378, 420, 421, 437, 439
citizen initiative groups 11, 19, 437
citizens and the state 1–4, 7, 9, 10, 13, 18, 23, 294, 419, 421, 429, 433–5, 438
city states, democratic 2
cleavages, societal and political 13, 228
cognitive competence 12, 13, 262, 271, 314
commitment and withdrawal 7
common good 386, 408
community, political 2, 344

competence, political 262, 267, 269
confidence, in institutions 298–303, 320
conflict, ideological 113, 217, 241, 252
congruence 3, 4, 8, 9, 349
constitution 328
credible alternative 6, 8, 324, 329, 421
crisis:
  of representative democracy 4–6, 9, 323, 324, 326, 350, 351, 354, 441, 442
  rhetoric 4, 5
culture, political 300, 349, 413
cynism, political 264–7

decisions, collectively binding 2
demands:
  of citizens 2, 4–6, 13, 323, 324, 326, 421, 431, 434
  new issue 11, 13, 14, 16, 18, 19, 22, 432
  new participation 11, 16, 17, 19, 22, 437, 438
democracies:
  in Eastern Europe 354–6, 368, 376–8
  in Western Europe 1, 7, 9, 323–5, 348, 351, 413, 419, 433, 434
democracy 2, 384, 386, 388
  direct 8, 9, 324, 390, 409, 420, 421
  functioning of 3, 332, 357, 358, 376
  idea of 2, 299, 347–50, 359, 383, 384
  meaning of 331, 332, 384, 385
  representative 2, 6–9, 13, 21, 267, 323, 390, 419–21, 431, 432, 435–9, 450
democratic consolidation 354, 355, 378, 379
democratic theory:
  collectivist 385–7, 390, 391, 409, 411
  individualist 385–7, 390, 391, 409, 411
democratization 355
deprivation, social 266